KL

5

NIGERIA: DILEMMA OF NATIONHOOD

CONTRIBUTIONS IN AFRO-AMERICAN AND AFRICAN STUDIES

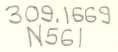

NIGERIA: DILEMMA OF NATIONHOOD

*An African Analysis of the
Biafran Conflict*

JOSEPH OKPAKU, Editor

CONTRIBUTIONS IN AFRO-AMERICAN AND
AFRICAN STUDIES • NUMBER 12

THE THIRD PRESS
New York

GREENWOOD PUBLISHING COMPANY
Westport, Connecticut

Library of Congress Catalog Card Number: 78–111266
ISBN: 0–8371–4668–2

Greenwood Publishing Company
A Division of Greenwood Press, Inc.
51 Riverside Avenue,
Westport, Connecticut 06880

The Third Press
444 Central Park West
New York, New York 10025

Printed in the United States of America
Designed by Peter Landa

CONTENTS

APPENDICES:

NIGERIA: DILEMMA OF NATIONHOOD

1

TURNING A NATION AGAINST HER PEOPLE— NIGERIAN ASPIRATION TO WESTERN EXPECTATION

Joseph Okpaku

The Myths of Western Objectivity, Expertise, and Scholarship

I. Suddenly one morning newspapers break forth with a headline "CRISIS IN THE CONGO" or "COUP D'ETAT IN GHANA—NKRUMAH OUSTED" or "MILITARY TAKEOVER IN NIGERIA–DREAMS OF DEMOCRACY 'SHATTERED,' " and the poor reader begins yet another exercise in unsuspecting misinformation as a reporter flies in from London to Lagos to come up, the next day, with a profound insight into the "deep-rooted causes of the present conflict."

Western scholars, some of whom may have spent a week or two in a suburban hotel as far from Nigeria as Cairo, and others, who may have flown over Africa sometime during World War II and by so doing qualified as "experts" on all aspects of African life from rural culture through sexual behaviour and industrial development to literature and philosophy—these scholars immediately go to work churning out authoritative proclamations. Most such proclamations, whether from academicians or reporters, have one thing in common—the profound simplemindedness of their interpretations, the often highly creative falsity of their "facts," and the uniform, boldfaced, arrogant ignorance. Somehow, the qualities of an educated man, such as the modesty of scholarship that used to be the mark of sound minds and the subtle qualifications and reservations that should characterize an honest reporter, are ignored or summarily dismissed. In the rush to pontificate on matters which these men are incompetent to comprehend, as much because of their embarrassingly minimal knowledge of the place and the people as because of their inability or unwillingness to understand the depth of the African mind, simple, easily consumable interpretations are presented to the innocent reader whose access to Africa is wholly dependent on these scholars and reporters. As if the survival of their culture were incompatible with the simple truth, these men desperately and almost viciously refuse to consider the possibility of the fact that the African mind is not just at least as complex as the Western mind, but in all probability perhaps far more so, because of the fact, all too easily ignored by the West, that the African mind derives from a cultural history that predates Western civilization.

Somehow, the opinions of the Africans, the Nigerians, the people who are the actors in the situation, are not sought after. And when they are nevertheless expressed, they are either ignored or dismissed. No one seems willing or able to consider the simple fact that a Nigerian born and bred in Nigeria and having grown up in that historical context of which the crisis is a phase, is perhaps likely to be more competent to offer the presumably non-partisan and open-minded American or European public a more meaningful insight into the crisis. It has never occurred to those who run the bastions of international communications, such as the Associated Press, United Press International, *The New York Times,* or the television networks, to employ the services of African reporters in order to provide their public with more knowledgeable information and more sophisticated and more sensitive interpretation of the dynamics of a situation the Africans are more acquainted with. On occasions when this issue is raised, the response is that the African, being "emotionally involved" in Africa, is unlikely to be objective on African affairs. When one points out that by the same token American reporters, who exclusively cover American affairs, are similarly emotionally involved in American politics and therefore should be regarded as equally unlikely to be objective, one is accused of being argumentative. To point out that this same prejudice (which is actually racist, or at least ethnocentric) is extended to America where white reporters may cover all stories while black reporters may only cover black stories—more as a public relations concession, since only whites cover the big black stories—to point this out is to hate white people. And if one goes further to question the mythical objectivity of white scholars and reporters that one hardly finds in Western scholarship and reporting anyway, one is either branded a "revolutionary," or it is immediately remembered that the cocktail glasses are empty and need refilling.

In the meantime, the scholars continue to pontificate, the reporters file their high-sounding dispatches, and the non-skeptical and highly uncritical American public, rather untrained in how to read the news, continues to swallow, myths, half-truths, nonsense and all, yet another headful of pretentious and misguided news coverage.

Somewhere what seems to be forgotten or perhaps deliberately ignored is the fact that since participants in a given situation will act in accordance with their comprehension of the situation, that comprehension remains the most important insight into the given situation. Thus, Western prejudices notwithstanding, the most important opinion on the Biafran crisis was and remains that of the Nigerian people themselves. Yet it is precisely this opinion which was not sought in all the international centers of concern. With rather great amusement, Nigerians all over Europe and America—and there are thousands of them—sat back and read the presumptuous proclamations of what in the American idiom would be called "quickie" experts who overnight had come to understand perfectly every element of Nigerian life. Some of these "experts" lamented the tragedy of the alleged collapse of what they once called the only "stronghold of democracy in Africa." Some sought to draw a pattern of violence across the entire continent in terms reminiscent of the old films of the "savage African." Others, with the remarkable ability of making up in prophecy what they lacked in scholarship, claimed that the crisis had been a long time coming and that they had always predicted it. In all their rhetoric, they forgot that not only had they, to the contrary, always predicted the best and most optimistic for Nigeria, but that many of them, bearing the titles of "special consultant" and "expert" by a definition of international expertise which beats fundamental common sense, had been responsible for giving the kind of advice that ultimately led to the Civil War.

This about face by these consultants with little concern for moral responsibility and professional integrity was later to make Nigerian officials very sore. It was to lead to a reassessment, by the country, of her friends and enemies—a critical attitude, long overdue and late in coming into being, one which had been effectively prevented by the hordes of foreign "experts" that flooded the Nigerian government system and almost choked it to death. Ironically, it was to take such a major disillusionment, arising from a remarkable show of bad faith, to awaken Nigeria from her stupor of naïveté and place her at last on the path of actual independent political behaviour.

II. The foregoing is crucial if we are to understand the extent of the anger Nigeria and Nigerians felt about the reaction of the world press to the outbreak of fraternal hostility that was soon to be called the "Biafran war." For years Nigeria took a humble and open-handed attitude to her development. She was told that there was a certain glorious and perfect state of existence called "Western democracy," and she believed it. She was told further that that democracy had certain rules which, if she observed, would make her reap luscious fruits of that glory, and she believed it. Then she was told that Nigerians, even those educated in the West, were not qualified to guide the country in the development of her public, scientific, industrial, political, and social life. Even that she believed. Thus it was only a matter of logic for her to believe the next argument, namely, that the only people who could give her expert advice were people from that so-called Western democracy.

So thousands of Western experts, many of them former classmates of Nigerians and a not insignificant number of whom had performed at a level below that of their Nigerian classmates at the universities in Europe and America, poured into every stream and gauntlet of Nigerian life and government. It became a common scene for a Nigerian to pick up the papers and read about some "authoritative" pronouncement by a former schoolmate who was certainly not known for his conceptual perception back in his own good old country.

With a combination of these factors and others, the very fabric of Nigerian government began to rip apart at every seam. These factors included the deference of Nigerian leaders to alleged Western expertise, the sometimes subtle, sometimes overt racism and cultural chauvinism of some of these Western advisers and their governments, and the consequent disregard and sometimes distrust of the young educated Nigerian, partly because he seemed to pose an ultimate but inevitable threat to the older and often less educated politician, and partly because some of these advisers, in order to maintain their privileged positions in Nigeria and to prevent the influence of the informed opposition to them by educated Nigerians, and to discourage their appearance and acceptance in the crucial positions of national policy-making.

So in the late 1950s British foreign policy, as expressed through Nigerian policies on education, encouraged the study of law and the classics while discouraging training in the sciences and technology. While this worked in providing jobs in Nigeria for British engineers, little did Britain know that from the study of Plato, Aristotle, and Cicero would come the call for political freedom. Little did Britain know that in the study of law lay the beginnings of the knowledge of the law that was later to lead to the demand for constitutional changes that were to lead to the demand for full independence.

The American version of intervention appeared in 1965; it took a form far more dangerous and saw the cooperation of an ignorant and very vulnerable Nigerian government. It came bearing the banner of a new and fascinating but meaningless concept called "over-education." American experts in Nigeria advised the government that for her rapid development she did not need Ph.D.'s or M.A.'s, perhaps only a few first degrees, and that the Nigerian government's focus should be on what Americans called "technical training"—a euphemism for "skilled labor." "Why get Ph.D.'s," they said, "when you can spend the same amount of money to get five or six [skilled laborers]? Ph.D.'s are only good to teach or to do research," they added, "and it is cheaper to hire American teachers and researchers."

So the word went out that Nigerians abroad were being over-educated and that they should be sent back home. In 1965, the officers of the African-American Institute, a United States government-sponsored agency, met with members of the Nigerian Consulate in New York and in an atmosphere of presumptuousness that could only have equalled the absurdity and stupidity of the situation, went down the list of Nigerian students who were graduating that year, most of whom had already received admission to top graduate schools in America, and proceeded one by one to decide who should get graduate education and who should not. Then, with consummate pomposity, they jointly issued orders to scores of young Nigerians to terminate their brilliant academic careers and return home to "help their country." Such "help" included the advice that they were needed badly in any field, their specific discipline and training notwithstanding. In response to the storm of protests from the angry and frustrated students, the African-American Institute had the audacity to recommend that engineers, who had been interested in research or university professorship, should take positions as English teachers and that scientists should apply for jobs in publishing. To most of these students, all of whom had been chosen to study abroad because they were at the top of their classes in their high schools, it became, reduced to elemental terms, simply, "work wherever you can work, and do whatever you can do, go home and just go home." Coming at the end of what allegedly had been a seemingly carefully thought-out plan for national development, this action could not but raise charges of intentional sabotage of the Nigerian future through the systematic sabotage of the education of the young Nigerian upon whom the future of the country ultimately rested.

Ironically, the Nigerian government through its consular attachés became an unwitting collaborator in this vicious atrocity against her own best interests. Whether there was a plot to destroy Nigeria as some of the students could not help but believe, or, as is more likely, whether it was sheer stupidity on the part of the American advisers to the Nigerian government (which supported the general charge of questionable competence on the part of these men by the students), the only relevant point is that the education of many bright Nigerians was forcefully terminated in 1965. Many of them, threatened with the withdrawal of their visas and passports, headed home leaving their brilliant futures behind. Only the few who were lucky enough to discover the illegality of the threat to withdraw their passports and visas were able to stay to continue their education.

This episode had its few humorous moments, as the following indicates:

A student, who was about to graduate with a B.S. in civil engineering and who had admission to specialize in structural engineering under two of the best known authorities in the field, received a letter from the African-American Institute to the effect that the Nigerian Consulate and the Institute had decided that he did not have a future in engineering and that his country needed him at home. Angry, he telephoned the Institute and the following conversation ensued:

"I received your letter and it hardly makes sense."

"I can understand your reaction," a female voice answered, "but we have given serious thought to it and, as you know, we always have your best interest at heart."

"Of course. Of course. Now, since you refused to receive a

collect call and I am paying for this call I will not debate with you. Let's get to the point. If I go home, what will I do?"

"Whatever you came here to study for. We have offered to find you a job. You know you are highly qualified."

"All right, so find me a job as a professor of engineering, and I will be glad to go home tomorrow."

"But we can't find you a job as a professor."

"Why not?"

"You are not qualified."

"I thought you just told me I was very qualified?"

"Listen." (It was then becoming clear that the lives of many Nigerians lay in the hands of some silly little New York girl seeking to justify a policy that was equally silly. She probably had nothing to do with it in the first place—the poor girl.)

"I am listening. After all I am paying for it."

"Look, be reasonable. There is a job opening in a publishing house."

"In a what?" and he slammed the receiver down before she could continue.

The 1965 fiasco was to keep many Nigerians away from the Nigerian Consulate in New York forever and to alienate a few of them from their government.

The first coup d'état in Nigeria was to take place less than six months later. And to many of these young Nigerians, it was long overdue.

III. And so as Nigeria strove desperately to aspire to the expectations of the Western world, sacrificing everything Nigerian as it bulldozed along this path, she won the meaningless praise of the West and lost the confidence and respect of her own people. As she blindly sought to be "the good boys," as an American newspaper once referred to her, she set aside all sensitivity to the interests of Nigeria and her people; and as she struggled feverishly to fulfill the empty dream of a so-called democracy without seeking its meaning or finding out if her Western mentors lived by the codes with which they sought to strangle her, she ignored the concerns of the Nigerian citizens, alienated her precious young intellectuals, and rushed headlong into disaster. Thus, at the United Nations, Nigeria was to use some trivial rhetoric to defend American intervention in Katanga to the anger and disillusionment of all the other African member-nations who had looked to her for continental leadership and to the deep embarrassment and shame of millions of young Nigerians who were at a loss as to how to excuse this degradation by a country they loved—for the Nigerian, like · any other African, is a passionate patriot.

These events and the feelings they aroused, constituting the international rape of an innocent, naïve, but good-natured and well-meaning government that was only trying to do what international diplomacy, pressure, and propaganda had told her was the only thing to do, were to lead, early one morning on the 19th day of January 1966, to a military coup d'état. That coup d'état was the prelude to the costly Civil War and the shedding of much priceless and precious—very precious—Nigerian blood.

Approaches to the Analysis of the Biafran Affair

There are at least two approaches to the study of the causes of any given crisis. One approach is to attempt to look at the series of events which led to the crisis. In this case we seek answers to such questions as what happened and where; who said what and why; who did what, when, and how. This takes us into the realm of fact and falsehood, of speculations, accusations, charges and counter-charges, and rumors.

Characteristic of this approach is the preponderance of myths and hearsays and the popularization of half-truths in the context which makes them easily digestible. Thus when a newspaper reporter totally unfamiliar with the Nigerian scene flies in from London or New York to cover the situation, and when he has less than twenty-four hours to file a report, the best he could devise is a story of what is most plausible and most obvious, which often may have nothing to do with reality. He interviews people in the streets (more often the waiters in his hotel, forgetting that waiters generally will say only what is consistent with the etiquette of their job), or he may get some "inside knowledge" from some second-rate official whose information is no more reliable than that of the waiter (except that his principal preoccupation with being an "insider" makes him less free with his lack of knowledge) and whose objectivity is no less subjective than that of a peddler, except that the latter is less deceived by a false sense of his self-importance.

The job of the reporter is made doubly difficult (and therefore his insight less meaningful) by the fact that generally the space allowed him to cover the issues is so limited that it is impossible to even establish the complexity of the situation. He is then required to cut or "simplify" his story, an assignment which invariably requires that the essence of the issue with all its complex ramifications is eliminated in the very process of simplification. The end product is a simplified story on a complex issue without its complex core which is the very essence of the issue in the first place. Thus, for example, it is "too complex" to explain, in less than one column of any newspaper, the different factors that led to the civil crisis in Nigeria. It requires more space, better insight, and greater knowledge to be able to explain that although Ibos ended up as the underdogs during the Biafran war, they were party to the federal government that immediately preceded the crisis; that the Hausas, although in a majority, had always been discriminated against in the "Christian" South where there were special ghettoes (Sabon garis) for them; that behind it all, although the Ibos were mainly Christians and the Hausas mainly Muslims, there were at least two other states, both Christian and in the South, which were on the federal side, and above all that all Nigerians, being human, were subject to the appeal of power and the complex dynamics of the conflict of generations, as well as personal and regional interests. Even if all of this did not take much space to express, it would be regarded as too complex (an assumption which substantially belittles the intelligence of the readership), and the story is, therefore, reduced to the simple and meaningless interpretation that the Nigerian crisis is a result of corruption, colonialism, the economy—conditions which could be applied to any political crisis in the world—and tribalism, an expression which, among Western journalists, has become a code word for "African."

The preceding description is based on the assumption—very ideal, indeed—that the journalist is conscientious, of a relaxed disposition (a more useful term than "objective"), and with no personal bones to pick. It also assumes that he does not have any difficulty in getting a visa, has no problems at the airport on arrival, and gets nothing less than royal treatment at the hotel. If anything goes wrong with these assumptions, experiences which every foreigner is sure to get in the reporter's own country, then we begin to get vituperations in the guise of news dispatches, and verbal lynchings of public figures who may have refused to grant an inconvenient and probably thoughtless request for an interview. This is also assuming that after a good dispatch the editor at headquarters has enough knowledge of the subject matter, especially the subtleties, to do a meaningful job of editing the dispatch. An honest job is, of course, not necessarily a meaningful or reliable job.

Another seemingly minor circumstance that may substantially influence the reporting is whether the reporter's chauffeur, valet, or guide is Yoruba or Hausa or Ibo, or from one of the smaller ethnic groups. With all these variables one can attempt to analyse a given situation. The end product, at its best, is a document with which to assign praise or blame.

Or one can approach the situation with an analysis of causality. Here we reduce the importance of most events to the level of catalysts and accidental triggers of a situation that was fundamentally explosive, thanks to factors that are far deeper than the events and facts that get debated and tossed around in the mass media. Thus, it is a fact of Nigerian politics that not only was the crisis long overdue, it had in fact been taken for granted by every Nigerian years before when foreign experts and reporters were fooling themselves with their dance macabre—their dance of mutual fascination—with Nigerian politics. What is therefore very important and what has not been given to the public is a thorough and highly informed analysis of not so much the events but the deep undercurrents that led to the situation that made the Biafran affair inevitable. Such analysis, it seems, can only be provided by people who are most familiar with every aspect of Nigerian life, its culture, its influence, its idiosyncrasies, its individual and national character, its humor and prejudices, and the complex mixtures and countermixtures of its people. This is what is attempted in this book.

Nigeria: Dilemma of Nationhood: An African Analysis of the Biafran Conflict brings together some of the best African minds in an attempt to analyse and synthesize the forces that led to a historic crisis in a major African country. The objective is to enlighten fellow Africans as well as non-Africans on the dynamics of contemporary African political life. In bringing these scholars together I deliberately chose to approach the issue from different angles and different disciplines in order to bring out the broadest and deepest insights into the subject. Furthermore, since it is a fact of traditional African life that it is not so important that people see eye to eye as it is that all points of view be expressed, this book is very African in that it contains different and sometimes conflicting interpretations and points of view on issues. What is important is that each interpretation is thoroughly documented, provocative, and comprehensive. As a result, after reading this book, one will not have been coerced into taking sides but rather will have been given such a diversity of convincing information and interpretation, so he or she will be better able to form an independent opinion.

This is no less important now that the war is over since the very willingness of these young scholars to work together on a book with others with whom they disagree sharply is the very essence of scholastic objectivity and political responsibility. It is the expressed hope of every contributing author to this original book that its greatest usefulness will be to fellow Africans. Our commitment is to the belief that the best of African minds must give their best to the analysis of African problems as they are the only people competent enough and with sufficient commitment to provide solutions to African problems. Some Western "experts" have tried to resist this, but others have come to realize that not only is it desirable that the most important opinions on African development be African opinions, but it is inevitable. Any resistance to this fundamental position, even if it succeeds temporarily and encourages alienation of African minds from the service of their own people, is bound to be short-lived and can only complicate unduly the inevitable transition from experts to bystanders of many so-called Western experts on African affairs.

It has been a gratifying experience writing this book, and we hope it will be other persons' meaningful experience reading it.

2

BACKGROUND TO THE CONFLICT: A SUMMARY OF NIGERIA'S POLITICAL HISTORY FROM 1914 TO 1964

Moyibi Amoda

The Development of Nigerian Political Parties

Gabriel Almond, in *Politics of Developing Areas,* defines a political system as

the interactions to be found in all independent societies which perform the functions of integration and adaptation (both internally and *vis-à-vis* other societies) by means of the employment, or threat of employment, of more or less legitimate physical compulsion. The political system is the legitimate, order-maintaining or transforming system in the society.[1]

There are many political systems, such as the Congo's, that are excluded by this definition where the question of legitimacy is the crucial political issue. Political systems threatened by revolution or civil war or colonial political systems where the functions of adaptation and integration are performed, even though the possession and use of physical force by the colonizing power is regarded as illegitimate by the subjects, are other examples. Almond's definition, however, can be applied with some validity to political parties in Nigeria.

The definition is more comprehensive than Burke's definition of a party as "a body of men united for promoting by their joint endeavours the national interest, upon some particular principle in which they are all agreed." The Burkean concept of the party assumes a national arena in which the national interest is known but in which groups differ as to the means of achieving the ends. In accord with this concept, citizens may form parties because of agreement on certain means. As a party, they can propose programs to the electorate; and their failure to satisfy national needs may result in the loss of office. While in office, however, their duty is to carry out the national mandate faithfully.

Groups which at the moment are not in office because their proposals are only acceptable to the minority of the population have to set themselves up as the people's watchdogs, pointing out where those in office have failed to do their duty, where the means proposed have been inefficacious, and how the opposition's programs will more efficiently further the national interest.

This role of the party best suits the parliamentary system of government with its opposition parties, cabinet, and parliamentary responsibility. With an educated community, with efficient means of communicating national needs and judging governmental performance, and with the consensual basis for accepting the rules of the game assured, such a system will succeed, as it has in Britain.

The parliamentary system of government is essentially dependent for its success on the existence of parties whose representatives agree on a common policy, work together in a united front in Parliament. It is the party system which renders politics intelligible to the electorate.[2]

With the ends of society agreed upon, the test of the party's performance can only depend on the excellence or efficiency of its program and the execution of this program. Hence discipline and a united front in parliament become important values in parliamentary government.

When, however, this concept of the party is transferred to a society still in flux, where the national interest is still in the process of definition, there are bound to be conflicts about the nature of political goals and about the political means with which to achieve those goals. Political contests become contests to define the goals to be sought by society. In the absence of moderation on the part of the political parties, conflicts may become total, one party's victory annihilating the other parties. Parliamentary government becomes very difficult to operate when disciplined parties are devoted not to working out those means which are most conducive to an accepted national end, but to discovering the extent that the constitutional means can be used to further particular ends. The electorate cannot give a mandate acceptable to all parties because it is split into many communities.[3] The goals of political parties are not understood by all in terms of a common language of advantage and/or disadvantage; meanings are ascribed them from imputation of their sectional origins, and Parliament, rather than being the institution where the national logic or idea is abstracted from the numerous and partially organized demands, becomes the arena of power where the temporal majority superimpose the will of all upon the general will.

The political history of the introduction of the Nigerian peoples into legislative politics supports this interpretation. To this history we now turn.

In 1914 the colony of Lagos, the protectorate of Southern Nigeria, and the protectorate of Northern Nigeria were amalgamated, thus creating a unified Nigeria under Lord Frederick Lugard, who remained the Bristish governor until 1919. In 1923 a legislative council which had been set up in 1861 with jurisdiction over Lagos was expanded and reorganized. The new council provided for four elected African members, although property franchise was still only granted to the inhabitants of Lagos and Calabar. Parties sprang up almost spontaneously, a pattern which was to repeat itself as constitutional devolution of power led to greater political activity.

From 1823 to 1947 Lagos was the point around which the political actors revolved. The quinquennial elections for the legislative council, the triennial elections for the Lagos Town Council (to which body the elective principle was extended in 1920), and the perennial issue of the status and headship of the House of Docemo were the central issues of Lagos politics from 1923 to 1938.

The crucial and dominant personality of this period was Herbert Macaulay, founder of the Nigerian National Democratic Party (NNDP). His supporters were the House of Docemo and the vociferous Lagos market women.

As parochial as the actual concern of the NNDP was, the founder envisaged for the party a much wider role. His long-term aspiration was to see an eventually free nation under the Commonwealth,

to secure the safety or welfare of the people of the colony and pro-

tectorate of Nigeria as an integral part of the British Imperial Commonwealth and to carry the banner of "Right, Truth, Liberty, and
Justice" to the empyrean heights of Democracy.[4]

The immediate goal of the NNDP was to win the Lagos election
as a means of protecting the economic and political interests of the
native traders and producers of Nigeria, to press for the Africanization of the civil service, and to promote the development of higher
education and the introduction of compulsory education throughout the country.

Macaulay's preoccupation with championing the rights of the
traditional ruler of Lagos against the colonial government, and
the insulating effect on his party of the indirect rule which shielded
the interior of Nigeria from the political influence of Lagos,
prevented the NNDP from becoming truly national.

In 1938 the young, educated elite united to protest the standards
applied to higher education (specifically the granting of degrees
under British University standards by Nigerian institutions, in
particular the Yaba Higher College), discrimination in civil service,
and the issuing of licenses to African lorry owners. The protests
became a movement, and the movement soon outgrew its modest
beginnings to become the first major attempt to build a political
party on a national level. Branches of the party, the Nigerian
Youth Movement, were opened in most of the larger towns and
cities; leaders included men like Ernest Ikoli (Ijaw), Samuel
Akinsanya (Ijebu), H. O. Davis, Dr. K. A. Abayomi, Dr. Nnamdi
Azikiwe (Ibo), and Obafemi Awolowo. The party's goals included:

1. abolition or reform of indirect rule;
2. representation of provinces, including the north, in the legislative council;
3. higher appointments in civil service;
4. representation of Nigerians in London;
5. attention to the problems of the farmer and rural communities;
6. aid and support to African business entrepreneurs;
7. improvement of conditions of service of African employees
in mercantile firms.

The tenor of the party's thinking was national, its reforms were
directed toward the removal of particular abuses (the indirect rule)

which prevented the effective politicization of the masses, and the abolition of discriminatory practices against Africans both socially and economically. While it sought greater African representation in the decision-making bodies of the government, it still accepted the framework that the British system provided.

The importance of the Nigerian Youth Movement lay in the fact that it was the last party in which most of the Southern political leaders who later played important roles in Nigeria would work under one banner. Azikiwe and Awolowo, symbols of two of the three major tribes in the country, men who have been prominent in making Nigeria what it is, were members of the same party, working for the same national ends, until 1941.

In 1941 the fateful Ikoli-Akinsanya incident [5] split the Movement and introduced the thorny issue of tribalism for the first time. A seat in the legislative council had become vacant with the resignation of Dr. K. A. Abayomi, President. Party protocol and precedent directed that this seat should be filled by Ikoli, next in command, but Akinsanya (Ijebu) chose to contest for the party nomination. After his bid for candidacy was thwarted, he and his backers, the Ijebus and the Ibos under Azikiwe, left the Movement, proclaiming that they had been victims of tribal discrimination.

Whether a case to back this charge could be made is debatable. Among the supporters of Ikoli there were prominent Ijebus like Awolowo who saw the issue as one of maintaining party discipline and precedents. Ikoli himself, on whose behalf the Yorubas were supposed to have acted, was not a Yoruba but an Ijaw. If there had been tribalism, it should have worked against him too. It can also be pointed out that Ikoli, as an editor of the *Daily Service,* had come into the newspaper market at a time when Azikiwe's newspaper enterprises, the most important of which was the *West African Pilot,* were experiencing some financial difficulties; the economic implications of this rivalry might well have been more important than the bogeyman of tribalism. Another reason for conflict could be Azikiwe's dissatisfaction with his minor role in the Movement—a movement, moreover, dominated by Yoruba intellectuals more conservative then he.

All of these factors could have accounted for the final break. The important thing was that a practical and political move was made and tribalism was called in to justify it. This might be called the most important political episode in the history of Nigeria because it set a precedent which has yet to be reversed.

THE NATIONAL COUNCIL OF NIGERIA
AND THE CAMEROONS

In 1944 a melange of improvement associations, clubs, labor unions, and tribal unions met in Glover Hall in Lagos to form the National Council of Nigeria and the Cameroons. Membership in this party was organizational. The original members included two trade unions, two political parties, four literary societies, eight professional associations, eleven social clubs, and one hundred one tribal unions.

The party's immediate goal was to secure the independence of a united Nigeria within the Commonwealth. Its ultimate objectives were to disseminate ideas of representative democracy and parliamentary government by means of political education. "Specifically, the objectives of the NCNC are political freedom, economic security, social equality and religious toleration. On attaining political freedom, the NCNC looks forward to the establishment of a socialist commonwealth." [6]

The NCNC started as a national party, a purpose which was reflected in the composition of its leadership: Herbert Macaulay (Yoruba), president, and Azikiwe (Ibo), general secretary. Its tour of the country in 1946–1947 to rouse the people against the projected Richard's Constitution gave it a national aura which no subsequent party has managed to equal. However, between 1946 and 1948, the tribal tensions which had been initiated by the Ikoli-Akinsanya dispute of 1941, coupled with the dissatisfaction of the Yoruba elite, who felt that the NCNC was dominated by Azikiwe and the Ibos, culminated in the tribal cold war of 1948. The fulminations in the Zikist *West African Pilot* and the Yoruba organ, *Daily Service,* were catalysts which exacerbated an already explosive civil situation in Lagos. Threat of war almost turned into civil war as members of both tribes began to purchase weapons. The temper of the times can be understood from the altercations of men who had labored for decades on behalf of the national cause. Sir Adeyemo Alakija proclaimed that

we were bunched together by the British who named us Nigeria. We never knew the Ibos, but since we came to know them we have tried to be friendly and neighborly. Then came the arch devil to sow the seeds of distrust and hatred. . . . We have tolerated enough from a class of Ibos and addle-brained Yorubas who have mortgaged their thinking caps to Azikiwe and his hirelings. [7]

One could see the Ibo acting out what Azikiwe was to give national significance when he depicted the national destiny, the Ibos' ineluctable destiny to conquer and rule the nation.

It would appear that the God of Africa has specially created the Ibo nation to lead the children of Africa from the bondage of the ages. . . . the martial prowess of the Ibo nation at all stages of human history has enabled them not only to conquer others but also to adapt themselves to the role of preserver.

The Ibo nation cannot shirk its responsibility.[8]

THE ACTION GROUP

The Yoruba's specific answers to the threats of the Ibo represented by the NCNC and the Ibo State Union (a quasi-cultural-political organization) were the Egbe Omo Oduduwa (1948), an equivalent to the Ibo State Union, and the Action Group (1951), a party deriving its initial energy from the Egbe. But it is necessary at this moment to focus on the Action Group as a political party. Its relationship to the Egbe will be discussed later when I try to relate the role of the tribal-cultural organizations as agents of political socialization on a pan-tribal basis.

Although the membership of the AG was to be on an individual basis without any social, religious, or class discrimination, the founders of the party intended to concentrate on the Yoruba section of the Western Region, with hopes of winning the election to be held under the new McPherson Constitution of 1951. The central committee of the AG was to consist of representatives from each of the twenty-one divisions in the Western Region, members of the Egbe Omo Oduduwa who were interested in politics. They were to be persons who could be relied upon to carry out a concerted program.

As stated in the Inaugural Address to the conference which publicly launched the AG at Ondo Province on April 28, 1951, the very basis of the AG was to be two complementary strategic guidelines of action:

1. To bring and organize within its fold all nationalists in the Western Region, so that they may work together as a united group, and submit themselves to party loyalty and discipline.

2. To prepare and present to the public programmes for all depart-

ments of government, and to strive faithfully to ensure the effectuation of such programmes through those of its members that are elected into the Western House of Assembly and the federal legislature.[9]

Its immediate purpose was to win the elections of 1951 to the Western House of Assembly. Its long-term goals were:

1. The immediate termination of British rule in every phase of our political life.

2. The education of all children of school-going age, and the general enlightenment of all illiterate adults and illiterate children above school-going age.

3. The provision of health and general welfare for all our people.

4. The total abolition of want in our society by means of any economic policy which is both expedient and effective.[10]

The party was prepared to use modern political means, programs, party discipline, and political manifestos to capture a parliamentary election, but realized that only with the support of the traditional leaders in the Egbe Omo Oduduwa could the party image be quickly and efficiently propagated. The instrumental use of the Egbe was a political necessity, since it was only through the Egbe and its traditional leaders that the new language of parliamentary politics could be effectively translated. The Egbe had evolved into an effective medium of cooperation between the new elite of the Western Region and the Yoruba chiefs. And among the people of Yorubaland, the influence of the chief was considerable. As Obafemi Awolo wrote in 1945, chieftaincy has an

incalculable sentimental value for the masses in Western and Northern Nigeria. This being so, it is imperative, as a matter of practical politics, that we use the most effective means ready to hand for organizing masses for rapid political advancement.[11]

This tactical use of traditional means to advance a modern political goal is important. It is one of the keys that unlocks the seemingly confusing mysteries of the Nigerian political scene.

THE NPC
The emergence of a highly disciplined party in the Western Region, combined with the necessity to organize for the elections taking place in all of the regions, had its political consequences in the

North and the East. The NCNC at its meeting in Jos in 1951 reorganized a party which had been almost moribund for three years, changed from organizational to individual membership, and launched a vigorous election campaign in the East and the West.

The first important political developments unfolded in the Northern Region. Before 1947 Northern Nigeria had been effectively screened from Southern political influence, due to a joint effort of the traditional rulers and the colonial government; it now found it had to organize or see the North captured by Southern political parties whose secular ideologies were inimical to the traditional regimes of the Hausa-Fulani emirates. In 1948 two cultural groups, the Bauchi General Improvement Union and the Youth Social Circle of Sokoto, both composed of young men interested in politics, amalgamated. Jamiyan Mutanen Arewa (Northern People's Congress) was the result of this merger.

The traditional rulers, suspicious of any political activity not controlled by them, did not support this political party at the beginning. The leaders of the Jamiyan were cautious reformers who knew that without the support of the native rulers they could never succeed. They made a special effort to convince the rulers that they were only interested in helping the traditional authority stave off the Southern political invasion. In return, they asked for a measure of reform within the native authority system, stating that

Jamiyan does not intend to usurp the authority of natural rulers; on the contrary, it is our ardent desire to enhance such authority whenever and wherever possible. We want to help our natural rulers in the proper discharge of their duties . . . we want to help them in enlightening the Talakawa [the mass].[12]

The party was regarded as containing radical elements, especially the articulate leader, Aminu Kano, who was for drastic curtailment of the power of the rulers. In 1950 Aminu Kano broke away from the NPC to form the more dynamic Northern Elements Progressive Union.

In preparation for the 1951 election, the NPC was revived and declared a "Progressive Political Party as from October 1st 1951." It had received the endorsement of the rulers who now planned to use it to stabilize their regime. Its leadership was drawn largely from the ranks of higher officials in the native administrations (emirates). Its program included:

1. Demands for regional autonomy within a united Nigeria.
2. Local government reform within a progressive emirate system.
3. The voice of the people to be heard in all councils of the North.
4. Retention of the traditional systems of appointing emirs with a wider representation of the electoral committee.
5. Drive throughout the North for education while retaining and increasing cultural influences.
6. Eventual self-government for Nigeria within the British Commonwealth.
7. One North, one people, irrespective of religion, tribe or rank.[13]

Cautious friendship should be extended to all the peoples of Nigeria, although it could not be overemphasized that only the Northerners could save the North.

The elections of 1951 found all three parties victorious in their respective regions. The NPC controlled the Northern Region, the Action Group the Western Region, and the NCNC the Eastern Region. Apart from the AG, whose leadership in the 1962 crisis led to a government dominated by a coalition of the NCNC and some former AG members, each region was dominated up to 1962 by one of these major parties.

This regionalization of the parties had manifold consequences for the nation. It led to the peculiar form of the federal setup of Nigeria, in which the Northern colossus dominates all the other regions combined. It led to the entrenchment within each region of a party drawing its greatest support from the largest ethnic group in the region. And as a consequence of this, although all claim to be national, no national party with effective support in all the regions has emerged.

To maintain a national front and to establish a government acceptable to all members of the federation, the NPC, which can secure a working majority in the Northern Region alone, has been willing to form coalition governments with the NCNC. An almost impregnable North, in a federal constitution based on universal adult suffrage, assumes that the Southern parties, to have any voice in the federal government, must content themselves with the junior partnership in a coalition which is dispensable to the senior partner. I shall explore the implications of this problem in the final section of this essay.

The Ideological Stance of the Parties

To the Western observer, the style and vocabulary of Nigerian political elites may appear contradictory, as tribal and particularistic values comingle with national and secular values in individuals or in groups. The spectacle of national leaders on the one hand enunciating the tenets of the socialist society to be achieved, while on the other hand cultivating tribal loyalties which contradict in their implications the national millennium to be sought, present some difficulties to the builder of political typologies. It is sloppy and unsophisticated analysis to label the parties tribalistic, and therefore traditional, only because they seem to be based on tribes. This analysis does not explain all the peculiarities and intricacies of the political attitudes of the elite. A more detailed analysis will show how, in the case of the Southern parties, the AG and the NCNC, traditional values have been employed to promote modern, secular causes; and how, in the case of the Northern People's Congress, a modern political instrument, the party, has been employed to stabilize a traditional, authoritarian system.

The Action Group, as a list of the founding members would show, draws its leadership from the ranks of educators (33 percent), the professions (19 percent), and business (35 percent).[14] There is and was no leader from the working class (in Nigeria these would be daily paid laborers) and very few from the labor unions. The AG represented the interests of a rising class of businessmen, lawyers, doctors, and educators, although its support remains until today in the mass whose aspirations it is supposed to further. "The Action Group is the party of the masses, with reverence for Obas, understanding for the rich, and complete identification with the aspirations of the common man." [15]

The AG's use of the traditional rulers has been a calculated tactical maneuver. The leaders of the party, in agitating for political concessions from the British, demanded local government reforms to limit the autocratic power of the chiefs. So long as the British used the native rulers to maintain its regime, it would have been tactical to fight on two fronts: against the British and against the native rulers. *The Constitutional History of Nigeria* shows the British desperately trying to reconcile popular demands with the autocracy of the native authority system. Under the McPherson Constitution of 1951, the traditional leaders still had a very important role to play. What is even more important is the fact that the so-called autocratic native authority systems, at least in the Western Region and in the North, still enjoyed much popular support.

Clearly the AG was founded with a realistic awareness of the fact that chiefs were destined to play a major role in local and national politics under the Constitution of 1951 which extended the franchise to millions of people on a semi-democratic basis. However, the powers of the Yoruba chiefs in the Western region were limited by custom and the chiefs, with few exceptions, were not averse to political co-operation with those members of the new elite who were prepared to observe the traditional proprieties.[16]

There was no doubt in Awolowo's mind that without the support of the politically crucial institution of chieftaincy, he would have been forced to discontinue the AG's activities. "I was under no illusion at all that if these leaders of the Egbe frowned on the new political project, I would either have to abandon it or think again."[17] If the Egbe had decided to enter into politics as it had contemplated, "I was quite prepared to have the Action Group disbanded, leaving the Egbe free to start its own political wing."[18]

But the Egbe support was secured; there was need for a united front against the militant NCNC. And with the AG in power, the chieftaincy, as an institution, was brought under the government's control. The parties' success on the national level meant that the constitutions to be written would be dictated by the interests of the class represented by the parties. The regional constitutions gave the assemblies the right to depose or make chiefs. The Northern party was a party of chiefs and had as one of its principles the preservation of the emirate system, while the AG and the NCNC were determined to control the chiefs in their respective regions.

The success of the AG's eleven-year "rule" (1951 to 1962) had shown the masses where effective power lay: the native authority system had been democratized; patronage and threats of deposition had made manifest that no natural ruler could oppose the government and reign (the Alafin Oyo, when he clashed with the government, was deposed); the party possessed the crucial power of sanction of appointment and deposition of chiefs. In 1958, for instance, only one of the fifty-four members of the Western House of Chiefs was identified as supporting the NCNC. So thorough was the party's control of the chiefs that even in the turbulent and violently anti-Action Group city of Ibadan, the majority of the chiefs were AG supporters.

The party's use of the Egbe Omo Oduduwa was also tactical. The Egbe Omo Oduduwa had been established in 1948 to preserve the Yoruba culture from the onslaught of the Ibos. Its program, apparently ethnocentric, included in its objectives:

1. cultural development.
2. educational advancement.
3. Yoruba nationalism "to accelerate the emergence of a virile, modernized and efficient Yoruba state with its own individuality within the federal state of Nigeria . . . [and] to unite the various clans and tribes in Yorubaland and generally create and actively foster the idea of a single nationalism throughout Yorubaland."
4. protection of chiefs "to recognize and maintain the monarchical and other similar institutions of Yorubaland, to plan for their complete enlightenment and democratization, to acknowledge the leadership of the Yoruba Obas."
5. Nigerian federation "to strive earnestly to cooperate with existing ethnical and regional associations and such as may exist hereafter in matters of common interest to all Nigerians, so thereby to attain to unity of federation." [19]

The Egbe, as could be seen from its program, was more than a cultural organization. Its program envisaged the creation of a political community, perhaps a constitutional pluralized monarchy (since Yorubaland had many Obas [kings] and chiefs), or perhaps an upper house of chiefs with a lower house of assembly. The latter now exists in all of the four regions. The Egbe represented members of the new and rising class: lawyers, doctors, businessmen, civil servants, and certain far-sighted chiefs who perceived that the locus of economic and political power was not local but regional and national. Their values were fundamentally non-parochial and non-traditional.

The logical outcome of the national struggle for power with rival groups meant the inevitable politicization of the Egbe. The AG and the Egbe, the former having the chiefs as protectors, and the latter supporting the leadership of the chiefs, could be merged with the mobilizing of a population predominantly illiterate, traditional, and tribalistic. However, once the party as the political heir of the British had reduced the chiefs, by constitutional means, to a politically subordinate position, it had to build its own support at the grass roots and establish its own legitimacy.

The party, as government, could use its power of patronage to secure the support of the elite. Its control of the marketing boards, finance corporations, and the National Bank ensured the continuing support of the bourgeois class from which it emerged. But in order to retain the support of the masses, it had to champion welfare programs. Thus, control of the masses became dependent on the provision of social services, economic development, and political stability.

On the regional level, the party had to play the part of the broker, meeting political demands with political means and attempting to forestall some future needs by careful planning. This is what Ayo Rosiji (onetime Federal Minister of Health) meant by "pragmatic" welfare statism, as contrasted with principled welfare statism. The former, centering on planning, was the keynote at the AG's inception, and has remained a first article of AG belief.

Elections became a contest of manifestos, promises, and counterpromises.

All parties base their appeals to the electorate on welfare state principles, and the several governments of the Federation, in particular the regional governments, devoted substantial and increasing proportions of public expenditure to the accomplishment of welfare programs; the provision of schools, hospitals, maternity centers, water supply systems—in short, the things that the rural people want and demand from representatives. In a sense, the welfare state is a cultural imperative of communal society: industrialization at the expense of welfare would require the repudiation or disregard of communitarian principles which have been affirmed by Nigerian leaders.[20]

It became imperative to preach that a rival party, because of its different ethnic base, would sacrifice the interests of the Yorubas for the advantage of its own ethnic group. It was also imperative to show that, when compared with regions controlled by rival parties, the Yoruba-dominated region was better off.

Contests between political parties grew more fierce, because they were also contests for the powers of government on which the legitimacy and support of the party could alone be based.[21] Against parties with similar programs and similar ideologies, the only "real" difference was ethnic difference and the exploiting of deeply ingrained prejudices. Thus it was the exigencies of power, not the inability of tribes to work together, that led the AG, and by the same token, its rivals, to invoke tribal differences.

THE NATIONAL COUNCIL OF NIGERIA
AND THE CAMEROONS

Most of what was said in connection with the development of the
AG is applicable to the NCNC. The remarkable thing about these
two parties is that the more their rivalry intensified, the more
indistinguishable their programs and ideology became. The placid
politics of "tweedledum and tweedledee" has unfortunately been
the exception rather than the rule when these parties compete for
office.

Just as the AG had its Egbe Omo Oduduwa, the NCNC had its
Ibo Federal Union (changed in 1948, during the tribal "cold war,"
to Ibo State Union). The difference was, however, that while the
AG could emerge as a political party only by working through the
Egbe, the Ibo State Union brought its mobilized mass support to
a party already having Ibo leadership. The NCNC had the leadership and the Ibo State Union provided the followers. It could
easily be asserted that the "tribalization" of the "National" Council
of Nigeria and the Cameroons was inevitable, as the bulk of the
101 tribal unions in the NCNC were Ibo unions. But this is an
oversimplification.

Between 1944 and 1948, when the NCNC was the only national
party, it spoke for the nation, and nationalists in all the provinces
rallied to its support. Its 1946–1947 tour of the country to
mobilize the people in opposition against the Richard's Constitution of 1946 brought to all the people of Nigeria, as the previously
Lagos-based politics had never done, the drama of national struggle. But the leadership struggle, first in the Nigerian Youth Movement, then in the NCNC, between the Yoruba elites, who until then
had dominated the political scene, and the more militant, aggressive, and articulate Ibo elites, who until the arrival of Azikiwe from
the United States in 1937 had been on the periphery of Nigerian
politics, was to rend the delicate fabric of the national movement
in two.

The struggle could be seen as a class struggle between the conservative, status-conscious Yoruba elite and the more egalitarian
and more dynamic Ibo elite. Press war and tribal recriminations
were to follow. The cold war had started. The Egbe Omo
Oduduwa was formed at the peak of the struggle in 1948. In the
same year the Ibo Federal Union was reformed as the Ibo State
Union, ostensibly to organize the "Ibo linguistic group into a

political unit in accordance with the NCNC charter." The national president of the NCNC was elected the president of the union.

With the loss of most of its Yoruba supporters, the NCNC became predominantly Ibo. To mobilize this base of support into one solid phalanx behind the NCNC was thus the goal of this party. Between 1948 and 1951, "tribalism and regional nationalism became not only the most legitimate but the most effective means for educated nationalists to secure power." [22]

The struggle between Nigerian rivals incorporated the struggle against the colonialists: the relative backwardness of the Ibos and the differential development of the West and East were imputed to the calculated plan of the colonialists and their Nigerian stooges.

The Ibo State Union had to carry the message of the NCNC to all supporters; in this struggle there could be no neutrals. The identity of the Ibos and the fate of the NCNC had to be inextricably wound together.

Tell them that the Ibo giant is waking from his stupor and is asserting his inalienable right in the scheme of things in this great country of Nigeria and the Cameroons. Tell them that the Ibo stands solidly behind the National Council of Nigeria and the Cameroons, and believes the NCNC is destined to weld this country into a federal commonwealth of politically free and equal nations. Tell them that in accordance with the Freedom Charter, we have answered the clarion call sounded by the NCNC for national self-determination of the various linguistic and ethnic groups of our blessed country towards the crystallization of a federal commonwealth. [23]

The McPherson Constitution of 1951 established the federal structure of Nigeria in its present form. The elections to the House of Assemblies in all the regions accelerated the drift toward subgroup nationalism and tribalism. "Educated Nigerians who aspired to fill the new positions of power and status opened up to Nigerians by that constitution realized that their most secure base of support would be the people of their own groups." [24]

From 1951 to the present, the NCNC has been overwhelmingly dominant in the East. The Party has had time to cultivate grass root support, and whatever political control the Ibo State Union had, has been lost. From 1957 to 1958, the intraparty rivalry between Azikiwe and his right-hand man, Mbadiwe, was settled at the party level, and all attempts to use the union as a mediator failed. The union contented itself with wishing that the disagreement would be settled amicably, but accepted the verdict of the National Executive Committee which expelled the rebellious group led by Mbadiwe. The electoral loss suffered by Mbadiwe in his own hometown and constituency indicated that when a choice has to be made between the union and party, the party will be chosen.[25]

The problem the NCNC leadership faced in 1964 was how to dissociate the party from its popular image as an Ibo party. We have seen that at the regional level this was almost impossible; political exigencies made the party predominantly Ibo in the region. At the national level, the leadership was certainly not predominantly Ibo. Yorubas occupied positions of influence in the National Executive Committee, and they had a proportionate share of ministerial portfolios. However, the fact that the NCNC strategic alliances compelled the National Executive Committee to grant representatives of these allies some say in committee decisions was indicative of the attempts of a more confident regional party to capture a national arena which it had once relegated to a subsidiary level in its politics.

The NCNC, like the AG, profited from intertribal and intratribal rivalries in the Western Region. This, rather than the fact that its program was national, was responsible for the success of NCNC in Ibadan, Ilesha, and the Midwest Region generally. Because local needs might make these coalitions temporary, the NCNC kept tight control over its one secure base, the East. Its national alliances remained peripheral to its regional operations.

The federal context in which the party had to function created pressure to make the adjective "national" in its title a reality. Its ideology since 1951 oscillated between support for a federated or a unitary Nigeria. Its leadership was certainly more nationalistic than the leadership of the two rival parties, the AG and the NPC.

Like the AG, the goal of the NCNC was the establishment of a welfare state. Michael Okpara, leader of the party, explaining his party's ideology, wrote that

having considered the various political philosophies carefully, namely Capitalism, Liberalism, Communism, and Fascism, we have come to the conclusion that the only philosophy that appeals to us is that of Socialism, where the means of production, exchange and social services are primarily a responsibility they bear through their government.[26]

The inconsistency of a socialist ideology and a leadership mainly bourgeois led to tremendous tension within the party. There was a struggle between the old guard, which Dr. Okpara (a medical practitioner) symbolized, and the young, ideological, and more radical wing, once isolated in the articulate but politically ineffective Zikist national vanguard. The issue was important enough to cause the national president, Azikiwe, to issue an apology for his wealth and his membership in the bourgeoisie.

It was true that Azikiwe's career did not fit easily into the traditional Marxist framework of the socio-political analysis. "How does one classify a populist banker whose political support lies primarily in the peasantry and the working class, and not in the new elite of which he is supposed to be the epitome?" [27] How does one classify the leader of a nationalist organization that seeks a socialist commonwealth, but whose political lieutenants are drawn from the most bourgeois element within the party? To the impatient demands of the young enthusiasts in the party he cautioned:

Let us not make a popular mistake by assuming a normal acquisition of wealth is wrong for society. It is not inconsistent with socialism for a socialist, through hard and honest work, to acquire a limited amount of wealth to enable him to co-exist successfully with his capitalist counterparts. It is not the volume of wealth that makes it obnoxious to the Socialist, but it is the use to which wealth is put that matters. If some of us had not accumulated wealth in the dim and distant decade when the oppressor was in his heyday, it would have been impossible to found this great party. . . . Nevertheless, the well-to-do among us must now use their wealth in a philanthropic manner, if they have not already been doing so. . . .[28]

The government's extensive involvement in the economy of the nation, a heritage of a colonial administration which had taken the responsibility for promoting the colony's economic development, was as far as the NCNC had gone toward socialism. It was also as far as any of the parties in Nigeria had gone. The government of Northern Nigeria controlled by the traditionalistic and authoritarian Muslim emirs was for socialism, if socialism meant government control; the government's responsibility was really the responsibility of the party in power.

However, since the interests of the rising classes of businessmen, professionals, and educators were well protected, and since it was from these classes that the party recruited its leadership, the logical step which all socialist countries should take, public ownership of "production, exchange and social services," was difficult, if not impossible, to take. At Jos, in 1962, the adoption by the AG of "Democratic Socialism" as the party's ideology split the party into two irreconcilable camps. If, in a party usually considered conservative (the AG), the militance of its radical wing can force the adoption of this ideology, then, in a party regarded as more liberal (the NCNC), the inconsistency of a bourgeois leadership and a socialistic party cannot but lead to a future ideological rift within the party.

THE NORTHERN PEOPLE'S CONGRESS

One of the strongest factors which made Lord Lugard adopt the indirect rule as a system of government in Northern Nigeria was the presence of an elaborate emirate system with highly developed administrative apparatus. The bureaucracy in the North has been closely tied to the emirate system since the Fulani conquest in the nineteenth century. With the institutions of the Northern People's Congress under the auspices of the traditional rulers, the party has drawn its leadership from the native administration. From tabulations made by R. L. Sklar in 1958, the principal occupations of 62 percent of the members of the National Executive Committee and 65 percent of the members of the committees in eight principal emirates of the North were officials or clerical employees of native administrations. In certain emirates, Sokoto and Adamawa, the NPC executive was scarcely more than a committee of the native administration.

It had not been difficult for the emirs to control nationalistic movements in the North, since the British and the indirect rule which gave the autocratic emirs more power, made Hausa nationalists particularly vulnerable to economic, political, and cultural pressures. Because their few Western-educated elite were employed by the native administrations either as civil servants or teachers, the Hausa could be influenced by threat of economic reprisal and other legal penalties.

The Northern administrative elite, which forms the backbone of the NPC, differs from the politically dominant new class of Southern Nigeria in so far as it is not deeply involved in business enterprise. Their lack of financial independence made them vulnerable to threats of economic sanction for political progressiveness.[29]

The Hausa business elite had always resented the "invasion" of the North by Southern businessmen, who were not only economic rivals, but also people of an alien religion (Kafaris—unbeliever), and thus had everything to gain by identifying their interests with those of the traditional ruler. The party also had solid support in the masses, the majority of whom, long used to obeying their leader whose right to rule was based on Islam, remembered that "Our religion is the religion of obedience." The NPC, therefore, was supported by the traditional ruling class, the native administration, official and employee occupational class, wealthy Hausa business-men, and the business elite in general. In addition, laborers organized by leaders of the NPC, and beggars who lived on alms tended to support the NPC.

The intensified desire to catch up with their more developed Southern counterparts, both politically and economically, led to the well-entrenched policy of Northernization. The educated class of teachers, skilled artisans, clerks, and semiprofessional elite, a class which Coleman called the "crisis stratum," found that the demand for services by the Northern government was more than they were able to supply. It was to their advantage to collaborate with the NPC, which was devoted to the mutual aim of keeping the eco-nomic and political market places out of the reach of their better equipped Southern competitors. Those who challenged the power structure, like Aminu Kano, leader of the Northern Elements People's Party, found themselves condemned to a long period of political ineffectiveness.

In the North it was very difficult to be in the opposition. Politi-cal reprisal was great. The borderline between political opopsition and legal offense was a very vague one, and opposition leaders often found themselves in prison, serving sentences for sedition or for endangering the peace by public criticism of the leaders of the government party.

The pan-tribal unity which Islam created also tended to rally everyone behind the religious leaders. Religion, economics, and politics were so thoroughly mixed that a threat to one was a threat to all. This, more than anything else, explained the impervious-ness of the Northern region to political influence from the Southern Nigerian parties.

The North was securely dominated by the NPC. Its electoral victories from 1951 to 1965 showed that its control was the nearest to a one-party state control in all of Nigeria. It had no ideology except insofar as the maintenance of the dominance of the chiefs and administrative elite was ideology. Its motto of "One North, one people, irrespective of religion, rank, or tribe" expressed its determination to mobilize all the peoples behind the party. Even in the Middle Belt area, where the agitation for a separate region was most intense, the acculturative effects of the Muslim religion were to the advantage of the NPC.

Of the three Nigerian parties, the AG, the NCNC, and the NPC, the NPC was the least dedicated to a united Nigerian nation. Its policy was stated in 1951 as "cautious friendship to all the other peoples of Nigeria," and this policy had undergone no considerable change. Its Northernization policy showed that the government still found it almost impossible to think on a national scope.[30] Thus we have the paradox of a party that ideologically and politically was the most parochial and traditionalistic placed in power at the federal level by the constitutional provision of universal adult suffrage.

The Role of the Parties in Political Development

I have already stated that the process of nation-building in Nigeria lies in the resolution of the conflicts between borrowed institutions and the indigenous political structure, and that the agents of that resolution would be the political parties. Implicit in this thesis, therefore, is the hypothesis that the process of political socialization and the emergence of the nation-state will depend largely on the successes and failures accompanying the socialization process.

I am aware of the traditional objections to this approach—objections to what appears to be a political determinism, possibly raised by my emphasis on political socialization as the integral aspect of the nation-building process. The relationship between the values individuals espouse as individuals, and those they share in groups and institutions devised to sustain and promote crisis-free transmission of change, cannot be explained by a static monistic analysis.

The development of classes, the availability of power, and the presence of trans-class values, all take on a mix which may aid or hinder the evolution of a community coterminous with the territorial limits of the state. The history of the peoples involved in the "nationalizing" process is also an important variable to include in a theoretical explanation of the task of community building.

Even with all these objections, it can be stated without too much distortion that all communities have had to grapple with the problem of establishing an institution to which all owe allegiance, the legitimate authority to which ultimate loyalty is given. Where peoples find themselves without such an institution, there is the threat of societal breakdown. This threat is especially increased when the peoples concerned share a history of common government that is only half a century old and have a complicated ethnic and cultural composition glued together by a foreign language; when the only visible symbols of the state are the government buildings, and the state itself is known as the government; and when the bulk of the population is traditional, illiterate, and unsure of what to expect from this "government," or how to make effective demands on its bureaucracy. In such a community the problem of community-building, a problem which for analytical purposes can be trimmed down to the task of inventing old institutions on which ultimate authority is reposed, is usually tackled by the elite. It is they who have the concept and enjoy enough psychic mobility and intellectual empathy to think in terms of an aggregate as large as the nation. Upon their dreams, their inventiveness, their capabilities, their dedication depends the gradual or revolutionary expansion of values conducive to the delineation of the community under construction.

In Nigeria, as in most of the recent African nations, the political parties were the institutional organizations through which the elite tried to function. Political parties, in an age which many have appropriately called the "age of politics," have therefore been the crucial modernizing factor.

The purpose of the third and fourth sections of this essay has been to show how the parties went about cultivating their home base of political support, from what class the party leadership was recruited, and how effectively or ineffectively other institutions, such as the chieftaincy which was traditionally the repository of social and political legitimacy, were incorporated. To determine whether this process of communal politicization led to the "nationalization" of the community and whether it was accompanied by the adaptation or rejection of native or foreign institutions, we have to sketch briefly what changes had taken place up to 1964 and what was the quality of this change. I shall deal with these changes under the following headings with the political party as the common denominator:

1. Political Party and Ethnic Factor
2. Political Party and Class

3. Political Party and Ideological Predilections
4. Political Party and Participation
5. Political Party and Administrative Service as Agents of Integration
6. The Effects of 1–5 on the Stability and Effectiveness of Governmental Institutions.

POLITICAL PARTY AND ETHNIC FACTOR

Since almost all of the major parties espoused the emergence of a Nigerian nation as one of their long-term objectives and certainly as an article of their ideology, we shall investigate how their programs assisted or militated against such an emergence. The major political parties we have seen had their main support in the ethnic group dominant in their region. The historical analysis in Sections Three and Four of this essay showed that the political strategy adopted in a federated setup was to use the ethnic and cultural differences to keep out rival parties. Political socialization was therefore on a communal basis. The tribalization of politics meant that individuals were not socialized into a national community. In a situation originally amorphous, no clear meaning of the national community to be built was imported by the leaders to the followers, nor was a national response by the followers possible, since they were appealed to only through their ethnic identity.

Only a national political party with genuine mass support in all the tribes would have been able to detribalize politics and make it the promotion of the national interests by available power.[31] Thus, to maintain power in the regional and federal parliaments, the political leaders found it strategically important to place tribe and party together. To remain in power without having to depend on any one ethnic group required that ethnic differences be played down and elections be waged on programs. But, since the programs were so similar in all the regions, the average voter on the basis of program alone found it difficult to make a choice. Uneducated citizenry and universal adult suffrage seemed to create a unit which required a conspicuous label to differentiate one political "good" from another.

The ethnic factor in a population predominantly illiterate made rational politics extremely difficult to achieve. The absence of a trans-tribal political party and the presence of political elites, torn between political exigencies and ideological commitments and unwilling to act nationally in terms of their political style, tended to

freeze the process of nationalization of the community, thus limiting community awareness to the regions. During this period
effective political community existed only in the regions.

The creation of a state on linguistic or ethnic bases provided
the governmental power, political and economic, to establish an
effective and viable community; but regional communities fed on
the fragile body of a national community which was unsupported,
as each of them was, by any emotional or psychological involvement of the masses.[32]

POLITICAL PARTY AND CLASS

The emergence in the political leadership of a "new class" was a
phenomenon remarkably characteristic of the Southern political
parties. Here politics was allowed a mobility described by James
Coleman as unparalleled elsewhere in recent history. We saw in
Sections Three and Four how the nationalist movements had been
fought on two fronts, one against the colonial system and the other
against the native administrative system which had excluded the
vocal elite from political power.

The new class composed of teachers, lawyers, businessmen, and
doctors formed the influential political and economic elite by their
domination of the native administration. The party's control over
the government gave it a powerful instrument of patronage. Its
control of banks, the marketing boards, and the finance corporations meant that the leaders could ensure the loyalty of the new
class by granting and withdrawing contracts, loans, and the security
of lucrative jobs.[33] The three regions, Northern, Western, and
Eastern, had banks controlled by the governments, and the use of
loans and extension of credit tended to be highly political. "In
sum," as Richard Sklar succinctly states, "commercial patronage,
including loans, marketing board licensing, and government contracting, is channeled through public agencies that are quasi-
political in nature and conception. *In all regions, these agencies
serve the political interests of the government party only* [italics
added]." [34] This explains why the loyalty of the "new class" was
predominantly to the system which allowed their position of dominance to continue, and why it was extremely desirable for those
aspiring to the "new class" to use politics as the medium of social
mobility.

Within the Nigerian context, the party substantially controlled
those institutions fundamental to the pattern of social stratification.

Electoral campaigns, therefore, took on added dimensions. The stakes were higher, since loss of an election might lead not only to loss of office, but also to serious financial and perhaps social repercussions. The fierceness of the campaigns, the use of all means to defeat the rival parties, stemmed from this use of politics as the social and economic motive force. The result was the perpetuation of differences, especially tribalism, and policies such as that espoused by the Northern Region's government, a policy of strict Northernization of the civil service, and perhaps of all economic opportunities. Thus intra-regional party struggle could be seen as class struggle between various new classes whose vested interests would be jeopardized by electoral defeats. This accounts for that phenomenon of "bench-crossing," of buying over members of the opposition in the parliament by the government party. This practice did harm to the meaning of elections, indicating not only the lack of a well-disciplined party and the fragility in the party system, but also the lack of an effective process by which the electorate could hold its elected representative to account. In a system where the support of the government opened great promise of patronage, both economic and social, it was difficult to resist the tempting offers of the government.

In the North we have seen that the wealthy businessmen, the school teachers, the native authority officials, and the Alkalis (Muslim judges and court officials) identified their interests with those of the government. Since the government's Northernization policy preserved the citadel of the Hausa chieftains, while at the same time shielding its peoples from the rivalry of Southern-trained businessmen, teachers, doctors, and lawyers, protection of the *status quo* was criticized and denounced, and the necessity for carrying out enlightened programs was increased. Some concrete evidence was required for asserting that one regime was better than another. Hence the inter-regional party struggle had the positive result of making the regional governments more receptive to new ideas and more willing to meet the needs, defined or undefined, of the masses who were still to develop the political mentality that saw the party as an instrument to satisfy public needs.

The tendency at the national (federal parliament) level was to keep the parties separate, preventing mergers (though not electoral and tactical alliances which left both party structures intact and unimpaired) from which a national and unifying party could emerge. Parliamentary coalitions at the federal level were usually on a *quid pro quo* basis, a consortium at a fundamental level, at least as far as preserving political support was concerned, to utilize proportionately the federal powers of patronage (limited to administrative jobs, ambassadorial and ministerial appointments), and to stabilize the parliamentarians' positions until the next elections. This type of coalition, based not on ideological similarity, but only on expediency, could work as long as the members of the coalition respected their spheres of influence. It was delicate and susceptible to pathological contortions even in times of relative quiet—but in crisis the coalition would disintegrate. This explains the curious but for a time "stable alliance" of the progressive and comparatively militant NCNC and the conservative and somewhat authoritarian NPC, a coalition which had taken various forms from 1953 to 1964.

The opposition was impotent, being composed of the party, which was regarded at the regional level as a potentially dangerous rival; but much more important, the members of parliament, depending so much on the party, were well disciplined and voted solidly for all government proposals.

POLITICAL PARTY AND IDEOLOGICAL PREDILECTIONS
It will be necessary here to regard the Southern parties as one category and the Northern party as another (with the exception of the Northern Elements People's Party, allied to the NCNC with whom it agreed ideologically).
The NCNC and the Action Group. Both parties adopted socialism as their goal. Socialism as functionally interpreted by these two parties was essentially the public ownership of the means of production and distribution, as expressed through the government's responsibility. In essence, it would be much like a welfare state in which the government attempts to meet minimum social and economic requirements of the citizenry. Its guiding concept was that of planning. It was thus a pragmatic socialism, a method of achieving the efficient use of available resources in a society where the public sector seemed to have a monopoly on the administrative techniques to meet social demands. This was socialism not as an ideology, but as a program.

The infusion of the program with a doctrine, commitment to a set of dogma and hence some form of ethos, tended to divide rather than unify the leadership of each party. In both parties the split seemed to take on the aura of conflicts between two generations:

the fairly conservative, bourgeois, pragmatic old guard, the effective leaders of the party, and the young, more militant avant-garde. This is obviously an oversimplification of the ideological division within the parties, but it certainly was valid as a statement of a recognizable tendency.

The "contradiction" of chiefs, affluent lawyers, rich landlords, and other similar persons leading a party purporting to march toward a socialist society may have caused some discomforts to ideological purists in the party. In 1958 Azikiwe had to defend the presence of the rich within a party motivated by socialism. Wealth was not bad; private enterprise was not bad; it was the use of wealth that should be questioned. This explanation was temporarily accepted, but continuous pressure towards explicit definition of the brand of socialism to be adopted never ceased. In 1962 the AG's adoption of "Democratic Socialism" caused a split between the militant wing backed by the National President, Chief Awolowo, and the more conservative group backed by Chief Akintola. However, the concern for ideology certainly remained at the theoretical level, except insofar as a rationale for government intervention in the economy, an intervention characteristic of the colonial government, was needed.

The parties certainly were not ideological, nor did individuals vote on ideological grounds. In the sense that we differentiate parties as Communist, Socialist, Christian Socialist, there were no ideological parties in Nigeria. If ideology means the acceptance of certain goals and certain institutional and attitudinal means to transform the existing system, then there were no ideological parties, at least as far as their political style and political acts were concerned. The predominantly pragmatic and eclectic approach adopted was flexible and philosophically utilitarian, though it permitted class differentiation. Essentially it sought to extend equality of opportunity and freedom of choice.

Parties tended to see themselves as instruments to provide solutions for needs expressed and unexpressed, one of which was economic development. They did not regard themselves, in practice at least, as the agents of a millennium. As Coleman puts it, parties view their goal as the satisfaction of the "national interests," the national interests being not the symbol of a way of life to be preserved, but rather the embodiment of their collective aspirations. As such, their principal emphasis is upon general goals such as universal education, higher standards of living, racial dignity, and "life more abundant," the motto of the AG. Thus ideology *qua* ideology was not an important ingredient of the political mixture in Southern Nigeria.[35] Yet ideology as a conceptualization of a way of life, a type of society, and types of citizens building this type of life does generate a community spirit. It is thus a systematization of the values and programs to effect these values. In mobilizing support for an ideology, participation is based on the total view of the millennium and the massing of empathy to include all who believe in the dream. Thus groups which unite, if this is part of their goal, apart from force or the practical considerations of cooperation to solve specific and geographically defined needs, must create and project consensus-building values. They must develop an ideology, a belief in a way of life and the gradual socialization of individuals into the value patterns conducive to the emergence of this way of life. Fourteen years was too short a time to evolve an ideology meaningful to all citizens.

Northern Region and the NPC. The religious conquest of the North by the Muslim Fulanis gave the resulting political system a cohesiveness which has become characteristic of the traditional Muslim countries. Islam, like Protestantism, encompasses more than worship; it is also a socializing and political force. While the social and political elements in Protestantism are implied, the Muslim faith explicitly designs a system which fuses both the secular and the religious worlds. It is a religion with an ideology, an ideology of brotherhood irrespective of race and rank. In itself it does not necessarily imply an authoritarian or democratic system. However, in the North where Islam came with the Fulani's sword, it was used to stabilize a highly stratified society. Side by side with the unifying message of the brotherhood of all races was the word, spread by force or convention, that "our religion is a religion of obedience," obedience to the "natural" rulers. The motto of the NPC, "One North, one people, irrespective of religion, rank or tribe," tended to weld the North.

Leaders of the dominant culture groups have espoused pan-regionalism rather than pan-tribalism. Indeed the NPC evolved into a political party from a cultural organization that encompassed many nationalities and tribes. This distinctive phenomenon in the social development of the Northern Region may be attributed to the universalist teaching of Islam. In part it may be a consequence of the fear of Southern domination, which grouped sections of the progressive Northern elite as well as the chiefs in the early postwar period.[36]

It is certainly true that the realization in the late 1940s by the leaders of the North that they were vulnerable to Southern "insidious ideologies" led to the willingness of the native rulers to employ the newly introduced weapon, partisan politics, to defend their system. However, the identification of Southern politics with an alien religion, Christianity, helped to make the Northern Region less receptive to the secular style of the Southern parties. The ideology described by the NPC's motto fused politics and religion in a region where there was essentially one established religion. The challenge to the political structure was therefore an attack on a way of life and a challenge to be uncompromisingly resisted.

The economic corollary of "one North, one people," with the North in supposed danger of Southern domination, meant the limiting of Northern resources to Northern exploitation, a regional autarchical restriction of opportunities, and Northernization which offered something to everyone.

Thus the problem of national integration was complicated by the difficulties entailed in marrying an absolutist, authoritarian, comparatively unified religio-political culture with a relatively more secular, pragmatic, but disunited culture. (In the South, the individualistic, militant, and egalitarian Ibos were much different from the class-conscious, essentially more conservative and urbane Yorubas. But both, in terms of their ideological stance and political style, were more alike and, therefore, stood together against the Northern Hausas and Fulanis.)

The South had no conception of what community it wanted, but it knew the plan to be somewhat socialistic, hence secular. The North, however, knew what it wanted. Its aim was to keep the past by using the tools of the present, to keep the North Muslim and under the emirs, but to use the modern tools of art and science to maintain the North at a competitive advantage with the South. Whether the North could contain the Orient and the Occident without being a victim of a cultural schizophrenia was doubtful. The universalistic and relativistic attitudinal complexes, when they co-exist within individuals, groups, or nations, lead to irrationalities. Whether the North, Islamic and totalistic, could fuse with the amorphous and secularistic South is yet another question difficult to approach.[37] The pathological disturbances of several Latin American countries have been traced by many Latin American specialists to the co-existence of traditional and secular values in all classes with the consequent inability of the society to develop a system in which ultimate loyalty is reposed. The labor and pain produce stillborns. Such co-existence in Nigeria, if fusion is even possible or conceivable, may lead to a like paralysis of will, and hence to the evolution of institutions too weak to contain the process of change.

POLITICAL PARTY AND PARTICIPATION

Northern Region. In the North the factors of religion, culture, and the closed political systems made political participation of the masses the endorsement of the *status quo,* because the elite were in control. Since the political elite comprised mainly the hereditary rulers and their kin, political mobility through election or any other political means was difficult for the middle and lower classes. Political mobility for the middle groups of society was controlled by the desires of the aristocratic elite. It is true that in the North the individuals most loyal to the emirs were employed in the native administration system, and the leaders of the NPC tended to be drawn predominantly from the native administration. However, since economic mobility was relatively more open and the Hausa businessmen and professionals were drawn from the middle groups, the loss of political power tended to be less painful, and thus acceptable.[38]

The social bond of Islam, the sense of obligation of the rulers to the led, and the fact that the middle groups had not ceased to identify with the lower classes to whom they charitably gave alms and attention made the masses less susceptible to radical ideas. The strength of the NPC lay in the solid faith of the masses in their leaders.

Southern Region. Within the two major parties, ethnic factors were the most important when explaining the political behavior of the dominant groups. Where there was opposition within a group, and thus an alliance with another political party outside the group, historical, religious, or class factors might be operative (for example, the socio-economic rivalry between the Ibadans, native settlers of the city of Ibadan and opposed to the AG, and the immigrant settlers, the Ijebus, wealthier and politically entrenched in the leadership of the AG). Of the two major groups, the Yorubas and the Ibos, the Ibos had the stronger inclination to vote in a block. The NCNC strength in the West depended heavily on the recent historical internecine warfare between major groups in Yorubaland (for example, despite the rivalry between the Ijebus and Ibadans, and the Ilesha and the Ile-Ife, the former voted almost consistently with the AG, and the latter with the NCNC).

While the power of patronage seemed to keep the "new class" loyal, welfare statism made the continuous support of the party by the masses more meaningful to them. Political participation in terms of voting might be psychologically fulfilling, but it had little political effect for the masses—most voting was a blanket endorsement of the party's candidates except in cases of intense constituent dislike for an individual. The development of class awareness and political education, and thus the detribalization of politics, was necessary to render the election an examination and selection of alternative programs presented by rival political parties. Without this, the masses needed generalized criteria, such as clan, tribe, or religion, in order to exercise any choice at all.

POLITICAL PARTY AND ADMINISTRATIVE SERVICE AS AGENTS OF INTEGRATION

Nigeria at its independence inherited from the British a well-established civil service, trained in the British tradition of non-partisanship. On it rested the gigantic task of assisting the government to formulate and execute policies.

The stability of the colonial administration depended to a great extent on the strength of the civil service. For the majority of the people, the bureaucracy was identical to the government. The buildings it occupied were the visible symbols of the government, and its civil servants the executors of the government weal. The extensive government involvement not only in public administration, but also in the development of the economy, meant a necessary enlargement of the bureaucracy.

The plethora of civil servants was therefore the corollary of welfare statism. The average individual for most of his daily needs, jobs, medical services, education, license for burials, etc., had to contact a bureaucrat, who controlled his destiny. He felt helpless before the bureaucrat, who participated in a power structure which he had never controlled and had not yet learned to control. He did not regard the administrative service as a bureau of servants; indeed, he regarded it as a master whose world of papers and endless delays must be endured. He saw the bureaucrat as responsible to the government, but he had not yet learned to see his election of government officials as his control over the bureaucracy.

The civil service as the arm of the executive interacted with the mass. Its program might help channel demands and expectations to and from the government. It could not, at the time, fulfill the role of political socialization by inculcating in the mass that it was a national institution subject to public pressures and control. The role of the bureaucracy as the administrative and information-gathering arm of the government followed the British pattern and was adopted in the political situation in Nigeria.

The granting of responsible government to the Western and Eastern regions in 1957, and to the Northern Region in 1959, instituted the ministerial systems. Cabinet and ministerial responsibility for policy execution meant the close cooperation of the bureaucratic elite and the political elite. Because the political elite were new to the task of administration, they relied greatly on the direction of the civil servants. The granting of independence did not lessen this reliance, but rather increased it. The regionalization of politics also led not only to the regionalization of the civil service, but introduced politics into the selection of the bureaucratic elite. Since the civil service was the major source of occupational mobility, especially for the majority of the educated elite, it was susceptible to political pressure.

The party extended its control over the civil service by co-opting the bureaucratic elite into the political elite. The politicization of the elite and of the civil service thus introduced pathologies already existing in the political system. Tribal and political considerations became important in recruiting the elite. High-level policy positions in the regions rarely went to individuals only on merit consideration. The Northernization of the Northern Region civil service was the public expression of a norm which the Southern parties followed in practice, although not in principle. In the federal civil service, the ministers tended to surround themselves with permanent secretaries and private secretaries of the same party and usually of their own tribe.

On the federal level, the coalition between the NPC and the NCNC meant the partition of the appointive powers of the federal government. The scandalous disclosure by the press in 1964 of tribalistic "packing" of certain ministries was an inevitable result of the patronage system.

The effects of all these developments on the civil service as an integrative institution were dysfunctional. The political promotion of an NPC, AG, or NCNC candidate into the top position in the ministry to adjust a political disequilibrium bred resentment among

civil servants who regarded themselves as more qualified by experience and tenure of service for the position. The lack of job security
and of promotion based on a non-political merit system weakened
the loyalty of the civil servants to the bureaucracy as an institution.

At the lower levels of the bureaucracy, employment and promotion in the civil service were more by merit. However, since politics
appeared to be a more rapid way to the top, the civil servants
possessed divided loyalties. While they depended upon the merit
system of the bureaucracy, it was an additional insurance to be
registered as party members. It was these groups, urban, young,
restless, and ambitious, who formed the "crisis stratum." It was
they who were already mobilized but found no satisfaction in the
conservative leadership of the parties controlling the country. They
were to be found in the Nigerian Youth Movement under Dr.
Otegbeye, in the Zik's National Vanguard, and in the militant wings
of the existing parties.

For the middle groups of the bureaucracy, composed of the bulk
of the "educated elite"—the majority of whom could find jobs only
in the civil service—neither politics nor the bureaucracy offered
any satisfaction. Here were the alienated, those disillusioned with
the administrative monotony and possessing too much imagination
to remain satisfied behind their desks and files. Here, also, were
ambitious and talented men who could find no hope of immediate
promotion because the bureaucratic elite was relatively young and
the usual attrition by retirement and death very slow.[39] Their
contempt for a government run by "illiterate" politicians and a
bureaucracy controlled by parties could result in a cynical acceptance of corrupt practices.

A decline in the efficiency and probity, and hence of popular respect
for government, is possible in view of the slight experience and the
absence of service traditions. The absorption of the developing educated class into bureaucratic office will prevent them from participating
in the political activities of the unofficial sector of society. A third
consequence will be the absence of a normal age spread within the
administrative hierarchy.[40]

Some decline in efficiency and probity could be accepted if this
was the immediate price to pay for the "immobilization" of the
politically mobile of the middle groups. But if contempt for the
government led to acceptance of a radical ideology to transform this

society, these groups would provide the leadership. Within the Nigerian context, such ideology to be effective would have to come by revolution. The price of revolution is blood, and this even the disillusioned elites were not yet prepared to pay.

The Effects of 1-5 on the Stability and Effectiveness of Governmental Institutions

I have defined national integration, in this essay, as the nationalization of the community, the community being coterminous with the legal territorial boundaries of Nigeria. A "successful" nationalization of the community, then, would take place when each individual, group, or class begins to feel that there is a stake, the highest stake, in the preservation of the continuous existence of the community; when loyalties to individuals, groups, or classes, for certain public actions, are subordinated to the national interest; and thus, by implication, when the ultimate sacrifice is paid in terms of lives and loss of liberty in critical situations so that the nation may live. The nationalization of the community is said to be successful when in public interactions both in the political and economic market places a functional and legal equality of participants is the accepted norm; where merit in the economic market place is the criterion for mobility; and where in the political market place the rule of law and the temporary expression of the "public will" resulting from an election is accepted as a guide for political behavior (at least until enough support is mobilized to change this "will"). Therefore, in a national community, a certain degree of public behavior and consensual political style is built into the polity. This is an ideal rarely attained, against which the effect of the five factors discussed in this section are to be measured.

It was found that the ethnic factor prevented the development of a national consciousness which could invest the national institutions with a primacy over other institutions. This ethnic factor, coupled with the relative absence of class considerations, also led to the lack of development or recognition of common interests which cut across tribes, linguistic groups, or filial associations. The existence of mass illiteracy and a minority of literate vocal elites resulted in a dichotomous development of class awareness. The majority and the illiterate, existing in a tribal or linguistic milieu in which ascriptive and achieved status depended on traditional criteria, were socialized into parochial class and caste values which had relevance only within a limited group or area. Their political consciousness, because of the active politicization of the tribe, had not grown beyond the regions.

The literate few, who as members of the business, professional, and administrative elite performed in the regional and national arenas, had developed class awareness which was politically circumscribed. They were the political elite whose social and economic development was closely linked with partisan politics. It is they who invoked the tribal loyalties to shore up their political support. As "nationalists" they were dedicated to a united Nigeria (whether it was legal unity, "communal unity," or economic unity, they were yet to determine). As politicians they employed the traditional symbols which prevent the emergence of this unity. They exhibited a political schizophrenia which in the Nigerian context was most destabilizing. Sklar's description of one of the nationalists, Adelabu, succinctly exposes this schizophrenia.

In principle, Adelabu was progressive, as his writings indicate, in national politics he was a radical. But in local politics he was too astute and ambitious not to appear as a conservative and a traditional. Therefore, he was not identified with the administrative reformers of the Ibadan Progressive Union of Youth; he publicly opposed court reform and was discreet in his criticism of the inefficient tax system. Throughout Nigeria he was admired for his militant nationalism. His colleagues in the nationalist movement respected him for his ideals, but people of Ibadan loved him because he was the idiosyncratic personification of their traditional values and their cantankerous hostility to imposed reforms.[41]

This duality of role performance was an asset, so long as the politician's roles in the local and national contests were separable.

In regional politics, the politician had to respond to local pressures. He could use his national or local image as the political strategy demanded. But at the federal level, where the national interests became paramount, the clash between the local and the national was inevitable. The strengthening of the particularistic rather than the national values weakened whatever national community existed. As an actor at the national level, he sought to reconcile national demands, which he helped to define, and local demands, which were imposed upon him by his environment. His entry into the national political arena depended on the votes of the non-national majority, but his performance in the market depended on his interpretation of what the national rules were. His inability to mobilize support outside his local group compelled him to fall back on the assured group support. Yet at the federal level, stability depended primarily on the acceptance of the rules of competition. If the regulating and arbitrating institutions threatened one or more of the competitors with ruin, the whole structure would be endangered as the threatened party might opt out of the federation. Stability might therefore be stability of the *status quo* or the acceptance of the rules of the game to channel political change.

It was therefore at the federal level that a few individuals, members of the political elite, responding to the inchoate national demands, were to decide whether Nigeria would exist or disintegrate. The December 1964 election in a way showed how fragile the national community was and how dependent on the ideological commitments of the political elite. The federation was threatened with dissolution, elections were seen as useless solutions to the political problem, there were street riots in the cities—these were the ominous symptoms of disintegration and unfinished nationalization of the various communities of the federation. However, the fact that the dissatisfied national leaders called only for boycotts of the elections, "talked" of "peaceful dissolution" of the federation should certain demands not be met, and their obvious unwillingness to advocate violence that might lead to civil war indicated at the very least the effort to "keep the Congo out of Nigeria" and to maintain the tenuous federal structure.

The army, the police, and the civil service were loyal to the government, as if it made no difference what "party" was exercising the constitutional authority of the government. The majority of the people waited, perhaps uneasily, for the decisions of the leaders. They allowed themselves to be persuaded that the results of the federal election would be accepted and the efforts towards constitutional reform would follow.

The compromise prevented the ultimate crisis, a crisis which began over the demands to use a constitutional reform to solve a political problem. The crisis still persisted, since the problem was as yet unresolved and had to be resolved if every election were not to lead to a nightmare of political disintegration. The means that the leaders chose for resolving the crisis were, however, very important. They chose reform, not revolution, and the redistribution of political power, not the destruction of the basis for political power, the nation.

This crisis during three weeks of December 1964 was not unforeseen. It was long in the making. It was implicit in the Richard's Constitution of 1946; it was unresolved in the McPherson Constitution of 1951; it was left for further negotiation in the Constitution Conference of 1957. The problem had to do with the distribution of power within the federation and with the creation of more states within the existing states of the federation. In the absence of a national consensus about what was to be divided, in the absence of an overriding loyalty in all groups to the nation, Nigeria, the problem of creating new states also merged into the larger problem of creating the national state itself. In arguing over the issues of new states, or in refusing to discuss the "insoluble," there was a tacit agreement that all debates would be conducted within a federal framework. The fact of negotiating and acting within this framework imparted an attachment to that framework. For most, the issue was not what framework should be adopted, but how it should be strengthened to enable it to withstand the strain of future demands.

The last section treats the election of 1964 with this problem in mind. The conclusion offered indicates in what direction the author thinks the political parties progressed in adapting themselves and those they led to their environment, and in adapting their environment to their own needs—and to the basic need, that of the nationalization of the various peoples that exist within the geographical and legal entity called Nigeria.

Elections And Issues of National Legitimacy

In the immediate postwar years, the Nigerian nationalists expected and demanded greater participation in the government. The sacrifices they endured on behalf of the British Commonwealth were to be repaid by British gratitude expressed in greater devolution of power to the Nationalists. The presence of the Anti-Colonialist Party, the Labour Party, in Westminster, increased Nationalist hope. The Labour Party was not unwilling to act in accordance with its avowed purpose, that of gradual liberation of the oppressed.

In 1946, the Richard's Constitution was promulgated. The objectives were:

1. to promote the unity of Nigeria,
2. to provide adequately within that desire for the diverse elements which make up the country,

3. to secure greater participation in the discussion of their own affairs.[42]

Though the constitution met a hostile public desiring more than mere "discussion in their own affairs" and sorely dissatisfied with the representational system which would leave most of the "discussion" to those already sympathetic to the government, the one innovation introduced into the Nigerian political structure, that of regionalization, was not criticized.[43] In fact, it was seen as a belated recognition of a principle long advocated, a federation in which diversity in unity, or unity in diversity, would be preserved.

Federalism was accepted by all the Nigerians, Nationalist and non-Nationalist alike, as the most suitable system for the organizing of a country diverse in its ethnic composition.

The rationale for such an approach seemed to have been provided by M. Venkatarongaiya, who wrote in *Federalism in Government* that

Federalism may be said to be the best kind of government for people among whom there is a considerable amount of diversity in respect to language, religion and culture and for countries which are vast in size and which contain provinces and sections with varying geographical and economic characteristics. In such situations, no other form of government can thrive so well and produce such good results as federalism does.[44]

Although it can be shown that federalism itself seems to thrive badly in a situation in which the various linguistic groups are interested in preserving their own identity (for example, English- and French-speaking Canadians), the thorny question of the distribution of power between the center and the federal components may become insoluble if adequate checks and balances to equilibrate the influence exerted by each region are not provided. Where the conditions defined by Venkatarongaiya exist, the process of preserving the linguistic and cultural differences results in the weakening of the unifying bonds. Linguistic autonomy soon merges into the desire for political autonomy. The dialectics of decentralization rarely produce a synthesis of a unity in diversity. Stability is achieved if the regional components are approximately equal in size and thus are able to form coalitions in which the diverse interests are well protected, and if the constitution provides for checks and balances in which the interest of the minority will find adequate expression.

The worst possible situation exists where there are not only linguistic and cultural differences, but where one state or region of the federation is so large that its influence overshadows those of the other states or regions. Thus, when Awolowo advocated the creation of several states along linguistic lines, the assumption was that none of the states would be large enough to threaten the other states within the federation; otherwise, the *raison d'être* for such a system would not have existed.

We advocate the grouping of Nigeria into various autonomous states or regions, purely on ethnical basis. Experience of other countries shows that this basis is more natural, and invariably more sasisfactory than any other basis. . . . It is a matter of general agreement that a lasting unity of the peoples of the vast country can only be achieved through federation and not fusion. Consequently it is absolutely necessary to lay the foundation for federation now dividing the country into the regions that will form the units of the proposed federal constitution. This undoubtedly is the reason why regionalization has been about the only acceptable feature of the Richard's Constitution.[45]

How large should a state be? Should there be as many states as there are linguistic groups? Awolowo had answered these questions when he made one of the criteria for the creation of more states the financial viability of the proposed state.

I hasten to add, however, that we advocate ethnical grouping only as the ultimate objective. We realize that if this basis is strictly adhered to at present throughout the country, some states would emerge which would be totally incapable of finding money to run their own affairs. We consider it desirable, therefore, that for the time being such ethnical groups as are unable financially to maintain their own separate states should be amalgamated with other larger and neighboring groups until they are able to maintain their own separate autonomous states. Such smaller ethnic groups should be free to decide within which larger groups they are willing to be temporarily amalgamated.[46]

Awolowo envisaged a federated system in which the unit would be the ethnic group, enjoying within the federation an autonomous existence. Whether this group will be so autonomous that the federation would become more like a confederation was not the important question he wanted to answer. He was more concerned with preservation of the integrity of the ethnic group within a "united" Nigeria. Political reality would soon lead to the abandonment of this theory and to the acceptance of larger aggregations as the basis of a federation with the problem of unity and diversity still unreconciled.

Azikiwe also thought along the same line, but he tried to reconcile the demand for linguistic states with the problem of economic and political unity of the country. If the boundary of the states were to be drawn to preserve the cultural integrity of each ethnic group, how was power to be shared between the group and the federal government? Were the states to be so small that the federal government was only to be given power to perform functions which the states could not otherwise perform?

I am opposed to the division of a great country like Nigeria with an area of 372,674 square miles and a population of about 25 million into three regions, because it is an artificial system and must inevitably tend towards Balkanization and the existence of chronic minority problems. I suggest instead the division of the country along the main ethnic and/or linguistic groups in order to enable each group to exercise local and cultural autonomy within its territorial jurisdiction.[47]

To reconcile the demand for cultural diversity and unity in diversity, Azikiwe agreed with the substance of the recommendation of the Nigerian Students Conference in Edinburgh in July 1949, which he maintained was in keeping with the Freedom Charter of the National Council of Nigeria and the Cameroons.

The Constitution of Nigeria should be based on some form of federation which would permit all the nationalities of Nigeria to develop to full political and national cultural maturity, while at the same time insuring that Nigeria as a whole progresses towards a more closely integrated economic, social and political unity, without sacrificing the principles and ideals inherent in their divergent ways of life.[48]

The demand that the constitution should permit the various groups to develop to "full political and national cultural maturity" implied that the states must enjoy a great measure of autonomy. However, the demand that the economic, social, and political unity of the country should be preserved implied that each state would have to sacrifice some of its autonomy for the greater good of the whole. If the "whole" were itself autonomous and independent of the parts, the sacrifice by the parts would be easier to make, since the balance would still be maintained among the parts. If the whole were to be supreme over the parts, the problem of reconciling cultural and political autonomy of the parts with the distribution of control over the whole by the parts could be a

Sisyphean task. Unity in diversity could be achieved if there were institutions to which the diverse parts owed loyalty and if the parts were equal and thus had equal say in the control of the whole. But short of these two alternatives, something would be sacrificed; either unity or diversity would have to be modified by politics.

The introduction of tribalism into Nigerian politics in the late 1940s and the regionalization of the political parties imposed a solution which froze the political *status quo* but left unanswered the delicate problem of power distribution among the entities in the federation. When, in 1948–1950, proposals for the revision of the Richard's Constitution were put before the Regional Conferences convened to discuss the issues, there was a choice between a unitary system of government (the whole should be supreme over the parts), the continuation of the three-regional setup, or a federation with many more states than then existed. The overwhelming choice was for the retention of the *status quo*. The choice was an admission that no one group enjoyed the support of the diverse groups to be entrusted with the task of governing the whole, and that the affairs at the center would be carried on by a coalition, a coalition which was acceptable even to those excluded from it.

Do we wish to see a fully centralized system with all legislative and executive power centralized at the center or do we wish to develop a federal system under which each different region of the country would exercise a measure of internal autonomy? If we favour a federal system should we retain the existing Regions with some modification of existing Regional boundaries or should we form Regions on some new basis such as the many linguistic groups which exist in Nigeria? Without exception all the Regional Conferences recommended a federal system of government with the existing three Regions as the units. But opinions differed on the question of boundaries.[49]

They could not agree on how the boundaries should be drawn. Since each group was bent on preserving its own region intact, the three major parties, the NPC, the NCNC, and the AG, which in 1951, 1953, and 1957 had to negotiate with the Colonial Office on constitutional questions, were unable to decide what should be an acceptable formula of revising boundaries or creating new states, though the Federation, as it was, was an unbalanced Federation. The Northern Region was bigger than the other regions put together. Its leaders, with the motto of "One people, one North, irrespective of rank and religion," would not discuss the partition of the North into smaller states. The other two parties, representing the Western and Southern Regions, accepted this incongruity, perhaps to preserve the unity of the country. They had to accept the Northern demand that it get at least 50 percent of the seats in parliament. The North made it clear enough that that was the irreducible minimum it would accept as a condition of belonging to the Federation, and the British strategy made this concession of the Southern leaders almost impossible to refuse, since they would only deal with a unified Nigerian delegation at constitutional conferences.

Thus the position of the Northern Region in the federation,

like that of Uttar Pradesh in the Union of India, creates great uneasiness about the future stability of the Nigerian Federation. In population as well as in size, the Northern Region is very much larger than the Eastern and Western Regions combined. It is therefore feared that this form of imbalance creates an ominous potential to the stability of a federation. John Stuart Mill, in discussing the federal form of government, pointed out that "There should not be any one state so much more powerful than the rest as to be capable of lying in strength with many of them combined. If there be such a one, and only one, it will insist on being master of the joint deliberations; if there be two, they will be irresistible when they agree; and whenever they differ, everything will be decided by a struggle for ascendency between the rivals." [50]

Between 1951 and 1953, Nigeria did not have to pay the price John Stuart Mill correctly set for such lop-sided federations. At the center, a national coalition, equally representative of the three regions, formed the Cabinet. In 1953, the North and South confronted each other on the issue of setting a date for independence. The South was united in its opposition to the North. The result was a threat by the North to secede. In 1964, the North and the South once again confronted each other; the result was a threat by the South (the East most vociferously, and the West and Midwest could be counted on to follow the East out of the federation) to secede.

In 1953, the coalition government of the NCNC, NPC, and AG had been split on the motion for independence from the British in 1956. The NPC opposed such an early date because they feared that they were not as equally prepared as the Southern Region for independence and that independence would only lead to Southern exploitation of the Northerners. Tempers flared, riots took place in Kano, and while the two Southern leaders, Awolowo and

Azikiwe, embraced each other, the Sarduana of Sokoto stalked out of the parliament muttering, "The mistake of 1914 has been revealed."

The Northern leaders' answer was the Eight-Point Programme, almost tantamount to a demand for secession, and the most important of these points were:

1. all revenue except customs should be levied and collected by regions;

2. there should be a central agency which should be non-political in nature, having neither legislative nor policy-making powers; and

3. Lagos, the capital city, should be made a neutral territory.[51]

The North, in effect, asked for a confederation in which the three regions would be completely autonomous, a customs union in which only the economic needs would bring the three regions together.

The Secretary of State for the colonies, Oliver Lyttelton (now Lord Chandos), declared on May 21, 1953, a stopgap solution, a solution which is the basis of the Constitution of the Republic of Nigeria. "Her Majesty's Government had regretfully decided that the Nigerian Constitution would have to be redrawn to provide for greater regional autonomy and for removal of powers of intervention by the center in matters which could, without detriment to other regions, be placed entirely within regional competence." [52]

The constitutional reviews of 1953 in London, and of 1954 in Lagos, gave the formal structure to the Federation. The three parties, following what has been described in Section Three of this essay, established themselves in the regions. At the center, however, a most curious but stable coalition sprang up between the Northern Peoples Congress and the National Council of Nigeria and the Cameroons. The NPC was willing to accept 50 percent representation, instead of seceding, in lieu of its demand for confederation, and this of course meant it had to ally with one of the Southern parties. The Action Group, much more than the NCNC, had been carrying on active political campaigns in the Northern Region; the AG challenged the NCNC in the East, and was the Government Party in the region where the NCNC was in opposition. The NCNC and the AG also were kept apart by strong personal rivalries, rivalries which started early in the Nationalist movement and had resulted in deeply engraved suspicions on both sides. Thus the two Southern parties, which logically should have formed a coalition since their programs and goals were more similar to each other than either was to the Northern Peoples Party program, could not act together. Perhaps this was good for the country, since a clearly defined North and South alignment might have frozen the line of political action and forced the North into carrying through its threat to secede. From 1955 to 1964 the NPC and the NCNC were in alliance in the federal parliament. "The coalition government was rightly characterized as a 'political *mariage de convenance*'. Yet the great surprise is that these two parties, different as they are from each other ideologically and temperamentally, have up to the present been remarkably successful in holding together their precarious coalition." [53] It is not surprising when it is known that there were certain rules of the game to which this coalition tacitly gave rise. One of the conditions, definitely necessary for the coalition to have been so stable and acceptable to the AG, was that both parties, NPC and NCNC, would leave each other alone in their respective regions, that the AG was prepared to accept a position of ineffectual opposition in parliament so long as its regional base of strength was not weakened and that the NCNC would accept with equanimity whatever unwholesome pressures were brought to bear on its Northern ally, the NEPU.[54] To institutionalize this *status quo,* rigid procedures for the creation of new states were inserted into the Constitution.

Alterations to section 3 of this constitution for the purpose of establishing new regions out of other territories shall be effected only in accordance with the following procedure.
(a) A proposal for the alteration shall be submitted to each House of Parliament and, if that proposal is approved by a resolution of each of those Houses supported by the votes of at least *two-thirds* of all members of that House, the proposal shall then be submitted to the legislative houses of all the regions: and
(b) if the proposal is approved—
  (i) by a resolution of each legislative house of a majority of all the regions or
  (ii) by a resolution of each legislative house of at least two regions, including any region comprising any part of Nigeria that would be transferred to the new region under the proposal.[55]

In 1962 the precarious balance was upset. The crisis in the AG leading to the schism in its leadership became a subject of national concern. A state of emergency was declared by the national parliament. The AG was in disarray, and the two parties in the federal government had taken more interest in the demise of a rival than in the preservation of law and order. The Western Region had been ruled since then by a government deriving its legitimacy from the Emergency Legislation, and no election was held from 1962 to 1965.

This episode demonstrated the power of the federal government. Its constitutional authority, which had not been employed because of the tacit agreement of the national parties to limit the federal government's participation in governance to the federal territory of Lagos to the promotion and coordination of the economic policies of all the components of the federation and to the conduct of foreign policy, was not invoked to effect a major change in one of the regions. The federal government had shown it had powers, powers which could be used by a party or parties, with the appropriate majority. Henceforth, the struggle to control the federal government would be fiercer if the federal government were not *primus inter pares,* but the most supreme political body.

From 1962 to 1963 there were signs that the coalition between the NPC and the National Council of Nigerian Citizens was under severe strain.[56] The NCNC, as a junior member of the coalition, had been given more ministerial positions than its numerical contribution to the coalition merited. It controlled three strategic ministries—finance, foreign service, and communications. Thus the attempt by the NPC to assume in practice what was politically a fact (the role of senior partner) led to resentment on the part of the NCNC. The sense of frustration and impotence at the continued self-assertion by the NPC increased as the merger into the Northern Region of the Northern Cameroons, through the United Nations plebiscite in 1962, gave the NPC an overall majority in the federal parliament, thus putting the NPC in a position to end the coalition when it chose to.

In February of 1964 the figures of the census taken in 1963 were released. The effect was electrical. It changed the whole political atmosphere of the nation and prepared the ground for the crisis later on in the year.

Prime Minister Abubakar Tafawa Balewa had magnificently violated all the rules of government by consultation when he let loose a bombshell that shook the very foundations of the much acclaimed Nigerian unity.

The month was February 1964, and the National Convention of Nigerian Citizens was rounding up its talk at the Kano Convention of the party. Then came the thunder-bolt—the release of the 1963 population census figures for the nation, the delay of which had caused quite a stir in the country. Instead of consulting his brother premiers from the other regions as was originally agreed (or if he did, he carefully side-tracked the Eastern and Midwestern Premiers), the Prime Minister acted unilaterally.

The figures released, and referred to as "preliminary" yet "final" were as follows:

Northern Nigeria	29,777,986
Eastern Nigeria	12,388,646
Western Nigeria	10,278,500
Midwestern Nigeria	2,533,337
Lagos	675,352 [57]

This lengthy quotation, taken from the maiden issue of the political magazine of the NCNC, demonstrates the effect of the census on the party. The figures showed two facts which could not be ignored if the census were accepted.[58] First, it established as a fact what had been feared for a long time, that the North alone could overrule all the other regions put together, that the North could now form a government solely on the votes it got from its Northern base. Second, it showed that the Eastern Region itself was no longer larger than the other two regions, the Midwest Region and the Western Region, thus weakening further its position as a strategic ally. The balance of power had been upset. The stage was set for the split. What the census said was simple; in fact, its strength lay in bringing to the fore the issue of boundary revision. It spelled out the short-term alternatives for the parties. The NPC would win any election in the future if the Southern party could not make any headway in the North and if it maintained its opposition to the creation of new states from the existing regions.

The NPC's control of the North was shown in Section Three to have been almost absolute; the cost of being in the opposition was not lightened by the native administration system which made political opposition criminal.

The constitutional barriers to a legal revision of the boundaries or creation of more states made this an ineffective method to reduce the preponderance of the North by breaking it into more states. Without the Northern acquiescence in the federal parliament, a two-thirds majority could not be obtained to pass the resolution for the creation of more states, and without this majority the bill could never become law; without the NPC agreement, no other two regions could pass the bill, for such majority must include the region affected. This was the impasse. Under such conditions NCNC and NPC could not be maintained on the former basis without adequate revision, especially when the more radical members of the NCNC were becoming impatient with their more conservative ally. The coalition was at an end. The NPC would seek other allies in the Southern Region to make its government more Nigerian; the NCNC would ally with other Southern parties and then attempt to fight the NPC in the North to achieve a national strength. While the NPC would attempt to identify its interests with those of the country, it maintained there was no need to change the *status quo;* the NCNC would accuse the NPC of tribalism and appeal to the voters first as citizens and then as members of particular social and economic classes. In this respect, the election of December 1964 was the first national election to be held —and it failed precisely for this reason. Christopher Johnson, in the October 1 issue of the *London Financial Times,* was nearer the truth than most of the actual participants in the drama itself, when he wrote:

The Federal elections which must be held before the end of the year have a two-fold significance for the rest of Africa. Both democratic forms of government and federal-type institutional structure will be on trial, and their future may depend on whether Nigeria continues to show that they are workable.

The staying power of Nigerian democracy is dependent on that of Nigerian federalism. The Northern Region, thanks to the controversial census last year, is entitled to more seats in the Federal Parliament than the other three regions put together. If the Sardauna of Sakoto, the traditionalist leader of the North, decided to use his superiority to control the federal government with no more than token support in other regions, the federation itself will be put under strain.

But if, as Sir Abubakar is said to prefer, a national coalition of all the major parties is formed, what becomes of the party system with its guarantee that there will always be a healthy parliamentary opposition to the government? The problem of the Northern Region's preponderance will only be solved as other parties get a chance to make inroads into the Sarduana's still somewhat feudal support. The forthcoming elections will show to what extent this slow process is already taking effect.[59]

That was precisely what was to precipitate the crisis, for the other parties did not feel they were getting a chance to wage an unmolested campaign in the North. From June to October, the alignment of all the parties under the NPC and NCNC banners was taking place. By October, when the campaign began, the lineup was as follows: the Nigerian National Alliance, consisting of the Northern People's Congress, the Nigerian National Democratic Party, the Midwest Democratic Front, the Niger Delta Congress and the Dynamic Party; and the United Progressive Grand Alliance, consisting of the National Council of Nigerian Citizens, the Action Group, and the United Middle Belt Congress.[60] As a fairly generalized description of the NNA (NPC, NNDP) and the UPGA (NCNC and AG), one could say that the former represented the *status quo,* and the latter the challenger to the *status quo.* It was the UPGA that defined the issues, that published manifestos, and that publicized malpractices of the NNA. The spotlight was on its campaign—it was energetic, optimistic, and boisterous. Its manifesto, styled the "People's Manifesto," posed the question, "What are the causes of the crisis and the moral dilemma in which our country finds itself today?"

In the first place, Nigeria came into independence without ideological orientation. From the early forties up to 1960 the one overriding aim of all social and political forces in Nigeria was the termination of foreign rule. To this end all other interests were subordinated. As soon as independence was attained in 1960, a community of interests ceased to exist among the various forces in the country. These forces began to group themselves broadly into two; those of reaction, feudalism and neocolonialism on the one hand, and those of progress, democracy and socialism on the other.[61]

In attempting to mobilize all the citizens to stop a mammoth North and to find issues which a national consensus could achieve, the UPGA had to go beyond the tribe, it had to think and act in terms of the totality of the nation, and it had to present a goal which was relevant to the problems faced by each class.

If regional parties had fed on tribal feelings in the past and if tribalism and socialism are incompatible, since socialism assumes a national consciousness in which class considerations are more relevant than the constricting ethnic loyalty, then regional parties become an obstruction to the construction of the socialist society. As an article of faith, UPGA would continue to support the idea of national parties and oppose regional parties. It is not difficult to see that one Nigerian nationality could hardly emerge on the basis of regional parties. All forms of extreme regionalism would therefore have to be openly discouraged and opposed.

If a young man from Kano [North] cannot feel at home in Ijebu-Ode [West] and a young man from Ibadan [West] feels like a stranger in Sapele [Midwest] and a man from Benin [Midwest] feels like a stranger in Enugu [East] and a man from Calabar [East] feels like a foreigner at Maiduguri [North], then we still have a long way to go before we can really claim to be one country.[62]

In the long run, the "one country" should be able to provide for all the classes within its jurisdiction. The narrowing down of the gap between classes by a better wage structure, the provision of more jobs in cities and in the rural areas, the judicious use of the monetary and fiscal system to expand the economy, thus providing the means and incentive for an efficient private sector to supplement the public sector— these become some of the necessary goals to work for on a national basis. The plan of economic development would see to the expansion of the economic infrastructure, then concentrate on rapid agricultural and industrial development; "the present practice of the federal government of practically leaving industrialism to the regions and private industrialists alone will be discontinued on the day we assume office by getting the federal government to enter industrialization in a positive and practical way. We shall lead the regions and private industry rather than be led by these." [63] Such a plan would seem to be relevant to the Nigerian situation, especially when within one year, 1964, the workers had shown their potential strength when they struck for three weeks and almost paralyzed the whole system of public utilities, when teachers in the Western Region were on strike, and when the continuous flow of educated but unemployed young men and women clamoring for jobs was flooding the cities.

If these represented the long-term goals, the short-term goals would deal with how the present system could be changed to make it amenable to national, rather than regional and parochial, thinking. In the *Nigerian Outlook,* Dr. Okpara wrote:

We hold the view that the two worst threats to Nigerian unity are the practice of regionalism which has now been carried into the political field and the fact that the most important principle of federation, namely, that there should not be any one state so much greater than the rest combined that it can bend the will of the federal government. Until these two threats are removed, they labour in vain who labour for Nigerian unity and solidarity.[64]

If the socialist program is designed to remove the danger of regionalism and substitute a rational consciousness as a norm of political behavior, the second and most immediate threat could only be removed by constitutional revision. The Constitution should be revised to equalize the strength of the various states, the federal government should be strengthened to make it more effective as a coordinator and director of national policy, and the powers of the federal government should be controlled by introducing a system of checks and balances between the executive, legislative, and judiciary arms of government.

We shall create new states in the North, the East and West along the lines of the old provinces. As this may give a maximum number of 25 states, some contiguous states may be allowed to combine on the principle of self-determination. We shall accompany this with a new revenue allocation to shift a good deal of the burden of social services to the federal government.[65]

The Senate would be given concurrent powers with the House of Representatives. Give the President executive powers for the electoral commission, the Public Service Commission, Census and Audit. The President would set up a permanent vital statistics commission to collect figures of births and deaths over a period of fifteen or twenty years to obtain accurate figures and avoid political conflict each time a census was taken. A permanent Judicial Commission to deal with tribalism, discriminatory practices, and violations of fundamental human rights would be created. This Commission "can initiate proceedings against these practices or act on the basis of genuine complaints or suits from citizens. . . ."[66] The implications of these proposals are obvious. The allocation of powers over the Electoral Commission, the public service, etc., removes these institutions from direct partisan pressures, depriving one party or parties of an important patronage leverage that could be used to the detriment of other parties. The necessity for having reliable census figures, not only for the more efficient reallocation of resources, but also for the fundamental issue of a meaningful exercise of suffrage and adequate representational system, need not be argued if the eventual goal is the development of an active participant society.

The creation of a permanent Judicial Commission to look into discriminatory practices, but more especially into political victimization during elections, would remove complaints that the legislative and judiciary powers of the incumbent governments were used to stifle opposition and would at least guarantee participants in the political game a fair chance to play out their parts. Parties would not find it necessary to hire a team of lawyers which would accompany the politicians in their compaigns to fight an obstructionist partisan legal system.

The sum of the UPGA Manifesto was thus an indictment of the present political system, its reforms, and the projection of the ideals of a militant nation through constructive programs towards a future where a national community would eventually emerge.

The Manifesto of the Nigerian National Alliance, when compared to the comprehensive one presented by the UPGA, was less exciting. It concerned itself with the improvement of the present system, the expansion of the public services within an unaltered federal structure. It did not take issue with the goals of socialism, nor with the revision of the state boundary; while it tried to match the UPGA in the making of promises, it announced no new ideology. It promised to see to the preservation and reformation of democratic institutions in the Republican Constitution. It would ensure fair and equitable distribution of the wealth of the nation and create equal opportunity for all people. It would accelerate the development of educational institutions to fulfill the goal of Nigerianization of government services. It would arrest the deterioration in spots.

Maitama Sule, director-general of the NPC Bureau of Publicity and Information, summed up the manifesto of the UPGA as envisaging Draconian policy to effect reform.

Indeed NNA raises this timely alarm because what is now promised by Dr. Okpara, for and on behalf of the UPGA, is compatible only to the midnight of horror with which Adolf Hitler proclaimed in June 1934 the Third Reich, knocking at the door of every opponent and of former friends and in that one night, cutting down hundreds of Germans of every class and clime.

What is more, the reputation which the little dictators elsewhere have established in the last brief decade, convinced us that the happiness of our people cannot be bought at the price of the kind of dictatorship which the UPGA now promises in exchange for unity and progress, however grand.[67]

The implication of this statement was also clear; the NNA would talk only in the terms that were meaningful to them; they were concerned with the people of Nigeria, not with the tribes or different classes within which they fell; in talking over such aggregates, the conflict inherent in the class concept would be resolved by defining it out of existence; also, if the NNA would not change the *status quo* and the UPGA could not get the necessary two-thirds majority to revise the constitution, then only a dictatorial regime could coerce the NNA into submission—hence the warning of the Third Reich and small dictatorships.

The election was therefore going to settle everything or nothing. The determination and vigor with which the UPGA carried on the campaign showed they believed they would succeed, or at least present such a united opposition if they lost that they could force some concession out of the NNA. In October, and even in November, the UPGA still anticipated victory; it glorified the masses and the fatherland. So confident was the UPGA that Okpara could say that no region or party would be allowed to opt out of the federation because it suffered an electoral defeat. "This will be unconstitutional; we cannot allow anybody to secede." [68] I am tempted to add, "We cannot allow the North to secede," for this is implied in his expectations of victory. Between November and December, however, disillusionment set in—the UPGA began to see the election would settle nothing. Between October and December there had been such a change that in December Okpara was talking of seceding from the Federation. The causes for this change were allegedly to be found in the continuous victimization of the UPGA candidates in the North.

Reports of violent attacks by hired thugs on UPGA candidates filled the press. Headlines like the following were commonplace, and increased in frequency as the election campaign progressed: "the UPGA candidate for Akwanga constituency in the coming federal elections, Malam Iliya Remi, was recently at the Lafia Alkali Court sentenced to two years' imprisonment with hard labor after being found guilty of unlawful assembly. The offence, according to the prosecution, was committed on September 24. . . ." [69]

With no protection from the law but that of the team of lawyers sent to keep candidates on the soapboxes and out of the jails, with charges of violent suppression of opposition candidates, and with forty UPGA candidates already in jail and twenty others denied registration, the announcement two weeks before the election that sixty-four NNA candidates would be returned unopposed to Parliament could only be seen as fraudulent by UPGA.

The North was the key to the whole election; 167 of the 312 seats would be contested in that region alone; of these, 64 seats were already declared secured by the NNA; the 103 seats which were to be contested could not be contested with the UPGA candidates in jail. If there was a fair election, perhaps the UPGA could get enough votes in the Middle Belt where the Tivs were already in arms against the Northern government, but with a state of emergency declared and with the imprisonment of UPGA candidates, the election result in the North could be said to be predetermined.[70]

The UPGA demanded the delay of the elections until the "irregularities have been regularized." [71] The irregularities were not regularized, the election was not to be postponed, the UPGA would not accept the result of an election which they could see was "predetermined," the call for boycott of the election was given, and the East, under Okpara, threatened to secede. We had gone the whole circle and were back where we started. How does one reconcile federalism with the uneven allocation of power characteristic of the component regions? How does one expect politicians to act with responsibility when the "possible" results of such action are defeat? To prevent the breakdown of communications between the various parts and the whole, the part with the preponderant influence must exercise this weight with moderation, must be generous in its use of political power, and must make some concessions to the smaller members of the federation.

The NNA, with its overwhelming influence, has not been generous or moderate in its use of power, nor was it prepared to make any concession to its opponent. The impasse is symbolized in the attitude and utterance of the two most crucial figures in the whole election, Chief Michael I. Okpara, leader of the NCNC and chief spokesman of the UPGA, and the Sardauna of Sokoto, leader of the NPC and the NNA. The Sardauna had faced the crisis with equanimity and was prepared to allow the Eastern Region, rich in oil, to secede peacefully if it insisted on a separate state.[72]

For Okpara, the practical solution was dissolution of the federation and then unification when the need for a concerted action forced itself upon the consciousness of each party. "For the UPGA—prudence was in all regions going in peace their own different ways. If future events bring home to us that strength lies in unity, and suggestions for federation are put forward from any source, then we should sit down and define our terms." [73]

The elections were held and were boycotted in the South. There was violence and talk of secession. However, the final, logical move was not made. At the last moment, when the leaders could have given the word, the word that would have led to secession in peace, or secession with civil war, none pronounced the fateful sentence over the federation. The President and the Prime Minister succeeded in working out a stopgap solution, necessary to allow tempers to simmer down. The election result would be accepted, elections would be conducted where they were boycotted, and a national coalition government would be formed.

The basic issue, that of constitutional revision, would be taken up sometime in the future. Time, at least for the next five years, had been bought. The question was, would it be used? Would the UPGA dissolve, with each party reverting to the much deprecated regionalism, or would it maintain a united front which would force the NNA into more progressive policies, both at the center and in the North? Would the NNA rectify the anomalous situation in the Western Region where the mobilization of public opinion on the national level would leave a new political taste in the mouths of those involved in the recent crisis? The explicit adoption by the UPGA of socialism as a goal of election and policy was a confession that politics, in the future, would no longer be the manipulation of a trusting electorate and unprincipled bargains among the leaders. The amazing alignment of all the political forces in Nigeria into two parties was novel in the experience of the Nigerian parties; it committed the parties to definite stands and policies; it introduced a new quality into the style of political behavior, the use of ideology, and the use of foreign policy (alignment and non-alignment) as election issues. The masses were promised deeds in the election manifesto, and masses that would strike for an economic end will not hesitate to use their political power to force the promotion of economic ends. That was why the election of 1964 was important in itself—it unleashed national forces which would direct the flow and tempo of future political behavior. It made the North realize to what extent the South could be pressed before the stability of the federation was jeopardized. It made the South face the long-hidden ideological inconsistency between a national pose and a tribalistic political behavior. The North forced the South to think nationally; the South forced the North to make a greater effort to seek Southern allies and to change its name, replacing "the North" with "Nigerian." Whether the

South forced the North to think nationally is the question. On
the answer depended the future of a stable federation.

Conclusion

This chapter has been in one way a stocktaking of the changes,
some of them almost revolutionary in their import, that have taken
place in Nigeria between 1944, when the first national party was
formed to direct the drive for independence, and 1964, when the
same party, because it felt its national aspirations could not be
fulfilled within the present system, talked of secession. The political
changes have been most important and most salient. An independent republic has emerged from a set of colonial holdings welded
together in 1914 by an imperial decree. The indigenous institution
of chieftaincy, previously the instrument of the colonial power
which it served in order to preserve its hold on the people through
the indirect rule system, had become subordinated to the government (in the Southern regions) and was now controlled by men
who had had no say in the halcyon days of the colonial regime, and
by men who would have no right to wield power under the traditional system. Because of the continuing importance to the mass of
the people of a tradition, derived from Islam, calling for unquestion-
ing obedience to those invested with authority, the traditional rulers
in the North successfully rode the crest of the nationalist movement.
They used the Northern xenophobia, coupled with the defensive
regionalism of the Northern elite, to strengthen their regime. In
this sense the confrontation of 1964 could be regarded as the
Southern attempt by the North to extend the Northern chieftaincy
hegemony to the South. The final resolution of the conflicts may
not be solely within the realm of the leadership elite. The silent
masses were asked in 1964 to throw off the shackles of tribalism,
to think in national terms, to evaluate a party's program by its
relevance to their daily lives; these masses, the so-much praised and
maligned people, might force a solution upon the leaders, if the
leaders proved inept and out of tune with the rumbling dissatisfaction from below. The implications of this for an orderly, continuous societal development are important. The leaders could
not expect the led to have any faith in the rule of law if these laws
were disregarded at will by those who were supposed to enforce
them. These leaders, in sabotaging existing institutions for the
maintenance of political supremacy, might inculcate an unhealthy

cynicism into those led, thus rendering themselves and the institutions they represented vulnerable to revolutionary attack. The vote would be respected if the exercise of suffrage had meaning, both in the making of meaningful choices and in the periodic control of the decision-making process. Parties would become more than an instrument of power, more than a means of meteoric social and economic mobility, and more of an instrument putting into effect popular demand or suggesting alternative solutions. In 1964 the implications seemed to have been recognized by the UPGA. Its manifesto clearly showed this concern with the transformation of the party into the instrument and executor of the public weal— it saw the necessity of protecting the national institutions from the effects of partisan manipulations of these institutions. Its final desire to sanction secession was symptomatic of the disillusionment and disaffection with the electoral process. The choice of non-recognition of the electoral process and the condoning of violence, even when the cause was "good," set a precedent which could be dangerous. Secession from a federation, like civil war, is the ultimate recourse available to the "oppressed," but it is the mark of good politics to make this the last recourse. Nothing succeeds like success, and nothing stabilizes like stability. Violence, by its very nature, is destabilizing and may unleash dysfunctional results to negate some, if not obliterate all, that the political leadership has tried to build. For every region of Nigeria, the message of 1964 was loud and clear—the message was reconciliation or conflict. The goal of national growth cautioned against conflict; reconciliation and the pooling of strength were the sensible alternatives. The ensuing conflicts, the pursuit of a course of violence, comprise the topic of the remaining essays.

Notes

1. Gabriel A. Almond and James S. Coleman, *Politics of the Developing Areas* (Princeton: Princeton University Press, 1960), p. 7.

2. *Report of the Special Commission on the Constitution of Ceylon,* CMD (1928) 3131, p. 41.

3. I am using Coleman's definition of community as a group of any size whose members have a consciousness of living a common life and sharing a common destiny. "There is a hierarchy of communities ranging from the family or village to the region or nation. The strength of community varies according to the size of the group, the intensity of social communication among its members, and the sense

of in-group identification. In the modern world, the nation is usually regarded as the terminal community." (James Coleman, *Nigeria: Background to Nationalism* [Berkeley and Los Angeles: University of California Press, 1963], p. 421.) Nigeria is in transition in the sense that for many the tribe is the terminal community, although the influence of the national community has given rise to inchoate community feeling at the national level. The question of "what tribe is he?" is still not irrelevant.

4. Constitution of Nigerian National Democratic Party (Lagos, Nigeria, n.d.), p. 1.

5. For a detailed explanation of this incident, see Coleman, *Nigeria,* p. 227 and Obafemi Awolowo, *Awo—The Autobiography of Chief Obafemi Awolowo* (Cambridge, Eng.: Cambridge University Press, 1960).

6. Nnamdi Azikiwe, *Zik: A Selection from the Speeches of Nnamdi Azikiwe* (Cambridge, Eng.: Cambridge University Press, 1961), p. 181.

7. Alikija in *Egbe Omo Oduduwa Monthly Bulletin,* June 1948 (typed copy); see Coleman, *Nigeria,* Chapter 16, "The Ibo and Yoruba Strands in Nigerian Nationalism."

8. *West African Pilot,* 6 July 1949.

9. Awolowo, *Awo,* p. 223.

10. Ibid., p. 224.

11. R. L. Sklar, *Nigerian Political Parties: Power in an Emergent African Nation* (Princeton: Princeton University Press, 1963), pp. 101–102.

12. *Daily Comet,* 29 December 1949.

13. Manifesto of the Northern People's Congress, 1 October 1951, in *Report on the Kano Disturbance,* p. 45.

14. See Coleman, *Nigeria,* pp. 380–381, Table 23. These are 1963 figures and represent the percentage of those elected into the regional House of Assembly. The figures for the federal House of Representatives are fairly comparable. However, for the purpose of this essay, the figures for the region will suffice.

15. Sklar, *Nigerian Political Parties,* p. 261.

16. Ibid., p. 106.

17. Awolowo, *Awo,* p. 221.

18. Ibid.

19. See Coleman, *Nigeria,* p. 345.

20. Sklar, *Nigerian Political Parties,* p. 504.

21. Ibid., p. 495. The use of patronage by parties: "the major institutions of Nigerian society, in particular those institutions which are fundamental to the pattern of social stratification, are closely related to and substantially controlled by the political parties."

22. Coleman, *Nigeria,* p. 350.

23. Ibid., p. 352.

24. Ibid.
25. Ibid. Mbadiwe and Azikiwe are members of different sub-tribes; Mbadiwe comes from the Orlu and Azikiwe from Onitsha. As a favorite son, Mbadiwe should have been elected. However, it seems as if the loyalty to the NCNC is not to the NCNC as a party but to Azikiwe, its founder. Since 1959 Azikiwe has turned over the reins of leadership to Dr. Michael I. Okpara, a capable, but certainly not a charismatic, leader. Azikiwe's decision to go to the center need not have necessitated his resignation as a leader. He perhaps wanted party leadership to be dissociated from his person. The party's continuing supremacy may be an example of a successful "institutionalized charisma," or the use of governmental powers to strengthen the party's hold. However, the almost uncritical support of the masses may still be due to the fact that the NCNC is seen as a party of the Ibo; certainly a rival party among the Ibo has yet to emerge.
26. Michael I. Okpara, "Before the Dawn," *The Nigerian Outlook,* 10 September 1960, p. 12.
27. Sklar, *Nigerian Political Parties,* p. 230.
28. Ibid.
29. Ibid., p. 323.
30. The Eastern Nigerian and Western Nigerian governments did discriminate in employment against applicants from other regions, but they never made this a policy or proceeded to a systematic dismissal of those already employed.
31. I am obviously ruling out the cases of groups which claim to be members of another party just because the groups to which they are opposed belong to the ruling party (for example, the case of the Yorubas of Ibadan, Illa, and Ilesha).
32. What I am saying here does not imply that certain groups did not think themselves to be Nigerians. They did; yet for the purposes of political and to some extent social interactions, their awareness of this nationality stopped at the tribal or regional boundary. Obviously this was a function of ecology or education. The educated, urbanized Nigerian was empathic and able to think in terms of the whole national structure, though he might not be able to act in all his interaction, public and private, as a Nigerian.
33. R. L. Sklar in his studies of the patronage system, the class structure, and the power of the political parties, noted that in the Western Region over 80 percent of the contracts awarded by the government during the period of his study (1954–1955) went to the members of the AG. "In every region the major instruments of commercial patronage are the regional market boards and regional development corporations." (Sklar, *Nigerian Political Parties,* p. 449.)
During the 1957–1958 crisis in the NCNC, a producer-buyer, Mr. Obioha, of sound financial standing, had backed the faction opposed to the national leader. Azikiwe is quoted by the *West African*

Pilot, 26 July 1958, and the *Daily Telegraph,* 9 September 1958, to have said, "The government [Eastern Region's] would be foolish to renew Mr. Obioha's produce-buying license in view of the fact that he had joined the Mbadiwe conspiracy to overthrow the government unconstitutionally." The conspiracy had been a party split in which the national leader was asked to resign. This move was defeated and the rebels were expelled from the party.

The equation of opposition to the party hierarchy with opposition to the government is indicative of the fusion of the roles of the party as an organized but private group of individuals, and the party as the temporary agent of the government. This tends to lead to the attitude that opposition to the party is opposition to the government, and hence conspiratorial. Public powers are thus used to punish private individuals for private reasons.

It is interesting to see how one member of the new class, Chief H. O. Davies, Queen's Counsel—the "Politician in the Flowing Robes"— viewed the "nouveaux arrivés." Talking about the social distance that suddenly develops between the electorate and the elected, he hints at the association of the new secularistic role of a politician and the traditional loyalty associated with power. Most of them acquired the title of chief, including Chief Awolowo, and Davies himself. They were the new men usurping old roles by new means. It is not clear whether it was a case of old wine in new bottles or new wine in old bottles.

Quoting from H. O. Davies, the minister, the highest of the political elites, does not visit his constituency with a feeling of a servant delegated to carry out the constituency's needs, or of a Burke defending himself by claiming the inalienable responsibility of politics in reconciling the expressed needs of the individual constituency and the politician's conception of the national interest.

His few visits to the village area, to open a new school, factory or hospital are heralded with pomp and ceremony. It is considered a great privilege if he accepts an invitation to preside over a social function in the town. The minister, who formerly eked out a miserable existence as party secretary, now has a sizable bank balance. While he lives in the palatial ministerial residence, he can afford to build a private house for himself. This anti-colonial comrade who was previously obliged to negotiate long distances on foot is now driven short distances in a luxurious car. Economically, ministerial government is a restratification of a society into a new form of plutocracy, at the top of which are the new well-to-do and all-powerful ministers. (H. O. Davies, *The Prospect for Democracy* (London: Weidenfeld and Nicolson, 1961), p. 72.)

34. Sklar, *Nigerian Political Parties,* p. 452.

35. Among the educated elite there was a ferment of ideological awareness. The university students, professors, labor leaders, and young civil servants in the government's bureaucracy did tend to be

ideological. But their political behavior was to a large extent still uncontrolled by ideology. The only real ideological party, Dr. Chike Obi's Dynamic Party, which consistently lost all the elections it contested, seems to have been rejected both by the elites and by the masses.

The party began with these values:

1. The party shall be a rigidly disciplined body even if this means drastic reduction in the number of the members.

2. When human beings form a body they surrender part of their personal freedom to the body. The bigger the body and the benefit derived from it by the individual who is a member, the greater is the apparent loss of personal freedom to the individual. The interests of the individual can only best be guaranteed by the interests of the individuals of the state taken collectively.

3. To guarantee the interest and security of the individual of the state, the party believes in:

a. Public ownership of all major means of production and distribution and of the defense of the state.

b. Making all economic and social plans from the point of view of the interest and welfare of the individuals of the state taken as a whole.

c. The day-to-day control and management by the people of the means of livelihood and defense of the state.

d. Political independence is absolutely necessary for the attainment of full freedom from cultural, intellectual and economic slavery.

e. The necessity of being active, energetic, and on the offensive, and of using all means of persuasion at its disposal beginning from the simplest methods first and following up, when necessary, with stronger methods. (Azikiwe, *Zik*, p. 330.)

The rejection of this curious amalgam of a militarized fascist political system with some socialist and individual (not necessarily private) enterprise is a rejection of an ideology alien to the system inherited from the British. It has no basis in tradition and requires a revolutionary change of the society. Curiously enough it could provide unity of tribes—but at what cost?

36. Sklar, *Nigerian Political Parties,* p. 326.

37. I used "secularistic," rather than "Christian," even when the South is predominantly Christian, because it is the influence not the religion, it is the greater exposure to Westernization not the conversion to the dogma of Western religion, that is important for this analysis. Religion is not an important political factor in the South (West and East), although this might need some qualification in regard to the East.

38. There are those, like C. Wright Mills in his *Power Elite* and E. D. Baltzell in *The Protestant Establishment,* who maintain that, while the United States may appear classless and open, the limit of political mobility for the majority of Americans is set by their being members or non-members of the power elite or Protestant establish-

74   MOYIBI AMODA

ment. The essence of the analysis is applicable in the Northern case, the middle groups accommodating themselves to a political situation, even though it was undemocratic, provided the economic market place was open enough to accommodate merit.

39. They go to London, all over the world, on scholarships for their education. They take tutorials and correspondence courses, they try to rise by education. Will they be members of the educated proletariat or not?

40. *The Character and Viability of African Political Systems— The United States and Africa.* (New York: The American Assembly, 1958), pp. 47–48.

41. Sklar, *Nigerian Political Parties,* p. 296. Chief Adegoke Adelabu was a prominent Nigerian Nationalist, leader of the anti-AG, and hence pro-NCNC.

42. Nigeria Sessional Paper, no. 4 (1945), Cond. 6599.

43. Ibid.

44. M. Venkatarongaiya, *Federalism in Government,* p. 183; see also Kalu Ezera, *Nigeria: Constitutional History* (Cambridge, Eng.: Cambridge University Press, 1960), p. 78. "Under the Richard's Constitution of 1946, there was a legislative council for the whole of Nigeria composed of: the governor (as president); 16 official members in the ratio of: 13 ex-officio and 3 nominated; 28 unofficial members in the ratio of: 4 elected and 28 elected indirectly or nominated. Of course it was to be expected that the governor would not nominate those on whose support he could not count."

45. Awolowo, *Awo,* pp. 176–177.

46. Ibid., p. 176.

47. Azikiwe, *Zik,* p. 109.

48. Ibid.

49. Kalu Ezera, *Nigeria: Constitutional History* (Cambridge: Cambridge University Press, 1960), pp. 228–229.

50. Ibid., pp. 248–249.

51. Debates of the Northern House of Assembly, Kaduna, 23 May 1953.

52. *Report of the Conference on the Nigerian Constitution of 1953,* no. 8934, p. 3.

53. Ezera, *Nigeria,* p. 215.

54. The creation of the Midwest State out of the West cannot be regarded as the weakening of the AG, since the Midwest had always voted NCNC and was regarded as a political liability.

55. The Constitution of the Federation of Nigeria, Chapter I, Article 4, Section 3.

56. The NCNC was changed from the National Council of Nigeria and the Cameroons to the National Council of Nigerian Citizens, when Southern Cameroon merged with French Cameroon to form the Republic of Cameroons in 1960.

57. *The Nation*, Official Organ of the NCNC, People's Magazine, vol. 1, no. 1. (August 1964): 19.

58. The figures were challenged at Supreme Court by the NCNC, but the Court ruled it was not justifiable—a technical fact which competent arithmetic ought to establish becomes a hot political issue.

59. *Financial Times* (London), 1 October 1964.

60. The Nigerian National Alliance:

1. The Nigerian National Democratic Party—formed from the splinter group of the AG and some former NCNC members—party in power in the Western Nigeria under the premiership of Chief S. L. Akintola.

2. The Niger Delta Congress—small mushroom party in the river provinces of Eastern Nigeria.

3. The Dynamic Party under Dr. Chike Obi, militant fascist ideology —small and inconsequential, at least by performance at the polls.

4. Midwest Democratic Front—opposition party in the Midwest Region.

The United Progressive Grand Alliance:

1. The NCNC, comprised of two branches, one based in the Eastern Region and the other in the Midwest.

2. The Action Group, the majority still under the leadership of Chief Awolowo, sentenced to prison for ten years for subversive activities following the 1962 emergency in the West.

3. The United Middle Belt Congress, strongly entrenched in the Middle Belt Region, comprised of non-Hausa groups—under its leader Tarka, it sought to carve out the Middle Belt state from the Northern Region.

61. "The People's Manifesto," *Nigerian Outlook*, 12 October 1964, p. 4.

62. Ibid., p. 5.

63. Ibid., p. 4. The general strike in spring 1964 involved over 80,000 workers, representing over 75 percent of industrial workers and 33 percent of all wage earners.

64. "Okpara Speaks on Crusade for Freedom," *Nigerian Outlook*, 14 October 1964, p. 5.

65. Ibid.

66. Ibid., pp. 4–5.

67. *The New York Times*, 29 November 1964, p. 16.

68. *Nigerian Outlook*, 6 October 1964.

69. Ibid., 9 October 1964.

70. The Tivs riots were serious enough for the Northern Region to declare a state of emergency, and for the federal government to send troops to quell the rioters.

71. *Time*, 8 January 1965, p. 18.

72. *The New York Times*, 31 December 1964.

73. Ibid., 5 January 1965.

3

CITIZENSHIP AND POLITICAL CONFLICT: A SOCIOLOGICAL INTERPRETATION OF THE NIGERIAN CRISIS

Peter P. Ekeh

Introduction

One of the major difficulties encountered in the numerous studies of African politics is the failure to point up the generic nature of problems and issues in African political life, which leads to an undue emphasis on the so-called "tribal" conflicts. For example, interpretations of the Nigerian crisis (like the Congo crisis before it) fail to look beyond concrete groups and actors for a more inclusive explanation. Any political conflict, whether in Asia or Africa, belongs to a class of human political behaviors. It is only by considering the generic nature of such conflicts that their more concrete African forms gain theoretical significance.

My attempt to explain the Nigerian crisis in this chapter will involve a theoretical perspective that has certain characteristics. First, it assumes that the Nigerian crisis belongs to a class of conflicts that could be found elsewhere, in Asia and Europe, both in the past and present. Second, I shall seek to explain the Nigerian crisis in terms of objective political experiences of various ethnic groups in the country which, I believe, flow from the peculiar arrangements of the Nigerian constitution of 1954. It is my impression that these factors explain a great deal of the variance of social and political life in Nigeria—at least much more than the attention to them hitherto would indicate. Third, my interpretation of the crisis builds on the comparative analysis of the elements of citizenship in the Western world and in the postcolonial societies of Africa, on the assumption that colonialism is to Africa what feudalism is to Europe.

The Nigerian crisis is a crisis of citizenship. The political conflicts that have arisen from differing attitudes to citizenship will be analysed in this chapter. The various factors associated with these conflicts are by no means as uniform as they appear at first glance. Various modifiers exist to define the intensities and salience of personal commitments to the elements of citizenship. It is the central claim of this essay that the *type of ethnic group* [1] to which one belongs is central to one's definition of, and relations to, political conflicts in Nigeria.

The strategy of searching for explanations and interpretations of African and Asian intellectual problems in terms of the conceptual schemes and theoretical perspectives developed from social experiences in the West is rewarding in many ways. For one thing, a theoretical unity is achieved, while at the same time comparisons bring to the fore peculiar problems in African political life. For another thing, the experiences in Africa help the comparative analyst to reexamine various assumptions implicit in Western-derived generalizations.

The more successful of the "modernization" studies are those which have sought to understand African and Asian problems by going back beyond the immediate European industrial past to preindustrial experiences in the West. Perhaps the most significant point of departure in this direction has been provided by Edward Shils' distinction between "primordial" and "civil" ties,[2] a distinction that clearly belongs to Tönnies' more inclusive *Gemenschaft-Gesellschaft*.

Geertz' definitions of these categories go a long way in pointing up their significance for political life in the new states.

By primordial attachment is meant one that stems from the "givens"—or, more precisely, as culture is inevitably involved in such matters, the assumed "givens"—of social existence: immediate contiguity and kin connection mainly, but beyond them the givenness that stems from being born into a particular religious community, speaking a particular language, and following particular social practices. . . .

The general strength of such primordial bonds, and the types of them that are important, differ from person to person, from society to society, and from time to time. But for virtually every person, for every society, at almost all times, some attachments seem to flow from a sense of natural—some would say spiritual—affinity than from social interaction.[3]

On the other hand, civil ties are characterized

. . . by a vague, intermittent, and routine allegiance to a civil state, supplemented to a greater or lesser extent by governmental use of police powers and ideological exhortation.[4]

This rather tenuous nature of civil ties may well be exaggerated by many writers, but the more symbolic significance of civil ties and the greater involvement and intensity that characterize primordial ties are real properties of political life in every society.

The most important element in the new tradition of "modernization" studies originating from Shils' distinction is the recognition that civil ties and primordial ties are not labels that characterize social relationships in different societies at different times. On the contrary, they are the centrifugal forces pulling the same persons in different directions at the same time. It is the sharp relationship between these two ties, especially as they concern the political elites of society, that renders this distinction a useful one in an analysis of the Nigerian crisis. In Shils' other terms, the elite is torn between its "will to be modern" by seeking to work with civil symbols and its "quest for identity" in primordial resources.[5]

This distinction between "primordial" and "civil" ties will be central to the analysis of the Nigerian crisis in the following pages. Both political conflicts and citizenship will be characterized in terms of this distinction, and various aspects of the Nigerian crisis will be examined by invoking it. In the first part of this chapter an attempt is made to provide definitions and theoretical considerations of political conflict and citizenship, especially in their "non-Western" (or more appropriately, African) forms. The rationale for this part is to provide a theoretical context for the analysis of the Nigerian crisis—in other words, to define the generic issues and problems of which the Nigerian crisis is a subset. Later, a more concrete evaluation of these concepts in their Nigerian form is made. The nature of primordialism and citizenship and their relationships to secessionist tendencies in Nigeria are examined in this section. This section is then followed by a brief evaluation, but by no means a description, of the events surrounding the "Biafran" declaration of secession. Lastly, I make an attempt to look to the future, by commenting on the possible trends that primordial forces and the elements of citizenship may follow in the future Nigeria.

General Considerations on Citizenship and Political Conflict

POLITICAL CONFLICTS

Africa has been involved in various types of conflicts, but the nature of such conflicts has not been clearly specified. Max Gluckman's picture of "tribal conflict" in Africa, for example, would hardly lead one to expect the type of conflicts experienced in Uganda, the Congo, or Nigeria.[6] The general weakness in such studies is that they assume that African conflicts are bounded almost entirely by primordial sentiments. It seems to me that although primordial commitments play a large part in many of Africa's major conflicts, there is also a civil side to them.

An argument that sees the Nigerian conflict in purely civil terms, however, would seem to be even more inadequate. In spite of the extravagant resort to the language of Marxist analysis by many scholars to characterize African and "third world" problems, many of our conflicts go beyond purely economic interests. It seems necessary for adequate analysis to differentiate political conflicts. In general, political conflicts may be characterized as either civic or primordial.

Primordial conflicts polarize the politically active members of society on some low-level ideological issue which can only be understood in primordial terms. It is the sacredness of a primordial grouping that becomes politicized and politically salient. Those who are involved in primordial conflicts consider their side to the issue as a symbol of a sacred grouping, the destruction of which would threaten their personal identity. In other words, the existence of the primordial grouping is considered critical to the identity of a group of people in a primordial conflict. Those who riot and go to war because of the introduction of a new language do so because they fear that the identity of their group would be destroyed.

In civic conflicts, on the other hand, ideas and interests are salient. Ideologies are the warp of civic conflicts. One fights to save ideas or interests that are valued, either because they yield personal benefits or because they are considered intrinsically important. Memberships on both sides of the polarized political spectrum are multiple and not restricted to a primordial principle.

Such a distinction compels the view that not all civil wars, so called, are civic conflicts. Indeed, a large number of the so-called civil wars are primordial conflicts. It is, of course, quite possible that the polarized sides in a conflict see it from different points of view. Some may regard it as an effort to save or destroy the identity of a group while others see it in ideological terms.

Is the Nigerian Civil War a civic or primordial conflict? It would be presumptuous to answer such a question in a paragraph. It may be a question with no definitive answer. As I shall try to argue, however, there is a large primordial component in the Nigerian Civil War. But there is variety to this. Part of the problem of this essay is to isolate the varying intensities of primordial commitment —or even civil commitment—by different groups in the events leading to the war. Did Nigerians go to war because they are Nigerians or "Biafrans" with a claim to civil commitments to a nonprimordial principle? Or was the war over the issue of primordial identities?

Some light will be thrown on such questions when we consider citizenship. How developed is Nigerian citizenship? The commitment to civil life in Nigeria is highly differentiated among different groups in the country, and I shall seek to identify the various groups in their citizenship relationships to Nigeria. But first the concept of citizenship, especially as it relates to its emergence in a new "nation," deserves careful attention.

THE STRUCTURE OF CITIZENSHIP

The hallmark of a modern nation-state is citizenship. The most dramatic way postindependence nationhood was brought hcme to many Nigerians was the requirement to obtain passports and travelling certificates before crossing the border to neighboring countries. Where before a Nigerian Yoruba could walk across the border to see his half-brother, a Dahomey Yoruba, he was now required to visit the Immigration Office for arrangements for such a trip. The idea of citizenship, in other words, is closely tied up with the nation.

For all that, citizenship is also a subjective feeling and the formal arrangements at an Immigration Office do not exhaust the meaning of citizenship. As T. H. Marshall puts it, "Citizenship is a status bestowed on those who are full members of a community." [7] The "community" may well be the nation, but the membership of a village may be regarded by an individual as of greater importance. The respect that a villager pays to the drumbeat of his locality may be a more effective symbolization of his citizenship than a meaningless national anthem.

The lack of a phenomenological component in the definition of citizenship by some of the leading writers in this area arises from the tendency of seeing citizenship as a legalistic imposition. But the implied definition by some other writers represents citizenship as a subjective phenomenon.[8] Considered in this latter sense, it may be said that citizenship denotes the subjective membership of a community and, therefore, the nation-state is only one of the possible focuses of citizenship feelings.

Structurally, citizenship has been defined as consisting of rights and duties.[9] The question that comes to mind is, what happens when the focuses of these rights and duties are different or when they are viewed with different intensities? What Bendix calls the "Great Transformations" in Western Europe, in which national citizenships were consolidated over a span of at least a century, indicate a gradual process of subjective identification with the nation-state. Banfield's description of the "amoral" familial patterns in southern Italy and Almond and Verba's findings in their cross-national studies clearly indicate that such citizenship feelings towards nation-states are not always as mature as the countries.[10] But the problem faced in new African nations is not one of lack of participation in national politics, but rather of varied loyalties to the civil nation-state and to primordial centers of power. Citizenship in the West broadened its base to the nation over generations with at least a modicum of psychic involvement by the individual. The danger of having different primordial and civil centers of loyalties competing with each other for the allegiance of the citizens was not as great in such a gradual transformation as that now faced in the new African states.[11] The importance of such gradual transformations, as in the West, becomes apparent when their effects on the duties and rights of the citizen are considered: the duties come to be defined centrally, at a national level, and the concomitant rights are sought in the idiom of national consciousness, or at least by organizations with a national base.

This situation of the "Great Transformations" contrasts sharply with what has obtained in Nigeria. "Independence" meant little more than a formal declaration. Citizenship duties were not dramatized in a way that could tie them to national consciousness, nor was the need for sacrifice to the nation part of the Nigerian political tradition in pre-civil war days. Rights were never really fought for:

the right to national independence was hardly phrased in citizenship terms. This is not to say that there was an absence of citizenship; rather, its definition was fragmented. There was hardly any legal or social process that necessitated the nation to emerge as the symbolic focus of rights and duties. Primordial centers were at least more important for a great number of people. In the following section I shall try to document the variety of citizenship feelings in the country and show how and why they varied with respect to the civil concept of Nigeria.

An analytical distinction seems necessary at this point. We may, in the spirit of this chapter, distinguish between primordial rights and duties and civic rights and duties, depending on the loci of allegiance or claims that the political actor makes. What is indicated here, then, is that there is a cluster of adult political behaviors and expectations that is styled as duties and another cluster that is styled as rights. Depending on the subjective meaning of politics and the patterns of political participation and cognition for the adult members of the society, they may have varying definitions of these rights and obligations. Individual members may come to feel that their taxes and military services are owed to their ethnic (primordial) groupings while being ambiguous about their rights.

Historically, rights have been a greater problem to the Western political system than duties. The duties of the members of Western societies, either to their overlords or to the most inclusive political unit they belonged to, were never in serious doubt. What were less sharply demarcated were the concomitant rights of the individual.[12] It is of some interest that T. H. Marshall differentiated rights without any accompanying attention to duties; that he did so seems to me to be indicative of the bias in the structure of citizenship in the West.[13] Depending on the period of history one encounters in the West, the problematic rights have varied from civil to political to social rights.

No such difficulties may arise in the rights of people in many postcolonial independent countries in Africa. Political "independence" conferred on most people both legal and civil rights, with great expectations of social rights on a national level. What do seem problematic are the duties of the citizen. There is no ideology at the national level in many of these African countries—with the possible exception of Guinea and Nkrumah's Ghana—justifying the nation vis-à-vis a multiplicity of primordial groupings as the appropriate benefactor of one's duties. On the other hand, there is at least a moral side to such duties to one's primordial grouping, as, for example, so-called voluntary contributions and a variety of other veiled taxes. The traditional rights which Nigerians expected from their ethnic groups have become either irrelevant in the new polity or otherwise absorbed by the civil order. Thus, while there is some expectation that the nation-state should be the final resort for one's (social) rights, there is a great deal of uncertainty in the matter of one's duties. If anything, the main focus of Nigerians' duties has tended to be the primordial order rather than the civil order.

THE DEVELOPMENT OF CITIZENSHIP AND POLITICAL CONFLICT

Transitions in the loci of citizenship have always posed crisis periods in history. In the West, the changeover of the elements of citizenship from feudal political loci to the more embracing civil order of the nation-state produced a "crisis in the relation of masters and servants" and "the crisis of domestic government." [14] The proper relation between duties and rights was constantly questioned and the premodern political structures of Western European nations were characterized by circumstances in which servants ". . . are not sure that they ought not themselves to be masters, and they are inclined to consider him who orders them about as an unjust usurper of their own rights." [15] While servants insisted on their rights of social equality, they were hesitant about their obligations to their masters; while masters insisted on their authority over their servants, they failed to embrace their traditional responsibility of protecting their servants.

Two factors were probably responsible for the eventual successful settlement of such crises of transition. First, the transfer of citizenship from localized areas to the national civil order was drawn over a long span of time, thus enabling such crises to be fully domesticated. This, of course, contrasts sharply with the rather cataclysmic nature of the call for full-fledged transfer of citizenship sentiments in postcolonial nations of Africa from primordial sources to the civil order. Second, there had emerged in the West an ideology that provided a platform for the negotiation of such crises of transition, namely, the contract. The age of contract in Western Europe called for a cost-benefit analysis, so to speak, of one's political activities. "No taxation without representation" is perhaps the most eloquent symbolization of this contractual spirit that was so pervasive at the critical juncture of the transfer of citizenship patterns from localized sources to the civil state.

In Western Europe there were two outcomes of the contract ideology: a prolongation of either the citizens' rights or obligations, once one set of these was redefined or transferred; and a strain towards having the *same* centers as the sources of one's rights and obligations. In spite of the crisis of transition which Tocqueville and Bendix have so eminently emphasized in the case of the West, the rights which the disadvantaged groups eventually claimed from the state were not at the expense of abrogating their obligations. Nor were the obligations left behind at their former localized base, while civil, political, and social rights were fought for on a group basis they became individual properties once they were won.

A third effect of the contract ideology on the transition of citizenship patterns should be noted. The contract ideology compels the individualization of social action, including political behavior. Thus, while civil, political, and social rights were fought for on a group basis they became individual properties once they were won.

All these features of the development of citizenship in Western Europe seem to contrast sharply with the main trends of citizenship development in postcolonial Nigeria. Needless to say, the period of intensive political activities within Nigeria (roughly between 1951 and 1967) is hardly enough to come to any firm demarcation of the paths of development. One can, however, hazard some foot paths. The lack of a contract ideology, or any equivalent ideology, needs no emphasis to bring it home. Citizenship is still largely a (primordial) group phenomenon rather than an attribute of individual political actors. More important is the trend toward having different loci for expectations and behaviors connected with rights and obligations. It does seem to be the case that prewar Nigerians, at least, had come to define their citizenship relations with the civil state in terms of, and only in terms of, their social rights, while their duties are withheld from the civil state and are either abrogated or otherwise located at primordial sources.

Since such a development is not peculiar to Nigeria, it may be worthwhile to state the issue here in more general terms. It is a major hypothesis of this chapter that *the rate of development or decay of, as well as the balance between, the rights and obligations of the citizens in any society are important determinants of the nature and type of political conflicts that develop in that society* (i.e., *whether they are primordial or civic*).

The following typology is intended to show the relationship between the rights and obligations syndrome and political conflicts within the state.

OBLIGATIONS

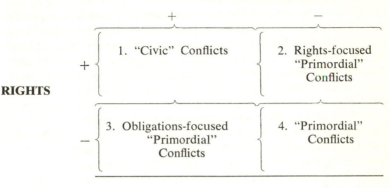

A "+" (plus) sign indicates that citizens in the society define and perceive their rights and/or obligations in terms of central state agencies and symbols. A "−" (minus) sign indicates that citizens in the society define and perceive their rights and/or obligations in terms of some primordial principle (language, race, ethnicity, religion, or territory). There are thus four possible cases, each of which shapes political conflict in a particular way:

1. In this situation citizens define their rights and obligations entirely in terms of the central civil order. If political conflicts develop in such a society they tend to be "civic" rather than "primordial." This situation, of course, must be regarded as an ideal one, only to be approximated by highly developed polities. England may be cited as providing an example of such a polity.

2. In this case conflicts are primordial, but they tend to be activated in terms of the demands of the various primordial groupings on central state agencies for the provision of social benefits. Prewar Nigeria offers an excellent example here. Social rights are demanded by various groups from central state agencies, while obligations originating from these sources are resisted. Political issues tend to be focused on the distribution of social benefits along primordial lines.

3. Ideally, conflicts in this situation should also be primordial,

but the salient issues here are obligations rather than rights. In a feudal society where the central state agency is assumed to protect the various units, while individuals are required to offer, for example, military service in return, we may envisage a case of this type. Individuals would tend to question the extent and legitimacy of their obligations.

4. Here is the extreme case of an agglomeration of primordial groupings massed together in a "nation-state." Most postcolonial "states" approximate this situation. Individuals in such "states" define their rights and obligations to the exclusion of persons from other primordial groupings. These elements of citizenship are seen entirely in a primordial idiom.

There are thus two cases ("2." and "3.") where the individual citizen is only partially related to the central civil order. In "2.," in particular, the usual rights he expects from his primordial groupings are either no longer salient or are now provided by the civil state. Rivalries between different primordial groupings come to be phrased in terms of the distribution of social rights but not with equal emphasis on equivalent duties to the civil order.

A few outstanding features of this typology should be highlighted. First, there is an assumption implicit in the typology that conflict exists in every society. The question is not one of "high" or "low" conflict, but rather it is of "primordial" or "civic" conflict in the society. Second, the rather facile assumption that there is no sense of duty in "developing" countries would be seriously questioned by this typology. What is argued here is that in certain instances the ideal-typical locus of citizenship, namely the nation-state, is false, and that there could be a dispersal of citizenship behaviors and expectations with respect to both rights and obligations. Third, it is important to emphasize that nothing in the typology indicates a unilineal developmental trend from "4." (primordial conflict situation) to "1." (civic conflict situation). If, however, "1." is defined as more advanced than "4." (a definition to which I would subscribe), then there are clear-cut possibilities that a reversal trend of decay from "1." to "2." or "3." (but hardly to "4.") is to be anticipated in many polities.

The rest of this chapter will be concerned with situation "2.," which Nigeria typifies. It is to be noted here that this type of conflict involves an admixture of civil commitments to rights and primordial commitments to duties.

The Nature and Patterns of Politics in Pre-war Nigeria

THE NATURE OF PRIMORDIALISM IN NIGERIA

The salience of primordialism for political action implies, first, that the people who are bound together by a primordial principle sufficiently see themselves as a corporate grouping worth perpetuating and, second, that their individual identities are tied up with the group's identity. A number of these principles may operate at once to heighten the identity of the group while others produce opposite effects.

This indicates that the salience of each primordial principle (race, territory, religion, language, or ethnicity) varies from society to society.[16] Because primordial attachments have been central to Nigerian political problems, it is important to examine the salience of each of these primordial principles in the Nigerian context.

Race. Race may be ruled out as constituting an important type of primordialism in Nigerian internal political conflicts. The absence of race consciousness, however, tends by default to throw into rather sharp relief other forms of primordialism that would otherwise be nonexistent or, at least, less salient. If Nigerians were critically aware of the fact that they belonged to a race that has been badly abused in its contact with the outside world, there might have been a valid basis for defining this area as a corporate primordial group of black people. Colonial education, both the Islamic and Christian religions, and a lack of adequate communications within Nigeria and between Nigeria and outside black communities have all robbed this concept of its value in the Nigerian political scene. The upshot is to make more salient less inclusive primordial principles in our political life.

Territory. If the absence of race consciousness has resulted in the lack of an all-embracing primordial principle that could include all Nigerians, territorial or regional groupings have tended to have far more complicated effects. In a society where communications have remained poor (mostly by oral means) and where one's measure of success is one's neighbors' wealth, territorial groupings have tended to embitter the relations between neighboring groups included in the same region. It tends to make more salient other principles of primordialism like ethnicity (tribalism) and/or language. The relations between Binis and Yorubas and between Ibibios and Ibos became much worse after the regionalization of

Nigeria in 1954. The tendency for neighboring ethnic groups to become enemies is a well-known feature of our political life. The relations between Urhobos and Itsekiris in the Midwest, or between Ibos and Ibibios, owe a great deal of their bitterness to common boundaries.

On the other hand, from the point of view of the whole of Nigeria, this overall tendency for neighboring groups to be at odds has promoted friendships between groups far removed. The beneficial results of this phenomenon for the integration of Nigeria cannot be overestimated. The strength of the Yoruba-AG in the old Eastern and Northern Regions, the popularity of the Ibo-NCNC in the Midwest (in the period 1954–1963—before the creation of the Midwest) and the friendships that existed between the Hausa-NPC and the Ijaws and, after the creation of the Midwest, the Urhobos and Itsekiris are perhaps among the most important reasons for the continued existence of Nigeria. That is to say, while territorial groupings, as a principle, have negative effects in heightening primordial definitions of neighboring groups, they have an important integrative function of promoting criss-crossing relations, especially between groups geographically separated.

Religion. Religion has been assumed by several people, especially foreigners, to be central to Nigerian politics. Chief Obafemi Awolowo, by every reckoning the earliest and most important exponent of a variety of primordialisms in Nigeria, wrote in 1947:

Above all, a deep religious gulf runs between the Northern and Southern portions of the country. The peoples of Western and Eastern Regions of the South, approach religion with remarkable moderation and nonchalance: Christians, Mohammedans, and so-called Pagans mix in society without restraint. The people of the North, however, are extremely fanatical about Islamism.[17]

It does not seem that Awolowo's blanket distinction between the North and South has proved valid. The distinction, however, is not without merit. Islam seems to have become rather domesticated in a way that Christianity has not: Christianity is still largely identified as a foreign religion and associated with the colonial power-structure, while Islam has gained a Nigerian texture. It should be mentioned that the brand of Islam in vogue in prewar Nigeria was far more conservative than that in places like Syria, Iraq, or Egypt. The nonenfranchisement of women in the North and the conservative interpretation of the Ramadan fast in the case of the working population and students are far removed from what is in vogue in more progressive Islamic societies.

This is not to say that religion has played an important part in our conflicts. It is interesting, indeed, that Ibo-NCNC, which was "Christian" in its leadership and membership, preferred alliances with Moslem-led parties while antagonizing Christian-led parties. Similarly, the Hausa-led NPC preferred as allies parties that were Christian in leadership and membership, while antagonizing "Moslem" parties like the Northern Elements Progressive Union. The reason for this curiosity is that regional factors, such as geographical proximity, were more salient in Nigerian politics than religion. Thus it happened that the NCNC was opposed to all parties in the East, the AG to those in the West, and the NPC to those in the North.

Language. Language has emerged as a controversial primordial principle in Nigeria, thanks to Awolowo's advocacy of the creation of states in Nigeria along linguistic lines.[18] There is an internal contradiction in upholding the principle of language; ethnicity and language differ in many cases, and ethnicity is an established important principle in Nigeria. There are millions of Fulani who today speak only Hausa, but nevertheless assert their identity with the Fulani as a distinct ethnic group. Nor would the Igalla and the Itsekiri peoples of the Midwest State take kindly to the idea of being called Yoruba, in spite of the striking similarity of their languages to the Yoruba language.

Awolowo has an Indian counterpart, Ambedkar.[19] Both feel that language is a universal primordial principle which is bound to triumph over all other primordial principles and civil ties. Neither seems sensitive to the fact that one of the strongest primordial groupings in the world today, the Jewish community flung all over the world, exists in spite of language barriers. Quite apart from this, it appears that the significance of language as a primordial principle rapidly decreases as the number of languages increases.

Of the four principles already considered—race, territory, religion, and language—none seems preeminently important in itself as a principle of primordialism in Nigeria. Nigerians have not generally rallied around any of these principles when the group with which they identify is threatened. But more relevant to the topic of this chapter, Nigerians have not usually defined their rights and duties in terms of their relationships to race, territory, religion, or language.

Ethnicity. It is ethnicity that has emerged as *the* principle of primordialism in Nigeria.[20] The significance of ethnic groups deepened with the increasing introduction of "democratic" processes. The "ladder" elections of 1950 emphasized the ethnic group as a basis of political power. The subsequent arrangements of constituencies along ethnic group lines gave expression to internal differentiations within various ethnic groups but, more significantly, to a clear-cut definition of the boundaries of each of these groups.

This last distinction is important. Internal differentiations in each ethnic group did occur, but they did not involve the disruptive conflicts that flowed from attempts to define the boundaries between various ethnic groups in terms of the sharing of political power. Most of those involved in the "within-ethnic" group power struggle were the old hands at colonial politics: chiefs, village heads, and wealthy civilians. The newer elements that emerged from the "democratization" of the Nigerian political process were the more "sophisticated" Western-educated Nigerians whose identities still lay with the ethnic group. The phenomenon known as "tribalism" was tied up with their manipulations—the attempts to increase the power of the ethnic group with which they identified.

The bitterness of the "between-ethnic" group struggles was due to a number of factors. First, by its very nature the struggle involved the sharing of the limited resources of a young and weak civil state to which these boundary-defining elements owed little or no duties. The award of scholarships, the provision of roads and water facilities, that is, all that might be called social rights, became the attributes of ethnic groups. While these rights were sought everywhere with great eagerness, "civic" duties were either being abrogated or severely limited.

Second, there is a new bearing in the definition of one's group identity. Traditionally, most Nigerians aspired to the level attained by their neighboring ethnic groups. But the new democratic processes introduced a new norm of comparison that made the old standards disturbing. The wealth of a neighboring group was now interpreted as an unfair distribution of common goods. Where before it was usual to level up, what was now required was to level down.

Third, the new civil arrangements either upturned traditional patterns of power relationships between neighboring ethnic groups or introduced new expectations of political power. The logic of electoral representation, once the "ladder" system was abolished, was "one man, one vote." In practice this meant that the new expectations of power of an ethnic group were a function of its voting total. In some cases ethnic groups that were the overdog became the underdog after an election, thanks to their small size. The size of the Ibos gave them a superiority that turned the balance of powers in Eastern Nigeria in a most dramatic way. Similarly, with the introduction of electoral processes Urhobos had expected a bigger share of power over the Itsekiris who had enjoyed political power out of proportion to their size. When they were outwitted by a subtle alliance of the Itsekiris with a bigger electoral block of the Yorubas, the Urhobos turned their frustration into a firm opposition to the Yoruba-AG party.

There is a sense in which it could be claimed, indeed, that the introduction of electoral processes (in the form of "one man, one vote") led to the power-defining phenomenon of "tribalism" that embittered the relations between various ethnic groups. Because the people involved in this new process had the techniques of Western politics and the academic wherewithal to pursue their identity goals, this mode of primordialism was often phrased in civil terms. Underlying all of this, of course, is the fact that civil politics was introduced into Nigeria at a time when the individual had no attachment or had no reason in fact for any commitment, to civil goals.

It is the point here, then, that ethnicity was sufficiently salient as a primordial principle for most Nigerians at the start of civil politics. Once civil politics made their impact the identity of the ethnic group became supreme. Although internal differentiations are an important factor in the outcome of many of the conflicts that followed, it is the new boundary "definition" of powers between ethnic groups that relate most directly to the history of political conflict in Nigeria. Before we pursue this matter further, it is important to consider the significance of the colonial experience for most Nigerians in their definition of their relations to primordial and civil centers of power.

COLONIALISM AND CITIZENSHIP
It would seem paradoxical to claim, as I have done, that the colonial era developed no significant civil centers with which Nigerians could identify—after all, the British lauded Nigeria as a case of successful colonial transition. Three apparently civil structures did emerge in the pre-independence period: the Civil Service, the Nigerian police, and the Nigerian army.

Of these three, the Civil Service was regionalized as early as 1954, although attempts to regionalize the police were successfully resisted, mostly by Nigerians from "minority" areas. The Nigerian army remained federal in structure, with no overt regional control. None of these were "melting pots"; indeed the Civil Service in each of the three regions became the rallying ground for ethnic group politics. The federal Civil Service was not completely insulated, but it was less abused by politicians fending for their ethnic group interests.

The Nigerian army has turned out to be the most sensitive area of Nigerian politics. In spite of all attempts to free it from ethnic group control, it was clear to many Nigerians, from the pattern of "quota" recruitment from each region, that all was not safe. The Nigerian police force, on the other hand, was to a much greater extent more Nigerian than any other service. Part of the reason for this phenomenon was due to the peculiar personnel structure of the Nigerian police force. A great many of the key officers and men, definitely the heads of the force for many years, were "minority" Nigerians who, as I shall argue, were prone to dilute their primordial commitments with greater cooperation with federal civil structures than other ("majority") Nigerians.

My intention here, however, is not to examine particular structures, but to consider how the colonial experience has shaped the orientations of Nigerians as citizens.

A major characteristic of citizenship in postcolonial societies, at least in Africa, is that obligations to civil centers tend to be much less emphasized than the claim for social rights from these same centers. The demarcation between civil and primordial ties is easy enough to identify in a colonial situation and was indeed encouraged by both British colonial administrators (especially through the medium of "indirect rule") and Nigerians immediately after independence.

Two reasons may be given for the greater emphasis on rights than on obligations. First, there is the doctrine of colonialism. Colonial powers invested great energies (especially via educational facilities in the teaching of history, religion, and English literature) to emphasize that their presence was in the interests of the colonized. Such overused concepts as "discovery" (of the colonized peoples), "intervention" (rather than interference by colonial powers), and "pax Britannica," loaded as they are, were clearly intended to tell the colonized that it is they, not the colonizers, who gained from the colonial experience. What the colonized peoples contributed to the development of their own society and to the development of the metropolitan center has usually been underplayed. This strategy unwittingly emphasized the rights of the colonized with respect to the civil center while de-emphasizing their obligations. Besides, it was the case that the image of the metropolitan center in the colonies is that of a wealthy overlord who spills money and goods to every needy person. The upshot is a situation in which individuals have tended to recognize their rights and to define their relations with the central state entirely in terms of benefits and social rights therefrom, but not in terms of obligations.

Second, this tendency has been reinforced by the struggle for independence, especially when such a struggle did not involve old (primordial) obligations or lead to the creation of new ones. A central strategy of the leaders fighting for independence has been to incite colonized peoples to resist whatever obligations they owed to the metropolitan rulers. It was not unusual to promise their followers to expect lower taxes and lighter obligations in general in the postindependence era. Poor performance at work and the avoidance of any type of colonial responsibility were hailed as patriotic acts. Needless to say, such habits tend to have a snowball effect. The ritual of independence celebrations did not usually differentiate national obligations from obligations to foreign rulers.

My position then is that on the whole, the colonial experience led Nigerians to emphasize their expectations of social rights from the civil order. But again it is important to point out that this tendency did not lead Nigerians away from their obligations to their families and ethnic groups. If anything, the colonial experience with its condescending distinction between "Europeanized" (later "Westernized") and native sectors of social life led more people to the "native" areas than to the "Europeanized" areas of social experience.

A comparative note is in order here. Colonialism is to Africa what feudalism is to Europe. They form the historical background from which Africa and Europe advance to modernity. As such, they have determined the peculiar characteristics of modernity in each of these areas. Feudal Europe operated by assuming that the duties of the citizen are given, not problematic, and the issues of citizenship centered around the rights of the citizens. It seems to me that this aspect of feudal Europe has been carried over to and consolidated in modern European societies, and their new off-spring in non-European settings. Especially in the West, rights have remained the bone of contention.

This process has been reversed for Africa by the colonial experience. At least with respect to the civil state, the rights of the citizen were developed full-blown with national independence. The colonial experience has produced the unanticipated result of lowering a sense of duty to the civil state, and this attitude has been carried over to modern Africa. Where rights are problematic for the West, we in postcolonial Africa may soon come to recognize that it is the citizens' duties to his nation that are problematic in our political life.

NIGERIAN FEDERALISM AND CITIZENSHIP

Almost every knowledgeable Nigerian agrees that our brand of federalism was awkward, but the evaluation of its incongruity varies rather widely. Generally, Hausa/Fulani speakers blamed any threats to the Federation on the intolerance of Southern politicians. Ibo and Yoruba complaints were that the size of the Northern Region was much greater than what could make for a good balanced federation.[21] The most extreme form of this viewpoint was that if only the North were not larger than the East or West, both in population and in land area, there would be no major trouble in Nigeria.

Complaints by other groups of Nigerians (whom I shall characterize as "minorities" and "marginals") were of a different nature—that the three majority groups in Nigeria, the Ibos, the Hausas, and the Yorubas, had all the powers in the regions as well as at the federal center, and that they themselves, totalling about half the population of the country, were reduced to second-class citizens. Representative of this viewpoint is Dr. Arikpo's complaint:

Nigeria moved from unitary to federal government [in 1954] and in the process created numerical majorities on the one hand and minorities on the other. This fact was to reveal itself as of the utmost significance for the future of Nigerian federalism.[22]

The year 1954 is definitely a most important date in the history of Nigerian federalism.[23] Although the East, the West, and the North had existed before then, they were only administrative units in the hands of colonial commissioners. With the 1954 constitutional arrangements, the Ibos, the Yorubas, and the Hausa emerged

as the ruling groups not only in their separate regions but
the center. Second, Lagos was separated from the Western
The emergence of Nigerians into power was not uniform; th
say, citizenship opportunities that followed the 1954 regionalization
of the country around the three majority ethnic groups created a
situation in which by a stroke of constitutional arrangements about
half the population of Nigeria was deprived of full citizenship
opportunities. It must be noted that there was no historical or
ideological justification for this sudden preeminence of Eastern
Region Ibos, Western Region Yorubas, and the Hausa/Fulani in
the Northern Region over the rest of the country.

The "rest of the country" represents over one hundred distinct
ethnic groups of varying population sizes, but with none of two
million. The land area covered by these groups is more than that
covered by the three majority groups. Over 90 percent of the
mineral resources of Nigeria lie in the areas occupied by these
varied small ethnic groups. I think it useful to distinguish among
these various groups.

The Hausa/Fulani in the North, the Eastern Ibos, and the
Western Yoruba, were *majority* Nigerians. The remaining groups
of Nigerians, more or less excluded from power in the regions and
at the federal center by the 1954 constitutional arrangement,
belonged to two distinct groups in terms of their relations to the
majority groups as well as their characteristic reactions to Nigerian
problems. They were *minority* Nigerians, who had no ethnic affiliations with any of the majority groups, and *marginal* Nigerians, who
had ethnic affiliations with one of the majority groups in the country but who by the 1954 arrangements were placed in a different
region. This latter category thus included Western Ibos, Lagos
Yorubas, and Northern Yorubas.

In terms of citizenship expectations there was a wide gulf
separating majority, minority, and marginal Nigerians from each
other. In the regions it was clear that only the majority Nigerians
could rule—a fact dramatized by the violent termination of Professor Eyo Ita from the Premiership of Eastern Nigeria in 1954.
The weak reaction of the minorities in the East, namely the formation of the UNIP, only pointed up the sad fact that all Nigerians
were not equal. Because the federal government was tied to the
regions, certain patterns became clear soon after 1954. First, only
political parties led by the majority groups could become politically
meaningful in a national context. Second, only a majority Nigerian

could become the Prime Minister or President of Nigeria. It was thus usual to characterize Nigerians as either an Ibo, Yoruba, or Hausa, or as a supporter of the Ibo, Yoruba, or Hausa. In other words, what counted in Nigeria was the membership of a majority ethnic group or support for the political party led by a majority group. Some of these facts become apparent from Map 1 and Table 1.

TABLE 1

Population of Nigeria (c. 1954)

Region	Population
East	12.00 Million
Majority (*Ibo*)	7.00
Minority	5.00
Marginal	0.00 (nil)
West	13.00
Majority (*Yoruba*)	10.00
Minority	2.50
Marginal (*Ibo*)	0.50
North	29.00
Majority (*Hausa/Fulani*)	13.50
Minority	13.50
Marginal (*Yoruba*)	2.00
Capitol–Lagos	
Marginal (*Yoruba*)	0.70
Total	54.70 Million

This unbalanced situation is the single most important factor in our history in the last two decades.[24] Early in the 1950s it was clear that the minority and marginal Nigerians were not going to take their new low status with amusement. The minority groups in the East turned away from the Ibo majority to either the Yoruba-AG or the Hausa-NPC. The minority and marginal groups in the West turned their political allegiance to the Ibo-NCNC for

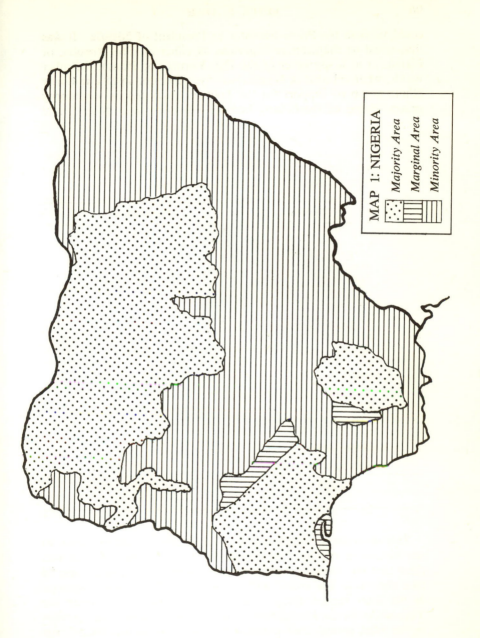

MAP 1: NIGERIA

Majority Area
Marginal Area
Minority Area

the most part, at least before the creation of the Midwest Region in 1963. In the North, a good section of the minority groups, particularly the Tiv, and marginal Yoruba intellectuals turned away from the Hausa-NPC to the Yoruba-AG. The reaction of the majority groups in each case was uniform: there was widespread oppression of minority (and marginal) groups in all three regions. It is therefore understandable that most minority and marginal Nigerians turned away from the regions toward the federal center, which at least gave a wider spectrum of protection to *all* Nigerians. They began to prefer the security of the federal Civil Service, and the centralized Nigerian police and the Nigerian army to the regional services controlled by majority groups. For the most part the allegiance of the majority groups to their regions was as strong as their attachment to their ethnic groups.

In fact, the conflict between civil ties and primordial ties in the new states, so correctly emphasized by Geertz, was mostly represented by conflicts between the regions and the federal center, between the autonomy of the regions and the survival of the Federation. In these conflicts the behaviors of majority, marginal, and minority Nigerians have differed quite widely. In broad terms it may be stated that whenever a conflict arose between a region and the federal center that could result in the secession of the region, there was a marked tendency for the majority group in the region to support secession, while the minority and, where they exist, the marginal groups resisted the secession; once the secession became a reality in any region, the marginal Nigerians ethnically related to the majority group that was seceding tended to support the secession.

Since secession has been the red devil of our political life, I shall consider the significant relationship of this distinction to the threats and failures of secession in all the three original regions in the country. But before I move on to this area, it may be worthwhile to state the meaning of the distinction for the elements of citizenship in Nigeria.

It is in order to begin with the citizens of Lagos. Native Lagosians have clearly only marginal support for the majority Yoruba. Their special status, beginning with their being labelled as the "Colony of Lagos" as distinct from the "Protectorate of Nigeria" in the hinterland, has given them a sense of distinction from the rest of Yoruba-land. Their claims to social rights—with special scholarship awards and other social benefits—clearly drew them closer to the concept of Nigeria than the Western Nigeria majority Yoruba. Their relations to the civil center of Nigerian political life was the one least mediated by the bonds of primordial loyalties. It seems fair to say that marginal Lagosians had a higher sense of duty to Nigeria than their majority kinsmen in the mainland.

The general pattern of politics in Nigeria came to be that the majority Nigerians' primordialism was sublimated in their attachment to their regions of origin, while the federal center represented now a civil center and now a primordial center—depending on who exercised power. The significance of their claims and access to social rights was greatly diminished by the fact that many of these benefits were mediated through the influence of their regional power structure. Thus those majority Nigerians who were recipients of federal scholarship awards were more likely to hail the politicians representing their regions (and hence their ethnic groups) as responsible for these awards.

The case of regions-based marginal Nigerians (that is, the Ibos in the West—later the Midwest—and the Yorubas in the North) was clearly different. In some cases they suffered the brunt of attacks directed at their majority kinsmen in another region by the majority ruling group in their own regions. Their affection for their regions was little, but they could not identify entirely with the region in which their kinsmen were the majority ruling groups; after all, they did not have access to the same benefits as their majority kinsmen. They were therefore more inclined to look to the federal civil center. They tended to embrace the federal Civil Service, the Nigerian police, and the Nigerian army with greater dedication than majority Nigerians.

All these tendencies became clearly marked in the experiences of minority Nigerians. In general, they looked more toward Lagos than to the regions. To put the matter in another way, in cases of choice or conflict between the federal center and the regions, their outlook was more toward the federal center. For many minority Nigerians, the regions symbolized the power structure of the majority ethnic groups. It is among minority Nigerians that a clear indication of duty to the nation began to emerge, at least in an incipient form. This is especially the case of felt obligations to preserve the nation.

All these remarks must, however, be interpreted in the light of the rather low level of communications that existed in the country. A more meaningful way of putting the matter is to say that these tendencies were greater for the more educated and elite groups among the different Nigerians that I have sought to characterize than among the illiterate.

SECESSIONIST TENDENCIES IN NIGERIA

Secession became a household word in Nigeria as early as 1954, when the majority Yoruba in Western Nigeria openly hinted about the possibility of secession, and indeed pressed for a secession clause in the constitution of Nigeria. No concept has appealed more to majority Nigerians, as a bargaining weapon, than that of secession—and no concept has been more dreaded by minority and marginal Nigerians than this notion of secession.

Minority and marginal Nigerians have usually responded to collective frustration in Nigerian politics by asking for a solution to problems in the idiom of the tenuous political system that existed in the country: thus such serious crises as the Itsekiri-Urhobo confrontation in 1952, the Tiv riots against the majority Hausa/Fulani rulers of Northern Nigeria, with consequent punitive actions against the Tiv, and the violent reactions of the Ibo rulers of Eastern Nigeria against Ibibio politicians were resolved by the due process of law in the Nigerian tradition. In each case the oppressed minority groups did not resort to defections from the Nigerian framework.

The response of majority Nigerians to collective frustration is totally different. The majority Western Yoruba were quick to threaten secession in the 1950s when it appeared that they were not gaining a great deal from the rest of Nigeria, and especially after Lagos was separated from Western Yoruba. Hausa and Fulani leaders also threatened secession in 1956.[25] The majority Ibos were the last group to threaten secession but anybody familiar with the style of Nigerian politics in the 1950s and 1960s would guess correctly that the Ibos were not immune to the temptation to which the two other majority groups had fallen victim.

Of course, the motives for threatening secession were not identical in all three cases. In general, the fear that any one of the majority groups would not share in the control of the power and resources of the Federation led to the threat of secession.

The threat of secession is not new to Nigerians. When in 1953 the present leaders of the NPC feared political and economic domination of the North by the South, they threatened secession. A few years later, the Action Group, faced with the combined opposition of the

East and North, and believing that the political influence of the West fell far short of its economic contribution to the prosperity of the Federation, threatened secession. In 1965 the leaders of Eastern Nigeria, finding that, despite the now favourable economic position of the region, their political influence was weakened by the NPC/NNDP alliance, threatened secession.[26]

This fear of the combined forces of two opposing majority groups by a third majority group emerges strongly in the thoughts of Ahmadu Bello. Isa Kaita's House of Representatives speech in 1959 struck a note that the Sardauna thought was worth quoting in his autobiography: "I rise to support the motion [Isa Kaita said]. . . . If the West and a section of the East feel that only their case should be heard and that they are not prepared to hear the other side, well, why delay the House?" And the Sardauna adds in his own frank way:

I then made the shortest speech that I have ever made and possibly one of the most important: "I arise to associate myself with the last speaker. The mistake of 1914 has come to light and I should like to go no further." I was referring to the Amalgamation that took place in that year between the old independent governments of Northern and Southern Nigeria.[27]

It should be clear that it was the cooperation between the East and the West that jolted the Hausa/Fulani leaders of the North. It is interesting that even at this early stage the Yoruba and Ibo, in spite of the use of East and West as terms of reference, had impressed their characteristics as majority groups. The "section of the East" in Isa Kaita's statement was really referring to the Ibos. The earlier threat of secession by the Yoruba was again no doubt occasioned by the joint views of the East and the North regarding the separation of Lagos from the West.

But why did the Hausas and Yorubas not secede? Again the Sardauna has given us the benefit of his frankness:

There were agitations in favor of secession; we would set up on our own; we should cease to have anything more to do with the Southern people; we should take our own way.

I must say it looked very tempting. . . . There were however two things of the most vital importance in our own way. The first was that the greater part of the revenue of Nigeria comes from customs duties. . . . Obviously we would have to collect our duty at our own borders. . . . Would an unfriendly South permit the free passage of our goods across their lands? . . . The second difficulty was similar to it. Would it be possible to send our goods down to the coast for shipment by rail or road? . . . We therefore had to take a modified line. We must aim at a looser structure for Nigeria in its general pattern. . . . This policy was gradually developed among us and we went over the Region canvassing our constituencies and influential opinion on its merits. We received a great deal of substantial support and reached a point at which we felt it desirable to put the matter to a vote after wide and public debate.[28]

Ahmadu Bello, in spite of his remarkable frankness in the passage quoted above, has not told us the pattern of support for the threatened secession and the idea of a looser Federation. Might it not be the case that minority and marginal fears about secessions and confederations were already taking shape at this early date?

Awolowo has not provided us with any discussion of the majority Yoruba threat to secede. However, his early support for the creation of the Midwest may give one some leeway to speculate that the existence of minority and, in our terms, marginal Nigerians in the West at that time was a main hindrance to the majority Yoruba secession bid.[29] Some evidence of the thoughts and strategies of Chief Awolowo, as the principal actor in the Yoruba West at that time, is the strong demand by Chief Awolowo and his supporters at this same time for the "return" of marginal Northern Yoruba to the West.

By far the most reflective and sober general statement on the meaning and consequences of secession has been that by Dr. Okoi Arikpo, a man of considerable experience in Nigerian politics. Dr. Arikpo was writing just before the "Biafran" secession became a reality:

The threat of secession is a convenient emotional expression of political frustration. But no regional leader seriously believes that it is a practical alternative to Nigeria's problem of adjustment to the modern world. Indeed no region of the Federation can afford to go it alone. The East, in spite of growing riches from oil, would be faced with an unprecedented employment problem if it broke away from the rest of the country. There are at least one million Ibo of Eastern Nigerian origin resident in other parts of the Federation, and if the East seceded, most of these would be forced to return there. The present leaders of Eastern Nigeria are too realistic to contemplate such an event with equanimity; besides the East is not linguistically homogeneous. The non-Ibo communities in the region would oppose secession to the point of breaking away from an independent Eastern Nigeria. And what is true of the East is true too of the North where, in addition to the dominant Hausa-Fulani linguistic group, there are several non-Hausa groups like the Tiv, the Birom and Yoruba who would passionately oppose the establishment of a separate Northern Nigeria, politically linked to the Arab world. On economic grounds alone, if on no other, the West and North could ill afford to secede. Indeed, the economies of the various regions are so complementary to each other that no severe fluctuation in the export price of one region's main primary product has ever produced violent fluctuations in the economy as a whole. . . . Nigeria's linguistic heterogeneity and diversified economy militate against secession while they favour closer union and central direction.[30]

The optimism expressed by Arikpo is more characteristic, of course, of the hopes and wishes of minority Nigerians than it is predictive of what was soon to follow: the secession of the East. But his two main points of emphasis, the economic integration of Nigeria and the aversion of minority (and marginal) Nigerians to secession, are most significant. It seems to me, however, that the aversion of minority and marginal Nigerians to secession is by far the most important single factor in sustaining Nigeria as well as being, more immediately, the single most important reason for the frustration of the Biafran secession. The economic factor would, in fact, seem to work in the direction of favoring secessions in many cases, especially when the region in question was economically well off.

It seems in order to make some generalizations about the various remarks in this and past sections. In the Nigerian situation, the relationship between primordial and civil ties emphasized by Geertz and Shils (the will to be modern and the quest for self-identity, in Shils' terms) may be phrased as follows: the primordial attachments of some 29 million Nigerians—Hausas/Fulani in Northern Nigeria, the Ibos in Eastern Nigeria, and the Yorubas in the West —were broad enough to accommodate the quest for self-identity and to provide a basis for the desire to be modern. In that situation, their attachments to the primordial source were much stronger than their attachments to the civil source, and their proclivity to defect from the civil center became very sharp. On the other hand, the primordial bases of some 26 million minority and marginal Nigerians provided some platform for self-identity but were quite inadequate for meeting the needs of modernity. The upshot is that this latter group of Nigerians, including some half-million Ibos in the former West and some one-and-a-half-million Yoruba in Lagos and in the former Northern Nigeria, was in general opposed to secessions in Nigeria.

More generally, then, we are claiming that the conflict between the quest for modernity and the need for self-identity is differently resolved for those who have a broad primordial base and those who have a narrow primordial base.[31] Where the primordial base is broad, both the need for modernity and self-identity are met in the idiom of primordialism, and primordial resources are given greater stress. Where, however, there is a narrow primordial base, only the quest for identity is met in the primordial idiom, and there is greater leaning toward civil commitments than in the first case.

The "Biafran" Secession

THE INTERPRETATIONS OF THE SECESSION

The dust of battle in the Nigerian Civil War has hardly settled and the recency of the crisis may be a major obstacle in the way of an objective evaluation of the events leading to the declaration of secession and war. Public relations agents and various international interests, notably the Vatican and the Catholic establishment in many countries, are so involved in canvassing their own points of view that one loses certain central arguments.

The most serious errors flow from attempts by foreign interpreters of the Nigerian crisis to lift incidents out of their contexts and interpret them against the backgrounds of their own history and prejudices. The various interpretations advanced by Western sponsors of the secession include notions of primordial conflicts that have been mentioned in this chapter. Differences in religion, language, ethnicity, region, and educational levels have been invoked to explain the motives for the secession.

I have already discussed the low political salience of religion in Nigeria. The nonsignificance of religion in the conflict is dramatized by the fact that the Biafran secession has polarized those who happen to be Christians much more than it has involved Muslims. As I shall argue later, those most violently opposed to the secession were not the Muslim Hausa or the Yoruba (a sizable proportion of whom are Muslims), but the greatly "Christian" minority and marginal groups in Eastern Nigeria, Midwestern Nigeria, Northern Nigeria, and Lagos.

The most eloquent argument for Biafran secession has been the claim of "pogrom" in Northern Nigeria. The Northern killings of 1966 have been some of the most terrifying experiences in the country, and there is little doubt that most of the casualties were people from the East, Ibos and non-Ibos (mostly Ibibios, Annangs, and Ijaws). The pattern of support for secession, however, reveals the main categories of Nigerian social life. The Northern killings were widely regarded by people in the East and Midwest as an overreaction by the Hausas (but also other Northerners) against the anti-Hausa coup, organized by Ibos, in January 1966, and the loss of Hausa civilians in Enugu and Port Harcourt. But secession was clearly opposed from the beginning by minority Easterners and Midwesterners. It could be argued, of course, that the motives for anger among the non-Ibo minorities in the East and Midwest, and even among the marginal Ibos in the Midwest, were different from the motives for anger among majority Eastern Ibos. For the minorities and marginals, the loss of relatives was experienced as a result of power struggle between erstwhile political friends and allies, the majority Ibos and Hausas. The lack of any solid basis for differentiating majority Ibos from the other groups in the East and Midwest could be blamed by the latter for such losses. For the majority Ibos (as it was for the Hausas and Fulanis before July 1967), it was a case of being beaten by former political friends and rivals in a fierce power struggle.

The irony of the Biafran secession is that it was occasioned by the breakdown in the relations between the Ibos and the Hausas, the majority groups that governed Nigeria at the federal center from about 1954 to 1966—the whole span of our prewar political history in which Nigerians were more or less in control of power. The antagonism of the Yoruba-AG against the Hausa-NPC and the rather bold attempt by the Yoruba-AG to win over all the minority and marginal groups in Nigeria in the federal elections marked out the Yoruba-AG as a "dangerous" political party for both the Ibo-NCNC and the Hausa-NPC. The liquidation of the Yoruba power structure, following the Hausa-Ibo coalition of 1959, was the joint responsibility of the coalition partners. As it happened, the imprisonment of Chief Awolowo and other AG leaders removed a common threat to both parties and marked the beginning of a bitter power struggle between them. The struggle for the control of the West led first to a flirtation between the weakened Yoruba leaders (a faction of whom was now led by Chief Akintola) and the Ibos, and then an alliance with the Hausas. In the famous

January 1966 coup, most key Hausa and pro-Hausa political leaders were killed.

Perhaps the single most important episode in the January 1966 coup was not the killing of the Prime Minister and the Premier of Northern Nigeria, but rather the killing of Northern minority military leaders in the Nigerian army.[32] At first this pattern of anti-Northern coup gave a false semblance of unity, by way of common cause, to the whole of the North and, later on, increased the hatred of Northern minorities to the Biafran secession. The July 1966 coup was a "Northern" coup in its joint operation by majority Hausas and Northern minorities.

My claim here should be clearly stated. The incidents leading to the 1966 coup and countercoup and the violence that followed was the result of a power struggle between the three majority groups in the country. The breakdown of the Ibo-Hausa coalition, following the liquidation of the Yoruba power structure, was the first signal of a physical showdown between the various majority groups. It was a clear-cut case of power struggle. Indeed, there is a sense in which it could be said that Biafran secession was impossible: whatever group won the confrontation to follow would eventually rule the country. The Ibos' seizure of the Midwest and their attempt to take the West and Lagos in the very first month of the war would seem to indicate that the Biafran secession was more like a stage in the ongoing process of power struggle than an intended clear separation of the East from the rest of the country. No one can now state exactly what would have happened if the Ibo forces had taken over Ibadan and Lagos, but it would have been most irresponsible for such military effort not to have been rewarded with the prize of controlling the capital of Nigeria and Nigeria's political power.

The Response of Nigerians to the Biafran Declaration of Secession

The secession game has been so long played in Nigeria that it seems relevant to evaluate the response of various groups of Nigerians once the threat to secede becomes a reality.

The call for a confederation, following the July 1966 coup and the incidents of violence in the North, was close to the choice of secession. That such apparently dedicated Nigerians as Tai Solarin could easily fall victim to the call for a confederation is not insignificant for an evaluation of the response of different types of Nigerians to the dangers of secession. With various "leaders of thought" parading around their own notions of what Nigeria ought to be or ought not to be, it seems clear that the "civic" commitment to the duty of preserving the nation came to the surface among minority and marginal Nigerians. This seems to me to contrast rather sharply with the apparent indifference of majority Hausas and Yorubas to the secession.

Majority Nigerians, in this case the Hausas and majority Yorubas, seemed little threatened by the possibility of the Eastern secession. Awolowo's statement that the West would secede "if the East was allowed to secede" seems to me to typify the majority attitude to secession. Colonel Usman's celebrated outburst at Aburi is slightly different from Chief Awolowo's stance, but it fits into the general majority response: "Let us take this question honestly, the East has not recognized the Federal Government. I think you better secede and let the three of us join together." [33] The minority reaction to the threatened Ibo secession was more varied. The Northern minorities seemed to have entertained for some time the artificial unity imposed on the North by the conflict with the Ibos, especially by the killing of Northern minority military leaders in 1966. But the harsh meaning of a separate Northern Nigeria for minority Nigerians in the North is not difficult to recognize, and one can safely say that Northern minority groups were far less inclined to permit the East to secede. The Midwest minority situation was far more certain. The nearness of the Midwest to the majority Ibos and the presence of marginal Ibos in the Region was a major threat. The rejection of secession as a means of solving Nigeria's political problems has always been a consistent position of Midwest politics.

The positions of the various marginals in Nigeria were of immense importance in the Biafran secession. The Northern marginal Yoruba (in Kabba and Ilorin) did not appear to have taken any critical position. However, the positions of marginal Midwest Ibos and of marginal Lagos Yoruba were of tremendous significance. The marginal Ibo position was understandably ambiguous: to be without their majority kinsmen in the East was distasteful, but their inclusion in the East would not basically solve their problems. They would remain rather marginal to Ibo power structure, even in the case of the latter possibility. By far the most critical was the case of marginal Lagos Nigerians. Their support for the projected Yoruba secession could have been fatal to Nigerian unity. As it turned out, they were quite hostile to secession, and they frustrated any major threat to the unity of the country.

The division of the country into twelve states, which was to be expected from the minority influence that followed the countercoup of July 1966, blunted any favorable reactions to the Biafran declaration of secession a few days afterwards. By this division, the influence of the North as an entity was considerably weakened, at least in prospect, by the creation of six states in the North. Three of these new states are predominantly majority Hausa states. The other three are marginal and minority states. Lagos was for the first time raised from its ambiguous status as the capital of Nigeria to statehood, with an addition of valuable new land excised from the old Yoruba West.

Minority Eastern Nigerians were immeasurably strengthened in their opposition to the projected Biafran secession, and in their expectations of citizenship opportunities in the new Nigeria, by the breakup of Eastern Nigeria into three states. The East Central State belongs to the majority Ibos, while the other two are minority states. The only state that retained its former boundaries in the new shake-up is the Midwest State, created from the Western Region in 1963 following a crisis in the region. The boundaries of the regions created by the 1954 constitutional arrangements and of the new twelve states are shown in Maps 2 and 3. In terms of their significance for shaping the political orientations and fortunes of Nigerians, the 1954 constitutional arrangements and the May 1967 creation of states are close competitors in our national history. I shall now turn to a brief evaluation of the political meaning of the new twelve-state structure of the Nigerian Federation.

The Meaning of a Multi-state Federal Structure

THE FUTURE OF CITIZENSHIP

A most important feature of the new multistate structure of the Federation is that the process of unequal citizenship, arising from the arrangements of the 1950s, is corrected. The anomalies in Nigerian federalism included, most significantly, the fact that the three majority groups that gained most from the Federation, and the members of which had the greatest citizenship expectations in the land, had the least sense of duty to the nation. What has emerged in the short history of the Federation is that minority and

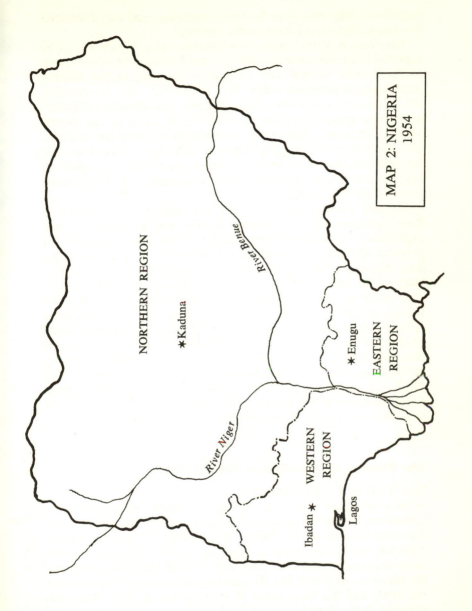

MAP 2: NIGERIA 1954

NORTHERN REGION

★Kaduna

River Benue

River Niger

WESTERN REGION

Ibadan ★

Lagos

★ Enugu

EASTERN REGION

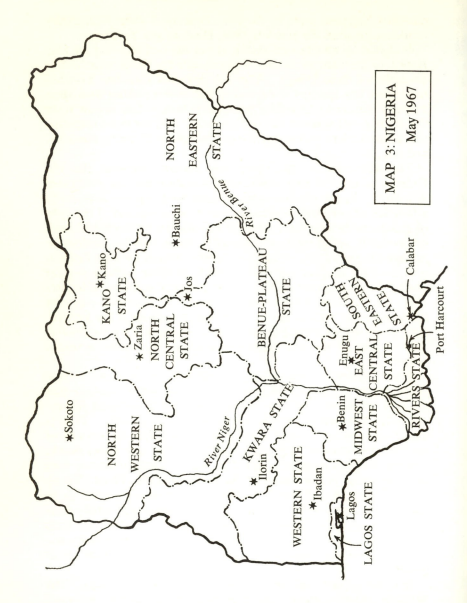

MAP 3: NIGERIA
May 1967

marginal Nigerians were by far more concerned about their duties to the nation than the majority Ibos, Hausas, and Yorubas.

It should be emphasized that it is not the fact of being an Ibo, Hausa, or Yoruba *per se* that is responsible for the peculiar political styles of these groups. After all, marginal Ibos and Yorubas have been less inclined to secession and power politics than their majority kinsmen. Objective social experiences that derive from the old regional makeup of the Federation were far more responsible for the various political styles attributable to majority, minority, and marginal Nigerians.

The difference in citizenship opportunities between the old Federation and the new multistate Federation may be illustrated as follows: by the old arrangement, leadership was not necessarily a function of personal competence but more a function of the type of group one belonged to. Thus, if the Biafran secession had been successful it would be near impossible for a non-Ibo Biafran to achieve the presidency of such a country. But in the new Federation, an Effik or Ijaw can achieve such an office without a great deal of hindrance, provided he has the required qualities of leadership. For millions of Nigerians, the irony of citizenship was that it was easier to achieve the leadership of the whole of the Federation, given proper arrangements, than it was to achieve the leadership of one of the old regions converted into an autonomous country.

The problem of citizenship, nevertheless, is far from solved. Understandably, federal Nigerian spokesmen stress the fact that the new multistate structure of the Federation is designed to prevent the domination of one ethnic group by another. This is important, but one should also be concerned with the pattern of the citizen's relations with Nigeria as such. The new states should also be designed in such a way that none of them competes with the civil center in the matter of the loyalties of the citizen. To do this, no state should remain as the spiritual headquarters, so to speak, of any primordial grouping. An illustration will clarify what I mean. The structure of the Hausa/Fulani states is such that each of them now appears as important as the others. Neither Kano nor Sokoto is now regarded as the center of the Hausa/Fulani ethnic group.

But this is not true of the other two majority groups. The Western State remains the Yoruba-land, to which marginal Yorubas in Lagos State and Kwara State may look to for primordial leadership. Similarly, marginal Ibos in the Midwest may be predisposed to look to the East Central State for spiritual and primordial leadership. On the other hand, if each of these "majority" states were split up into at least two states, such dangers would be minimized. What I am saying, in effect, is this: the new twelve-state structure has solved the problem of liquidating the category of "minority" Nigerians. They may now feel equal to the rest of their countrymen in their citizenship expectations and opportunities. However, it does not solve the problem of marginal Nigerians. As long as the Western State remains the headquarters of the Yorubas, and as long as the East Central State remains the center of core Ibo power and culture, no Lagos and Kwara Yorubas and no Midwest Ibos are likely to achieve any major office at the federal center. In the case of Kwara Yorubas and Midwest Ibos, they would tend to be distrusted by various other groups in their respective states. My prediction is that, if the East Central State and the Western State are not split up, then these marginal Nigerians in Lagos, Midwest, and Kwara states will have lower citizenship expectations and opportunities than their fellow countrymen.

One more citizenship problem remains. It has been my point throughout this essay that, on the whole, Nigerians have an exaggerated notion of the social benefits that the citizen should expect from the state. On the other hand, the concept of duty to the nation is minimal and, in some cases, nonexistent. A correction is urgently needed, and the material for that correction is available. It is not that Nigerians have no idea of duty; rather, the problem is the locus of the citizen's duty. Until now that locus has been largely primordial. This has been encouraged by the emphasis on primordial membership as a meaningful way of relating to the central state. It seems to me that the new state structure affords the opportunity of curtailing this preeminence of primordial relationships. Stated in another way, we should narrow the scope of primordialism to the family and community. This is why it is important to see to it that no ethnic group has a distinguishable center where its power rivals that of the state in its claim on the duties of the citizen.

The success of our Federation will depend largely on how much we can demonstrate that civil commitments and primordial attachments belong to different areas of our political behavior and that they need not conflict. As our nation embarks on industrialization and complex agricultural undertakings, resulting in new aggregations in urban centers or in the growth of larger rural towns, the benefits of primordial commitments should become of tremendous advantage in adjustment problems. To return to a stage where the establishment of one's identity in the primordial nexus threatens the foundations of our civil society is to take a backward step.

THE FUTURE OF PRIMORDIALISM IN NIGERIA

If the experiences of the last fifteen-odd years have any meanings at all, they are that primordial attachments are enhanced by civil politics and are greatly subversive of civil commitments. But primordialisms are by no means unbridled. Social structural arrangements are largely responsible for the pattern of responses by various types of Nigerians to national problems. The rigid positions of majority Nigerians on many issues, as contrasted by the subtlety and flexibility of minority and marginal Nigerians, can only be interpreted in a social structural framework. It is for this reason that many Nigerians now believe that primordial conflicts (especially what Nigerians like to call tribalism) will diminish. But what does that mean?

I expect more conflicts in the new Nigeria. But I expect that they will be "civic" rather than "primordial" conflicts, and that they will be tackled in the idiom of civil commitments to the nation. In a real sense, the Nigerian civil war represents a conflict between those who were fighting for equal citizenship expectations and opportunities and the direct relationship of the citizen to the civil center, and those who were fighting for the supremacy of majority ethnic groups. The defeat of the Biafran secession may eventuate in a feeling of low expectations of gain from appeals to primordial principles. However, that would not be the end of primordialism or primordial conflicts.

For one thing, there are countervailing strategies, to be employed by those who want to retain their primordial bases of power. Less disruptive primordial conflicts within the states may be expected in the sphere of defining the power arrangements between the various ethnic group elements in the states. Time is needed for the domestication of such primordial conflicts, but their solution will become easier if the rights and duties of citizens are better defined in our educational system and eventually in our cultural system. One suspects that the "codes of honor" suggested for the country are often misdirected. It is for the younger ones—in the family, in elementary schools, in secondary schools, and in universities—for whom we should devise "codes of honor." Might it not be important to devise a citizenship course to be taught in our elementary and secondary schools? We should learn to turn our schools into "melting pots" where Nigerian citizenship is forged and where the individual learns the scope and limits of his rights and duties.

One more note about the nature of primordialism in Nigeria. A curious aspect of Nigerian political life, often irritating to black Americans and West Indians, is that it is devoid of race consciousness. This in itself would be a most welcome thing if Nigeria had more than one race, although it would be less likely in such a situation. But is this a realistic attitude in a continent which is becoming ever less black because of South African, Rhodesian, and Portuguese anti-black policies? After all, every fifth black man in Africa is a Nigerian. Should we not regard it as part of our duty to be sensitive to the rights and burdens of black people elsewhere in the world? That could be a platform for a more inclusive primordialism, making the current extravagant significance attached to ethnicity less important. But this is a marshy area: there is need for a more skillful leader to survey it.

Conclusion

I have attempted to place the Biafran secession in a Nigerian political context. By so doing some details are inevitably neglected or underemphasized, but it is my feeling that a clear understanding of the events leading to the conflict, as well as the nature of the conflict itself, requires a knowledge of Nigerian political styles.

All too often, Nigerian problems have been discussed in the idiom of "tribalism." It has been my point in this essay that the political behaviors of Nigerians will be best understood if related to social structural arrangements. The reason an Ika Ibo or a Lagos Yoruba is less inclined to secession politics than his kinsmen in the East Central State or the Western State has to be sought in such social structural factors.

It has been the point of view of this chapter that the 1954 constitutional regionalization of Nigeria around the three majority groups shaped the political structure of the country in a very important manner. Although these three groups have wielded a great deal of power in the Federation, the great variety to Nigerian political history lies with the minority and marginal groups. If indeed Nigeria had been made up of just three majority ethnic groups—Ibo, Hausa, and Yoruba—she could not last for even one year. Because of the possession of powerful primordial bases, the three majority groups have shown very little interest in the survival of the nation. They have displayed a remarkable skill in fighting for their rights from the civil state, but their duties as such have been for the most part withheld from the civil state. On the other hand, marginal and minority Nigerians have displayed an incipient sense of duty to their country, especially in the area of felt obligations to preserve the country.

If one looks to the future of Nigeria with hope, it is because the trend is toward the arrangements that have led to this incipient emergence of a sense of duty to the nation among marginal and minority Nigerians. The success of Nigeria will depend on the degree to which primordial forces can be so domesticated that they operate within, rather than to the destruction of, the Nigerian civil framework.

My preoccupation with internal differentiations in Nigerian social arrangements should not be interpreted as indicating that non-Nigerian, external factors were unimportant for the declaration of the Biafran secession. It seems fairly certain that once the baseline for a collision course was set up in Nigeria, there were outside interests sufficiently anxious for civil strife in Nigeria to finance a secession bid. Internal arrangements do explain what factors led to international involvement, even if they cannot explain the pattern of that involvement. The internationalization of the conflict has come to mean, of course, that there is a new element in Nigerian politics. The significance of that new element will have to be weighed in the future.

1954 and May 1967: these are important dates in Nigerian federalism. Between these dates Nigeria experienced changes that many European countries did not experience in a century. Perhaps 1967 bodes well for the future of Nigeria; 1954 was definitely a mistake!

Notes

1. Throughout this chapter I shall use the term "ethnic group" for tribe.
2. Edward Shils, "Primordial, Personal, Sacred and Civil Ties," *The British Journal of Sociology* 8 (1957): 130–145.

116 PETER P. EKEH

3. Clifford Geertz, "The Integrative Revolution" *Old Societies and New States* (Glencoe, Ill.: The Free Press, 1963), pp. 109–110.

4. Ibid., p. 110.

5. Edward Shils, "Political Development in the New States," *Comparative Studies in Society and History* 2, nos. 3–4 (1960).

6. Max Gluckman, *Custom and Conflict in Africa* (Glencoe, Ill.: The Free Press, 1955).

7. T. H. Marshall, *Class, Citizenship and Social Development* (New York: Doubleday & Co., 1965), p. 92.

8. For an eminent example of this phenomenological approach to citizenship, see Gabriel A. Almond and Sidney Verba, *The Civic Culture* (Princeton: Princeton University Press, 1963.)

9. Reinhard Bendix, *Nation-building and Citizenship* (New York: John Wiley & Sons, 1964).

10. Edward C. Banfield, *The Moral Basis of a Backward Society* (Glencoe, Ill.: The Free Press, 1958) and Almond and Verba, *Civic Culture*.

11. It seems important to emphasize the point that the primordial principles most salient in Europe and many parts of Asia are so inclusive that they bestride nations. Ethnicity, especially in its African form, poses a greater disintegrative problem than a world religion.

12. What Bendix, following Tocqueville, characterized as a "crisis in the relation of Masters and Servants" (*Nation-building,* pp. 52–54) must be interpreted as a short-run crisis of transition that flowed from the changeover in the direction of obligations rather than a total rejection of obligations.

13. Marshall, *Class, Citizenship.*

14. Bendix, *Nation-building,* pp. 52, 53.

15. Alexis de Tocqueville, *Democracy in America* (New York: Random House, 1945), II, 195.

16. See Geertz, "Integrative Revolution," for a discussion of these five principles.

17. Obafemi Awolowo, *Path to Nigerian Freedom* (London: Faber & Faber Ltd., 1947), p. 49.

18. Obafemi Awolowo, *Thoughts on Nigerian Constitution* (Ibadan, Nigeria: Oxford University Press, 1966).

19. B. L. Ambedkar, *Thoughts on Linguistic States,* cited in Geertz, *Old Societies,* pp. 106–111.

20. The use of the word "tribalism" to characterize attitudes and behaviors based on ethnic affiliations seems to me to localize the concept without offering us the benefit of linking it to similar attitudes and behaviors in Western and other non-African societies.

21. The following statement by Ezera is typical of such Ibo-Yoruba complaints: "It has been generally accepted that one of the cardinal attributes of a successful federation is that no one unit should be

allowed to be so powerful as to overrule the other and bend the federal government to itself. In Nigeria, this cardinal principle was brazenly violated. Since the Northern Region was much bigger than the other regions combined, it tended to create not only an understandable fear of domination in the minds of the other smaller regions, but also an ominous threat to the stability of the Federation as a whole." Kalu Ezera, "The Failure of Nigerian Federalism and Proposed Constitutional Changes," *African Forum* 2, no. 1 (Summer 1966): 19.

22. Okoi Arikpo, *The Development of Modern Nigeria* (Baltimore: Penguin Books, Inc., 1967).

23. Changes that began in 1950 through 1953 culminated in the 1954 federal structure; it must not be imagined that 1954 was a violent changeover.

24. I interpret the oft-mentioned size of the North as an imbalance in the differentiation of powers between the three majority ethnic groups. If the North were no bigger than the other two regions, in both land area and population, most of our more pressing problems would have been the same as they turned out to be.

25. Alhaji Siv Ahmadu Bello, *My Life* (Cambridge, Eng.: Cambridge University Press, 1962), p. 135.

26. Arikpo, *Development*, p. 145.

27. Bello, *My Life*, p. 133.

28. Ibid., pp. 135–136.

29. Obafemi Awolowo, *Awo—The Autobiography of Chief Obafemi Awolowo* (Cambridge, Eng.: Cambridge University Press, 1960), p. 182.

30. Arikpo, *Development*, p. 146.

31. Shils, "Political Development in the New States."

32. These military leaders assumed a great deal of political significance in many minority areas of the North, because important politicians from these areas were jailed or otherwise were lacking in the exercise of power.

33. Nigeria, Federal Ministry of Information, *Proceedings of the Meeting of the Nigeria Military Leaders* (Peduase Lodge, Aburi, Ghana, January 4–5, 1967), p. 20.

4

THE NIGERIA-BIAFRA CONFLICT—A POLITICAL ANALYSIS

Okwudiba Nnoli

↙ The Nigeria-Biafra crisis represents the most serious and intense of all inter-African conflicts. In terms of the toll in human resources, it is unparalleled in the history of Africa. Like all wars it was not capricious but the consequence of a severe set of contradictions which existed and still exists between the two belligerent groups. Originally initiated by Nigeria to remove these contradictions, the war has generated certain contradictions of its own.

The conflict has brought about a higher level of tension between the belligerent groups, an excessive use of violence within and between the groups, and a severe breakdown in the lines of intergroup communications as well as an increased distortion of information.

Thus new factors have compounded the prewar situation and created new conflicts between the warring groups and within them. A new blurred and buzzing confusion has been imposed on the existing ones, so that a whole new set of conditions has arisen that must be taken into account in any discussions of peace. Peace must mean the imposition of a meaningful and endurable order and justice on the old and new forces whose present combination provides the main obstacle to the present and future peace in Nigeria.

Life may be looked at as a continual search for a more durable peace in that the individual attempts to reduce the ambiguity of experience by establishing more suitable and stable patterns of expectations which have relevance for him. All individuals carry on this search for order or peace in varying degrees. Each out of his confrontations with reality builds an ordered image of reality for himself.[1] Such an image is never congruent with the objective reality but is the motivating force for the individual's actions. Images have a dynamic nature and do change. Actions based on them change accordingly. What is significant, however, is that no change of actions is possible unless there is some change in image. It is the process of image formation and change that is referred to as the "perception of reality."

Perceptions have practical significance for the individual. Opinions vary according to individual differences in perception and preconceptions of reality. Perceptions are usually formed by taking in only those elements of experience that are relevant to one's ongoing processes and interests. Consequently, no one's opinion contains every aspect of reality because the world is too complex and confusing to make this possible. Nevertheless, the individual is desirous of generalizing situations on the basis of his limited experience which encompasses the totality or reality. The result is usually a gross oversimplification in an attempt to avoid being immobilized by indecision and ambiguity.

This short discussion of perceptions and images has two strong implications for the search for the peace in Nigeria and Biafra. First, on the part of outside observers of this tragic drama, certain and varied models of reality were used to impose order on the events of the conflict. Consequently, many Americans, for example, tended to see the conflict by analogy with the American Civil War. Russians equated it with the situation that existed in Congo-Kinshasa when Katanga seceded from the unitary state of the Congo Republic, and many African states approached the conflict with a deep fear of Balkanisation as they anticipated possible situations within their respective countries which contain diverse ethnic groups.

More important, the belligerents brought different perceptions and images to bear on the issues of the conflict. It may be granted that much of what normally would be regarded as the result of perception is propaganda designed to win the sympathy and support of outside observers by playing on certain dimensions of their perceptual processes. Nevertheless, certain other aspects of the conceptualisation of the situation on the part of the groups involved remain their genuine perceptions and images of the realities involved in the conflict. Perceptions become very significant in situations such as the Nigeria–Biafra conflict in which mutual trust, good faith, and good will have been destroyed.

When a group of young Nigerian army majors, motivated by the best ideals and principles of their country, attempted a coup on 15 January 1966 to replace the incumbent civilian government, their immediate purpose was to establish a new regime and end the chaos and virtual state of anarchy in Western Nigeria. Many citizens praised and admired the courage and action of the revolutionaries and welcomed the consequent military regime that came to power.[2] The reasons were obvious. The political leadership since the time of Nigerian independence in 1960, in its pursuit of the psychological and economic rewards of power, had shown itself insensitive to the plight of the masses of the people—the workers and peasants.

The government—whether advertently or inadvertently—seemed to be protecting the interests of the forces which were systemically exploiting these workers and peasants. Such forces included the local bourgeoisie whose financial power was being felt increasingly, the new labour aristocracy composed of senior civil servants and university teachers and related personnel who forgot the masses in their desire to reap the fruits of Uhuru, and, of course, the neo-colonialist forces represented by the Shell-BP monopoly and other capitals which exploited most of the oil and other resources in the country. In addition, the exploitation of the rural areas by the cities continued unchecked. In this respect dissatisfaction among workers came to a revolutionary head in the disastrous general strike of 1964 when the whole country was virtually paralysed.

In other respects national morale was at its lowest level because the leadership had become incorrigibly corrupt. Morality in public service was becoming a rare exception, and despondency among the population was reaching alarming proportions. National resources were diverted in order to consolidate the elite's hold on power. For example, as the Coker Commission amply demonstrated, the Western Nigeria Marketing Board funds, ostensibly reserved for social and economic development projects, were cleverly reallocated through a complex chain of banking, construction, and real estate institutions to key Action Group leaders for use in waging the 1959 federal elections and for generally strengthening the party at regional and national levels.[3]

At the personal level, the political elite equated the possession of power with conspicuous personal consumption usually at public expense. To the elite such consumption underlined the need for personal economic power and thus the economic exploitation of the people. To aid the process, they capitalized on the parochial and ethnic loyalties in the country and in the process increased inter-group hostility. Emphasis was on the distribution of the national cake with no reciprocal emphasis on baking this cake. The concept of "chop politics" was popularized to the detriment and stagnation of national development.[4] The results of such politics were evident in the acts of continual brinkmanship which became part of national life and which were exemplified in the 1962 Action Group crisis, the census crisis of 1963, the federal election crisis of 1964, the Tiv disturbances of 1964–1966, and the Western election crisis of 1965. Practically every significant issue gave rise to a serious political crisis.

Thus the coup of January 1966 was welcomed by many Nigerians with the greatest outbursts of national enthusiasm ever seen in the country.[5] There was a chance for a new beginning toward the recovery and reassertion of the national self. But the event was a shock to the plans and expectations of the imperialist, capitalist, and neo-colonialist forces in the country who were led by British monopoly capitalist interests. They saw in the coup a serious setback to their control of the country. When these forces successfully recovered from the shock of the coup, their propaganda machinery helped to create and consolidate in the Northern Nigerians a perception of the coup as an Ibo plot designed to destroy Hausa-Fulani oligarchical and reactionary power and thus to ensure the domination of the whole country by the Ibos. Some of the political and administrative blunders of the new military regime, which unfortunately had usurped the power which properly belonged to the revolutionaries of January and who were not motivated by the same ideals and zeal, helped to augment, confirm, and sharpen these perceptions.[6]

As the picture of the January coup became increasingly distorted as a result of the capitalist, imperialist, and neocolonialist propaganda championed by the British Broadcasting Corporation and the British High Commission in Nigeria, such perceptions and images became increasingly negative, and hostility toward the Ibos by the Northerners became possible. Unscrupulous politicians urged on by British imperialism seized the opportunity to show their pent-up hatred of Ibos.

The result was the harrowing waves of remorseless genocide

against the Eastern Nigerians resident in Northern Nigeria in May 1966, within the Army in July 1966, and, with the greatest fervour, destruction, and vengeance, in the North and elsewhere where Northern Nigerian soldiers were stationed, in September, October, and November 1966. In all, over 50,000 Easterners were gruesomely murdered; countless others were maimed and horribly mutilated. Over two million others, deprived of their habitation and livelihood in parts of Nigeria other than Eastern Nigeria, became refugees in their Eastern Nigerian homeland. The consequences were enormous; the best in statesmanship was needed if the country were to avoid impending complete disintegration.

It was obvious that the resultant crisis was of a different kind from the previous crises which had characterized Nigerian political life. Such previous crises were strictly political in the sense that they were struggles for power involving mainly the political elite. This time, however, the problem was sociological as well. The masses were deeply involved at levels of greatest relevance—life and death, earning a livelihood, and obtaining shelter. This point is extremely significant, because the masses operating at a level of subnational rather than national consciousness are not the greatest custodians of the national interest. This is especially true in such new states as Nigeria where forces of parochialism and subnational or ethnic loyalties are much stronger than the rudimentary forces of national unity and national interest. Furthermore, unorganised mass action when it materializes is much less controllable than elite behaviour, because chaos and anarchy are usually the consequences. "It is impossible to understand the depth of feelings in Eastern Nigeria. The mood is very ugly. For a long time the military Governor has had to work hard to keep these feelings from boiling over. There are feelings of revenge, and strong feelings of wishing to be left alone to build new lives in their own homeland consistent with Eastern dignity. Compromise is now a dirty word. The people demand that the future be settled at once. They are unwilling to accept any sacrifice of principles for some idealistic sense of unity they now realize never really existed." [7] It is always politically dangerous to allow the masses with the wrong political loyalties to effect direct rather than indirect rule especially when the masses have been seriously aggrieved. A good display of restraint, wisdom, and understanding was demanded by the situation. This, however, was not forthcoming.

It must be recognized that the social milieu of the new states, including Nigeria, is one in which the family is very closely knit. The extended family system prevails. In addition, within such families and in the society at large a very high premium is placed on human life far and above other values. The loss of Eastern Nigerian lives in the pogroms of 1966 was so extensive that most families of the region were directly involved. In addition, an enormous refugee problem resulted with its attendant economic consequences.

The matter was all the more explosive because of similar experiences of less magnitude, which the people had suffered in 1945 and 1953. Perception of individual and group security on their part became very serious, practically engulfing all men, women, and children. Accompanying such perceptions, of course, were negative feelings toward the other Nigerian groups, particularly the Hausas who were seen with very good reason as intent on their extermination. The North, fearing retaliation by Easterners, also felt insecure. In this state of affairs one group's actions especially in the area of armaments was interpreted as an imminent threat to the existence of the other group. A conflict spiral came into existence.

One of the most serious blunders of the Nigeria–Biafra conflict was made with regard to the conflict spiral which emerged after the pogroms of 1966. Unlike the leaders in January 1966, who attempted to placate the North which suffered most from the coup, the federal military regime rendered no apology, took no concrete steps to reassure the Easterners of their security and rights within Nigeria, and gave no meaningful assistance in the massive refugee problem. On the contrary, they subjected the Easterners to economic persecution. The Aburi agreements which were designed to correct this state of poor statesmanship were later disregarded by the Lagos regime.

The sad and morally painful fact was that outside the East practically no other group in Nigeria or elsewhere saw the massacres as posing a serious national problem or, if it did, was courageous enough to say so. Each ethnic group retreated into a womb-like isolation as if indifference and the passage of time would make the whole problem go away. The few non-Eastern intellectuals who dared to appeal to the nation's conscience were either jailed or driven into exile. Nigeria at the time seemed morally anesthetized. Under such circumstances the conflict would only continue to escalate making warfare inevitable. This widespread indifference for the Easterners' plight on the part of the Nigerian groups was then perceived by the persecuted Easterners as confirming their previous contention that they were being deliberately pushed out of the Nigerian federation and exterminated. The international community like the proverbial ostrich also hid its head in the sand of domestic jurisdiction of states.

The most significant political consequence of this pogrom and the resultant movement of populations to their respective sociocultural areas was the destruction of the interhuman network which, in fact, was the Federation of Nigeria. The country had disintegrated and ceased to exist. The basis of the political contract which established it had disappeared and the contract had become void. The immediate task of recreating another common political unit from the components of the previous ones called first for serious efforts at social engineering.

Economic Factors

What is the genesis of the mutually hostile and escalating perceptions which led to the massacre of the Easterners and the resultant conflict spiral? The answer lies in economics. To say that tribalism is the cause is to leave unexplained the cause of tribalism itself.

The consequence of the many different subnationalities living within Nigeria was the development of a self-interested kind of ethnic loyalty in which X's stuck together and favoured X's just as Y's and Z's did their own groups. Politicians seeking office and the spoils of such office fanned the fears and animosities of their followers into xenophobia in order to ensure their election as the protectors of ethnic interests. Few people were confident enough of their own ability to advocate a merit system of hiring and promotion. Only very few among the well-educated persons found it in their interest to favour selection on the basis of merit. Others preferred the security of at least being able to rely on tribal preference wherever it was possible to exploit it. Nepotism was rife. Interethnic hostility increased.

The dynamics of this form of behaviour was self-reinforcing and self-fulfilling since it was in the interest of individual Nigerians to aid their own at the expense of the others. Each X feared that he was regarded as an X by any Y or Z and would, therefore, be discriminated against by them. He believed that he could in turn expect preference from any X in a position to help him. It was in his interest to promote X's and to demote Y's and Z's. If any X, Y, or Z did not favour his own kind, he would get no preference from his kind in return and no one of the other groups would show him preference over his own people. As a result any person who got outside the system of tribal preferences was nowhere. There seemed to be no end in sight for this phenomenon which increased in intensity as more and more people became educated and jobs became scarcer. No number of states or any type of bourgeois political revolution can solve the problem thus posed. A socialist revolution is the only solution. It was not forthcoming. Consequently, this defensive, negative, fearful set of socioeconomic relationships among the tribes of Nigeria continued and reached its worst height after May and July 1966 when it was no longer only a matter of discrimination against the Easterners but of wiping them out ruthlessly.

This socioeconomic dynamic is made more problematic by the nature of the political economy of the country. In the African setting, including Nigeria and Biafra, the importance of who gets what is very great. To begin with a developing country necessarily possesses such extremely limited resources that the competition for them is extremely intense. At the same time the government is the major source of the distribution of welfare goods and services, a point which makes it clear that economic demands would be political. Where the gross domestic product is not increasing rapidly, as was the case in Nigeria before the crisis, the demands of one group for a larger share of the national cake entails a smaller share for some other group. Thus intergroup jealousy and hostility arose and increased in Nigeria.

On the other hand, the absence of industrialisation on a wide scale in the former Federation of Nigeria meant that class formation was not so advanced that a majority of the people thought in class terms. Identity was linked to sociocultural characteristics. The politics of allocation thus became the politics of location. And finally, the real basis for legitimacy in the country was the promise of performance in the economic sphere. To base legitimacy upon economic performance is, of course, risky and highly expensive especially in a situation where elections are conducted along the lines of Western democracies. Politicians can promise all manner of benefits to their parochial and ethnically based constituents who cannot think in broader national terms, but in order to fulfill their election pledges they must then encourage nepotism, ethnic economic chauvinism and corruption. Thus interethnic hostility was maintained with the subsequent grievances and jealousies reinforcing the original hostility. Only in a socialist society, where the exploitation of the masses by the elite for their own economic and political benefits has been eliminated, where candidates for political office are chosen for their commitment to social and economic justice, for the individual as well as the nation, and in which a greater emphasis is paid on baking the national cake than in sharing it at the individual level, can the disastrous economic consequences of interethnic economic rivalry be completely abolished.

The phenomenon commonly called "tribalism" is in fact the result of elite frustration in a capitalist system in which different ethnic groups compete for social services. The fact of capitalism means an acceptance of inherent inequality within the system. In the African environment where the majority of the individuals are not oriented toward events beyond their ethnic environments and their loyalty is first and foremost for that group, there exists a great potential for a rationalization of failures in the struggle for power and wealth in terms of the hostility of the other ethnic groups. The Nigerian leaders capitalized on this potential.

The fact still remains that the masses of Ibos, Hausas, Yorubas, and other ethnic groups in the country had more in common economically than they had with their leaders. Their common and logical cause lay in joint solidarity against the exploitation of the capitalist and imperialist forces in the country. The leaders on the other hand sabotaged this solidarity by playing on the feelings of ethnic division latent in the masses. No one would argue that the bulk of the Nigerian masses benefitted from the division of the "national cake." It was being shared among the elite of Ibos, Hausas, and Yorubas. The masses were used as pawns to support or oppose one or the other factions seeking this wealth. In the end they were pitted against themselves. Thus the real conflict—a struggle by the masses against the exploiting elite—was diverted into one among different segments of the exploited masses. This is precisely the function of "tribalism" in a capitalist system—to divert the attention of the masses from their exploitation by the elite and if necessary to divert an imminent elite-mass struggle into one involving different segments of the masses. Consequently it was the masses that bore the full brunt of the Nigeria-Biafra war in terms of death, starvation, and other forms of hardship and suffering.

It must therefore be accepted that in spite of the existence of different ethnic groups in one country, without capitalism and its acceptance of inherent human inequality which can easily be translated to mean inherent group inequality, there will not be tribalism. Socialism is the answer to the problems of tribalism. Consequently one does not hear of such problems in socialist countries, while the United States, Canada, Great Britain, and Belgium are still plagued by them. But the stranglehold of imperialist and neocolonialist forces on the Nigerian federation was so strong that socialism could not be established. The leadership was not dedicated to it but was steeped in capitalism. It remained and still remains, however, the only true solution to the country's problems.

Political Factors

Any re-creation of a political system on the basis of the components of the former Federation must take the realities of these components into account. The first and foremost reality is the size of the major groups: the Hausa of about 15 million, the Ibo of about 10 million, and the Yoruba of about 12 million. These groups cannot be equated with the ethnic groups in many other African countries; their sizes vitiate any such equation. In fact they are more like nation-states and by themselves are larger and even more viable than over half of the African states. And they are very many times bigger than any of the smaller groups of the former Nigerian Federation. The consequence of this reality is that no settlement for the association of the components of the former unit can work without the voluntary acceptance and participation of all these three groups. It is politically naive to expect that a solution could be imposed on any one or combination of them.

The second reality is the pervasive sense of parochialism and ethnic chauvinism of the individuals in these groups far and above their loyalty to a common nationality. The concept of a Nigerian nation has not been accepted by any significant proportion of the population. This means that negotiations on the basis of the least common denominator other than force, if possible, is the realistic method of approach to constitutionalism. With this knowledge coupled with the experiences of the pogrom, it is extremely naive to equate the Nigeria–Biafra conflict with the American Civil War or the Katanga secession. Again it was the poor statesmanship of the Lagos regime in its failure to recognize the importance of these two realities in the scheme of the conflict that is responsible for the fact that the crisis led to war. There must be justice for the minority groups, but reality dictates that no political arrangement can be worked out without the voluntary acceptance or acquiescence of all the major groups. The real problem lies with the inadequacy of the leadership and the socioeconomic system and not in the number of states. Equality must replace inequality as the foundation of the new system. In other words socialism must replace capitalism if any meaningful progress is to be made in solving the problems that led to war.

One of the significant consequences of the poverty of leadership and the capitalist nature of Nigeria was the tremendous amount of power which the different regions wielded over their respective affairs. The regions tended to perform for the individual the function of the ultimate decision-maker much better than the central government. Some of the results of this dispersal of state power to the regions and its concentration at the regional level are evident in the numerous political crises in which the regional interests were preponderant, such as the census crisis of 1963, the federal election crisis of 1964, the Western elections of 1965, and the conflict between the Northernization policy of the Northern region and the Nigerianization policy of the central government.

In time, regional cohesion, authority, and political unity encased in definite territorial frontiers contributed to a sharp sense of separation between the regions. Each looked to its own administrative center, evolved its own political disputes and compromise, and drifted away from its neighbours in political culture and understanding. The pursuit of individual and group power in national politics, which was backed by regional power and commitment, generated conflicts of interest that pulled the regions further apart in economic, political, and ideological considerations. Sovereignty in terms of the cohesion and integration of the federal state was yielding to the sovereignty and cohesion of the regional entity. Thus at the internal level sovereign power was highly divided and dispersed contrary to the doctrine of indivisibility, a characteristic of sovereignty. Given the same type of leadership and the same socioeconomic system, the creation of more states in the country will increase rather than diminish these tendencies. A socialist leadership and socialist reorganization of the country remains the answer.

What are the prospects for a socialist leadership in the immediate future? In the light of the stage of capitalism and the power of the neocolonialist forces in the country only a socialist revolution is likely to bring such a leadership to power. The neocolonialist network in the area may best be understood by a discussion of the external intervention in the crisis.

The Extent of and Reasons for External Intervention

In fact the war between Nigeria and Biafra provides a good case material for understanding the influence of the external factors in inter-African conflicts. The conflict became so deeply and widely internationalized that its solution depended to a large degree on London, Moscow, and Paris. In terms of its consequences for the human and material resources of the peoples involved, the war does not have any parallel in the history of Africa. The role of external involvement in generating these consequences is significant.

External diplomatic and military intervention in the conflict was largely absent at the outset of the war in July 1967. Great Britain first officially announced a policy of neutrality and imposed an embargo on the supply of arms to both sides. Similarly the United States and France adopted a neutral position. But British and United States neutrality at this time stemmed from their conviction that Nigeria would achieve a speedy military victory over Biafra.

When these expectations failed to materialize and Biafra was able not only to withstand the initial Nigerian invasion but also to threaten Lagos after capturing the Midwest, the showcase image of Nigeria built up over the years by the British and the Americans against the evident realities of the area was in mortal danger. In addition, British economic and political interests in the area were threatened. And these interests were both significant and extensive. For example, in his annual statement for 1967, the chairman of British Petroleum, referring to the closure of the Suez Canal as a result of the Arab-Israeli war of June 1967, pointed out that his company's problems would have been easier if the war between Nigeria and Biafra had not broken out. "Nigeria had assumed added importance because of its geographical advantage by comparison with oil which had to be moved around the cape." [8] Although in 1966 Nigeria's share of the British oil market was only 10 percent, this percentage was increasing. Commenting on the

British Petroleum Company's prospects in 1966, the *Financial Times* of London observed that "there is no doubt that the Nigerian oil is going to be very big indeed" and that what the oil companies had done so far was "small beer compared with progress they expect in the next few years." [9] As the British increasingly perceived their Middle East oil supplies as unreliable they "made very great efforts and spent very large sums to develop alternative sources in Nigeria." [10]

Since the British have always felt that their oil and other interests would be better safeguarded under the control of the conservative leaders of Nigeria than under the more progressive and nationalistic Biafrans, it was to be expected that the British oil companies as well as the shipping lines and commercial companies would support Nigeria against Biafra. The intervention of the shipping lines and commercial companies in support of Nigeria dated from the time of Nigeria's embargo against Biafra. The sudden decision by the Soviet Union to grant Nigeria's desperate request for arms in September 1967 hastened the decision of the oil companies to support Nigeria. Just as suddenly the United Arab Republic agreed to provide Nigeria with a squadron of Egyptian pilots. Great Britain immediately dropped its public position of neutrality, lifted its arms embargo and came out militarily, economically, morally, and diplomatically in support of Nigeria. Although these external interventions were weighted against Biafra, she nevertheless had a few foreign friends. Portugal provided her with landing rights in Lisbon following the Nigerian blockade of her territory. Later France declared herself in favour of the Biafran right to self-determination while five countries granted her diplomatic recognition.

Consequences of Intervention

External intervention has serious consequences for African societies. Since the intervening forces of the big powers are more powerful than the domestic forces, the outcome of the conflicts greatly affecting the nature and processes of African life are usually determined by the external power. Consequently African independence and initiative are constantly diminished and the true form of African development is suppressed by the imposition of external and unrealistic standards and structures. For example, the Nigeria–Biafra war was absurd. War is only a means toward the achievement of certain political objectives.[11] In conflict between hostile groups it involves the use of lethal weapons to kill, wound, or capture individuals from the opposing side.[12] If violence is thus central to war, it is self-defeating and absurd to use it as a means to allay the fears of violence from the attacking group. Subsequent to the pogroms in the North and other parts of Nigeria in which the Biafrans lost many lives and much property, the greatest obstacle to the unity of the component parts of the former Federation of Nigeria lay in the widespread belief by the Biafrans that their persons, group, and property were insecure in Nigeria. It was obvious, therefore, that the use of force by the Lagos regime could only increase this insecurity and thus intensify rather than resolve the existing tensions.

Nevertheless it may be granted that the British and the Nigerians in their misperceptions of the situation contended at the outset of the war that Biafran independence was not supported by the vast majority of Biafrans. Consequently they estimated a quick surgical operation involving an extremely limited number of casualties. The war, however, continued for over two years and at the cost of over two million casualties, most of them civilian victims of starvation, in the full evidence of the support of the vast majority of Biafra for Biafran independence and sovereignty. External intervention, particularly the British support of Nigeria, prevented the logic of absurdity from forcing an end to the conflict. As the war dragged on, Nigerian and Biafran, as well as humanitarian, interests became increasingly lost from sight while the interests of the significant intervening powers assumed greater importance.

Linkage Groups and Intervention

If intervention in inter-African conflicts is thus fraught with undesirable consequences then the problem of understanding and controlling it must start with the identification of links between domestic forces and the external forces which seek or are sought to intervene. These connections are the linkage groups with roots in both the African domestic system and in an advanced country.[13] In order to use the concept of linkage groups, we must think of the boundaries of societies in terms of marked discontinuities in the frequency of transactions and response. Thus Karl Deutsch conceives a modern society as a "multiple market for goods and resources based on a market for factors of production. It includes mutual responsiveness of units as regards the market for labour, for land, for materials and services, a multiple market for credit which is capital and a multiple market for governmental services." [14]

In such societies linkage groups are units which couple the internal decision system and the external environment. A big foreign company, for example, offers the community in which it operates much more than its products. No company is an island. It operates within the context of its community and its society at large. In its research activities, its recruiting programs, and its use of investment funds, the company makes its influence felt in the community. Thus it has couplings to the domestic market of goods and services, to the tax system and to the political and other institutions of both the host country and the mother country. Consequently it influences development in the community by integrating its economic purpose with the wider human and social activities which go on in the community and society. The access which such groups have to the population of the society facilitates their involvement on one side or the other of the conflicting currents within the society.

Linkage groups unite power and interdependence in interstate relations. They are the instrument by which states seek to achieve their middle-range goals of maximizing the resources and benefits they derive from their external environment. In this sense they act also as the basic structures of interactions and interdependence among states. They link the resources and environments of different states. Basic to the interest of states is the desire for a certain minimal level of subsistence in food, security, and sustenance of mates. Above and beyond this level, however, states also wish to maximize the benefits which their members need to make life more comfortable. They need more resources than are required for bare subsistence. As the power of a state increases, its ability to use external resources to raise the level of wealth and comfort of its members also increases. The extent of its linkage groups in other states, therefore, increases. Thus the big powers maintain more significant and diversified linkage groups in their external environment than the lesser powers and are, therefore, more successful in using these structures to achieve their middle-range objectives of foreign policy.

This union of power and interdependence in the concept of linkage groups is very crucial for understanding activities, including wars, which go on in African societies. It provides the crucial variable for explaining external intervention in inter-African conflicts. As a result of colonial experience, the boundaries of African societies, when they are defined in terms of transactions and mutual responsiveness, are not confined to the national geographical limits. Rather, they include many groups and subsystems which have roots in the external environment, particularly in the former metropolitan country.

Many commercial and other companies operating in Africa are part of parent organisations with headquarters in the former metropolitan countries and are therefore extraterritorial. For example, John Holt and Company Ltd., one of the two largest non-mining companies operating in the former Federation of Nigeria, is a company owned by a British family now in its third generation. The six directors of the company are all members of the family, and each is a working manager. All the shares are held by the Holt family. Similarly the banks in Nigeria were largely extraterritorial enterprises. Barclays Bank D.C.O. is a subsidiary of Barclays Bank Ltd. of England. The Bank of West Africa is owned largely by Lloyds Bank, the Westminster Bank, and the National Provincial Bank of Britain, as well as by the Standard Bank of South Africa, while the Midland Bank of Britain is represented on its board of directors. Consequently, each of the "Big Five" in British banking was represented in Nigeria. In such extraterritorial enterprises, both the directorship and ownership of capital are extraterritorial. The headquarters are located in Britain and are divided into departments. In the former Federation of Nigeria their business was run by local headquarters under area managers.

The linkage groups in prewar Nigeria were many and operated in various aspects of Nigerian life. Their number and variety affected external intervention. The more numerous the groups, the greater are the possibilities that they would align with the conflicting parties. Similarly, the more varied their activities, the greater is the possibility of alignment in domestic conflicts. Such alignments inevitably place their interests in jeopardy should the ally be defeated. Under such circumstances, the more variegated the groups, the greater the danger and threat to external interests in the area. The number, variety, and scope of activities of some of the linkage groups in the former Federation of Nigeria are discussed in detail in Margery Perham's book, *Mining, Commerce and Finance in Nigeria*.[15] She points out, for example, that the United

Africa Company (UAC) was probably responsible for 41.3 percent of the total import and export trade of Nigeria. It had large wholesaling and retailing establishments run chiefly by subsidiaries, such as Lagos Stores Ltd.; it ran various processing plants connected with the export business, such as the bulking plants for palm oil, the clarified butter factories at Jos and Kanos, and the sawmill at Sapele, probably the largest in West Africa.

The UAC acquired long leases over 12,400 acres of rubber and palm oil plantations in Southern Nigeria. Its leases covered roughly 75 percent of the total land leased to non-Africans and Africans. In addition, it ran some manufacturing establishments, such as the singlet factory in Lagos and some engineering services especially for motor vehicles. It also owned the only cold storage plant in the country as well as lighterage, coastal, and river services and controlled West African Publicity Ltd. The company owned all the shares of some thirty-seven companies and the controlling interest in twenty others. The UAC is controlled by Lever Brothers and Unilever. It is the chief subsidiary of Unilever in the British colonies and ex-colonies.[16] These business interests of the company naturally coincide with those of the parent company, Lever Brothers and Unilever Ltd. Unilever's other subsidiaries in Nigeria include Kingsway Stores, Pamol Nigeria Ltd., and African Timber and Plywood (Nigeria) Ltd.

Another very significant linkage group which took roots in dependent Nigeria was the Shell-BP Development Company of Nigeria. By June 1967 the company had spent £150,000,000 in its establishment of the oil industry in the country and at that time was exporting 500,000 barrels of crude oil a day.[17] Before the war, the company's nineteen oil fields in Biafra accounted for 10 percent of Britain's oil imports. In 1962 the Nigerian Minister of Mines and Power signed an agreement with Shell-BP Petroleum Refining Company of Nigeria Ltd. whereby the latter would be responsible for the construction and operation of a refinery and the federal and regional governments would have 50 percent interest in the project. The remaining shares were to be held equally by the British Petroleum Company Ltd. and the Royal-Dutch Shell Group of Companies. The refinery was opened in November 1965, and output in 1966 amounted to 1,549,000 tons.[18] During that year Shell-BP also was commissioned to build a lubricating oil blending plant at Apapa and a liquefied petroleum gas plant at Port Harcourt. The development of its oil and gas resources had been Nigeria's most significant event in recent years with petroleum having firmly established itself as the principal export and Britain as the chief beneficiary. For example, total Nigerian sales to Britain in 1965 exceeded £100 million for the first time according to the report of Barclays Bank D.C.O. in Lagos. The total value of exports to the United Kingdom in 1965 was £112.8 million, an increase of about £24 million over the previous year. Although Britain also increased her purchases of Nigerian fruit and vegetable materials and plywood veneers, petroleum accounted for the greater part of the increase in exports.[19]

Apart from the linkage groups introduced into the African states as a result of colonialism, others have resulted from the imperative needs of development. External financing of the country's projects is as old as Nigeria's railroad, the first of her great public works. Professor Frankel calculated that £75 million was invested in Nigeria from abroad from 1870–1936. About £40 million of the total was private capital, the majority of which was investment by trading companies followed by the mining companies.[20] In March 1962, Nigeria estimated the capital cost of the public sector of her 1962–1968 six-year development plan at $1.895 billion.[21] During the preceding seven years, consumption and investment had exceeded gross domestic product.[22] And for the following six years Nigeria could hardly discontinue her reliance on external financing if she were to fulfill the objectives of the plan. Most of the foreign investment was assignable to British companies. In his report to the shareholders in 1961 the chairman of Unilever Ltd. stated that Nigeria "is the country in which we have our greatest investment in Africa, £48.5 million." This figure was the largest overseas company investment in the country. The absolute amount allocated to manufacturing by the UAC, Unilever's principal subsidiary in Africa, increased with the approach of independence. During 1959 and 1961, the UAC placed more than 43 percent and 47 percent respectively of the year's capital expenditures in Nigeria in this category.[23]

Among the commerical non-company sources of industrial capital in Nigeria are a significant number of British corporations. Through the John Holt Investment Company Ltd., the trading company of that name has invested in a number of industries. The Colonial Development Corporation (CDC) was established in 1948 by the Parliament in London. Its purpose was to invest in the British colonies. Before independence in 1960 the CDC had approved capital expenditures in twelve projects, including the Nigeria Cement Company, the Investment Company of Nigeria (ICON), Ikeja Industrial Development, Northern Development (Nigeria) Ltd. (NDNL), and the Industrial and Agricultural Company Ltd. (INDAG) of Eastern Nigeria. The Commonwealth Development Act of 1963 restored the CDC's full powers of operation in the former colonies and changed the name to the Commonwealth Development Corporation. INDAG, founded in 1959, had invested in an aluminium-rolling mill and an asbestos-cement plant and had loaned £30,000 to a Nigerian who was producing powdered clay, a substitute for Benthonite, needed for Shell-BP's oil drilling. NDNL was set up in November 1959 with a capital of £1.25 million. By late 1961 it had invested £50,000 in a bottling plant and a smaller amount in a tannery. During late 1964 NDNL was reorganized as Northern Nigeria Investments Ltd. (NNIL). The total resources of this company in 1966 were £4.6 million shared equally by the CDC and the Northern Nigeria Development Corporation (NNDC).[24] The Commonwealth Development Finance Company (CDFC), which helps to finance development projects undertaken by Commonwealth private investors and enterprises, is 45 percent controlled by the Bank of England. CDFC was the main sponsor of ICON and organized the bulk of its capital subscription. It also loaned £1 million in 1960 to the Dunlop Rubber plantation, and £400,000 to a cotton yarn-spinning mill in Kaduna in 1963 as well as making a number of industrial investments.[25] Other British investment groups included the Overseas Development Corporation of Barclays Bank D.C.O. and the Nigerian Tobacco Company's Marine Investment Ltd.

These British investments in Nigeria were facilitated by the fact that the country was a member of the sterling area of the international monetary system. Together with other members of the area she pooled her foreign exchange reserves in London for the settlement of international transactions. She also used the British pound as a reserve as well as a trading currency. An essential feature of the informal arrangements of the sterling area in the existence of a highly concentrated banking system spread over the area. A few big commercial banks with head offices in London command vast assets and control much of the commercial credit and enforce financial discipline through informal agreements. Although the Central Bank of Nigeria, established in 1950, applied some controls on the expatriate banks, the power of these banks had not been drastically reduced.

Barclays Bank D.C.O. and the Bank of West Africa had since before World War II controlled the larger share of banking in Nigeria. The banking and insurance firms included, apart from the Bank of West Africa and Barclays Bank D.C.O., the two British insurance companies, General Accident, Fire and Life Assurance, and Royal Exchange Assurance. Until after World War II the British Royal Exchange Assurance Group was in marine, fire, and automobile insurance with life and endowment policies being of minor importance. As with the pension funds, the insurance companies until recently have had most of their reserves invested in London.

Britain virtually controlled not only the banking system of Nigeria but also the stock exchange. The Lagos stock exchange was originally operated by the then major buyer, ICON. Subsequent to the transformation of ICON into the Nigerian Industrial Development Bank in January 1964, John Holt (Nigeria Ltd.) took over this function. It dealt in three categories of securities, stocks of the government and registered companies, stocks of overseas companies that conduct operations in Nigeria, and other overseas securities. And in 1962 Nigerian Acceptance Ltd. was set up by John Holt as a merchant bank in Nigeria. Thus British investments were able to dominate Nigerian financial life.

Extensive linkage groups connecting Nigeria and Britain had also been introduced through British bilateral aid to the country. The magnitude of Nigeria's dependence upon external capital prior to independence, when compared with Ghana is revealed by the fact that 40 percent of the funds for the Nigerian Federal Development Plan of 1955–1962 had to be secured from abroad when Ghana's were implemented almost wholly with her financial resources.[26] During the colonial era Britain supplied practically all the aid required by the country. Before 1960, the Colonial Development Corporation and the Colonial Development and Welfare grants controlled by Britain ran the aid programmes. Colonial Development and Welfare grants in the first fifteen years following World War II amounted to nearly $75 million.[27] In the words of the Nigerian Minister of Commerce and Industry in 1961, "we are not unmindful of the debt we owe to the United Kingdom and it is entirely appropriate that the first major industrial mission to visit us after independence should come from British industry." [28] Between 1960 and 1964 Nigeria relied heavily on British aid. In honour of her independence she received a grant from Britain equal to the amount that was outstanding from the earlier allocations of the Colonial Development and Welfare Fund. The grant amounted to $15 million and was meant as capital costs of higher education projects in early 1961.[29]

Between 1961 and 1964 British loans to Nigeria through the Commonwealth Assistance Programme amounted to $30 million. This is in addition to the loan of $33.6 million made in 1960. And through its Aid for Surplus Capacity Scheme Britain made a loan of $4.5 million available to the country. This brought the total British loans to $68 million and the total British aid to Nigeria in 1964 since independence to over $90 million. This amount does not include the $9 million British financial commitment toward the Niger Dam Project.[30]

In 1965 British bilateral aid to Nigeria rose by 80 percent from £5,798,000 in 1964 to £10,307,000. Of the latter, £8,317,000 was in loans, £670,000 in grants and £1,320,000 in technical assistance.[31] Prior to 1960 Britain supplied most of the required external skill and technical assistance to the country. Through the Special Commonwealth Aid to Africa Programme (SCAAP), Britain spent £184,000 in equipment and experts in 1963. This is only one of the several means of British technical assistance to the country. The rate of such aid is estimated at about $3 million a year.[32] In fact according to statistics on persons overseas publicly financed by Britain in December 1965 there were 678 in Nigeria, 85 in Gambia, 63 in Ghana, and 38 in Sierra Leone. The figures for British volunteers overseas are: Nigeria 141, Ghana 66, Sierra Leone 48, Gambia 14.[33]

Thus linkage groups connecting Nigeria and Britain were many and existed in practically all significant aspects of Nigerian economic life. This is the consequence of the shortage of capabilities on the part of Nigeria. In many cases these groups were significant sources of employment for the population of the society; and thus they controlled to some degree the loyalty of the population they employed, especially as welfare benefits were scarce, the nation was weakly integrated, and loyalty to the national decision apparatus had not been consolidated. For example, before the war Shell–BP ran its own large trade school in Port Harcourt. Selected graduates were then sent on scholarship for further studies especially to the Yaba Technical Institute and the engineering school at Zaria. This is in addition to the large number of persons employed by the company both as permanent part-time and summer employees. In the political, social, and cultural spheres, similar linkage groups also existed. For example, the conservative and reactionary leaders of Northern Nigeria constitute a linkage group which was politically and diplomatically advantageous to Britain. The Anglo-Nigerian relations of friendship between 1960 and 1965 were the result of the trust which the British had in Balewa and his government. The latter did all in their power to protect and promote British interests in the area. In fact these relations were so good that Britain found it useful to convene a Commonwealth Conference in Lagos in early 1965 to counteract the decision of the OAU that its members should sever relations with her over UDI in Rhodesia at a time when law and order had virtually broken down in Western Nigeria and Lagos.

The Diversification of Linkage Groups

Another important factor in the relationship between linkage groups and external intervention in inter-African conflicts apart from the extent and variability of the groups is the degree of diversification of their sources. Linkage groups are indicators of interest and therefore the stake which one country has in another. Such stakes increase with the concentration of the groups from a single source and heighten the desire of the interested power to intervene to protect her interests. Foreign policy is first and foremost in the service of national interests and these include the activities of groups in the external environment. Trade, foreign aid, access to communications facilities and political resources, sources of supply, and foreign markets are for most states absolutely necessary to enable them to provide for increasing social welfare. For countries such as Britain, where agricultural and other resources are very limited and the size of the market for industrial goods is small, there is a great need to use other states to achieve this goal. It is the linkage groups that make it possible for a state to exploit a foreign market, ensure supplies not available at home, establish access to communications facilities, and in general make it possible for a state to maximize the use of external resources for the welfare of its citizens. It is in the interest of the state, therefore, to protect these groups and to aid them in the accomplishment of their aspirations.

For example, in 1966 British Electric was awarded a contract worth £1.2 million for a switchgear by the Nigerian government. The company was also supplying four of the water turbines for the Kainji Dam Project.[34] These contracts, of course, meant more profits and benefits to its British shareholders and managers. Similarly, a record profit of £371,000 for the year of 1965 was reported to the annual meeting of the British West Africa Corporation (BEWAC) founded in 1946 to export lorries, trucks, and tractors to Nigeria. The profit represented an increase of £206,000 over that of the previous year. Also in 1965 the John Holt Investment Company of Nigeria made a profit of £128,000. It immediately announced an increased dividend of 11 percent, 2 percent more than the previous year. Total dividends thus became double what they were three years earlier.[35] John Holt Investments had interests in a range of industries, such as cement, contracting, cigarettes, paper converting, and oil milling. These profits were used to raise the standard of living of the shareholders and owners of these companies and generally to increase the welfare benefits of the British people. To such foreign countries an African country in which their linkage groups predominate and are highly concentrated becomes a significant unit in the calculus to use external resources for the benefit of their population. Thus Nigeria was important to Britain. British linkage groups were the most numerous in the country and enjoyed a high degree of dominance over those of the other countries. For example, the British share of total external investment in Nigeria was 50 percent in 1961, 34 percent in 1962, 50 percent in 1963, 56 percent in 1964, and 52 percent in 1965.[36] The fact that Britain was the former metropolitan power as well as her close friendship with the Balewa government accounts for this high investment rate.

The Significance of the Resources

In other respects, the relationship between the linkage groups and external intervention varies with the significance of the resources exploited by the linkage groups. Where resources of strategic importance such as oil exist, linkage groups facilitate intervention much more than in other situations. Thus British intervention in the Nigeria–Biafra conflict and her nonintervention in Sudan where the South is resisting Northern tyranny can only be understood in terms of the absence of any strategic resources to be exploited by the British in Sudan and the presence of oil in Biafra. As the British military and other support of Nigeria increasingly dictated the pace and duration of the war, the initial contradictions which gave rise to the conflicts were gradually superseded by the imperative and logic of who controls Biafran oil. The British support of the now infamous "quick kill" policy was based on the understanding that it would lead to an early resumption of oil shipments to Britain. In fact, the oil companies aided the Nigerians in their invasion of the oil-producing centers of Biafra.[37] It is very doubtful that British intervention would have been massive and unreasonable if British oil interests had not been affected by the conflict. It is no coincidence, for example, that Belgian intervention in the Congo against Lumumba was preceded by the support of the rich mining companies for Katangese secession. Similarly British intervention on behalf of Nigeria and against Biafra was preceded by the Shell-BP petroleum company's payment of oil royalties to Nigeria instead of Biafra.

Linkage Groups and the Cohesion of Society and Government

As Professor Rosenau argues, the nature and extent of the linkage groups are such that the national society is no longer the only factor in the legitimization of the society. The structure of power and influence also includes non-national elements represented by these linkage groups. These non-members of the national society participate in the processes of allocating values and coordinating goal-directed efforts. They not only engage in bargaining with the system but actually bargain within it.[38]

In some cases, the activities and resources of the linkage groups enable them to penetrate regions of the country not easily accessible to the central government. A good example was the penetration of the riverine areas of the former Federation of Nigeria by Shell-BP because of their mining activities, the UAC and John Holt because of their commercial activities, and the UAC, John Holt, and Elder Dempster companies as a result of their water transport activities. Thus the linkage groups may be more relevant to the lives of the people in a region and more knowledgeable of the area than the central government itself. Biafra claims that Nigerian invasion of the riverine areas of her territory was facilitated by these groups which provided navigation charts, weather information, and up-to-date maps of the areas, as well as some transportation for the invading troops.

Since the linkage groups are usually subsidiaries of parent organizations with headquarters in the advanced countries, their roots in African society are much weaker than their roots in the advanced countries. In addition, the African state is less powerful than the advanced country, and as a result of its underdevelopment, it needs the roots of the linkage groups more than the advanced country needs the internal roots in any one African society. Because of this relationship, therefore, the influence of the advanced country in the African society as a result of the presence of the linkage groups is bound to be strong. It may therefore intervene in a conflict in the African society to exert this influence in favour of one of the parties involved.

In another respect, a linkage group becomes much more susceptible to external influences if it is weakly integrated within the national society. If it retains very strong attachments to the mother country, it tends to identify more with its interests than with those of the African society. When the two interests come into conflict, it is more likely to champion the external interests. Most of the British linkage groups in Nigeria before the war were weakly integrated in the national society. They were racially and culturally different from the rest of the society. They also differed from the rest in terms of wealth and status and therefore in values and attitudes. Since social homogeneity contributes to integration, it was difficult for them to be effectively integrated into the Nigerian society in such a way as to retain their primary identification with Nigerian rather than British interests.

The linkage groups may also become significant in the life of the society and susceptible to external inputs if the national government is ineffective in satisfying the aspirations of its population. Essentially, governmental effectiveness is necessary to maintain internal integration of the linkage groups in the society. Ineffectiveness, on the other hand, generates pressures for new, different, or external forms of integration which facilitate the identification of the linkage groups with their mother countries. Thus the linkage group is more likely to hold out and prevail in a society if the domestic system is more fragile, whereas a highly cohesive national system with a high capacity for adjustment and learning may be able to absorb the impact of external influences and retain its linkage groups with partial autonomy but without allowing them to influence significantly the domestic activities of the society.

The preceding discussion demonstrates that the strictly internal character of an inter-African situation declines as the extent of linkage groups within the African society increases. Since linkage groups thus play a part in delimiting internal matters, they are more clearly instruments which facilitate intervention. They generate pressures in the advanced countries to protect their interests. The larger the interests, the harder it is to risk the return on it, if only the return in terms of good will. The British support of Nigeria against Biafra, for example, stems first and foremost from the British desire to protect the interests of her linkage groups in the area. These interests were perceived as threatened by Biafran independence. In the process the imperatives of British national interest prevailed over humanitarian interests and even the genuine interests of the Nigerian and Biafran peoples. In a war whose origin is predominantly human and whose consequences raised serious humanitarian concern all over the world, persistent British supplies of arms to Nigeria was morally reprehensible and must be condemned by all men of good will.

Britain, nevertheless, was not alone in her intervention in the conflict. The Soviet Union, France, Portugal, Egypt, and Algeria also intervened. These other countries, however, do not maintain significant linkage groups in the area. The Egyptians and Algerians, for example, are linked to the area by their Muslim brotherhood with the Northern Nigerian Muslims, but the number of such linkage groups is low and the variety is very limited. The others have their reasons for intervening which may be political as in the case of the Russians, economic as with France, and strategic for Portugal which benefits from any inter-African conflict that draws attention away from the brutal repressions in Portuguese African colonies. Similarly, intervention is also the result of domestic motivations; obviously the Biafrans and Nigerians sought these interventions for their own reasons and benefits.

It has been the thesis of this essay, however, that, in terms of the nature of the conflict resolution as well as the consequences for the African society, the crucial intervention is that facilitated by linkage groups. Without British intervention in the Nigeria–Biafra war, the conflict would not have lasted as long as it did in spite of the other interventions. In other words, any attempt by Africans to control the externalization of their conflicts must grapple with the problem of the intervention of their former colonial powers, and this intervention is facilitated by the numerous linkage groups they maintain in Africa. These constitute the critical variables in understanding external intervention in inter-African conflict. The British argument that Russia would displace her influence in Nigeria if she stopped her arms supply to the Lagos regime was meaningless because Russia lacked the necessary linkage groups to make the desire for such influence worth the cost as well as to consolidate such influence. In fact, the continued presence of British linkage groups in Nigeria made this possibility low since they bargained within the decision system of the area and enjoyed certain leverage there.

In summary, linkage groups are crucial in facilitating external intervention if they are numerous, varied in their activities, originate mostly from one advanced country, involve strategically important resources, or exist in a situation of low social cohesion and high governmental ineffectiveness. Each variable is significant enough in isolation. When they all operate in a situation, however, they tend to reinforce each other and thus magnify their roles in facilitating intervention. This reinforcement occurred in the Nigeria–Biafra war.

Since all interventions cannot realistically be eliminated, an attempt to control the external involvement in inter-African conflicts must emphasize the minimization of those interventions related to linkage groups. Such an emphasis must focus primary attention on controlling the linkage groups. The direction of such control must follow logically from the above dynamics of their influence. The number of such groups in a state must be drastically reduced. This action would call for a carefully thought out program of self-reliance which aspires to maximize internal potential resources.

In this regard the issue of nationalization must be faced. It destroys the roots which the linkage groups maintain in the external environment and therefore removes some of the middle-range interest maintained by an external power in Africa. Such an act must also be followed by the Africanization of the groups in order to fully integrate them into the African state. If nationalization and/or Africanization is unacceptable then the sources of these groups must be widely diversified. This action would reduce the stakes of any one external state in an inter-African conflict situation thus lowering the compulsion for her to intervene. Finally the need for a cohesive African society and government cannot be overemphasized. This necessitates a leadership which conducts its affairs in such a way as to prevent the actualization of the conflict potential in the state. For this purpose a highly dedicated socialist leadership is all the more indispensable.

Towards Peace in Nigeria

The disintegration of the interhuman, sociocultural, and economic network of the former Federation of Nigeria in 1966, as a result of the massacres of Easterners and consequent movement of populations to their native homelands, has been consolidated and even made worse by the war. The avoidance of intergroup contact with Nigeria has become, as a result of previous experiences, the ideal among the Ibos. Continued intergroup disequilibrium and intergroup institutional stagnation have been the consequences. Any return to peace in the area must face the task of re-creating this interhuman network and these intergroup institutions. This in a sense is the primary and initial task of any peace formula, for no political settlement will be adequate in the absence of such a network, no matter how rudimentary. Otherwise, a situation of intergroup apartheid is inevitable with all its possible repercussions. This process of re-creating intergroup institutions and an inter-human network is, of course, made very difficult by the psychological consequences of intergroup hostility. Consequently, it is a process that is bound to take a long time. Intergroup political associations must follow closely the evolution of those institutions and network if they are to be meaningful, realistic, and lasting.

Economically, the country's economy has been strenuously strained. The blockade imposed against Biafra, as well as the fact that geographically it constituted the main theatre of military operations, means that the destruction of economic institutions has been greatest in the East. Those institutions not destroyed have suffered stagnation. In addition, the currency situation in the East is bound to be a problem for a very long time. Reconstruction of the torn economy and the rehabilitation of the displaced persons must be undertaken in good faith if they are to succeed.

The long-term answer to the problem of reconstruction, re-habilitation, and development is socialism and self-reliance. In the former Federation of Nigeria, for example, the chief hindrance to a more rapid development was not really the size of the Nigerian market or the scarcity of capital, or even the scarcity of trained personnel, although all three of these were important. The most significant barrier was the complacent, routine, almost lackadaisical attitude toward Nigeria's problems which were the results of a very low political consciousness and commitment at the national level. While there was much overt activity and a strong motivation for personal gain, very few people thought critically about the gross shortcomings and inefficiencies in the production process. Almost no time was devoted to innovation, perhaps the most critical variable in a country like Nigeria with considerable resources, ambitious labour, and an amorphous but definite will to develop.

As a result of political considerations, Nigeria's economic integration left much to be desired. While there was commerce between regions, the most important exchange was services through the free movement of peoples. An illustration of regional economic chauvinism at the time was exemplified in the case of the cashew nut oil press near Enugu. The Northern government refused the use of this equipment for pressing groundnuts produced in the South, because it was not in the interest of the North to do so. It set up its own equally inefficient mill. This sectional economic chauvinism had been growing, as the individual became more and more oriented toward the region, thus undercutting the presumed benefits of Nigeria's size.

The answer to this problem does not lie in the creation of tribal states within a federal Nigeria because of the political factors concerned. As long as there is no firm commitment by the masses and leaders to the national level of action and loyalty remains at the state level, then tribal apartheid will result. This separatism will be made more destructive by a heightened deterioration in the pervasive kind of competition, better described as "scheming to do somebody else out of what he has for your own benefit." The emphasis on redistributing or capturing resources rather than on creating more will be magnified manifold. As long as attitudes and motivations remain unchanged and negative, conventional macroeconomic efforts will lack force to bring about a dynamic effect on the economy. The poorer states would seek to be parasitic on the richer ones, and economic interactions assumed to be a stimulus for their development would lead to an exploitation of the richer areas and the capturing of investments, for political reasons, which would more rationally be placed elsewhere. In fact, there would be little positive interaction.

There is only one appropriate political solution for these problems posed by the focus of political loyalty at the subnational rather than the national level. This is the creation of political arrangements based on programs of socialist reconstruction of the former Federation of Nigeria. What is involved here is the removal of transethnic loyalty to an ideological level of the state which emphasizes social justice, mass ownership of the instruments of production and distribution of national resources, the predomination of the interests of the workers and peasants who constitute the overwhelming majority of the population, and the removal of all exploitative forces which fan the fires of intergroup hostility. This arrangement would realize the brotherhood of man which is the true interest and conception of human relationship on the part of the masses. The workers and peasants would be highly conscious of their interest and destiny, both alone and in combination with similar progressive forces in Africa and the rest of the world, laying emphasis on improving the productive forces of the state for the benefit of all citizens regardless of sectional and parochial interests. To bring about this state of affairs, a social revolution is required.

The fact is that justice and development, the only means toward genuine rehabilitation and reconstruction in Nigeria, cannot be ensured as long as the basis of domestic social and economic organisation is capitalist and there is a great dependence of the state on the international capitalist system. Inherent in capitalism is inequality. In economic terms this means that someone must do the dirty work so that others may be rich. There is exploitation. As a result of the phenomenon of tribalism described earlier, this inequality in Africa finds operational expression in a hierarchical arrangement of ethnic groups in terms of their benefits from the economic distribution in the system. In postwar Nigeria, the defeated Ibos are the most likely victims of this economic inequality and exploitation.

Socialism on the other hand rejects this inherent inequality. It seeks to transform the society in such a way that all the structures which encourage inequality are eliminated. Free education must be established up to the university level with the primary and secondary aspects of it made compulsory, unemployment must be outlawed, health benefits provided free for all the citizens, and public transportation made available efficiently and easily to the masses of people. Under these conditions the need to amass wealth, which is the basis of the conflicts that lead to an acceptance of inequality, is diluted. People may then work more in cooperation than in competition. They are then in a position to accept the equality, dignity, and self-respect of their fellow countrymen.

This socioeconomic reorganisation is almost impossible without the country's making a clean break with international capitalism. The existence of linkage groups from that system encourages domestic capitalism and, as we have seen, leads to external intervention in domestic affairs of the African states with all its consequences. In this respect the question of nationalization of foreign enterprises must be faced. It is the first step towards national self-reliance. It removes the linkage groups in the country and thus clears the blurred boundaries of the state and makes it difficult for informal access and external intervention in domestic affairs to take place.

It is the merit of self-reliance that it realizes the political implications of economic relations. In the contemporary atmosphere of informal access and transnational politics it seeks to prevent informal attack and control.

Self-reliance controls but does not prevent external interaction with other states. In order to effect this control, it must rely on the power of the Nigerian peoples. If the leaders are reactionary, selfish and corrupt, the masses will be dispirited. But if they win the confidence of the people, which they can only do by the vigorous elimination of class and ethnic privileges, they can successfully mobilize them behind state actions.

Economically, self-reliance encourages local initiative and the maximum utilization of internal resources. Thus the latent energy of the country is transformed into the manifest energy for development. Foreign investment and aid are assessed strictly on the benefits they provide for development and not welcomed uncritically or treated with automatic suspicion and disdain. Economic and other relations with the advanced countries must be on the basis of interdependence and mutual benefits rather than dependence and exploitation. Self-reliance realizes that imperialism, both the old military style and the new monetary form, is not only morally reprehensible but also socially and economically detrimental as far as the general needs of the people are concerned. Only by an emphasis on socialism and self-reliance may the vast resources of the rural areas be turned effectively towards the development of the state.

It is therefore the task of all well-meaning people who wish to see peace established in Nigeria to encourage all actions which may make possible the adoption of socialism and self-reliance in the country . Otherwise violence is bound to recur either along ethnic lines or along lines of urban-rural, interelite, elite-mass, traditional-modern, interregional, interlinkage, and other contradictions in the society.

Notes

1. Kenneth E. Boulding, *The Image* (Ann Arbor, Mich.: The University of Michigan Press, 1956), pp. 6, 43.

2. Major General Aguiyi-Ironsi formed a military government when it became obvious that the young majors could not consolidate their coup.

3. See Federation of Nigeria, *Report of the Coker Commission of Inquiry into the Affairs of Certain Statutory Corporations in Western Nigeria* (Lagos, Nigeria: Government Printer, 1962), 4 volumes and Charles V. Brown, *Government and Banking in Western Nigeria* (Ibadan, Nigeria: Oxford University Press, 1964).

4. "Chop politics" refers to the contention among leaders of political parties, most of which had ethnic predominance, that the resources of the Federation must be evenly distributed among the different ethnic groups. Everyone must have a share of the national pie. The concept was popularized in the ranks of the NNDP led by Chief Akintola and was used as a slogan by him for joining the NPC in a coalition—thus the Yorubas would get their share of things.

5. Evidence from the following reports in the newspapers: Editorial, "The New Regime," *Daily Times,* 18 January 1966; Back page, "NCNC and AC Back Military Rule, *Daily Times,* 18 January 1966; Front page, "Labour Unions Happy," *Morning Post,* 18 January 1966; Editorial, "Road to Survival," *Morning Post,* 19 January 1966; Front page, "NPC Supports the Military Regime," *West African Pilot,* 19 January 1966; Editorial, "Best Hope for Democracy," *Morning Post,* 20 January 1966; Editorial, "Words of Gold," *Morning Post,* 21 January 1966.

6. It was unwise for General Ironsi to attempt to unify the administrative machinery at the time he did in May 1966. Awolowo and the other political prisoners should have been released by him and a constitutional conference called immediately to work out a new and more suitable arrangement while the Army continued to purge the public service of corruption and mediocrity.

7. Report of Colin Legum's interview with Chiniua Achebe in *The Observer* (London), 6 March 1967, p. 1.

8. Reprinted in *West Africa* (London), 20 April 1968, p. 464.

9. Ibid., 7 May 1966, p. 521.

10. Ibid., 20 April 1968, p. 464.

11. This point was made famous by Carl von Clausewitz's statement that war is a continuation of politics by other means. Carl von Clausewitz, *On War* (New York: Random House, Modern Library, 1943), p. 41.

12. Quincy Wright, *A Study of War* (Chicago: University of Chicago Press, 1942), p. 700.

13. On linkage groups, see Karl W. Deutsch, "External Influences on the Internal Behavior of States" and James N. Rosenau, "Pretheories and Theories of Foreign Policy," both in *Approaches to Comparative and International Politics*, ed. R. Barry Farrell (Evanston, Ill.: Northwestern University Press, 1966).

14. Deutsch, "External Influences," p. 6.

15. Margery Perham, ed., *Mining, Commerce and Finance in Nigeria* (London: Faber and Faber Ltd. 1948), p. 51.

16. Ibid., pp. 55–65.

17. *Shell Magazine* (London), February 1969, 49, no. 728, pp. 1–4.

18. Barclays Bank D.C.O., *Nigeria, An Economic Survey* (London, 1963), p. 27.

19. *West Africa* (London), 30 April 1966, p. 491.

20. Reprinted in Alan Sokolski, *The Establishment of Manufacturing in Nigeria* (New York: Frederick A. Praeger, 1965), p. 178.

21. *The New York Times,* 6 March 1962, p. 6.

22. Ibid.

23. United Africa Company, *Statistical and Economic Review,* no. 28 (London, 1966), p. 53.

24. Sokolski, *Establishment of Manufacturing,* p. 185.

25. Ibid.

26. O. Olakankpo, "Foreign Aid and the Plan," *The Nigerian Journal of Economic and Social Studies, 4,* no. 2 (July 1962), pp. 116–130.

27. Okwudiba Nnoli, "Economic Decolonization and Inter-State Politics in Africa: The Case of Ghana, Guinea, Mali, Nigeria, Senegal, and the Ivory Coast" (Ph.D. diss., Stanford University, 1967), p. 196.

28. Speech by Bukar Dipcharima, Nigerian Minister of Commerce and Industry, January 1961, in Federation of British Industries, *Nigeria's Industrial Renaissance* (London, 1961), p. 45.

29. Nnoli, "Economic Decolonization," p. 197.

30. Ibid.

31. *West Africa* (London), 27 August 1966, p. 977.

32. See the Special Commonwealth African Assistance Plan (SCAAP) Report for the years ending 31 March 1960, 1962, 1963, and 1964.

33. *West Africa* (London), 27 August 1966, p. 977.

34. Ibid., 13 August 1966, p. 921.

35. Ibid., 8 January 1966, p. 41.

36. Central Bank of Nigeria, *Economic and Financial Review*, 5, no. 2 (Lagos, Nigeria: December 1967), p. 1.

37. The Biafrans consistently maintained this point.

38. Rosenau, "Pretheories and Theories," pp. 62–68.

5

THE RELATIONSHIP OF HISTORY, THOUGHT, AND ACTION WITH RESPECT TO THE NIGERIAN SITUATION

Moyibi Amoda

Philosophy, History, Thought, and Action: Their Theoretic Connection

There have been crises in the African states since their independence — economic, social, cultural, and political conflicts often resulting in the overthrow of those in office, a change of political regime, and sometimes involving the rotation of elites. But only two crises have threatened a political unit with virtual extinction: the Congo crisis and the Nigerian Civil War. Of the two, the Nigerian example presents the clearer case of an African state in a postcolonial situation, involving issues which are clearly of domestic origin.

What makes the Nigerian situation paradigmatic is not the fact that it involves an independent sovereign nation, but rather that it evinces the typical anomalies which make the framework of an inherited polity problematic. The crisis is important, therefore, because it involves a question of the redefinition of the political authorities, political regimes, and political community; and for almost all the African states the problem of nation-building consists in exactly that, in making a particular definition of authority, constitution, and citizenship authoritative and consensual. Thus the issues which have engendered the Civil War in Nigeria are potentially capable of producing similar political conflagrations in most of the African states, since the political contexts of action in most of these states are very similar.

152

The Nigerian case is also typical in terms of the issues, real or imaginary, to the extent that they offer ideological points of political mobilization. Thus actors and observers have tried to reduce the conflict into such terms as "tribalism," "sectionalism," "religion," "moralism," "ideology" (Cold Warism), "humanitarianism," "imperialism," or "neo-colonialism," each reduction presenting its proponents areas of affective fixation.

But much more important than what the Civil War is potentially capable of meaning to non-Nigerians, in terms of conflict resolution, is what it means to the Nigerian people themselves, as a process of political education. A threat to a people's existence is the most startling, most traumatic, and most efficient way to mobilize them politically; this is one of the reasons why wars have always provided an effective crucible for the melting of disparate groups into one national mold. To the Nigerian who was unable to identify with the flag, with the anthem, with the strange and foreign proceedings in parliament, those symbols translated by the taking of life have become living forms *presenting* the projected context of desired political actions. From a man to whom politics was essentially epiphenomenal, peripheral, and noteworthy only in terms of its banality and corruption, his very survival now rests solely with the instruments of politics. He has become a political man. Formerly unaware of the impact of foreign involvement in domestic crisis, apt to classify states in simplistic ideological compartments of naive stereotypes, incapable of seeing that interest politics could yield bizarre but rational political combinations, this Nigerian has become sensitive to political nuances; he divides audiences, peoples, nations, clubs, etc., primarily in terms of their attitudes to the Nigerian crisis. It is because the Civil War is such a primary and ruthless process of political education that it is such a paradigmatic showcase. It is because the Civil War has been such a startling revelation that the problem of the political understanding of how people go about comprehending such crisis situations is an urgent intellectual question.

When the question is put in this way, it is possible to construe the purpose of this chapter as the contention that an intellectual and epistemological question is more important than the more obviously direct political question of inquiry into the motives of political actors. To put this construction on my question is to state what appears on the surface to be a paradox, that is, that there is a world of actors out there and a world of theorist-spectators in here, and that to understand that world of actors out there, one must study them from this world of the theorist-spectators. This apparent paradox resolves itself if we are understood not to be addressing ourselves to a situation of social and political disorganization, that is, to a situation which assumes on the testament of the actors themselves, an agreement on certain basic goals and disagreement about certain institutional means for their realization, to which disagreement and its resolution the theorist-spectator can contribute his specialized technical knowledge. On the contrary, we are concerned with certain situations in which the framework of politics and social life (that is, situations in which the definition of what is authority, what is a rule, what is a citizen)[1] is the node of disagreement. In such crises the gap that separates the actor-participant and the theorist-spectator vanishes, since both are simultaneously attempting to reconstruct the discredited political paradigm, to give meaning to its rules, to describe and ascribe roles to each citizen and cluster of citizens. Both are simultaneously attempting to find the root causes of the anomalies in such paradigms and to construct alternative paradigms with which they can give meaning to contemporary action, offering criticisms and prescriptions to the degree that their stipulated paradigms coincide with or diverge from those of opponents.

In such a context the theoretic word immediately becomes ideology; political programs become iconic representations of theoretic visions; statesmen become philosophers on their own behalf and philosophers—ideal type for the political scientist—hunger for the position and status of founding fathers. It is not mere accident that such situations have furnished us not only disproportionate numbers of theorist-actors and actor-theorists, but also disproportionate instances of persecution of men of letters, for it is precisely in such situations that speech is immediately relevant. Because such emergent situations lead to the amalgamation of roles and to easy corruption of the distinct roles of theorizing and acting, a professional self-consciousness is more than ever demanded of the actor and theorist when the political context reveals itself as emergent. This is why we said that the understanding of how men go about comprehending their political role becomes an inquiry into crucial intellectual and moral assumptions that direct and undergird political observation. It is a task requiring urgent attention because the word of explanation or justification carries with it the responsibility for the prescription of certain policies, policies which involve the collective fate of a people or sectors of a people. It is in such a situation that the dictates of action make the separation of the roles of observation and acting difficult and lead to the seduction of reason by passion.

Yet while the intimate connection of words and deeds must be recognized, the distinction between the activities of producing relevant words and deeds must be maintained because, close as they are, the two activities concern two distinct subject matters and operate by different rules of selection, organization, and criticism; in short, the two activities, theorizing and acting, operate with different epistemology and different methods and entail different sets of responsibilities. It is a sensitivity to this intimate connection between the ideological impulses of theorists and actors that informs the following quotations from Hegel and Meyerhoff.

One word more about giving instruction as to what the world ought to be. Philosophy in any case always comes on the scene too late to give it. As the thought of the world, it appears only when actuality is already there cut and dried after its process of formation has been completed. The teaching of the concept, which is also history's inescapable lesson, is that it is only when actuality is mature that the ideal first appears over against the real and that the ideal apprehends this same real world in its substance and builds it up itself into the shape of an intellectual realm. When philosophy paints its grey in grey, it cannot be rejuvenated but only understood. The owl of Minerva spreads its wings only with the falling of the dusk.[2]

Man's existence is history; or "life and reality are history, and history alone" as Croce said. Thus history and not the City of God, is the key to a philosophy of Man and Society.[3]

What is implicit in Hegel is not only that philosophers, theorists, scientists, and actor-philosophers, actor-theorists, and actor-scientists would attempt to instruct themselves, their pupils, their governments, and other governments on what the world ought to be; what is obvious is not only that they would claim authority to order and re-order the world. This Hegel knew was part of the intellectualist perspective, part of the heroic impulse that drives actors and theorists to participate in politics directly or in sublimated politics in the world of academe. The crucial import is not the philosopher's claim to authority, but the basis of this authority.

The philosopher, whether actor or observer, foreign or indigenous, can only have subjects for thought when the acts of politics have been done—when they are cut-and-dried after their process of formation has been completed. It is this statement that embodies both the theory and the program of history. If philosophy is not merely to be a sorting and classification of hard but dead facts according to criteria of classification extrinsic to the facts themselves, the cut-and-dried actuality of past life has to be given life again. The hand of the clock has to be made to run backwards. There has to be, as far as the human imagination is capable of artistic reconstruction, a playback of what has transpired, a repeat performance of a unique act. Understanding what has been done, the key to philosophy as Meyerhoff puts it, is therefore not the classification of dead facts, the connection of categories by a chronological string, but the apprehension "of this same world in its substance," this world which has passed.

It is a task performed under the most arduous conditions, when the facts appear to be dead, when they are not bathed in the floodlights of obvious emotions and motives. Understanding and changing the world is therefore not to be achieved by mere use of a stereotype as explanation. To be prepared for an intellectual understanding of the world, the philosopher must be capable of the artistic activity of self-transformation and self-transportation from his parochial point in his cultural habitat into the action-situation of those actors, the consequences of whose deeds present the philosophic problems of understanding.

On the other hand, the actor dealing in situations in which philosophy (in terms of dispassionate inquiry into the meaning of things) is absent deals essentially with ideology. He acts *cum ira*. His actions are presented not to elicit objective inquiry but as an appeal to a commitment. He uses history and philosophy, but from an interest-bound position. His facts are by nature stereotypic; they are symbolic presentations of subjective feelings. Each fact in his official history-beads is connected to the others with specific emotive threads to produce the total effect of mobilization for a cause.

The subject of philosophy is the dead and actualized world. Action, because of the contingent and fluid setting in which it manifests itself, must of necessity live off the systematized knowledge of the past; action assumes history and philosophy, although its use of history and philosophy is subject not to the rules of history and philosophy, but to those of action. It is the function of philosophy and history to make the silent facts of the past talk relevantly to the present, to put life into past deeds and into past conceptions of the world in order to provide living men the material to build their ideals.

It is within this context that an analysis of historiography as it concerns the Nigerian situation becomes extremely important, for here we are charging philosophy with the task of comprehending the nature of actuality, the destruction of the postcolonial amity binding the various segments of the Nigerian society. Only with such an understanding can the ideas which interpret the past and posit attainable possibilities become directive, architectonic, and relevant. However, were this the understanding which actors and observers of the Nigerian situation had of their roles, there would be no need for an historiographical critique of Nigerian tradition. It is because the search for explanation of the Nigerian Civil War has revealed the perennial habit of resorting to a one-factor thesis, with the corollary dependence upon stereotypes, that one must be sensitized to the gap between philosophic history as I have portrayed it, and the political historiography which is characteristic of observers and actors alike.

I have attempted to present the subject matter of this chapter in very general terms. I shall now endeavor to make my case more specific. In order to identify who is the actor and who is the philosopher, who is committing what crime against what reason, etc., it is helpful to conceptualize the following groups as inhabitants of a two-by-three matrix:

	Actors	**Philosophers**
Foreign	Foreign actors	Foreign philosophers
Nigerians at home	Nigerian actors at home	Nigerian philosophers at home
Nigerians abroad	Nigerian actors abroad	Nigerian philosophers abroad

I have divided the political universe into the realms of actors and philosophers. I have further divided the actors and philosophers into three categories: foreign, Nigerians at home, and Nigerians abroad. The result is a division of the population into six groups: foreign actors, foreign philosophers, Nigerian actors at home, Nigerian philosophers at home, Nigerian actors abroad, Nigerian philosophers abroad. In this essay I will be limiting myself to only sectors of some of the groups.

For example, I shall be referring exclusively to American philosophers, instead of to all possible foreign philosophers who are interested in the Nigerian situation. I do this because of my particular familiarity with America. I shall not have to specify who the foreign actors are, since it suffices to rely on the current schema of international politics and to use the government of any country as the unit of a foreign actor. Neither is it necessary for me to make the distinction between the individual and group actor, since the type of argument that I am advancing makes such a distinction meaningless. It is also not especially important for me to indicate the particular patterns and instances of action undertaken by each government of each foreign philosopher, for this is not that type of analysis. I know that the reader realizes that Nigeria, being a member of the international arena, has by virtue of such membership created international interest in its domestic affairs. It is enough to show here that, if there is need to act, understanding the basis upon which decisions are made entails judgments based upon particular conceptions of what the issues of politics are in Nigeria. Finally, in discussing the Nigerian abroad, I will be depending most heavily on experiences among the Nigerians in the United States, in particular those in the San Francisco Bay area of California. The pattern elsewhere is unlikely to differ appreciably.

The American philosopher, an Africanist, begins his analysis of an African political problem with assumptions as to what is political and what is not political, what is a problem of development; he makes assumptions as to what is wrong with the society, what is the gap between the desired goal and the available resources. Typically he has assumed that the public declaration of the African leader constitutes a public commitment to a goal and that, having understood the logical import of that goal, this understanding provides him with the reliable knowledge which would serve as a basis for political analysis and prescriptions.

On the basis of his expertise he could be, and often is, consulted by the government when a problem arises in his area of specialization. What I am saying should not be construed to mean that Africanists make United States policy with respect to Africa. The United States government need not even follow the advice of the expert. However, as soon as it has been admitted that the Africanist is consulted, we have also admitted that the Africanist does wear two hats, that of a philosopher and that of an actor, and whereas his impact as a philosopher may or may not be negligible, the consequences of his role as actor become immediately politically relevant since the institution within which he acts can significantly alter the state of affairs in the area of his specialization. Moreover, when the United States government or some private foundations have to send experts on politics or administration overseas, they must recruit these experts among the Africanists and once more the basis of selection becomes the earned reputation as philosopher whose subject matter is African politics. Should his advice be accepted and put into practice, his political vision becomes a political program affecting the collective life of millions of African people.[4] And again the intimate connection between the two roles, that of philosopher and that of actor, is obvious.

Moreover when the indigenous philosopher abroad undertakes his philosophical education, he is exposed to what the Africanists consider to be the subject matter of political inquiry; he is educated not only in a particular mode of analysis, but also in a complete political cosmology which constitutes the basis of the Africanist epistemology. Thus, the Nigerian philosopher at an American university becomes the student of the Africanist who is professor and consultant. In terms of his professional role, the Nigerian philosopher abroad is socialized into a particular cosmology, and this cosmology generally becomes the only professional basis for his identifying what constitutes political meaning in the area of his birth. To the extent then that his audience consists of American professors, he has to justify deviation from the acknowledged expert in the field, yet not in terms of the fact that he is African and therefore has by virtue of that fact alone a special intuitive knowledge which his teachers could not have, because they are foreign. Rather he has to justify deviation from his teachers in terms of the commonly accepted language of discourse, in terms of an epistemology acceptable to his teachers, which means accepting the Africanist cosmology as a basic premise while disagreeing with the Africanist with respect to the validity of conclusions asserted from the commonly accepted premises.

The point is that, even in the process of philosophical education

*in an American university, the African student desiring a degree in
African politics has to accept the authoritative definition of the
Africanist as to what is political and what is not political, what is
an interesting problem and what is uninteresting, what are the
legitimate criteria of criticism. If he were to reject all these, he
would still have to defend his rejection in these very terms or else
he could not communicate with his professors. And what is more
radical, were he to question the very basis of the political epistemology—the underlying political cosmology—not only would he not
be able to talk to his professors, he would be challenging the very
basis of their authority both as professors of, and as consultants
on, African problems—and at this stage of the game a philosophical misunderstanding becomes a political misunderstanding.*

But were we to assume what is frequently the case, that the
Nigerian philosopher abroad *believes* in the Africanist political
epistemology—for this is what he is being asked to do when he
is promised a professional degree—he also begins his political
analysis by assuming a political cosmology identical with the
foreign philosopher, for the categories which he accepts subsume
a commitment to a particular political ontology and to a particular
political metaphysics. He has before him similar thought tracks as
those available to his mentors, and he has to store and process his
data along the same conversion patterns defined by these tracks.
In a way, he also becomes an expert on the same basis as the
foreign philosophers, and, like them, he attempts to create a
political world recognizable by the profession of philosophers. The
only significant difference between the Nigerian philosopher abroad
and his Africanist mentors is a difference in terms of which government (or governments) has their loyalty. In any case, we see a
possible pattern of relationship between the philosophers, African
or foreign, and the same connection can be made for the African
philosopher now returned home and the foreign philosophers who
were his teachers.

The indigenous actor defines the situation immediately. And to
the extent that he defines political development in terms of affluence based on criteria by which foreign philosophers analyze and
interpret activities productive of affluence in their own communities or to the extent that he defines development as the successful
adaptation of a particular foreign institution to local needs or to
the extent that he defines these goals as being the Africanization
of certain political processes borrowed from a foreign area of the

world, to that extent it is possible and necessary for the actor to rely on political and philosophical experts from the area in which the imported institutions originate. And to the extent that this is the case it is possible for the foreign philosophers to claim the world of the indigenous actor as a subject matter understood through their academic categories.

The conjuncture of these assumptions creates dual tendencies. First, it induces the foreign philosopher to posit an idealized model of his society as the goal of political development (and this cannot be dismissed as ethnocentrism, for the indigenous actors, like the Israelites of old, are asking Samuel to give them a king).[5] Second, it creates the subject matter for him, for to the extent that a common political culture spreading from the Americas and Europe into Africa is assumed, to that extent does it become the legitimate intellectual function of political scientists to gather data from their areas of specialty to illustrate the local conditions which may necessitate certain forms of alteration of the political processes concomitant with this universal political culture. If there is a universal political culture, the Africanist becomes the political scientist interested in African problems. The criteria of what constitutes a problem are dictated by the discipline of American political science. And the Africanist has a subject matter as an American political scientist talking to a predominantly American audience only if the African political actor has defined a subject matter, that is, the goals which he thinks his society ought to pursue.

Hence, in dealing with a particular problem of politics that the actor confronts, it becomes necessary to see how the actor defines himself politically—how he has chosen his problems. And we expect that, if the African actor defines his political world in sociological and psychological terms peculiar to his experience as an African, the mere fact that such a definition is expressed in political, social, and psychological categories of a certain kind would make the public world expressed not immediately comprehensible to the American philosopher interested in studying such public phenomena, even if the American philosopher's intention is to study such phenomena, be they African, Chinese, or Indonesian.

We would expect this to be so because the statement that a philosopher in his role as a philosopher should be able to comprehend the categories by which all men attempt to make sense of their experience, provides the philosopher only a formal logical understanding of categories which are empty of specific content. Once the categories are particularized, that is, made the vehicle of expressing the individual perception and cognitions of social experiences, the philosopher must, of necessity, be a participant in the experience expressed by the categories the universal meaning of which he knows through his formal training as a philosopher; or he must be able to justify his reliance on the reports of members in the particular social group which *has chosen* to express its feelings in terms of these categories.

However, with respect to the American Africanist and the African actor, we have, until recently, been given the impression by both the Africanist and the modern African that no such gap in social and psychological understanding exists. It appears that the African actor defines his problems and his world in such terms as are immediately comprehensible to the American Africanist. And it appears that the American Africanist implies that merely to have been given a training which all American philosophers should have provides the American philosophers both the general philosophical categories and the particular social expression of those categories irrespective of the particular society that the philosopher may choose to study. And it is here that the sense of a paradox in the claim of the American philosopher and in the self-definition of the African actor appears.

For it ought to strike us as paradoxical that an African political actor, creating a political subject matter comprehensible to an American philosopher who is speaking immediately to a predominantly American political and intellectual audience, should be assumed to be existing *simultaneously* in a political cosmos *similar to and different from that of the American actor;* yet how else can logical understanding of the meaning of similar words (similar words used by Africanists and African political actors) provide simultaneously orientations to the social and psychological meanings of these words, unless we assume not only a similarity of political personalities, but also similarity of processes of thought, similarity of political experiences, and similarity of political consciousness? In short, do we not have to assume that the African and the American actors are not only inhabitants of the same political universe but also similar products of essentially the same processes? This indeed is a paradox. For the African political scene has been treated by political scientists as a novel context for carrying out the experiments of political modernization. And if the African situation is novel it must not then be identical to the American situation.

This paradox is further complicated precisely because the African political actors seem to have defined their situation as essentially part of a continuum ranging from the underdeveloped (or "developing," or "primitive," or "new") nations to the developed nations. And if it must be recognized that the African actor defines the political actuality, we are compelled to accept the actor's self-definition as the unit of analysis. One then ought to ask in what respect the African situation is different from the American situation, since intuition tells us that the American political experience is not similar to the African political experience to the degree assumed by the Africanist epistemology or by the formal statements of the *significant* political actors in Africa.

One must ask whether or not there is a case of false consciousness involved and, if so, who is falsely conscious. One must ask why, if the Africanist and the African actor are in agreement as to the similarity of their political universe, even if the African actor's adoption of a foreign reference group indicates not African actualities but African aspirations, why recognized modes of analysis required for cogent description and interpretation of political problems are applied with the least rigor when the subject matter, African political problems, is a subject of political science. Why would stereotypes do as political explanation in Africa, and not do as political analysis of American government or American political behavior?

Once these types of questions are raised we are brought to the central problem of this chapter, the philosophical understanding of how Nigerian actors and intellectuals come to know the political world within which they find themselves and which they help to alter.

Definition of the Nigerian Political Situation

We indicated earlier that the Nigerian case as an illustration of the chronic problems arising out of inquiry into African politics was paradigmatic in nature. We indicated that it was so in terms of the audience interested in it, the issues raised by the Civil War, the scope of political conflicts, and the opportunity for political education afforded by such a crisis.

What we must now do is to indicate how the groups which we

have singled out have explained the Civil War and then trace out the implications of such definitions in terms of both political historiography and political sociology . And in order to provide more than negative criticism, we will suggest some alternative ways of understanding politics while respecting the distinctiveness of political activities and philosophical inquiry. In the ensuing comments we will focus upon elaborating the following themes:

(1) That American philosophers demonstrate a penchant for looking at the problem of political development as essentially a problem of social disorganization. Hence, they assume that the opinions of the leaders express the summary of popular opinion at the most, or, at the least, the summary of the opinion of the most significant political sectors; that the leaders' political values express popular values or the values of the most significant elites; and finally that the problem of political inquiry is the problem of searching for suitable political structures and processes which help to remedy the social problem. We contend that these assumptions are inappropriate because they entail a political situation different from that in which the actors actually find themselves.

(2) That African actors operate with two conflicting sets of assumptions. On the one hand they assume that the problem of political development is a problem of social disorganization and they therefore seem to assume the permanence of inherited colonial political values, even though there may be differences in terms of how the inherited institutions are made to work and to what extent institutional innovations should go. On the other hand, these actors behave as if their political arena is emergent and prismatic. By emergent I mean that they see their situation not as defined but as in the process of being defined; no framework is unalterable; the fluidity of the political environment necessitates continuous effort at adaptation of institutions to their environment and continuous work to control the political forces whose identities are still only partially known. They also seem to construe the situation as prismatic, in that they see their immediate political goal as the acquisition of power. They assume that everything in the political arena is a resource, real or potential, and that the political game is a zero sum game. In other words, what I lose, my enemy gains. The rules of the game are viewed as weapons of power and hence not sacrosanct. Finally, they view everyone as self-seeking and a partisan of a clique—there are no philosophers, just actors.

These assumptions indicate an instrumental orientation towards the political world in a context where there are no commitments to any particular definition of the game. This then makes the problem of political development not a problem of social disorganization but a problem of social ontogenesis. It is a problem of creating a political society in which actors accept and adhere to a common political framework and common rules. In short, the problem is the creation of a political cosmology and the propagation of a political language with which actors could negotiate their way through the recurrent problems of social conflict.

Nigerian Actors and Nigerian Philosophers Abroad

Realizing that the Nigerian student (potential philosopher and actor by citizenship) has been compelled by the situation to explain the origin of the crisis to himself and to others, we take a look at one organ of the Nigerian students, *The Nigerian Students Voice*. The selection is taken from the issues published early in the crisis when the Nigerian students were still undivided along the lines of cleavage that divided the political actors at home. Let us begin with the Editorial of the October–December 1966 edition. The Editor-in-Chief, J. B. C. Ugokwe, begins:

When some young Nigerian Army officers relieved the *Nigerian masses* of the burden of an *unpopular civilian government*, most people had brighter hopes for the future of Nigeria. Of course, we regretted the innocent lives that were lost, especially in the Army. We feared the consequence of the coup because of the *cyclical nature of coups*, especially considering the fact that *"justice" was not done in all parts of the country*. But we rejoiced at the facts that: the "rebels" surrendered to the official Army Command; that the Army was called upon to govern the country until order was restored; that *the Army embarked on a unitary form of government* and a search for *honest* public officials.

We had faith in the Army. It was progressive, internationally distinguished, intellectually enlightened, efficiently disciplined and *supposedly* unified. We believe that a unitary form of government and an honest class of public servants are Nigeria's best instruments for a rapid political, social and economic progress.[6]

The first sentence of this editorial appears to be a causal explanation of the overthrow of the civilian government: It was unpopular. There is an acknowledgment, although somewhat impatient, of the political cost involved in the displacement of the civilian regime. There is an expression of slight regret that "justice" was not done in all parts of the country. The political problem is defined as the restoration of order by the institutionalization of a unitary government. The qualifications of the Army for undertaking this task are seen as its progressiveness, its international distinctiveness, its efficiency and discipline, and its solidarity.

Taking a closer look at these assertions, assertions which represented the dominant feeling of Nigerian intellectuals in the early phase of the civil crisis, we are struck by their lack of logical coherence. Although we recognize that as a set of statements portraying a particular sentiment they make sense, they nevertheless reflect that dangerous lack in our political awareness, the seeming ignorance of the implications of our preferences. It was assumed that the civilian government was overthrown because it was unpopular. This indeed was the case. But there was by no means a clear definition of what constituted popularity. Who was unpopular to whom? Did all the major sectors of the political community perceive similar symptoms of this unpopularity? More important, was there a common perception in the key institutions of the central and regional bureaucracies of what constituted the political malaise? What was in fact the relation between removing the civilian government and the institutionalization of a unitary government?

None of these questions occurred to us until the "cycle of coups" indicated the seriousness of the crisis and the relentless but predictable consequences of unpremeditated political actions. The Nigerian intellectual simply accepted the political actor's definition of the situation and built a structure of expectations on this basis. The civilian politicians were charged with being unpopular, the military regime proclaimed a war on corruption and a restoration of honest government, and we Nigerian philosophers accepted those statements as a causal analysis of the situation. Yet had we been attuned to our responsibilities we might have asked the questions raised above before taking a position on the issues.

For it would have been important to know what there was about the political context of action which produced this systemic unpopularity. An attempt should have been made to know whether the crisis in the Western Region, to the extent that it involved all the governmental units in a struggle for dominance, meant, in fact, complete alienation of all relevant publics from their official representatives. We could not assume that the unpopularity of the government had provided such a political education that the disparate population of each region had become welded into a "mass." Neither could it be assumed that the political crisis had produced the political consciousness necessary to evaluate our political history, to diagnose the ills of the polity as attributable to the malfunctioning of particular institutions, and to prescribe a change from a federal to a unitary form of government as a cure for these ills.

In no way did the charge of unpopularity entail all those assumptions upon which the case that "justice" be done so glibly rested. It was assumed that dishonesty had been the bane of the civilian regime, but no attempt had been made to show in what respect dishonesty was attributable to the rules of the game, the political definitions of authority, the political distribution of rewards and obligation, or the definition of the context of politics. One was still no nearer to a political understanding of the past, and the prescription of unitary government clearly indicated the lack of appreciation of the contemporary context of political action, since it was precisely that demand for unitary government which was the issue of conflict at home.

Dr. Alexander D. Acholonu, in the same edition of *The Nigerian Students Voice,* focused on tribalism as the root cause of the Nigerian crisis. He began with a definition of the "tribe":

The ethnological meaning of the word "tribe" is a group of persons or clans descended from a common ancestor and often under common leadership. A tribe has a dialect and a feeling of kinship. "Tribe" and "tribal" are convenient terms for indicating that a people still follows custom rather than state law. . . . Being tribal *implies incompartibility* [sic] *among people of the same country. It indicates that the people are sectional or ethnocentric.*[7]

Tribalism thus defined is termed by Acholonu as the "opium of national unity in Nigeria." The political society is seen as a conglomeration of ethnic groups with distinct origins. The system of indirect rule is cited as a reason for the rigidification of the "feudal" and anti-modern structures of the Northern Region. The missionary education is seen as the process for the inculcation of modern attitudes in the South. Tribalism is seen to have been excited by the politician who not only created parties along sectional lines but also "looked on power as an end in itself."

They, in their thirst for power, united their various groups around themselves. They constantly and desperately preached the consequent subjugation of ethnic groups if they refused to vote for them. In the North, the Ahmadu Bello Youth Organization was formed to translate into action Ahmadu Bello's dream of ruling Nigeria forever. In the West, the sympathizers of Awolowo and his followers formed the Awolowo Youth Organization to oppose Akintola's band of thugs; while in the East, Okpara's Youth Brigade paraded around as a successor to the Zikist National Vanguard.[8]

The crisis of Nigeria therefore lay in the chronic propensity of politicians to resort to tribal considerations in their political dealings. Tribalism, in the context of political actors who regarded their state as an artificial creation of the British, was further exacerbated by a constitutional arrangement which meant the intensification of parochialism.

This constitution, *inter alia* brought about regionalization of civil service, regional rivalry and thus augmented tribal sentiments. *Regionalism,* or, *tribalism* entered into many things in which superior national representation was needed. When youthful energy was or is to be generated to demonstrate Nigeria's manpower and prestige, tribalism warped it. . . . Tribal animosity actuated by regionalization reached its climax in 1964 when the Northern Nigeria House of Assembly passed a resolution to revoke leases held by Southerners (mainly Ibos).[9]

If tribalism was the "opium of Nigerian unity," the solution then could only be its eradication and the subsequent imposition of a unitary constitution:

[Ironsi] had taken the right step [in] the right direction by banning the old regional parties. He abolished regions and renamed them provinces. But he may have put old wine in a new bottle.

The greatest challenge we present-day Nigerians have is to fight tribalism which so far, has proved to be the opium of our national unity. We are a people of diverse origins. We are faced with the problem of learning how to live together regardless of our origins. Recent events in Nigeria are a display of unyielding determination to change the *status quo.* The future of Nigeria is in grave doubt. The doubt can only be cleared by us.[10]

We have quoted extensively from Dr. Acholonu because he attempts to explain genetically the cause of the Nigerian crisis. Dr. Acholonu adopts a nationalist perspective. The colonial history is reviewed and the relation between the social structure and the inherited political institutions is depicted. A whole generation of political actors is dispassionately put on trial and condemned for its tribalism. The sense of concern for the survival of the nation permeates the essay. This article from an Ibo represented the best articulation of the new nationalism that all Nigerians were advocating.

But having said this, one must ask again to what extent this was a realistic appraisal of the history of the country.

What strikes me in reading Dr. Acholonu, to the extent that his position is indicative of the position of Nigerians abroad, is the expression of political innocence which bordered on naïveté. It was enough for us to say tribalism was the cause of the Nigerian crisis. But what indeed is tribalism? Dr. Acholonu describes it as the political style of ethnic groups bound together by a common institution. However, this does not imply incompatibility or sectionalism or ethnocentrism as he suggests. Like him we have assumed too quickly that because a political society is pluralistic it is therefore tribalistic. Yet, we know that Switzerland is a pluralistic society with a federal constitution, but there too, factors sufficient to define the Nigerian society as tribalistic are not sufficient to describe Switzerland as tribalistic. Neither can the Anglo-French conflict in Canada be described as tribalistic.

If there was tribalism, what then could have compelled a political elite, educated in the modern institutions, to cultivate tribal differences? Dr. Acholonu suggested the additional fact that the politicians were concerned solely with power. This again was a popular stereotype which all the Nigerians abroad seemed to have uncritically accepted as causal explanation. But this fact in itself may or may not be related to tribalism. It is possible for a political class devoted to private aggrandizement to be bound by a gentleman's agreement to exploit the national institutions for private ends, to extract public resources for the development of private fortunes, using ethnic support as the ticket to the national and regional arena. Yet these are political goals and they do not entail the communitarian antipathy suggested by tribalism.

Furthermore, a closer look at the Nigerian situation would clearly reveal that this "tribalism" had nothing to do with the ethnological tribalism. There was something about the political context of Nigeria which made periodic appeal to sectional interests politically necessary. Indeed, it would have been politically unwise for a political actor not to have been "tribalistic." Once

this perspective was accepted, a Nigerian desiring institutionalization of a national political culture would have realized that the fault
that we are tribalist, was not in particular men, but in our institutions, and the problem of shifting the society from "tribalism" to
"nationalism" would then be seen not as a problem of social
disorganization but as a problem of social ontogenesis.

But a program of social ontogenesis could only be realistic after
a thorough analysis of the political history. From this vantage
point the colonial history becomes revealing. For it must be
realized that the Nigerian colonial state was established by the
British to erect an efficient and effective administrative state, not
to carry out a program of political development. When Nigerian
leaders assumed power, two possibilities were open to them:

(1) They could replace the British political elites, using the
inherited colonial institutions for the same end, namely the maintenance of political control.

(2) They could use the inherited colonial institutions for a more
ambitious goal, that of developing a national political consciousness. This goal would necessitate a development of some sort of
esprit de corps among the political class.

Who would replace the British and how would they be selected?
Here indeed was the first problem to be solved. For unless there
was amity and a tradition of cooperation among the various sectors
of the Nigerian leadership, the very creation of a political vacuum
would result, not in the replacement of the British by a solidaristic
national elite, but in a scramble for power within the context of
the colonial administrative state. Because it was not in the colonial
administration's interest to compel the formation of a national
consciousness, because there was no history of comingling among
the various peoples of Nigeria, because the process of transfer of
authority from the colonial state to the emergent political society
meant setting up political processes which, to the extent that they
were democratic, mirrored the existing social patterns of the
Nigerian colonial societies, the context of politics was defined in
such a way that there were no free-floating national resources that
could fix the direction of flow of political transactions.

This meant that the promise of authority meant the control of
existing political institutions. Yet the mechanism for political
competition for this authority entailed the creation of political
agencies for the acquisition of power. Where the only national
problem equally relevant for all sectors was the acquisition of

authority, what then was more practical and effective than the creation of political parties? What was more sensible than to use the most efficient resource, an appeal to sectional interests? The farmer—Ibo, Hausa, Yoruba, or Urhobo—had recognized the supremacy of the British overlord, but how was he to accept the replacement of the British by a leader from a group which may have always been a political enemy or at least from a foreign and distant group?

The easiest way to make such a population accept the new state and become voting citizens was for each group to generate its own leadership. And there were leaders in each group who had no basis for leadership unless they were granted votes. To be consciously regional became the most political thing to do. To develop the largest regional coalition by choosing individuals capable of being elected in their own constituency was the most effective technique. The political process was directed at the capture of power, in a milieu in which organizations had to be erected for the achievement of the opportunity for political participation, and in a context in which there was no overriding loyalty to any rules of the game. In such a situation where the political framework itself could be used as an instrument, politics could not be anything but a series of tactical maneuvers. The sure basis of power in such a fluid environment had to be the periodic appeal to the voting populations still politically imprisoned in traditional group definitions.

If this had been our perception of our past, we would have been less hasty at the outset to condemn the civilian leaders, our first set of founding fathers. We would have been more sensitive to those systemic problems which compelled the reliance upon sectional support for electoral purposes. Indeed, we would have long been apprehensive of a political structure operating with two sets of contradictory norms. The inherited colonial institutions had been based upon recruitment norms which ensured compatibility between the structure of authority and the criteria of selection of the incumbents of these roles. In the native administration the local authorities were chosen from the groups traditionally accepted as figures of authority. The colonial administration was in the hands of the British. And imperative coordination between the two structures of administration was provided by the British imperial regime. But this coordination could not be transferred along with the transfer of authority from the British to the Nigerian political class. It was beyond Britain's duty to create a political class which would be as powerful as the British colonial estate. In fact had Britain attempted to do this, there would have been a legitimate reason to charge her with leaving behind an appointed political class, a puppet regime to carry on British political interests camouflaged in Nigerian political dress. In short, she would have been charged with replacing direct colonial control with indirect neocolonial control.

Thus, in examining Nigerian political history through the perspective of politically induced ethnicity, we find that tribalism was not the cause of the country's political instability; if anything, tribalism was only a symptom of that instability. The real root of the problem is the existence of a social situation which made it impossible to generate a unified national class capable of controlling adherence to the rules of the game or of maintaining the integrity of the political process.

The disturbing conclusion to this examination of the political perspectives of the Nigerian abroad is the fact that it shows what type of political knowledge undergirds our stated position on the crisis at home. We had taken positions with but a cursory political introspection. We were not in a position to estimate just how serious the crisis was going to be. We thought that with the restoration of law and order and the replacement of corrupt politicians with honest bureaucrats, peace, progress, and stability would be achieved. Our hopes, however, were not based on a proper appreciation of the type of political forces which had been unleashed. We hoped that somewhere, somehow, and through some mechanism, notions of political limits would be imposed. To compound the confusion we uncritically accepted the political statements of actors at home and attempted to choose the least offensive possibility from the host of propagandistic utterances. Thus, we found ourselves in a car without brakes heading towards a precipitous cliff, without realizing it until the sudden crash of the car awakened us with a startling jolt, and we knew that this was no longer a play but a matter of life and death.

True, as Dr. Acholonu said, the future of Nigeria was in grave doubt. But neither he, nor the host of other Nigerians whose remarks could furnish us with the same instruction in political innocence, was aware of the difficulty of the task that was entailed in "clearing the doubt." One solution that was surely not the way to clear the doubt was what we did. We did not realize that the very fact that we were abroad meant that each of us could not have been directly involved in the crisis at home; nor did we see that singly and collectively we were part of a group that was about to be disinherited and robbed of a home, and that this very fact meant that we should remain together in attempting to sort out the mess being created by our founding fathers.

Lacking this realization, we instinctively followed the cues coming from home. We all rushed, each acting first and postponing thought, to the aid of our fathers. We took sides and having taken sides began to philosophize about the origins of the dispute, forgetting that this process of thought immediately rendered impossible both objectivity and the raising of the framework of the Nigerian polity above the level of ideology. In this way we rendered it impossible for the actors at home to perceive an alternative way of escaping from the quandary they were in. For it would definitely have put a different complexion on the crisis if the Nigerian community abroad had been united, even at the time that our parents and sisters and brothers were being slaughtered and maimed. This required introspection into the origins of the political madness raging at home; it required a stoic calmness born, not out of indifference to life, but out of the appreciation of the tragic folly that is possible when conflicts take certain turns and involve people in certain situations.

But instead of maturing under the stress of political tragedy, we were brittle and cracked under the pressure. The first impact of the blow scattered the political community abroad. When we recovered and began to gather together, we found ourselves in different political groupings which were the isomorphic mirror of the groupings at home. Having abdicated the philosophic role, accepting the ideological pronouncements of the actors at home as historical explanation and as the only realistic program for the future, our contemporary thoughts and actions could only be the imitation of the contemporary thoughts and actions of the actors at home. We were in the position of the Communist parties in the Stalinist era and had to wait for new party lines and new party directives before we could form an opinion on the events which, like the caprice of nature, disturbed our worlds. In short, having abdicated thought and entered into combat without knowing the terrain or the reasons for the battle, we had also lost complete control of our political universe. The only human thing left for us was imitation, and the only decent originals we could mimic were the actors at home.

Nigerian Actors at Home

In discussing the group of actors at home I will limit myself to the spokesmen of the Nigerian government. My reasons for doing this are twofold:

(1) In a situation in which the stakes are states, any attempt at defining the political reality about which there is conflict is ideological; it is ideological not because it may not be true but because, by being a standard against which to contrast and compare the actors' definition of the same reality, it renders judgment on these actors' definitions and therefore threatens the ontological basis of their position. It is this reason which makes me rule against attempting to speak on behalf of all the participants in this dispute. I will therefore not speak for Ojukwu or for those who share his beliefs.

(2) The government has chosen to defend the integrity of the colonial inheritance. It has chosen to keep all the sectors of the country together. It is its responsibility to know why the colonial inheritance was jeopardized, what made a civil war possible, and how to prevent future civil wars. Its perspective upon what has happened becomes critical in assessing the possibility of its success not only in containing the divisive forces within the existing framework of politics, but also in moving the actors away from the framework of war into the arena of peaceful resolution of political conflicts.

In testing the understanding of actors one does not proceed in the same manner as one does in analyzing a philosophical statement. In analyzing a discursive statement one typically operates with notions of logical validity, logical consistency, fixed definitions of key terms, and coherence of arguments. But in the question of action, actors deal essentially with ideological statements, mythical discourse, inflamed orations, and normative injunctions. Logical consistency may or may not be efficient, given the type of goals, the type of means, and the type of costs one is willing to entertain. But one can accept the expressed values of the actors, hope that they know what they want, hope that they want what they desire with some degree of passion, and hope that they are sensitive to a logic of self-interest with which one can assess the moves which are productive or counterproductive of the goals desired.

In assessing the Nigerian actors therefore we can attempt to see whether the expressed policies of unifying the country in a form which would prevent the recurrence of the crisis tallies with their perception of the origin of the crisis which created the problem of political and social disintegration. Let us examine the statements issued by the proponents of the Nigerian government's case with the understanding that nothing that is said constitutes a moral judgment as to the worth of the case. Rather, I am writing from the understanding that only a philosophical comprehension of the past constitutes the basis of an intelligent foundation of history, and that an ambiguous picture of the past can only mean the transfer of that ambiguity into the context of the present and the future. I shall quote extensively from the official statement of the Nigerian government on the crisis, which attempted to provide the historical background of the present crisis.

Commenting upon the fact that the bright economic future of the country had not been matched by a corresponding hope in the political stability of the country, the government continues, in *Nigeria 1966:*

The pre-independence election of 1959 left a permanent scar on the body politic which the joys of independence could not heal. *The division in the political ruling class was mainly along regional lines,* the Northern Peoples Congress in the North, the National Convention of Nigerian Citizens in the East and the Action Group in the West.

The Action Group crisis of 1962 marked the turning point in Nigeria's political life. The subsequent state of emergency in the West followed by the uneasy rule by the National Convention of Nigerian Citizens/United Peoples Party Coalition Government and then the Nigerian National Democratic Party ushered in political tensions and violence undreamt of in our parliamentary life.

Other political crises which followed the 1962 Western Region Stalemate included the Census controversies of 1962 and 1963 and the 1964 Federal Election resulting in the Constitutional impasse. Even the general strike of June 1964 which began as a protest by the workers was almost converted into a political crisis by those bent on seizing power at all cost. *There was thus a continuing crisis of confidence among the accepted political leadership.* An apparent political realignment of political groupings emerged from this series of crises. The main political parties in the country were regrouped under the two giant Alliances—the United Progressive Grand Alliance and the Nigerian National Alliance. The subsequent "broad-based" government of the two Alliances was formed by the late Prime Minister, Alhaji Sir Abubakar Tafawa Balewa, to keep the country together *but unfortunately that government included many personalities who had been discredited by a large section of Nigerian public opinion. The public was equally restless with the widespread corruption and abuse of office by highly placed persons.*

It was in this climate of general disillusionment with the political *ruling class that certain officers in the Nigerian Army sought to use the army, created for the defense of the fatherland and the protection of the citizen, to attain purely political ends.* Widespread violence followed the Western Region Election crisis of 1965 believed by many honest Nigerians to have been rigged on a very large scale. *But the revolt in the West only provided the occasion for some officers in the Nigerian Army to use the army to attain political ends.*

There had been a similar attempt during the 1964 Federal Election constitutional crisis which was foiled by the prompt intervention of army officers who did not believe in the military seizure of political power from civilians. On that and subsequent occasions, the army officers plotting to seize power were assisted by some civilians, including politicians. It is to the credit of the former civilian Federal Government that in the interest of peace, no army officer or civilian was subsequently punished for the planned military coup of December, 1964.

The tragedy in using the army to resolve purely political questions is that a military coup usually brings in its trail tragic episodes in which violence and cold-blooded murder is the order of the day. The experience in Nigeria since January 15 has followed this familiar historical pattern which all men of goodwill are now trying to arrest. *It is unfortunate that the pattern of killings both on January 15 and July 29 followed mainly tribal lines.* This has, therefore, tended to heighten tribal distrust particularly as between the Ibos and Northerners in the army.

Some observers, particularly foreign commentators, have seen in this unfortunate pattern a kind of genocidal warfare. Just after the January 15 military uprising, these observers were trying to convince the whole world that there was an Ibo masterplan to wipe out the Northern ruling class. After the July 29 army mutiny, these people now say that there is a Northern plan to kill all the Ibos. *The Supreme Military Council has decided on measures which will convince every Nigerian wherever he may be in the Federation, that the armed forces of the Federation will henceforth protect him irrespective of his tribe or origin.*

The Event of 15th January, 1966

As far back as December, 1964 a small group of Army Officers mainly from the Ibo ethnic group of Eastern Region dissatisfied with political development within the Federation began to plot, in collaboration with some civilians, the overthrow of what was then the Government of the Federation of Nigeria and the eventual assumption of power in the country.

The chief plotters were Major C. K. Nzeogwu, Major E. Ifeajuna,

Major D. Okafor and Captain E. N. Nwobosi. Others connected with the plot were Captain Oji, Major C. I. Anuforo, Major I. H. Chukuka, Major Ademoyega, Captain Gbulie, 2/Lt. N. S. Wokocha, Lt. B. O. O. Oyewole, Major T. Onwuatuegwu, 2/Lt. Azubuogo, 2/Lt. Ojukwu.

The 1964 Plan was designed to take place at Enugu during the annual shooting competition of the Army which is normally attended by all senior officers of the Army. *The plan leaked, most senior officers kept away and the plan was temporarily abandoned.*

The 1965 Plan by the same officers which was executed on 15th January, 1966, was hatched out finally in Abeokuta during the All Arms Battle Group Course there. *That course was originally planned to be held in Kaduna in Northern Region. But suddenly the Officer Commanding the Nigerian Army, the late Major-General Aguiyi-Ironsi, changed the venue and ordered that the course should be held in Abeokuta. All the officers involved in the plot to overthrow the Government were given assignments to do at the course.*

Exercise *Damissa*

There are five Battalions in the Nigerian Army. Prior to the Abeokuta course, three of these were commanded by Ibo officers. One of the two not commanded by Ibo officers was the one at Enugu commanded by the late Lt.-Col. Adekunle Fajuyi (a Yoruba officer). *To pave the way for an almost all-Ibo command, Major-General Aguiyi-Ironsi sent Fajuyi to conduct the Abeokuta course. So on the eve of the coup, four of the five Battalions of the Army were under the command of Ibo officers.* This was done to facilitate the commands in case members of the army revolted against the coup.

The coup was termed among the plotters "Exercise Damissa" which translated from its Hausa language means "Exercise Tiger."

Although the original plan stipulated that the action intended by the plotters should take place simultaneously in all the Regional capitals (Kaduna, Ibadan, Enugu, Benin) and Lagos, all available information indicates that there was in fact no intention to carry out the plan in Benin and Enugu. In Benin, an Ibo man of Mid-West origin was Premier and head of the Regional Government while in Enugu another Ibo man was Premier and head of East Regional Government.

[The coup was executed and accepted.]

Fate of Plotters

For a period of about seven months thereafter, every Nigerian hoped that the country would go on to achieve greater progress in development generally.

But there was the vexed question of the fate of the plotters of the January 15 incident. Some Nigerians thought of them as heroes in leading the overthrow of the much hated politicians, but their killing of innocent army officers, mainly from Regions other than their own, inflicted a major wound on the Nigerian Army famous for its disci-

pline. It is unfortunate that a decision one way or the other was not promptly taken in this regard. When it was learnt in some quarters of the army that those directly involved, although detained in various prison establishments of the country, were being paid their regular salaries plus other allowances, the hitherto smothered feeling that those concerned should have been brought to book according to military tradition apparently began to show expression in the impatience of a section of the army. **The already charged situation reached an explosive point** when a very strong rumour started circulating that there was a further plot to annihilate army officers and civilians from the same Region as most of those who had been killed in January. This was the immediate cause of the events of July 29.[11]

As often is the case in difficult moments, an attempt to examine the declared position of one's government is seen in some quarters as an expression of disloyalty and lack of patriotism at the most or a display of lukewarm support at the least. Whatever may be the feelings of those who read this, I do not think it is necessary for them to question my loyalty. I am a Nigerian citizen. I too have come to the painful decision that, irrespective of what the past may have been, there is no sufficient reason for one to wish for or support the demise of that political unit to which I have decided to give my primal loyalty, *viz* the Sovereign Republic of Nigeria.

But having said this, it is obvious that the facts which compelled me to my conclusion that Nigeria must exist as established in 1960, are not necessarily the facts which led others to the same conclusion. I agree with the Nigerian government that whatever political conflicts may have originated within the framework of the 1960 Federation ought to be solved within a political arena that is commensurate with that framework. But I also believe that the facts of the past are capable of being put together in diverse ways and could lend themselves to distinct, and sometimes contradictory, interpretations. Further, in terms of the spirit of this chapter, which is directed at an attempt to delineate an attitude toward political events, it is a necessary duty to inspect the pronouncements of the spokesmen of the Nigerian government if only to understand the fit between their declared purpose and the type of political temperament reflected in their pronouncements.

This being the case, one thing must strike the careful reader of the extensive quotation from *Nigeria 1966:* the events are arranged in a form that purports to function as an historical explanation.

Yet, apart from the very broad and unrevealing order of chronology, there is no apparent logical connection between the facts reported. There are no arguments, no expressed basic premises, no rules of inference by which the logical entailment of each premise could be checked; in short, unless one already shares the point of view of the Nigerian government and already holds the values and perspectives of the spokesmen of the Nigerian government, unless one already has the same psychological experiences and reactions as the authors, not only would it not be apparent why certain facts were selected, why they were arranged the way they were arranged, but it would also not be clear in what sense the facts are used. In other words, there could be no way of knowing why certain events among the chaos of political actions originated by the civilian politicians and the army had become so salient and paradigmatic. What appears at first glance to be an analytical history of the events of 1966 is in fact only an official history, and hence the key to its understanding could be furnished, not by the statements and propositions contained in the account, but by a political set of values which make the psychological meaning of the official history public.

For instance, we are told that the political system as inherited and operated by the civilians had, by 1966, been rendered illegitimate by the systematic corruption of the political elites, that everywhere there was mass disillusionment and alienation, and that the political regime was bankrupt. We are told that "It was in this climate of general disillusionment with the political ruling class that certain officers in the Nigerian Army sought to use the army, created for the defence of the fatherland and the protection of the citizen, to attain purely political ends."

What is one to make of this ambiguous conclusion? If the political elites were truly unpopular and resented, if their continued political dominance was anathema, one would expect that a people, alienated and disaffected from the rulers that they have selected and honored, had the reserved right to remove these leaders who in the popular opinion had by their unabashed corruption "rebelled" against their constituency. The problem would be whether or not there were constitutional means for effecting this desired political action. If the only constitutional means of turning politicians out of office was the electoral system and if the political class had demonstrated their willingness not to use it legitimately but to corrupt its application, then the alternatives seem to be either the perpetuation of a situation of political malaise and civil unrest, or the application of some extralegal means for removing the detested politicians.

What would be important for those who wished the fatherland well would be a search for a political agent in whom all could trust, and who, motivated by a public spirit, could be trusted to perform a painful but necessary political operation and restore health to a troubled and diseased polity. Thus, if the army were the only political agent capable of doing this, its intervention in politics would still be in defense of the fatherland. The question then would not be whether or not the army should perform an additional and novel task which the political exigencies of the time had thrust upon it, but whether or not the leadership within the army was motivated by this public consciousness. For the army may have the capabilities of intervening in politics since it enjoys a monopoly over the resources of violence. But the important thing in terms of its political involvements would be whether it was capable of acting as the protector of the state, that is, of intervening to protect the framework of politics, without itself becoming one of the partisans in the conflict, or itself becoming the very body within which the divisive political disputes were to be resolved.

Thus when the Nigerian government mentions that some of the sectors of the army interested in intervention were also interested in political ends, it could be saying three things: (1) that the army should have been used to restore faith in the system. It should have intervened to turn out the political rogues as Christ turned out the avaricious money lenders defiling His Father's temple; (2) that the army should have intervened in politics, but not as partisans of the politicians who had provided the *raison d'être* for that intervention, the implication of such a statement being that somehow the military's intervention in politics had produced a situation in which some members of the army were now in collusion with the politicians whom they were supposed to chastise; (3) that irrespective of the nature of the political conflicts, there has always been a sector of the army interested in not just being soldiers, but also inflicted with the mania to be politicians.

There is no way of knowing which of these three alternatives is logically connected with the political history that preceded it. There appear to be two things happening, political conflicts within the civilian regime and political conflicts within the army. The reason for connecting them is not expressed. The basis for the political crisis among the politicians is given, but the basis for the political conflict among the army elite in terms of their response to the corrupt political situation is not given. Or, rather, the reason given for the apparent conflict in the army is differences in attitude towards *a theoretical problem,* that of whether or not the military under any circumstances should intervene in politics. But when we couple this concern with a theoretical constitutionalism of military morality with the total unrest, complete disintegration of law and order in the former Western Region, carnage in the streets of Lagos, and the emergence of organized political banditry, for the army to have remained in the barracks or merely to have performed police functions and executed orders issued by a group that they themselves regarded as the sole perpetrators of the political crimes that had put the country into the throes of this crisis, would have been like Nero—they would have been fiddling on the theoretical problem while Nigeria burned. The "Nigerian Army created for the defence of the fatherland and the protection of the citizen" would have been politically irrelevant and socially redundant.

The conclusion one draws is that there could have been no serious disagreement that some type of extralegal intervention was needed (especially if what was legal was what the corrupt politicians defined as legal), since the spirit of the law was already dangerously contaminated. There could have been no serious disagreement about what agency should act, knowing that the alternatives were the labor unions, the civil bureaucracies, the police, or the armed forces. One can only conclude that the Nigerian Armed Forces, even though they were the logical agents to act *pro patria,* in themselves did not possess, apart from the mere monopoly of the instruments of coercion, the organizational form or the organizational authority to intervene as an integral agency. They had neither an institutionalized organizational culture into which membership had been socialized, nor the organizational power to control the behavior of members when involved in a new task, a political rather than a purely military task.

In fact the army, still a fragile organization rather than an established institution, was caught in the same difficult situation which had rendered the political corruption of the inherited institutions possible. For as soon as the army, a collage of individuals recruited from the various social groups of the Nigerian society and reflecting the structural strains in the society, was involved in a situation in which, in order to survive it had to act nationally, it found itself victimized by the systemic propensity of all-Nigerian politics to be converted into sectional politics. The army needed a national political consciousness to provide each of its sectors with a common political vocabulary and a sense of what were significant stimuli and what responses were appropriate to them. But what it had was a professional ethics appropriate to routinized police functions within a colonial regime. Thus, at the time in which it was required to act, it needed to have inculcated its members with a national professionalism. The army to survive then, to restore health to the Nigerian polity, required the complementary ideologies of nationalism and professionalism. Army leadership would be secure to the extent that the national ideology was internalized and made operative within the army. This would prevent sections of the army from being mobilized on parochial and tribal grounds. The professional ethics would have ensured the integrity of the military organization, the stability of its role structure, and the predictability of adherence to the line of command, without the authority of the instructions being questioned because of the ethnic definition of the incumbent of office.

These structural problems of the army, rather than *ad hominem* explanations of the difficulties within the army, ought then to be the context within which specific political men in the army should have been discussed. Such considerations underlay the concerns expressed by some spokesmen of the Nigerian government at the early stage of the civil disturbances. The military intervention was therefore welcomed as legitimate and no one argued in the early phase of the crisis that the military had the right to intervene; in fact, such was the spirit of enthusiasm engendered by the military government that Chief Adebo, the Nigerian Chief Representative to the United Nations and one of the country's most trusted bureaucrats, could argue in Paris with a representative of the World Bank that the army's intervention had been Nigeria's saving grace. The military government had not only allayed fears that Nigeria would collapse under the burden of controlling and containing inflammable rivalries between parties, but it was also maintaining law and order in the face of diffused attacks on all types of authority, as well as containing

the tensions within the army itself—between the leaders of the coup and their admirers on the one hand and those rather indifferent soldiers who took over power on the other. The Northern Region has not erupted, though on the face of it, it does not stand to gain by the events of January 15. The new regime has maintained an impressive momentum allowing no anticlimax or disillusionment to spoil its popularity. *One obvious danger now is that it still may not be able to convince the North that it is a genuinely national regime.*

Internal strife in the army seemed a real possibility in the regime's first week. Shots were heard inside the barracks. There was an attempt on General Ironsi's life and the leaders of the coup were either imprisoned or went into hiding. There was also bitterness about the seemingly needless death of popular senior officers, especially of Brigadier Maimalari and Colonels Pan and Mohammed (all Northerners) and Brigadier Ademulegun (a Westerner). General Ironsi seems to have handled this with restraint. To make his regime respectable he had to deal firmly with those coup leaders who had blood on their hands; he seems to have done this without making a witch hunt of it.

The placatory gesture of appointing a Northern Emir's son as military governor was greeted with cheers even in Sokoto, home of the dead regional premier. "Both regimes, the old and the new, came to us from God," commented the Sultan of Sokoto's chief scribe, while the Sultan himself has prayed for the success of the new regime. Sokoto was the spoilt darling of the Sardauna of Sokoto's regime, yet even here his passing was accepted quietly. If there are misgivings about what has happened, the death of the Sardauna has left nobody to express them. In fact the last few weeks have demonstrated what people have long suspected about the North; its divisive tendencies are stronger than the cohesive ones. The "Ibo coup" idea will doubtless lose its force when it is fully understood that even if the coup was an Ibo one (which is by no means proved) this is largely academic because the men who carried it out are not now in power. This is not yet fully realized because of the secrecy that still surrounds the fate of the plotters.[12]

Not only does this quotation bear out the confused situation that actors and observers alike had to make sense out of, it also clearly reveals that, irrespective of what might finally come to be the verdict, it was by no means certain whether or not there was a coherent history merely waiting to be uncovered behind the events of 1966. Thus there seemed to be too much willingness to ignore contradictory statements about the same event, to clamp facts into molds which they barely fit, a too ready reliance on stereotypic judgment and the use of scapegoat explanation in the official history of *Nigeria 1966*. It is not the veracity of the facts identified that is questioned, but rather the arrangement of those facts and the rationale for extracting certain types of interpretations from them.

For a government involved in a context likely to infect it with the same malady that destroyed three generations of political groups (the destruction of the civilian politicians, the decimation and rearrangement of the postcolonial military hierarchy, and the splintering of the Nigerian Army), there did not seem to be a healthy respect for the facts of that situation. There was still a belief that the evils that had befallen us were due to evil men; there was not the realization that not only is the road to hell sometimes paved by good men with good intentions, but, further, that certain political situations, because of the pattern of behavior they tend to induce in order for actors to survive, tend to corrupt men and foil their expectations.

Thus, if we were interested not in having a scapegoat for this occasion, but in producing an historical explanation which would consist of facts that all well-intentioned observers, foreign or indigenous, would accept, we would be interested in finding out just what systemic factors made it impossible for the military to act in concert.

Why, for instance, would a coup which in January 1966 was welcomed as a national salvation, come to be regarded as a sectional coup by July of the same year? Consider Nigerian reactions in January 1966: "Two weeks after the army rose and swept away the civilian establishment in a few hours there is idealism in the air and talk of a 'New Nigeria.' No more corruption, no more tribalism and nepotism. In the place of self-seeking politicians, discipline and self-sacrifice. There seems no lack of the will to work hard." [13] There was hope and optimism in the air. There was not only going to be a new Nigeria, but the new Nigeria was going to be built on a surer foundation than the old Nigeria which had been brought to a final but unmourned demise. Ironsi, in the spirit of the new Nigeria, set a Commission of Inquiry into motion.

The commission's terms of reference were:

To identify those faults in the former constitution of Nigeria which militated against national unity and against the emergence of a strong central government, to ascertain how far the powers of the former Regional Governments fostered regionalism and weakened the central government, to consider the merits and demerits of (a) a unitary form of government, (b) a federal form of government as a system of government best suited to the demands of a developing country like Nigeria—without hampering the emergence of a strong, united democratic Nigeria. The Group is to suggest possible territorial divisions of the country, to examine voting systems, electoral act and revision of voter's register. It is to consider the merits and demerits of (1) one-party system, (2) multi-party system, as a system best suited to Nigeria, and the extent to which party politics fostered tribal consciousness, nepotism and abuse of office; to determine the extent to which professional politics contributed to the deficiencies of the past regime, and the extent to which regionalism and party politics tended to violate traditional chieftaincies and institutions, and to suggest possible safe-guards. The Study Group will be served by two joint-secretaries and assisted by a working party to be set up on a Nigeria-wide basis and will submit its report to the Attorney General of the Federation.[14]

In brief, the crisis not only provided an opportunity to examine the specific reasons why the defunct regime generated the type of crises which it did, but more broadly, it was an opportunity to examine the degree of viability of the inherited political institutions, and whatever new political philosophies or forms of institutions might be adapted within the Nigerian social milieu. At this point the army was still seen as a unit with General Ironsi its legitimate spokesman. Underlying the program of work was the assumption that, although there might be disagreements about the utility of specific programs, there would be no fundamental disagreements about the basic goals of the military regime. More important, there would be no questioning of the legitimacy of the military hierarchy to guard the progress of the state, and there would be no disintegrating attacks on the integrity of the military organization.

To understand why these hopes had not only dissipated in July, but why the country was involved in a deeper crisis which made the January events a holiday in paradise, should be the concern of a government bent on preserving the state *in toto*. We suggest that this understanding is the only guarantee against the propensity to build on a naive foundation of unfounded optimism. One would suggest that the recourse to *ad hominem* explanation by the authors of *Nigeria 1966* suggests rather an uncomfortable fact—there might still be a lack of appreciation of the tremendous difficulties which an elite must confront when attempting to win a war, to carry out a social revolution in terms of creating a new political consciousness upon which a stable unified amicable association of Nigerian citizens may be based, and to carry on institutional development not only to cope with the destruction in materiel and public confidence attending the war, but also to provide the basis for economic development and the equitable distribution of the ensuing social wealth.

For instance, it is my belief that the present crisis is due primarily to the type of political situations that actors find themselves in, and not to the evil of politicians. (I have yet to find a state where politicians are not regarded as corrupt, a state in whose history political corruption has not played a large integrative and positive role.) But in order to understand why this is so, one may try to answer the question of why one perception of the military coup in January 1966 was replaced by a diametrically opposite perception in July.

I am struck by the fact that the political involvement of the military placed it in a situation in which it was likely to be endangered, for the situation had factors in it which could unleash the centrifugal forces within its organization. Perhaps a military government in exactly the same situation as the Ironsi government, and charged with the task of holding and developing that state for whose existence it is now fighting, would be glad to learn from the mistakes of its predecessors. In terms of this pedagogic interest we may attempt an alternative interpretation of the events between January and July 1966, which, without denying the existing facts as to the intentions of actors both past and present, nevertheless places more emphasis on the structural constraints upon actors and the tendency for such constraints to leave only certain options open to actors. These options, when taken, seemed to lead to the escalation of the very conflict which the decision to act had been intended to attenuate.

Assuming the existence of certain political alignments and culture, what exactly were the implications of having the military intervene to rescue the fatherland from its predators? This is why we must know what the coup meant. If the coup meant anything in terms of who would be responsible for directing the ship of state, it was that the country would be under the dual leadership of two bureaucratic systems of organization, the military and the civil service. If it is further realized that the military organization, because of its limited involvement in civil government resulting from its professional expertise and social function, could not be an effective partner in the formulation of policies, it would then be seen that the effective but informal policy-making organization within the government was the civil service. The military did not have to initiate policies, but it could veto them. Thus there could be four sources of conflict within the government: (1) a conflict between the civil service and the military, (2) a conflict between coalitions of groups within the army and within the civil service, (3) a conflict within the civil service with the army playing the role of the arbiter, (4) a conflict within the army with the civil service arbitrating the dispute.

It is possible to indicate that the second alternative seems to be the type of alignment fraught with the possibility of conflict, since it appears that the effective ruling group within the national government was a coalition of top-ranking civil servants (mainly in advisory positions) and the top military rank of the military hierarchy. It is suggested that because of the Southern preponderance within the civil and military bureaucracy, most of the men who occupied such high positions were likely to be, and indeed were, Southern. Also, one could not deny that the composition of the Supreme Military Council and the Federal Executive Council, the two highest executive agencies, was also predominantly Southern.

The Federal Executive Council was composed of: (1) Head of the Federal Military Government and Supreme Commander of the Armed Forces (Southern), (2) Head of the Nigerian Army (Southern), (3) Head of the Nigerian Navy (Southern), (4) Head of the Nigerian Air Force (?), (5) Inspector-General of the Police (Southern), (6) Deputy Inspector-General of Police (Northern).

The Supreme Council was composed of: (1) Head of the Federal Military Government and Supreme Commander of the Armed Forces (Southern), (2) Head of the Nigerian Army (Southern), (3) Head of the Nigerian Navy (Southern), (4) Head of the Nigerian Air Force (?), (5) Military Governor, Northern Nigeria (Northern), (6) Military Governor, Eastern Nigeria (Southern), (7) Military Governor, Western Nigeria (Southern), (8) Military Governor, Midwest Nigeria (Southern).

The instruments of power were clearly in the hands of Southern elements. But this in itself is not a necessary or sufficient cause for the July mutiny. What is more important is not how this preponderance was used but how it was perceived to be used by all the groups interested in the activities of the central government. The question then is how such a preponderance, attributable to the initial headstart which Southerners had made in institutions whose orientations were essentially bureaucratic and national, was used so that it could be construed as furthering particularistic and ethnic interests. This is an important question because merely to say that the government was controlled by Southern elements within the government is not to imply that there necessarily must be a divergence of interests or divergence of interpretations of interests. It is suggested that if the army leadership and the civil bureaucratic leadership were all equally committed to, and were exclusively motivated by, a shared national ideology, the accidental preponderance of members of certain ethnic groups would have had no political significance. What happened?

One way of answering this question would be to ask what happened to the Southern group such that it became differentiated into an Ibo and a non-Ibo group. What happened to lead to the confrontation of the Ibo and the Hausa groups? My feeling is that the immediate source of the disillusionment was specifically political, but that, for the purpose of mobilizing support and true to the political style of the corrupt politician whose demise everyone vociferously celebrated, these specifically political causes were escalated into diffuse primordial ethnic ideologies which, in the absence of effective institutional controls, proved to be catastrophic. Since the effect of the January coup had partly led to the maintenance of the stratification of authority within certain bureaucratic establishments and to a restratification of authority within others, conflicts had been generated and, because of the structural alignment of forces within the bureaucracies, specific political differences within the bureaucracies became transformed into ethnic differences. The coup had resulted in a shift from a Northern to a Southern domination of the federal government.

Also, the abrogation of regional governments, and hence explicitly the abandonment of regional protection for the dominant ethnic groups within each regional civil service organization, would consequently have led to further Southern domination in each region. In quieter times, when it could be hoped that there would be love and amity between the groups involved, it would have taken a lot of persuasion to reassure those whose privileged positions would be jeopardized by the shift of the political center from the North to the South, that a centralized unitary government would give equal protection to all. The basis of such trust in the benevolence of the central government would have been a public or private assurance that political considerations would be operative in the reorganization of the bureaucracies; that is, for the sake of successful accommodation of interests there would be a concomitant agreement to accommodate these conflicting interests by compromise instead of by adhering to the apolitical bureaucratic rule of promotion by merit and expertise.

In other words, the South would have had to agree that it too would accept some amount of sacrifice, instead of insisting on all of its prerogatives, for the sake of national unity. When the nature of the game was civil politics, the North had monopolized power. Similarly, when the game was bureaucratic politics, the South was monopolizing power. And just as the exclusive Northern domination had been the main structural anomaly in the old regime, in the same way was the exclusive Southern monopoly of administrative power the main structural anomaly in the new regime. The problem, as it had been in the old, was how to reconcile the dictates of political power with bureaucratic meritocracy, how to find an acceptable formula of exchange such that sufficient Northern power could be converted into Southern managerial expertise, and vice versa.

If this line of argument is correct, one could surmise that the operation of the central government did not offer enough political reassurance to all the relevant publics. What it did to break what was at best a fragile national coalition into ethnic factions within the various governmental agencies remains to be empirically determined. It was clear that the policy of immediate unification, the famous Decree No. 34, certainly led elements in the North, who to that date had made almost all the sacrifices in terms of loss of authority, power, and privileges, to believe that they would continue to make all the sacrifices.

Nigeria 1966, the present government's report on the crisis, presented a reasonable picture of the state of affairs in the North. Commenting on the growing uncertainty as to the political future of the North as important Northerners read the events, the report states:

Thus a feeling of resentment and fear was created in the minds of the ordinary people. This was further emphasized by two widely advertised incidents at the Army and Air Force recruiting centres at Zaria and Kaduna where people believed Northerners no longer had a fair chance in the new recruitment into the Army even though the selection was quite open. *The ex-politicians who were unpopular to start with found that people were prepared to listen to them. The Northern Civil Service Union also started to agitate* by writing to the *New Nigerian* newspaper.

This was the state of affairs in the North when the "Unification" Decree was announced on 24th May, 1966. Besides, there are related issues in which are involved (i) University Students of Northern origin in the United Kingdom and at Ibadan, Lagos, Zaria and Kano, (ii) ex-politicians and (iii) civil servants. In about February, 1966 the students in the universities started writing in the newspapers that only Federation and not a unitary form of Government was suitable for Nigeria. This was carried on to the civil servants, especially those in the junior grade.

Meanwhile, in the North the local petty contractors and party functionaries whose livelihood depended solely on political party patronage became active. Most of them, like their counterparts in other Regions, were indebted to either the Northern Marketing Board or the Northern Nigeria Development Corporation. They were the hardest hit by the change of government especially as all those indebted to Marketing Board and the NNDC were made to pay up their arrears. They resorted to whispering "campaign," rumour mongering and incitement, aided and abetted by other factors. *They are the elements most close to the ordinary people and they have utilized that to create a public opinion which is very strong and potentially dangerous against the authorities.*

When the NWOKEDI Commission was appointed, most of the Civil Servants in the Federation, particularly in the North, were apprehensive and convinced that *there was a preconceived plan to "bulldoze" the unification of the Civil Service through*—come what may. On the 24th of May, the "unification decree," a major constitutional and political step which had not been widely discussed was announced, along with the dissolution of political and tribal parties decree. The key words in that announcement are: "The Regions are abolished." In whatever way it was put, it was bound to give offence to those who had already made up their minds against unification. The May 29 disturbances in the North followed.[15]

The key point in this extensive statement is that the proposal of unification threatened the whole gamut of political interests and political groups in the North. It was not so much that centralization could not be the cure of the Nigerian ills, but that it offered no protection to the displaced Northern political elite, a protection which regionalization had offered. It was possible that the North would have endured the loss of her political leaders and of her dominance at the center, if it could have been assured that some version of the Northernization policies would be continued. The January coup had shattered the established power structure in the North, but the crisis was also an opportunity for a new circulation of elites. The North seemed to demand, as the least condition for remaining in the state of Nigeria, the guarantee that it could have the power to protect its political resources from the very real possibility of Southern usurpation.

In fact what the Nigerian government reported expressed by the Northerners in 1966 had already been expressed sixteen years earlier, in an editorial published in *Gaskiya Ta Fi Kwabo* on February 18, 1950. What was expressed was the fear that without established institutional guarantees the vital interests of the North would be jeopardized by the withdrawal of the British:

Southerners will take the places of the Europeans in the North. *What is there to stop them?* They look and see it is thus at the present time. There are Europeans but, undoubtedly, it is the Southerner who has the power in the North. They have control of the railway stations; of the Post Offices; of Government Hospitals; of the canteens; the majority employed in the Kaduna Secretariat and in the Public Works Department are all Southerners; in all the different departments of Government it is the Southerner who has the power. . . .[16]

Loss of power, lack of power, the prospect of a continuous loss and lack of power constituted the sum total of the political expectations of the displaced and displaceable Northern political and bureaucratic elites. Within this context all that was needed was a pretext, a reasonable facsimile of a case not only that the sole benefactors of the recent coup were Southern, but further that this had been the plan all along. Given such a potential source of emotional sympathy, all that was needed was for a group to supply a public reason which linked the multitude of private dissatisfactions, and to identify a palpable agency as the cause of their private social misfortunes, and all hell could break loose.

If these reasons were sufficient explanation for the May 29 disturbances, as *Nigeria 1966* suggests, a position which I lean towards, the disturbances demonstrated to the disgruntled Northern groups that the federal government was not in a position to institutionalize Decree No. 34. For having broken the law and not felt the heavy hand of the government as a reprisal, no clearer demonstration of a loss of authority and legitimacy could be furnished. One implication of this for the federal government would have been for it to reduce its activities to a level commensurate with the level of power and authority it could effectively control. This would have meant the recognition that the army could not solve the Northern problem through the Decree, and that the army could not pacify and reduce the North if it came to a confrontation. For there would have been no quicker way to instigate a civil resistance in the North than for the federal government to have sent a contingent of its army, not only to restore order, but to punish the culprits as well. There would have been a spectacle of predominantly Northern soldiers led by predominantly Southern officers, in a situation where the popular Northern officers had been killed in the coup led by the army, marching against a Northern population. This required a professional and national army, an army different from that at the command of Ironsi's government.

What the foregoing would have entailed for the Ironsi government, or for any other government with the same function, would have been either the abandonment of political centralization or the establishment of political guarantees to protect the interests of the Northern "organizational dispossessed." The government, for obvious political reasons, could do neither. It could not turn its back on the national program of the January coup without facing the threat of a coup from the junior officers. It could not initiate a program of guarantees without confronting the resentment of Southern civil servants who could still remember the similar and distasteful policies of the Balewa regime. And furthermore, it seemed unable to prevent the alienation and factionalization created by its policies.

In short, the government could not purge or impose a cohesion over the various forces which it had to control in order to enjoy national authority and legitimacy. Once the military and civil institutions were split by these conflicts of interest, it was possible for them to be "contaminated" by the latent and repressed conflicts existing within the greater social environment. The intrusion of ethnic and particularistic values into the various bureaucratic organizations could be expected to generate greater political conflict, since these organizations, being hierarchical and totalistic, brought the antagonists into direct confrontation. It is suggested that the bureaucratic organization, such as the army or the civil service, lacking the space required for political bargaining and political insulation of authority, must either adapt the relationship between its instrumental and expressive values to the environmental pressure (that is, become more ethnic, more tribal, more infected with parochial divisiveness) or face the destruction of its organizational life.

Although this is a choice which most organizations have to face, this choice is most pressing for a highly structured and hierarchical organization like the army, for the role structure calls for specific behavior and requires greater authority and power to restrict the actors to the performance of new tasks in situations of role conflicts. And because a lot of coercion is required to induce conformity to role behavior in such contexts, especially where there has not been a long period of time for these institutions to develop adequate socializing and incentive mechanisms, authority roles are, of necessity, conspicuous. The relationship between the superordinate and subordinate role incumbents must be specific. Given the coercive basis upon which this relationship is erected, assuming that we are dealing with a fragile organization without an established institutional culture and in a situation in which its members find their organizational role in conflict with their social roles, legitimacy must rest upon the acceptance by both the top and bottom ranks of the leadership hierarchy of a common set of instrumental values. Since an organization held together by instrumental values lacks the cohesion of an organization having a cementing base of expressive values, conflict over these instrumental values makes it possible for the whole organization to fall into disrepute, since cohesion can be achieved only by a reliance on successive injections of coercion to keep the organization functioning.

These considerations allow me to suggest that the Nigerian army, once a national organization, was unable to adapt itself to the environment which its intervention in politics created. The consequence of this maladjustment was the rapid deterioration of the faith of its rank and file in the nationalistic values upon which its role structures were based. Once the legitimacy of the top leadership in the army became questionable, the values of ethnicity became all the more relevant as a basis of group differentiation, especially as the organizational matrix increased rather than decreased the opportunities for confrontation. In other words, neither the Hausa lieutenant dealing with the Ibo captain, nor the Hausa sergeant in contact with an Ibo lieutenant, saw the captain or lieutenant who happened to be Ibo; rather, they saw the Ibo who happened to be a captain or lieutenant. Given this decay of organization and remembering the costs of the January coup and the group which paid most for it, it is possible to see why the second coup was anti-Ibo.[17]

The important point flowing out of this analysis so far is that we seem to have isolated a syndrome of relationships which allow for specific political issues to be transformed into ethnic issues, irrespective of the political group and the differences in their political interests or professional styles. And for a government interested in controlling its future, the understanding of this structure of constraints seems critical, for the present situation is bound to throw up isomorphic sets of issues, only this time the East would replace the North in the equation. It therefore must be of primal concern whether or not the form of leadership, the residue of trust, and an articulated national program would be present to render possible the amalgamation of the "organizational dispossessed" by incumbents of the integrating institutions in a manner which would render politically irrelevant the chance coincidence of the political and ethnic divisions.

We shall return to a concluding statement on the problem of Nigerian political reconstruction. So far we have been concerned with the types of considerations which go into providing a reliable historical background to the contemporary political crisis, and we shall now turn to considering the perspective of a foreign philosopher, an Africanist, James O'Connell, who has written on the problems of political integration, the Nigerian crisis being his illustrative case study.

A Foreign Philosopher: James O'Connell

"POLITICAL INTEGRATION: THE NIGERIAN CASE"
In considering the format of this section, I had three alternatives: (1) I could review the general theoretical and methodological assumptions of Africanists in an effort to indicate the type of perspectives they were likely to bring to bear upon the Nigerian situation; (2) I could limit myself to authors on Nigerian themes and cull regnant assumptions, theoretical and methodological, and from these deduce the probable model those authors would have applied for the understanding of the crisis; (3) I could do what I decided to do, select an Africanist dealing immediately with the Nigerian crisis.

James O'Connell is one of the most sophisticated analysts of African politics. He has consciously braved the usual pitfalls of most foreign observers; there is virtually no recourse to stereotypes or clichés. He attempts to adapt social science theory to the facts, rather than compel the facts to fit into imported theoretical molds. In fact, he demonstrates a sympathy for the subject of his analysis, a sensitivity that enables him to recognize persistent structural patterns where a coarser approach would have led to loss of critical insights. I have therefore not been motivated by an animus against foreign observers. My concern is to understand where the limits are for a position of external observation, and to understand what type of knowledge, both from the viewpoint of science and from the viewpoint of concerned actors, can issue out of such perspectives.

It is obvious from his writing that James O'Connell intends to speak to two constituencies, the social science constituency of which he is a voting member and the Nigerian constituency, since what he says concerning the present situation stems from the conclusion of his essay, which functions both as a theoretical lesson and as a possible basis for policy prescription. He begins with a definition of political integration:

Political integration which involves collective and interrelated actions to promote certain mutual interests, usually ranging over matters of welfare, order, and defense, takes place on several levels. This chapter is concerned with political integration on the level of the Nigerian State. Integration is a relative concept and there are degrees of integration on the level of the state. At the very least the members of the social group comprising the state must be willing to hold together to promote mutual interests and not to wish to break away to do this within another state or in separate states.[18]

In the context of the chosen case study, Nigeria already presents a case where some actors have chosen to opt out of the state. Is this therefore a case of disintegration, or of integration? If the definition serves any useful function, it should serve to identify not only which aspect of the phenomenal world James O'Connell wants us to focus on, but also the meaning of that aspect that has been given a privileged status. Finally, once the meaning of the definition is known, one wants to see how it facilitates the understanding of a social reality which otherwise would remain chaotic. The definition of integration presented here seems to cover all types of social actions generally and all political actions specifically. For all political actions involve collective and interrelated actions, and they may promote interests in such matters as welfare, order, and defense. And certainly politics takes place on all levels. This being the case, we are given a theoretical perspective which purports to deal with political integration and a definition which points at a subclass of social actions, politics; no logical connection exists between politics and political integration unless we specify just what problems of social actions involve certain consequences for a given political unit which necessitate our identifying the political implications of social action in terms of some category labelled "integration."

On the whole, O'Connell's article has not contributed much to the store of knowledge which social scientists have about the problems of integration and disintegration at the state level. He has applied intuitive judgments as to what factors should be included within the essay on political integration. And I can only surmise that, if Hazlewood accepted this as a case advancing the theoretical knowledge on integration and disintegration, he also was applying private intuition in making that decision. It is true that, if in social science there are no public definitions of what constitutes integration or disintegration, but rather there is the feeling that both constitute a problem, an empirical case can be made for wanting to study phenomena of integration or disintegration if only because of the type of political consequences attending the problems. Yet we would then have a community of social scientists, each using the same words and meaning different things by them, each reading case studies and finding something of relevance, the criteria of significance being private.

To say that O'Connell has not contributed much to the theoretical fund of knowledge on political integration in political science does not mean that he cannot say anything of significance to the actors in Nigeria. As a matter of fact, his essay indicates that he had a vivid appreciation of some of the problems of social disorganization confronting the Nigerian political society. For instance, he recognized the repeatable pattern of the process of politics whereby social competition in the absence of a national electorate resulted in the mobilization of the voting constituency according to ethnic considerations—a pattern which some observers have erroneously labelled "tribalism," but which he correctly styled as competitive modernization.[19] From the identification of this pattern of politics he could predict that, if actors chose to carry out a program of political centralization and, still lacking a national ideology, had no resources other than those now available, or even if a certain group drawn from only one or two ethnic groups had a national ideology which involved loss of power and authority of other relevant publics drawn from other ethnic groups, then such an attempt was bound to lead to an appeal to ethnicity and hence a corruption of those national programs. This is so because the only commonly accepted criteria with which to judge the motivations of political actors would be the notion that individual political loyalty could not be counted upon to extend much beyond his primary group, which in nine cases out of ten is coterminous with the ethnic group.

Moreover, he could have predicted from his description of the basis of political affiliation that structurally no Nigerian political party could have been expected to function as a mobilizational party or as an organizational weapon. Indeed, the parties were a conglomerate of individuals capable of winning the support of their constituencies, even though each constituency had issues peculiar to it. And, in fact, it is in this respect that political science could have been of service to African actors. Although it could not serve as a theory of action for all political systems, it could nevertheless provide a matrix for understanding the theoretical implications of certain types of political desires, where it is possible to identify the content of action and the issues of conflicts.

Knowledge issuing from such an approach of external observation could be of use to political actors, although the utility of such knowledge stems from a clear delineation of the situation in which actors find themselves, a definition of the issues of interests, and a specification of the type of problems emerging from action performed within the defined situation. Such a mode of political analysis belongs to a long and honorable tradition of political science and political philosophy. The history of political thought furnishes many paradigmatic examples. Starting with contemporary comparative political science it is possible to select certain political problems—it may be a problem of social mobilization (*à la* Karl Deutsch), a problem of political institutionalization (*à la* Samuel Huntington), problems of transforming a political organization into a political institution (*à la* Philip Selznick), the problem of conducting a social and political revolution through the agency of a political party (*à la* Merle Fainsod or Franz Schurmann), the problem of the acquisition of political power (*à la* Michels or Fred Riggs). One could then, on the assumption that a given political elite are concerned with similar problems, examine what their available resources are, the pattern of political situations, and the nature of the constraints under which they must operate, and from these factors calculate what types of normative, structural, motivational, or behavioral changes have to occur for there to be any hope of effective movement towards such a goal.

Indeed, were political scientists attempting to be theoretically relevant to actors in the type of political situation which we have described as emergent and prismatic, there is a paradigmatic model that could be profitably copied. They could follow in the footsteps of that imaginative Florentine, Niccolo Machiavelli. For he too was dealing with a situation which was emergent and prismatic. He was addressing a political group, the *condottieri,* a group of political entrepreneurs who were primarily interested in advancing their private political ambitions, a group of men who were not restrained by tradition, patriotism, or the fear of God. He was attempting to provide a political education for these men, to teach them that prudence and wisdom could pay politically.

A theorist attempting to teach such an unruly group could only hope to arrest their attention by demonstrating that he had a political knowledge which could prevent an actor desirous of quick political gains from committing disastrous political mistakes at the least, and at the most providing himself a safe institutional protection. Such a theorist had to have at his fingertips a catalogue of types of political actions, knowledge of their possible consequences depending on the effect of such factors as the personality of the actor and historical accidents. Moreover, the theorist had to be sensitive to the rules of action, both in situations in which a public morality is operative and in situations where political corruption is the norm.

Above all, he must realize that the survival of actors is his primary concern, for no actor would listen to a political theorist who counsels him to commit what is tantamount to suicide. In other words, the theorist must be capable of not confusing his private preference with existing situations; he must be able to teach the actor to be a lion or a fox while teaching the actor how to move to situations in which all his rivals can act as men. This requires the theorist to be thoroughly familiar with the history of political actors in all possible situations from which relevant political lessons can be drawn. Hence, not only must he be knowledgeable about comparative politics, political sociology, and history, but he must also be thoroughly familiar with the current political history of actors. We must expect him to know the actors better than they know themselves (especially when we realize that actors tend to rely more on ideology than on philosophy, more on action than on reflection).

If we measure Africanists against the model of a neo-Machiavellian theorist, we find that they operate under different rules. They are concerned with values which have not been supplied to them by the actors they counsel. They worry about whether or not there can be democracy in Africa; whether or not a one-party system is a totalitarian party; whether or not a political party is mobilizational or reconciliational. They wonder whether charisma can be transferred, whether these is a West African political party, whether machine politics is more effective than a Maoist political party. They seem to assume that the actors are naughty pupils that must be taught their lessons and their etiquette. Solemn head shakes and pedagogic "I told you so's" are sanctimoniously issued. There is no appreciation of the responsibility of actors and of the fact that political, and often biological, survival are at stake. There is no knowledge of the political psychology of their clientele; and there is certainly no indication that they are aware of certain types of recurrent problems which motivate actors to cope with foxes and lions that represent their perception of their opponents. Not having been schooled in political history, and certainly having forgotten their history of political theory, and regarding contemporary comparative analysis as a source of political labels rather than a source of theories to be made operational, and having a disdain for philosophy and elementary principles of logic, they lack the empathy and imagination required to develop the political wisdom of a Machiavelli.

And since Africanists on non-African "experts" on Africa, like their colleagues in the social sciences, are unwilling to examine the Communist societies which are coping with the problem of altering the pattern of political constraints that engender corruption and political prismatism, they are unable to speak to the realities confronting political actors. They are too sanctimonious and conceited to be neo-Machiavellians, too much ideologues and marshmallow liberals to countenance the logic of examining what cost in human freedom is necessary to use the state organizations as the agent of social revolution. And they certainly are not aware of the political model which the ancient Israelites afford. If one were to be a victim of the naive scholarship which has made the name and approach of Machiavelli anathema, if one for political reasons did not dare offer as models Mao Tse-Tung, Lenin, Stalin, or Castro, and if one were unwilling to dig into one's history to find out just how his society solved the crises of legitimacy, nation-building, centralization of power and authority, economic development and distribution, and participation for fear of discovering that all along their history had stood in dire need of a theodicy, one might at least have no objection to using the Holy Bible as a source of isolating an ideal-typical case of the problem of social ontogenesis.

NIGERIA AND THE BOOK OF EXODUS—MOSES AND POLITICAL MOBILIZATION

The Book of Exodus furnishes this ideal type. It has provided theorists in the past with the example of Moses as the Founder. (It inspired, to name only a few, Hegel, Marx, Rousseau, and Weber, all great thinkers whom social scientists dare not disavow.) Exodus ought to be inspirational to those presently concerned with the problems of social ontogenesis.

In the plight of the Jews in Egypt we find a group that had become politically demoralized, a population of serfs, a population lacking in political hope and enslaved to a present that they were powerless to change. Like the American Blacks or the deracinated colonials excellently portrayed by Fanon, they had turned their hatred of their oppressors upon themselves. Unable to strike down their oppressors, they themselves became the only safe outlets for their hostility. They served a God who seemed unwilling to come to the rescue of His people. There was therefore no basis for concerted political action. They lacked a political consciousness, since their misery only filled them with anguish, and were compelled to turn their attention from a concern with the public and political to a concern with the private and personal.

Then Moses appeared. He was the paradigm of the charismatic leader. Born of Jewish parents, he had received his political education at Pharaoh's court. Unlike the people he was to lead, he had had a privileged education, an insider's knowledge of the Egyptian system. To translate the foregoing into a language suitable to our concerns, he had an expert knowledge of the idealized operations of the Egyptian political system. Like most naive members of the ruling elite, he had no knowledge of the sufferings undergone by the poor upon whose backs the ship of state was lodged. And he certainly had no notion of his own true history since he identified with the Egyptian-ruling elite. He might have been naive but he had a spontaneous way of responding to injustice, of empathizing with the victim, no matter what class the victim might come from. Thus, we see a second characteristic of Moses, a sensitivity to human suffering and an identification with the plight of the benighted.

He would have continued as the naive good-hearted Moses, unaware of the oppressive conditions surrounding him, had he not been an eyewitness to the maltreatment of a Jew by an Egyptian guardsman. It was his response to the oppression, *his slaying* of the Egyptian guard, which separated him from the Egyptian system. By his action he renounced his part in the continued oppression of the Jews, and by the act through which he achieved a political identity, he had isolated himself from both the Egyptians and the Jews. When Moses acted, it was without calculation, but with reference to some private ethics which could not abide oppression. He had acted *morally,* although without realizing the full consequences of his action.

He now offered himself as a leader of the oppressed Jews. But the Jews asked what his credentials were. It was not sufficient that he had acted heroically. It was not sufficient that he had rebelled against the almighty monarch by slaying Pharaoh's servant. Those who would see the charisma of the African political leaders stemming from similar heroic deeds performed during the national liberation movements can see that heroic deeds may constitute claims towards expectations of leadership. But heroic deeds do not necessarily imply the possession of charisma, for the audience beholding these deeds may or may not interpret them as an external observer may be prone to do. Moses's presumption was questioned; he had no traditional right to expect to be granted authority, in the very same way as a Mosaic leader coming from one particular ethnic group or class in Africa may be denied authority because he lacks such traditional claim to authority within his group and among the other groups over which he claims leadership. Moses had to create the basis for his leadership. He had to create the basis for his authority. In his enforced and temporary seclusion from Egypt and his people (a process which we can take as symbolizing a retirement from public action for some length of time), he developed his political character and consciousness. He sought, and found, a divine guidance. In other words, he had to convince himself that his desires for public service did not originate from private and selfish motivations, but from a vocation which he was powerless to refuse.

Moses became God's spokesman. His authority to speak came from God, not from the people he had been *chosen* to lead. He was then commissioned to go before his people, with the assistance of an eloquent brother, Aaron, an interpreter and intermediary between Moses and the people. Moses confronted his people and Pharaoh, and in the confrontation he provided a political education for both. He proved who was the more powerful of the two, Pharaoh or Jahweh; in other words, he showed his people whom to fear, and in so doing freed the Jews from the paralyzing fear which had made it impossible for them to rebel against their oppressors. In the context of power, Moses had to compete against Pharaoh's magicians—the possessors and monopolists of political knowledge in Pharaoh's court. He had to convince Pharaoh that the latter's magicians were incapable of matching God's power, and that he, Moses, had a knowledge which was more relevant to survival in the world.

This process implies that one of the ways of detaching people from old loyalties, thus rendering them available for a shift in loyalty, is to destroy their faith in the traditional gods and the traditional beliefs about what is practical knowledge. It further implies that one accomplishes this, not by decrying tribalism, for instance, but by creating a situation in which reliance upon the traditional idols is shown to be based on false foundations, false in the sense that in the situations which matter most one cannot count on the protection of these idols. One has to accompany this negative criticism, demonstrated by the verification of public predictions, by offering an alternative god whose protective power is demonstrated in the situations in which the traditional gods were bound to fail. Moses had to know very intimately not only the powers of his antagonists, but the limits of his own powers as well. He had to be able to define situations in ways which would render his action a political education to his audience. He had to be able to supply his audience with the same political grammar and the same semantic structure with which to identify the signification of his political action. In elegant contemporary parlance we would call this "political mobilization."

Having mobilized his people, having raised the price for the continual retention of the Jews so high that it was unprofitable for Pharaoh to keep them any longer, he now had a people to lead and a place to which to lead them. But note that in this process

Pharaoh did not liberate the Jews out of love for the Jews; he relinquished political control over the Jews only when their political leaders made it too inconvenient for the monarch to continue his domination. Note also that Pharaoh attempted to recapture political control. In those days he sent his army; in these days the modern Pharaoh works less directly, and sometimes his presence is revealed by cries of "neocolonialism."

Furthermore, the achievement of political independence did not mean for the Jews the achievement of social integration or nation-building. They may, as a group, have been defined as non-Egyptians. It would have made no difference if Pharaoh had given them, or they had given themselves a constitution, a common flag, an embassy in his capital. These would not have made the Jewish people a community or a viable political state. Their cohesiveness as a people had still to be fashioned in the desert. They had to achieve complete social isolation from outside interference. They had to be free to make their own mistakes. They had a curtain of sand around them, and for forty years (symbolizing the period of a generation, the birth of a people free of the heritage of subjugation) they underwent the travails of social development.

Read Exodus and find out how difficult this process is. Read about the continuous rebellion from God and Moses; read about the intertribal conflicts; see the story of Nigeria foretold thousands of years before. See a people liberated from their past, having no clear picture of the future, undergoing existential sufferings and deprivations, and lacking faith in their leadership revert to political categories which made their universe orderable. See them choose for themselves gods other than their political God who brought them out of bondage. Witness the harsh but necessary reprisals visited upon the rebels by God, the purge of the community by God, where many are killed in order that the rebellion may be stifled.

But see also that Moses stood between his erring people and God's anger. Even in their sin Moses still identified with them. Even in the application of violence to reorganize the society, private interests were not allowed to corrupt public actions. The interest of the community as a whole was always paramount, and the perpetuation of the society was the primal concern. There was an economy of violence—the dose was measured to cure the disease, and the interest in the health of the whole person was the only consideration.

The successful forging of a social consciousness therefore required the presence of certain factors. The context of actions compelled the necessity of having recourse to a set of political means. Moses had to respond to the political exigencies as he confronted them, his only guidance being a faith in his God. This is not a description of a dogmatist. We do not find Moses with a cookbook, a recipe of appropriate political poses; we do not find him a victim of philosophers of action, with a universal panacea for all problems identified by a universal theory of social ontogenesis. Within the context of a political problem, Moses, concerned only with the preservation of the group's unity, consulted with his God. God spoke and Moses, after reflection and conversation with God, vigorously applied the solution that he thought best. Here is an actor in whom are fused a knowledge of history and a knowledge of philosophy. Here is a leader in whom philosophy and history provided the materials which were transformed by a coherent system of political beliefs. These three ingredients served as the framework within which he understood the meaning of social problems, a framework through which he could communicate with others and in accordance with which he evaluated the political advice which he so eagerly sought.

With the problem of social ontogenesis solved, with the formation of a common social identity among the disparate groups constituting the social body that had migrated from Egypt, with the formation of common social categories of thought and the definition of a common social basis for social competition and the resolution of social problems, and finally, with the institutionalization of a common basis for the selection of leadership, the problem of formulation of the political regime, the political authorities and the political community had to be tackled. So far Moses had relied on inherited traditional laws to cope with the disputes that had arisen. Each group had been brought into the political society through the separate identification with Moses and through Moses to God. There was, in our popular lingo, vertical integration through Moses to God. There was no lateral integration between the groups. To coordinate such a group politically it was sufficient for Moses to employ *ad hoc* compromises between the traditional laws and God's messages. Each group could control its own affairs, provided it operated in accordance with the spirit of God. To the extent that this was the case, to the extent that authority was embodied in Moses and the groups were tenuously held together only by his demonstration in each crisis that his explanations were more reasonable because they were more efficacious, there existed a fragile political entity with little resilience to withstand the shocks of political storms. If we look to Africa today, we can find numerous examples that are almost structural isomorphs of this Hebraic political society.

So fragile was the political organization that, in the absence of Moses, a figure whom, in Apter's felicitous phrase, we would today call the "Integrative Integer," the society began to crumble and they asked Aaron to give them a god. With Moses gone, who was to connect them to each other and to the ontological principle that ordered their delicate universe? Thus, to forge a social community out of these tribes, it was necessary for Moses to transfer his "charisma," to create political institutions which would serve as the framework within which the future history of the people would be enacted. The framework would become a political cosmology in which God would be institutionalized through His laws. Moses could then disappear from the scene.

The process of this "transfer of charisma"—or what in the tradition of political philosophy has been treated from Plato onwards as a problem of founding—did not imply merely the enactment of laws, the formulation of a written constitution, or the creation of a political party. Moses could be a founder and a lawgiver, because his leadership was widely recognized. He had helped found the people and shape their social consciousness. He had been the personal representative of the powerful God whose footsteps made the world tremble. He had led the people through their painful odyssey. He had helped them focus on one set of political metaphysics and political ontology. He had a people who had been prepared to receive the laws, a people who had been forbidden recourse to a competitive source of laws.

This constituted the context for the act of bringing God's laws to the people. And the Decalogue, enveloped in an aura of drama, was anchored in notions of the divine. The basis of legitimacy from then on could not be questioned. The basis was not personal wealth, tribal loyalty, or possession of an army, but adherence to God's laws. The Decalogue constituted a public religion, the basis of the political culture. Symbols dramatizing the new political identity were fashioned, and the covenantal ark was placed in the front of the march towards the Promised Land, an ark to be borne at all times, an ark testifying to the residence of God among His people. This political religion constituted not only the definition of the state but also that of citizenship, the definition of the tone of politics and the pattern of predictable expectations. Incidentally, this model of the founding of a political state is evident in most political theorists who have concerned themselves with the problem of founding, from the paradigmatic example in Plato's *Republic* to Machiavelli, Rousseau, Hobbes, and Hannah Arendt.

I have concerned myself at length with the question of Moses because it is the most concise example that I could find in which all the problems confronting Nigerian political actors in particular, and African political actors in general, are exhaustively treated. I do not suggest that this ideal type should serve as a program of action; there are other functions of ideal-typical analysis. What I am saying is that if this model, dealing with a given historical example, helps us to isolate the problems and to generate certain hypotheses, we have a theoretical base from which to start. We have a model to impose on the novel facts of reality, and we can see the degree of fit or lack of it. In the context of the expressed political preferences of actors we have a basis for suggesting possible factors which may aid or impede successful actions. We can suggest what had been the costs to previous actors in the pursuit of certain lines of action and hope that the calculus of interests would make the actors choose prudently and wisely. Social analysis could serve a useful function in helping observers and actors make sense out of the chaos of political events that are enacted daily, but the tenor of my remarks so far should clearly indicate that I have not been too satisfied with the orientation of the social scientists who have addressed themselves to African politics in general, and to Nigerian politics in particular.

I am afraid to task the patience of anyone who has read this far and, as the saying goes, anything that has a beginning must have an end, and this chapter, believe it or not, must end. Hence I must hasten to the conclusion of my piece.

Conclusion: Participant Observation and External Observation

We have been arguing so far that, in situations in which political philosophers attempt to provide not only materials for thought but also a basis upon which political actors can build their ideals, such an intention requires the capacity of philosophers to know and understand the nature of the facts which the actors have enacted. The philosopher must not only know these discrete facts, he must be able to reconstruct from them the structure of the political world which was the context for these acts. His re-creation cannot be merely a flight of fancy; it must be a world which the actors, with some help from the philosopher, can recognize as either identical, or remarkably similar, to that in which he had once operated. It is when the actors see that the ills of their contemporary political world stem from the structure of the political world which they have always taken for granted, but which has now been reconstructed and placed before them, that they can become available for conversion, that they can begin to see the necessity for a change of the frame of reference.

This idealized relationship between philosophy and action, between the theorist and actor, is useful only to the extent that it has revealed the gap between the actual relationship between philosophers and actors and that model presented by Hegel. I have been struck by the fact that the political theorist coming to examine the nature of the world in Africa in general, and Nigeria in particular, has not come equipped with a structure of philosophical themes. His theories have not been an orienting compass. Instead of helping to reconstruct the historical context within which actors have played their parts and identifying the case with reference to certain philosophic considerations, he has not only relied upon the actors to provide the case, but he has also accepted the actors' definition of the situation. In this way he has, either through his personal preference or through certain social dictates, come to see the situation as essentially one of social disorganization.

We have however come to a conclusion, one which is justified by the Nigerian Civil War: that Nigerian actors in the past have been operating on a double standard. The actor in office has seen his public task as the rectifying of a socially disorganized world; the actor out of office has seen the actor in office as using all the instruments of state power as tools for the maintenance of his supremacy, as not holding anything sacrosanct, as believing that every political organization can, and must, if necessary, be used to maintain power. The actor out of office has cherished the hope of subverting the actor in office by employing every trick that works to upset the balance of power. When the actor out of office has replaced the actor in office by means fair or foul, he too wants to rectify a socially disorganized world so that his system of domination may find a stable basis. Such a situation—in which all political instruments and political programs are seen as counters in the game of power, in which all goals are strictly private, and in which there is no common political tradition that enjoys national consensus—we call "prismatic." And when this is complicated by the fact that the only stable basis of social organization is the primary group, the attempt to make an inherited political constitution operative for all these primary groups boils down to the attempt to create out of these many distinct primary groups a corporate group to forge vertical and lateral linkages between groups and between individuals. This is a problem of social ontogenesis, not a problem of social disorganization.

In the context of a prismatic emergent politics with the goals as social ontogenesis or nation-building and state-building, a political analyst must approach the problem in a manner radically different from the theoretical approach now employed. He must assume that at some specific moment in time and space, remote or recent, in the political society presenting him with these problems, individuals and groups, even when forcibly brought together into a corporate group, would continue to remain in that group to the extent that they perceived needs which could be partially or totally satisfied within the context of the corporate group. For the analyst, it is irrelevant at this point how these groups have come to the perception that they must forego their autarchic parochial existence and participate in a larger political society. For he must realize that the political elites, desiring to create a state out of a conglomeration of ethnic groups, must: (1) be able to frame the parochial problems confronting each group in national terms, such that these ethnic groups may see in that national problem the isomorph of their ethnic problems and thus perceive the necessity for a national social organization—this is the problem of nation-building; (2) concern itself with the question of resolving the actual or possible conflicts between these ethnic groups resulting from the process of integrating similar and dissimilar group needs along an acceptable social hierarchy of needs—this constitutes the problem of state-building.

When these two problems are combined with the notion of resource scarcity which initially awakened the distinct ethnic groups to the possibility of help from outside their boundaries, it must then strike the analyst that this combination introduces into the political order the seeds of consensus and of conflict. The consensus element helps individuals to remain committed to the organization and to accept its space as the context within which their needs should be fulfilled. That is, it allows for the continuation of membership (a factor contributing to political integration).[20] The conflict element results from the frustration of needs of some or all of the individuals included within the political order.

This element of conflict is the aspect we want to focus on if we are interested in the problem of political disintegration, and hence in the process that leads to situations where peaceful resolution of conflicts is replaced by recourse to violence for the settlement of political disagreements. Political and social structures and governmental and partisan organizations become associated with the structure of frustration and satisfaction. In other words, they become associated with a structure of emotions. In such a context we do not have a simple dichotomy—those benefiting from the *status quo* feeling satisfied, and those not benefiting feeling frustrated. The assumption is that some or all the needs of each individual are fulfilled for each individual to accept membership. (When all the needs of an individual are totally denied by others within the same corporate group, we have a necessary condition for the withdrawal of loyalty by that individual or group who finds his or its membership consisting solely of duties without rights.)

Thus, among those benefiting from the existing social and political arrangements, the feeling of satisfaction is simultaneously associated with an anxiety which springs from the desire to preserve that which caters to their comfort. For those unfulfilled by the *status quo,* a feeling of frustration is associated with hope— hope born of the conviction that the present structure of power is contingent upon, and reversible through, additional investment of social effort. (And when frustration and absence of hope are combined we find a powerful reason for a group to consider seriously an alternative arena for the satisfaction of felt needs.)

Anxiety, hope, frustration, and satisfaction become intertwined into a complex of emotions or attitudes. These attitudes are then the emotional predisposition to respond to social cues in terms of whether or not such cues indicate the probability that a particular action would increase or diminish the state of frustration or satisfaction, and, by implication, a means of identifying and evaluating the significance of political actions and actors. They are therefore mechanisms for the mutual orientation of ourselves and others, and they have an historical genesis. In a social context dominated by power relations, such as the Nigerian situation, political attitudes orient the individual in instrumental directions and further add to the contingent nature of the social order. The quest for stability engendered by the desire for maintaining the existing calculus of gains and losses makes it necessary for political elites to consider a movement from power relations to authority relations.

The process of *discovering* authority in the existing power relations entails the process of constructing a *legitimization formula*. This process consists of: (1) the *rationalization* of the existing structure of support and dissent through the production of an *official history* of the society up to that point in time when the claim for authority is being made; (2) the attempt to inculcate attitudes in the relevant audience towards the existing social arrangements by the construction of mobilizing social myths. The myths are models of social situations, involving stereotypic portraitures of those who agree or disagree with the authority figures; they contain emotions, attitudes, and beliefs imputed to individuals or groups involved in the social relations. They are to become the basis of faith. And it is through this systematization of historical rationalizations (the production of ideologies *à la* Mannheim) and myths that social values are engendered. Certain types of intentions become right; certain types of social arrangements are seen as fair and equitable; these and not those types of behavior are most appropriate.

The journey from needs to values is not a direct one and, as a matter of fact, the proponents of values are at pains *to find an impersonal and divine origin for such values.* However, the consequence is the identification of existing politics with the legitimate politics. The *integration* of society begins with the attempt to structure society in accordance with the predominant social values, and by implication, to instill in all individuals similar attitudes and beliefs with respect to the social and political *status quo*. Hence, the process of achieving social stability, the desire to move from a purely coercive situation of power being assumed, consists of the attempt to propagate the belief that those needs, emotions, attitudes, and myths associated with the preferred social situation are the only *logical* empirical deductions from the general set of values which all do, or should, accept.

It is from this process that the pattern of prejudicial categorization of individuals or groups stems. Not only is conflict the context in which myths are created, but myths are the contexts in which groups are differentiated. We have described political myths as the symbolization of idealized society which involve stereotypic images

of values, social structure, social behavior, and social actors associated with that order which is approved or disapproved of. In
myths, individuals or groups are opposed to those individuals or
groups one shares beliefs with. But this is not all. For the dichotomy of foes and friends also becomes the dichotomy of two types
of men, two types of groups, two types of political natures. The
differences between friends and foes are seen to be more than the
specific differences of disagreement on certain social issues. They
are generic differences of human nature. And in this way a hierarchy of human nature is created, such that the higher category of
which one is a member is that of fellow worshippers, friends, and
the superior. The differences between the higher and approved
category and the lower and disapproved category of human nature
are essential differences which are not caused by social existence
but are anterior to any social arrangement. Hence, the specific
social differences between these groups are true signs of the generic
differences between them. When this occurs, when we see specific
social differences used to justify a judgment that particular social
categories are natural categories, we see the manifestation of
prejudice, of ethnic thinking, and of the tribalization of social
existence.

Thus, certain needs, emotions, and attitudes are associated with
certain social problems and certain social situations. A hierarchy
of social groups, created by differential access to resources of
power, is associated with these attitudes in the context of the social
problems and social situations. The characteristics of these social
categories are transferred to the individuals within each category.
In this process the structure of emotions, attitudes, beliefs, and
values associated with the mythical stereotypes become "real" in
the definition of the "human nature" associated with a particular
group. And the values, attitudes, and propensities of individual
members of each category become an icon of those of the group.
The individual no longer has to act in order to be known. His
history and character are already revealed in the knowledge of his
group membership.

Prejudicial categorization therefore seems to be possible: (1)
where the typology of social problems and social situations taken
as the context for the revelation of the individual and group
characteristics is restricted to a convenient set and hence excludes
other relevant and revealing social situations in which other facets,
usually contradictory to the official categorization of characteristics,

are visible; (2) where judgments proper to those involved in the social situations are extended to cover those not involved in them, thus leading to the problem of over-generalization; (3) where there is no full appreciation of the self-interested nature of social interaction, that is, where differences arising possibly from conflicting needs tend to be attributed to differences in character instead; (4) where there is the tendency to project cues, needs, emotions, and attitudes, not only upon a particular group but on all similar groups as well, whether these groups are involved in similar or dissimilar social situations and whether they are actually motivated by those desires, emotions, and attitudes. Whatever the factor or combination of factors facilitating prejudiced categories, the categorization takes place in the context of orienting emotions. The search for categories is not dictated therefore by mere "facts," but by facts which justify the emotions. The category once chosen, its characteristics once defined, a definition of needs once ascribed to the group, the responsibility of society for fulfilling these needs are assumed to be no more and no less than that which the nature of the group entails. Where nature is the basis of the justification of demands upon society, politics becomes the servant of such an ontological justice. The difference in the treatment of these groups is then shown to flow out of the essential and natural differences between the types they represent.

We have offered a constructive abstraction of the types of problems, types of situations, types of perspectives, pattern of conflicts, and types of rationalization which characterized actors' definition of their social situation. As an ideal-type construction it is not a description of a specific social group and need not be identical with a specific corporate group. It is a model culled from historical observations of the actors' world, the basis of the order imposed on all these discrete observations being the theorist's perception of what constitutes their logical and social nature. What this provides is a paradigm through which an observer may attempt to discern the implicit order in the political drama of which he is an audience.

Being an ideal type of the situation of prismatic politics, being an ideal type of the process of changing the frame of reference from that of political prismatism to that of consensual politics, it means that the theorist need no longer depend completely upon his private intuition and the actors' definition of the situation. The paradigm allows him to argue from analogies, to appeal to certain accepted theoretical assumptions, to apply certain rules of argument. In short, it allows the observer to give the facts of observation public definitions in accordance with acceptable logic of discourse. More important, it provides the observer categories which are created with the specific orientation to the actors' world, and which allow him to examine the actors' world with reference to a theoretical perspective which is understandable both to the actors and to other observers (for we must not forget that, if the ambition of the observer is to speak relevantly to these two audiences, observers and actors, he must be intelligible to both).

Further, the possession of this paradigm protects the observer from falling into the easy trap where observation is not controlled by an articulate theory, the trap of mistaking the actors' ideologized facts, ideologized history, ideologized definitions of problems and other actors, for philosophical facts, philosophical history, philosophical definitions of problems and actors. The actor may have very good reasons for putting particular constructions on the situation. His purpose is to mobilize support and assure a commitment to him, to his position, and to his program. He is not interested in facts for truth's sake, which is precisely the theorist's initial interest, for it is this which gives him the authority to offer the known truths as the basis for the development of future ideals. And it is only when the theorist has a way of discerning political truths from political exaggerations, when he has a refinery within which he can separate the facts from their ideological ornamentation, that he can begin to reconstruct for himself a plausible picture of the world as the political constraints allow. It is then that he can have an inkling of the plausible picture of the political world which the actor carries in his head, for he must know when an actor is lying or speaking the truth, and he must be able to make an actor admit that he has lied.

Only in this way can an observer help an actor avoid becoming the victim of his own rhetoric, a prisoner of his own fantasies, especially if it is possible to mobilize a following in terms of such myths. And it prevents the observer from committing the more dangerous error of accepting the actor's myths as authentic history, for if he does this, he has to base his prescriptions and predictions upon this putative history. An actor may be wise in not heeding the warning of such a theorist because he has enough grasp upon reality not to fall prey to his own political chicanery. On the other hand, it is possible for the actor to accept these prescriptions on faith, and honestly attempt to institutionalize them. At this time he must certainly encounter the resistance of the groups who see the "founding father" not as God's spokesman, but as a self-interested politician. Such a situation leads to the attempt of a self-appointed elite to compel others to be free, and we are no longer so naive as to ignore the possible consequences of such policies.

Finally, use of this paradigm prevents the irresponsible theorizing which is primarily focused on creating a name within the political science discipline, an intellectual approach which renders the discipline irrelevant and pernicious to the world of actors, especially if political scientists also desire to become policy advisers. To realize the most beneficial exchange between theorist and actor, especially upon the problem of social ontogenesis (nation-building), actor and theorist must be capable of interchanging roles, for just as only an actor with a theoretical eye can appreciate a theoretical fact, in the same way only a theorist with an actor's eye can appreciate a political fact. But this exchange of roles will not be possible if both actor and theorist err in confounding a problem of nation-building in the context of prismatic politics with the problem of social disorganization. Both must see the world as it is. And in this case, it is the theorist's task to help the actor see the world as it is. Would it not be a dismal state for the medical profession if the doctor had to accept the untutored patient's diagnosis of his ailments as a scientific diagnosis?

The means to achieve this rapprochement, especially between the foreign observer and the indigenous actor, are not easily procurable, for the foreign observer must be able to *die culturally,* that is, be able to see his own society and other societies from a perspective which is consciously formulated and by a process independent of his parochial socialization within his own culture. He must be able, as it were, to crawl out of his cultural cocoon and make himself available for a sympathetic socialization into the culture he wishes to study. For the African actor this rapprochement requires that he decolonize himself, that he be able to perceive himself as his own man, knowing his own mind, and that he be able to know why he desires what he desires. It means, above all, that both the observer and the actor must have an historical consciousness of their growth, an historical consciousness of the political cosmogony within which they were born and into which they were socialized. They must have an historical consciousness of their character, a knowledge of how they have come to be what they are.

For only when the observer and the actor are conscious of their own identity can they know and sense what is common in their experience, what is different in their experience, why the world appears the way it appears to them, and know how to devise the symbolism with which to bridge the gap that may exist between both, how to apply the same political epistemology in identifying not only what is a problem and what constitutes a solution to that problem, but also the most effective and efficient method to attain that solution.

What dying culturally means, therefore, is the comprehension of the culture into which one is born. It is understanding not only how social facts have come to be defined one way rather than another, but also why they have come to be arranged in one way rather than another. It means understanding not only one's place in the scheme of things but how one has come to be placed there as well. What is more important, from the perspective of a sociology of knowledge, he must begin to appreciate just how his perception of the world, his basic assumptions, his basic dislikes and likes, are or are not a product of his particular place in the political and social cosmos of which he is a member. Such a consciousness does not come without self-education and self-cultivation.

But before one can be ready to work, one must be aware of the need to know, one must feel that ontological impetus. A person deeply in pain, in agony, or wrapped in obsessive fears, is not available for such work. He is too engrossed in himself; he is too conscious of his pains. All the attention he directs outwards is intended to seek the cause of pain and to procure a cure for that pain. He does not treat external reality with respect; he ignores psychic or social events which do not attenuate his agony.

Similarly, one completely ecstatic about himself and about his society is completely absorbed in the source of his delights. He dwells in his joys and wants to expand his source of joys to assure the continuity of his happy situation. Such a person has no need to be critical of his situation, is not aware of the suffering of others, is insensitive to nuances, is not aware of any other sources of pleasure, and, hence, cannot conceive of an alternative state of affairs to that which he enjoys. Differences annoy him unless they add to his pleasure. They merely present a situation whose rationality he cannot perceive, since the consequences of such social action lead to different results from those to which he is psychologically attuned. Such a person, when he concerns himself with

others, does so only to the extent that such effort naturally leads
to the perpetuation of his ecstasy; he naturally wants to make the
world identical to that aspect of it which satisfies him. He is not
an apologist, but a crusader, and he cannot appreciate why other
men desire to be different. He is by nature ethnocentric, and his
time perspective is completely ahistorical, or historical only to the
extent that he knows which factors in his past existence have
contributed to his present state.

How then does a man become historically conscious? He
becomes historically conscious when he begins to be aware of some
ontological lack, an awareness which can come only when his
mind is not completely absorbed in his pain or in his ecstasy, when
he can achieve a distance from the source of his anguish or his joy.
He begins to attempt to identify what it is that he lacks, how and
why this lack makes his inherited schema unfulfilling in terms of
the expected consequences from acting with respect to it. He begins
to attempt to discover what in his values, in his personality, in his
attitudes, in his vocation or avocation, what in his social situation
by becoming problematic presents him with issues of interest.

In this search for clarification he is a participant-observer, he is
an actor and an observer of his actions and those of others. He
attempts to construct a paradigm of his social order and his place
in it. He begins to see if he can identify the rhythm of social action
through the aid of such a paradigm. When he thinks he has
detected this rhythm, and thus identified the structure of action,
he attempts to pinpoint those factors in this structure which cause
his lack. When he begins to have an inkling of this by acting and
simultaneously reflecting on his action within his explanatory
paradigm, he begins to have a basis for prediction; he can base his
action on a hypothesis derivable from his paradigm and wait to see
if the predicted result is verified by the actual result. The more
confidence he has in his explanatory schema the more his actions
become based on a theoretical foundation. And through his action
he comes into conflict with those whose actions, whether based on
reflection or merely automatic, embody different principles. By
this dialectical confrontation in action, he begins to appreciate what
it is about the positions of the others within his culture which makes
them see the world similarly or differently. Through social conflict, he begins to construct the alternative paradigms which he
experiences in interaction with others. And it is through the comparison of his paradigms with the other paradigms which he can

discover in his society that he begins to develop a theory of his society, a theory of the society as he wants it to be, and an awareness of the difficulty of bringing others around to his viewpoint.

However, it is clear that the process of developing a theoretical consciousness is not based on science. Neither is it based on divine revelation, magic, or some other claims by which men and societies assert their preeminence. It begins from the experience of a lack, it proceeds from self-observation (what is observed may have been well put together or badly put together, but it is a result of either a good artist or a bad artist), it issues from actions in social situations within which one accidentally finds oneself by virtue of birth or citizenship, and from reflection upon those actions (and again the quality of reflection may be high or low, for what is reflected upon may be sublime or ridiculous). It becomes formalized through further social interactions and dialectical encounters; it ends in an affirmation of faith. One may then proceed to find a basis for that faith by an appeal to animism, magic, philosophy, religion, or science, but one must realize that the epistemology, whether scientific or magical, only serves as a basis of assuring that one's structure of beliefs is reasonable; it is not the cause of those beliefs. The epistemology is led to and serves a metaphysics which issues from experience in action.

One may attempt to argue for the relevance of this private vision for others, one may attempt to make the personal problem a social problem. However, the process for doing this is the recognition of the situation of one's audience, the recognition of the structure of constraints that impede or aid their activities, the recognition of their objects of fears and dislikes. It is the *creation* of a structure of explanation which orders all these fragments of knowledge, making this structure recognizable to one's audience, and therefore making the audience recognize the similarity or identity of their situation with one's own situation and in recognizing this similarity, come into awareness of the relevance of one's solution because they begin to know the sense in which one employs explanatory symbols. This is not the only way to make a private vision public. It is, however, one of the ways which avoid imposition, which avoid using one form of coercion or another in bringing one's theory into the world. And this is the process that one employs to enter into a foreign culture, to know how to develop that language which makes the communication of distinct experiences possible, which makes the availability of common sets of interpretative criteria possible, which makes the sensitivity to the unique and common in other people's situations, culture, values, and idiosyncrasies possible. It is this which makes possible the development of empathy and sympathy and the interchange of roles we spoke of earlier.

That such a process is difficult, I admit, but that it is necessary if observers and actors are to benefit from a cumulative process of growth, I do not doubt. And that this process is mandatory for an observer, whether foreign or indigenous, who wants "to give instruction as to what the world ought to be," I have had no intellectual or moral reason to reject. If it makes the price of pontificating to the world rather high, this is done not out of malice, but out of a concern for the discipline of philosophy and out of affection for the world of actors. To do less would be laziness, to demand less would be criminal. Therefore, in setting the standards where they ought to be set, we are putting the social analyst where he must begin with the assumption that politics, like other forms of social action, finds expression not in one but in many and distinct political universes, and where he must begin to appreciate the fact that the problems confronted in each social cosmos align the social values in their operational connection to the experiences of the actors and to the psychological meaning attributable to those values. He must realize that a reliance on logic as a tool of understanding the culture of the group he chooses to observe may *at best* give him a lexical definition of the meaning attached to these values, a formal understanding of the structure of motives and behavior issuing from adherence to these values, knowing full well that the attempt to understand the dynamics of social experience through formal definitions places him at a disadvantage. For he may not know what empirical model is extracted from the formal model. He may not understand the social and psychological rules of transformation through which this is done. The observer may assume that, because of the identity of these logical terms to the logical terms employed by actors in the system from which he comes, an identical political psychology explains the behavior and motivations of the actors which he now studies. However, this is a frivolous assumption, at the least, or an ethnocentric or egocentric assumption, at the most.

We will expect that the observer becomes aware that he must also understand the psychological meaning which the actors give to their experience. "Dying culturally" allows him to do this, freeing him from his cultural inhibitions and blinders and allowing him to imagine himself in the situation of the actor, to attempt to feel the pattern of emotions which would cause one to see the world in a particular way and interpret and judge the meaning of events from one, rather than another, perspective. When he perceives himself as capable of recognizing why, out of a range of possible choices, an actor makes a particular choice, when he can, on the basis of an understanding of the actor's psychology, in a specific political context, with reference to a specific political problem, predict the behavioral preferences, he can consider himself attuned to the actor. Both are on the same wave length and he now has a chance of understanding and appreciating the actors' motivations. This achievement gives him the privilege to address the actors. It serves as the knowledge upon which his opinion is based, and it allows the social analyst to make relevant to the actor's situation the fund of comparative knowledge defining his professional competence. With such a training he deserves to be a philosopher, a teacher, and an actor's counsellor.

We finally turn to the actor. In order to appreciate advice and learn the maximum from the social analyst the actor must understand the world in which he acts and how the world ought to be arranged. He must know himself, why he is moved to act and what objects excite him. It is within this context that he identifies his problems and seeks advice. Obviously, this process must vary for actors depending upon their situation and their problems. I am not attempting to speak for all actors. I address myself to the African actor in general and the Nigerian actor in particular. For such an actor to discover himself, to feel his identity, to know his history, what agitates him, and how he has come to be where he is, he must decolonize himself. We prescribe this because it is our understanding that what he achieved through political independence was less than complete knowledge of himself. To explain why this is the case we must understand what colonization truly meant. Colonization, in our understanding, was total. It involved political colonization, the replacement of one political system by another, a revolution from without. It included social colonization, that is, the rearrangement of the society to fit into the colonial scheme, the rearrangement if need be of social stratification in all the relevant fields of activity to ensure harmonious integration of the social order into the colonial order. It entailed economic colonization, that is, the forcible linkage of the colonies' system of production and distribution through the colonial administrative state to the imperial economic system, which became the coordinator of economic activities throughout the colonial empire. Above all, it meant a cultural colonization, the degree of which varied with respect to the difficulties of integrating the colonial culture within the imperial system. At the least, cultural colonization meant the establishment of a hierarchy of cultures, if only to provide legitimacy for the colonial regime. For if political colonization was effected through recourse to military conquest and fraudulent treaties, to base a system of domination on mere power relations would have been to rest the elaborate structure of colonial imperialism upon a fragile and fluid base. Political relations based on mere power relations legitimize rebellion, for the powerful do what they want and the weak suffer what they must, and the weak do what they must to get out of the position of underling. The fragility of basing social relations on mere power relations provides the impetus for the holders of power to move from recourse to coercion to an appeal to authority—hence, the necessity to create a myth of legitimacy.

Thus, as already said, the attempt to make colonialism legitimate leads to the establishment of a hierarchy of cultures, with the higher culture on the totem pole having the right to rule over the lower culture on this totem pole. The consequence of this is a process of a rewriting of the history of the colonized people such that their past logically leads to a colonial present. There are now institutionalized two worlds, that of the colonizing and that of the colonized, that of Prospero and that of Caliban. Sometimes Prospero deigns to leave the world of Caliban alone if Caliban has already accepted his inferior status; sometimes Prospero alters sections of Caliban's world if Caliban threatens to use his autonomy to the detriment of Prospero's world; sometimes Prospero holds before Caliban the prospect of an improvement in the latter's status, but it is made clear that there are ontological reasons why Caliban can never be Prospero's equal, that at best he can only be a bad copy.

Therefore, in addition to hierarchies of values and of institutions, there is also a hierarchy of model personalities. The ideal colonial accepts his place in the colonial scheme and desires to be like his master but understands that due to his ontological deformity he cannot be like his master, regardless of the superficial resemblances between them. The deviant, the troublemaker, desires to be like his master. He feels and thinks he has the potential to be not only like his master, but better than his master. It is the colonizing regime's duty to remove the latter possibility, to restrict aspiration within the context of that which is permissible, and to attempt to convert the colonized into the acceptance of his permanent inferiority.

While this is the logic of colonization, the process in itself does not necessarily have to be so patently obvious. The end result is all that matters—the integrity of the entire process being maintained by the willingness of the colonial administrative state to resort to coercion. The actual process does take place within this context of colonial domination, within the context of a colonial administration whose presence has to be explained without reference to the tradition or principle of legitimacy of the groups colonized; the whole process takes place with the assistance of the missionaries, the educational system, the economic system, and the entire structure of duties and privileges of the colonial order. In short, for the indigenous colonial born into the colonial order, unaware of the precolonial era where his ancestors not only could look the colonial administrators in the eye but, in fact, placed themselves at the level of the monarch whose servants the administrators were, to the colonial subjects who had not witnessed the traditional order being corrupted and subverted by the colonizers, this colonial subject has the choice between a traditional society already corrupted and made amenable to the colonial order, and the colonial order itself. His socialization takes place within the colonial grid. His perception of history is restricted to the scope set by the colonial order. His mind is an assortment of facts cut to the specification of the colonial order, and even when he reacts against the colonial order, he reacts with a personality shaped by that order. Colonization is therefore both the institutionalization of a revolutionary change of the traditional society (although the goals institutionalized are those of administrative control and administrative exploitation) and the creation of a new man; the native is changed into the colonial man.

Nationalism, or the struggle for independence, to the extent that it involves merely the desire to achieve political autonomy, to replace the colonial authority with a Nigerian authority, means the Nigerianization of the colonial administrative state. To the extent that the Nigerian elite concerns itself with political independence, it still has its social, economic, and cultural life colonized, and it is not necessary that the British be present physically to exercise this control. To the extent that there is external economic control there exists a situation in which an elite may initiate a program or want to initiate certain policies. But, because it lacks control of its economic institutions, it lacks control of an essential ingredient of power. What compromises in autonomy are involved in such a situation is an empirical question, but it is this possibility which renders theoretically interesting the problem of neocolonialism. The social structure may continue to remain colonial. Status hierarchy, articles of prestige, and social etiquette may be a copy of the colonial order.

What this means is that the stuff of politics, the articles over which men quarrel, their objects of love, are copies of the colonial order. It means that the postcolonial history is an attempt to deny the colonial definition of the colonized, an attempt to show that by the acquisition of power he achieved an ontological grace which allows him to be that which had been denied to him, a perfect copy of the colonial master. And, finally, if decolonization does not extend to the cultural level, what we then have is the mind of the independent state still enslaved to the colonial master. Thought proceeds within colonial grooves, and the churches, schools, and governmental institutions still continue to produce citizens specifically cut to the colonial specification. The models of personal growth, of economic arrangements, political arrangements, and police-military organizations copy the colonial patterns. The style of action and structure of rewards are all shaped after the colonial cultural artifacts.

In brief, cultural colonization is the institutionalization of a colonial mentality. It therefore seems to follow that there is nothing automatic in the process of nationalism which leads from the acquisition of political and military autonomy into social, economic, and cultural decolonization. Complete decolonization means total revolution, a revolution as complete as the colonizing revolution, and as radical as the penetration of the colonial order required. But this process of decolonization requires a political elite that "dies culturally," the death being a death within the colonial order. It requires an elite who have acquired an historical consciousness and have begun to realize that their brothers, sisters, fathers, mothers, husbands, and wives are still embalmed in the colonial mold.

The process of liberation is the attempt to educate people about their past, to restore everyone to the psychic level of his precolonial ancestors. Total decolonization indeed means that the postcolonial elites have achieved the status of psychological equality with their precolonial ancestors. They are now their own men; they are now ready to be the architects of their new future; they can now begin to use the inherited materials as elements in the new creation that begins to take shape in their eyes. But for this to be possible the cultural death issues in the production of both a philosophy of the colonial history and a philosophy of action. For these to become social, for these to awaken people from the colonial sleep, a political elite must make it its vocation to educate people into consciousness. The vocation must also be an avocation, for without a steadfast commitment and an unswerving devotion, a politically independent people will continue to re-enact their colonial past.

The thought of a country stumbling through history in a somnambulistic daze, the thought of the perils that could attend a political society whose lack of identity is complicated by its situation in a context where there are no constraints upon its members, the thought of a reckless adventurism which could threaten the society with destruction, the very possibility of political corruptibility in a setting where the mechanisms are absent for the restoration of political health to the polity and moreover the realization of the fragility of the social order and knowledge that when this home is destroyed there might be no other, all these considerations should lead a political elite to the same level of solicitude, the same intensity of patriotism, as Machiavelli showed for his native Italy rent asunder by pervasive political corruption. It will not be amiss if we redirect the appeal made by Machiavelli to Lorenzo de' Medici to the Nigerian political elites, for they also preside over a country that is being maimed and that is threatened with dismemberment. It will not be amiss if we demand the same amount of care for the well-being of our native land as Machiavelli demonstrated for his. Here is Machiavelli's prayer for Italy, a prayer which should be revitalized and inculcated in the Nigerians' consciousness.

And although before now a gleam of hope has appeared which gave hope that some individual might be appointed by God for her redemption, yet at the highest summit of his career he was thrown aside by fortune, so that now, *almost lifeless,* she awaits one who may heal her wounds and put a stop to the pillaging of Lombardy, to the rapacity and extortion in the Kingdom of Naples and in Tuscany, and cure her of these sores which have long been festering. *Behold how she prays God to send someone to redeem her from this barbarous cruelty and insolence. Behold her ready and willing to follow any standard if only there be someone to raise it. There is nothing now she can hope for but that your illustrious house may place itself at the head of this redemption,* being by its power and fortune so exalted, and being favored by God and the Church, of which it is now the ruler. *Nor will this be very difficult, if you call to mind the actions and lives of the men I have named. And although those men were rare and marvellous, they were none the less men,* and each of them had less opportunity than the present, for their enterprise was not juster than this, nor easier, nor was God more their friend than he is yours. . . .

This opportunity must not, therefore, be allowed to pass, so that Italy may at length find her liberator. I cannot express the love with which he would be received in all those provinces which have suffered under those foreign invasions, with what thirst for vengeance, with what steadfast faith, with what love, with what grateful tears. What doors would be closed against him? What people would refuse him obedience? What envy could oppose him? *What Italian would withold allegiance?* This barbarous domination stinks in the nostrils of everyone.[21]

The prayer addressed to the Nigerian liberator is not to be confused with the specific request Machiavelli made of the House of Medici; it is the spirit of the request which we want to convey. It is the jealous concern for a ravaged country, the indignation about the unwanted suffering, the desire for vigorous remedial action, and, above all, the fact that the task, even though seeming on the first encounter to offer gigantic resistance, is within the capacity of human will to accomplish. The task for Machiavelli was the recapture of a political autonomy, that which we would now call "nationalism." There was no question about the national identity of Italians, for colonization had been merely political and not as pervasive as it was institutionalized in Nigeria.

But the task for the Nigerian political elite is no longer the acquisition of political autonomy, although it may include measures to safeguard that autonomy. The task is far more difficult. It is to recapture an independent mind, to recapture political space, to accomplish a political renaissance; it is the task of the radical decolonization which we have described. However, as important as this task is, it is merely the beginning. Decolonization, even in the way we have used it, is not an end in itself. It is liberation from the shackles of colonial history. It is a movement from the past.

It does not contain an automatic path into the future. The process of decolonization frees the elite to take an objective look at the present political mess. It allows them to achieve the distance of a spectator, to see how the political evils to be eradicated are embedded either in men's chronic habits, or in the political organizations, or in the political situations, or in the political problems which agitate men.

The recognition of how the past has led to the present, while not presenting a guaranteed passport into a calm and productive future, presents objects upon which political imagination may dwell and fashion a way from the dismal past to a future charged with creative potential. This, in itself, constitutes a tremendous task in political education, and the poltical elite must educate themselves before they can educate the citizenry that has afforded them their privileged position. And the process of political education means, if it means anything at all, not the attempt to sell a popular line to a gullible population, not the attempt to slander any citizens or groups of citizens, but the courage to present those facts which represent the closest approximation to historical truths enacted by the collective populace. Above all, it means a commitment to a philosophical understanding of the past, and an understanding which political exigencies may tempt us to corrupt or reject. The commitment to the historical truths as unraveled by political philosophy also issues out of the love we have for our fellow citizens, our brothers in the same predicament, from the respect which we show to ourselves in confronting the past which we have wittingly or unwittingly fashioned. It is the other half of our patriotism.

If there is any doubt as to my meaning, what I am trying to say is best depicted by the response of Socrates to the Athenian political elite who ordered him to desist his quest for social and ethical truths:

I shall never give up philosophizing and urging you and making my point clear to everyone I meet, saying what I always say: "My good sir, you are an Athenian, a citizen of the city which is greatest and most noted for its wisdom and power; are you not then ashamed to be worrying about your money and how to increase it, and about your reputation, and about your honour, instead of worrying about the knowledge of good and truth and how to improve your soul?" And if anyone contradicts me and says that he does worry about his soul, I shall not let him off at once and go away, but question him and examine him and refute him; and, if I think that he does not possess virtue, but simply says he does, I shall reproach him for underestimating what is most valuable, and prizing what is unimportant. *I shall do this to everyone I meet, young and old, stranger and citizen—but particularly to you citizens of Athens, because you are nearer me in blood.*[22]

Socrates helps us to clarify the point we have been laboring to make, that when we say that the capacity to plan the future intelligently depends upon the political wisdom which man has been able to garner by a philosophical analysis of his history, philosophy in these terms is not a subject confined to apolitical academicians; it is not a concern with a recondite subject; it deals, if we may put it into American slang, with the "nitty gritty" of life, the definition of the goods that men love and quarrel over; it deals with knowledge of the possibility or impossibility of arriving at some solutions to present problems, with the basis of the most intelligent way to plan a social order. Philosophy is not therefore what a political elite may do only on Sundays, or when it writes a manifesto; it is the basis of action. It is the link between the past and the future, the only guarantee that men will not continually reenact Adam.

This brings us full circle to the point where we began. And if I have devoted the bulk of my space to metatheoretical problems, to philosophical issues concerned with social existence, rather than with specific political issues, it is not because I am insensitive to the task of defining the issues that agitate the present. Partly, my avoidance of discussion about the present Civil War and speculation about the future stems from the fact that others in this volume will be dealing with this aspect more competently than I can. Partly, it stems from my temperament, for I feel uncomfortable in a situation in which I have to deal with political ideologies as statements of facts, for what is it that actors in a dire conflict such as the present one are most naturally prone to produce, philosophy or ideology? I will answer my own question—ideology, of course, for it is their essential and legitimate task to mobilize support. But that is not my task.

And this brings me to the final reason why I have left political journalism and political fortune-telling to those more skilled in political tactics and strategies. It is the consideration that, unless political actors have a realistic definition of their situation, an intelligent understanding of how they got into that situation, an awareness of how and why their situation presents them with the type of problems that disturb them, it is not easy for them to plan scientifically how to remedy that situation. If the Nigerian actors do not have a proper appreciation of the constraints that have continued to bedevil their political universe and threaten it with extinction, how can they guarantee that when the opportunity presents itself they would be able to make the necessary provisions against a recurrence of the macabre events which constitute the coups and Civil War? And unless Nigerians know their minds, how can they learn from their own experience and from others? If foreigners are not sensitive to their own history and cognizant that their perspective on life is not deterministically defined by their citizenship, how can they appreciate a foreign world and be attuned to its dilemmas? And, finally, if the political world is deranged or capable of derangement, does that not present to him who has no disdain for the political world the duty of bringing thought and action into a more intimate relationship?

Notes

1. See Chapter 3 of this volume.
2. George W. Hegel, *Philosophy of Right,* preface.
3. H. Meyerhoff, ed. *The Philosophy of History in Our Time.*
4. For further discussion of this point, see Chapter 8 in this volume.
5. See Joseph Okpaku's article on the African intellectual, "Let's Dare to be African," *Africa Report,* October 1968, pp. 13–16.
6. J. B. C. Ugokwe, Editorial, *The Nigerian Students Voice,* 4 (October–December 1966): 3. (Emphasis added.)
7. Dr. Alexander D. Acholonu, "Tribalism as the Opium of National Unity in Nigeria," *The Nigerian Students Voice,* 4 (October–December 1966): 5. (Emphasis added.)
8. Ibid., p. 7.
9. Ibid., pp. 6–7. (Emphasis added.)
10. Ibid., p. 8.
11. Federal Ministry of Information, Lagos, *Nigeria 1966* (Apapa, Lagos: Nigerian National Press Ltd., 1966), pp. 4–8. (Emphasis added.)
12. Federal Ministry of Information, Lagos, *News from Nigeria,* 29 January 1966. (Emphasis added.)
13. *The New York Times,* 30 January 1966.
14. Quoted in *West Africa,* 2 April 1966, no. 2548, p. 391.
15. *Nigeria 1966,* pp. 8–9. (Emphasis added.)

228 MOYIBI AMODA

16. Quoted in translation in *Report on The Kano Disturbances,* p. 43, which is quoted in James S. Coleman, *Nigeria: Background to Nationalism,* 3d ed. (Berkeley: University of California Press, 1963), p. 362. (Emphasis added.)

17. I have not the space to explain why the Southern hegemony broke into Ibo and non-Ibo and how the Ironsi regime became associated with the Ibo group, but I will suggest that some of the reasons are to be found in the very intense rivalry within the federal bureaucracies between the Yoruba and Ibo officials, for instance.

18. James O'Connell, "Political Integration: The Nigerian Case," *African Integration and Disintegration,* ed. Arthur Hazlewood (London: Oxford University Press, 1967), p. 129.

19. Ibid., p. 181.

20. See the previous section on James O'Connell and the problem of political integration.

21. Niccolo Machiavelli, *The Prince* in *The Prince and the Discourses* (New York: Random House, Modern Library), pp. 95–96, 98. (Emphasis added.)

22. Plato, *Apology* in *Paideia, The Ideals of Greek Culture,* trans. Werner Jaeger (London: Oxford University Press, 1963), II, 38. (Emphasis added.)

6

SECESSION, FEDERALISM, AND AFRICAN UNITY

M. Nziramasanga

After one of the meetings of the Organization of African States to try and resolve the Nigerian crisis, President Nyerere of Tanzania was quoted in the press as expressing surprise at the number of African leaders who were not very enthusiastic about a negotiated settlement and who hoped for a solution through a military victory, preferably by the federal military government. This might appear to be in contrast to the OAU effort to stop the conflict, but the OAU has advocated negotiations based on the idea of a united Nigeria. The idea of unity is embodied in the charter of the organization and was expressed during the Congo crisis. To the Organization and the existing state governments, the present states making up the OAU and their borders are considered inviolable; secessions by regions or federations or republics are to receive no encouragement from the OAU as an organization. A few challenges have been thrown at this agreement on the unity of federations, and this chapter seeks to find some of the common characteristics of the secession attempts, and their immediate effects on the African states singly and jointly on the issue of international cooperation, whether political or economic.

Secession movements have been either regional, playing down tribal or ethnic identification, or tribal, with a major tribe in a region associated with the movement. The Katanga attempt in the

Congo might be taken as an example of a regional secession movement, and the Nigerian Civil War as a tribal secession movement.
There are, of course, other factors involved in any attempt to break
up the union of a state.

A brief outline of some previous attempts may help to clarify
these factors, and also limit the circle of reference by eliminating
internal disorders resulting from a coup, an assassination, or other
changes in personalities at the top which do not result from an
election. The states to be looked at are Ruanda, Burundi, Uganda,
Congo (Kinshasa), Sudan and Chad.

Ruanda–Burundi

The most advertised source of disintegration seems to be tribalism
—whether the tribe wanting to secede resides in a distinct territory
of a federation, as in Nigeria, or the racial issue (another form of
tribalism) surpasses all internal borders and pervades the whole
society, as in South Africa and Rhodesia. Among the independent
African states, Ruanda and Burundi have had political strife with
the opponents grouped more or less along tribal lines. The two
states had been a German colony until the end of World War I,
when the League of Nations made them a trusteeship of Belgium.
The Belgian government decided to split them up before they
gained independence. In 1961 the United Nations organized elections in Ruanda, and the result was an overwhelming victory by
Parmehutu, a party led by the Hutu, one of the major tribes.
Ruanda became independent on July 1, 1962, while Burundi
remained a monarchy. The Tutsi of Ruanda, though a minority,
had held power in the country since their arrival around the
fifteenth century. Their ruler, the Mwami, was the absolute overlord, and the Hutu as well as the Twa were their vassals. The Tutsi
wished to return to the old days of the Tutsi monarchs, rather than
maintain the republic with Hutu domination. A coup in October
of 1961 resulted in the death of Crown Prince Rwagasore, the only
likely successor to the Mwami Mambutsa. Thousands of Tutsi fled
the country into Uganda and Tanzania and formed secret organizations designed to overthrow the government. Two raids on the
country occurred, the most serious in December of 1963, when
about three thousand Tutsi men, women, and children invaded the
border; they were poorly armed and were defeated. In the reprisals

against the Tutsi that followed, ten thousand to fourteen thousand persons were reported killed, especially in the Gikongoro prefecture. [1] The refugees in Uganda, Tanzania, and the Congo still remain a problem, since they have not been absorbed into the country of their refuge, although there have been attempts at resettlement in Uganda.

Uganda

The Tutsi in Ruanda cannot be said to be secessionists; yet as a tribe they wanted to revert to a monarchy in a state which had attained independence and in which they were a minority. It was not a secession attempt because their power did not have a territorial base. In Uganda, on the other hand, the old monarchy of Buganda had the desire to secede from a newly federal state. In 1900 the Uganda Agreement established the rights of the Buganda kingdom, as distinct from those of the territory. It established the authority of the Kabaka of Buganda to rule through the native council or Lukiko "in a manner approved by Her Majesty's Government." This was in contrast to other areas in Uganda where the chiefs were appointed rather than traditional. [2] The Agreement served to entrench very early the power of the established chiefs in Buganda, while the process of appointment of chiefs in other areas probably resulted in a more fluid situation and made the later political transition an easier process. In negotiating and signing treaties with the British, the Buganda considered that the negotiations were conducted among equals and that this automatically granted them autonomy. [3] Thus the Buganda opposed federalism and interference from the territorial government as far back as the 1920s. When the negotiations began for a united state and again later when there was talk of the formation of a federation of the three East African territories of Kenya, Uganda, and Tanzania, the Buganda expressed fears for their independence. The Kabaka at first sought assurances that the federations would not be forced upon his people and sought secession of the kingdom from the territory in 1955. But the Buganda Agreement that followed in effect incorporated the kingdom into a federated Uganda. The central government, recognizing the problem and hoping constitutional provisions would forestall trouble, made various conditions and concessions on questions of finance, education, and health to overcome the kingdom's desire to secede. Four years later the government of President Obote felt confident enough to break its alliance with the Kabaka. In February 1966, Obote suspended the federal constitution and took over the presidential powers of the Kabaka. On May 23 Buganda staged a feeble revolt against the central government. The motives of the revolt are still not very clear. The central government reacted swiftly, supressed the revolt, and on June 10 took over administration of the kingdom. Since then the central government has seized the initiative and continued to press for the gradual weakening of the secession forces.

Congo

Federalism in Uganda was an attempt to solve territorial and tribal conflicts of interest. The Buganda kingdom felt it had the strength and economic viability to go it alone. The separatist movement in Katanga also seems to have been strongly influenced by this economic well-being. The desire to become a separate political entity had early beginnings in Katanga, though at first it was the white settler's attitude. Economic wealth from minerals was the chief source of the feeling of independence, and the vital role played by Katanga as a supplier of minerals during World War II helped to fan regional pride.[4] There were attempts to set up an autonomous dominion allied with Belgium, or a political federation with the neighbouring Rhodesias; the latter idea persisted through the 1950s. A provincial government led by the Conakat party sought diplomatic recognition from Belgium and the United States for an independent Katanga to be declared before the Congolese republic attained sovereignty.[5] After full sovereignty was attained on June 30, 1960, trouble started with the issue of Africanization of the army. A mutiny ensued; Tshombe called for Belgian intervention in Elizabethville and soon afterwards declared Katanga an independent state. Like Uganda and unlike Nigeria, Katanga's apprehension about the new Congolese state was not based upon fears about the viability of the constitution; it was based on the earlier notion of greater opportunities for an independent region which controlled its own destiny and did not have to share its supposed wealth with the rest of the new nation.

Sudan

Such fears of domination sparked the struggle in the Sudan between the Islamic north and the south. Sudan gained its independence on January 1, 1956, one of the early states to do so. The first mutiny in the south had been in 1955, when some northerners had been killed in the south. During independence negotiations the south was promised some local autonomy, but these plans were never carried out, and both the civilian and military governments which followed carried on a policy of assimilation of the south. The northern government blamed the British policy of isolating the south in pre-independence days as the chief cause of the rebellion that followed.[6] The latest military government has made overtures of peace and promised some autonomy to the south over internal and regional matters, but the south's distrust and hatred of the north does not seem to have diminished.

Chad

Chad has similar regional problems, but with religious overtones. The country had an unstable government before it attained independence in 1960. There was resentment in the predominantly Muslim north against southern dominance in politics. In February 1960, the Muslim parties formed a coalition, the Parti Nationale Africaine. The leaders were fired from the Council of Ministers by President Tombalbaye. Through several maneuvers the PNA was allied with Tombalbaye's party, the Parti Progressiste du Chad, to form the Union pour le Progres du Tchad. Divisive forces persisted, however, and in 1963 a plot against the government led to the arrest of influential Muslim leaders of the north for trying to split the north and south in order to align the north with Sudan. Since then French troops have been stationed in the country to help the government fight what the President terms "bands of brigands."

The crises which these governments have faced after independence point to the nationalist leaders' failure to realize the fact that they were inheriting divided rather than united states; when they had an idea of the tensions, they often lacked knowledge of the power or extent of these divisive forces. As a result, there were few provisions made in the constitutions to help prevent a region from resorting to secession, short of using force, or giving the minority a stake in the country large enough to dissuade them from wanting to break off. The fight for independence was not so much a fight against the old order as it was a fight to seize control of the existing system. In almost all cases the political ideology that existed at the time was adopted with few modifications. While such systems can and probably would work when time is not a factor, they can turn out to be unsatisfactory in countries working against time and with multiple issues to solve.

In British history major problems arose one at a time, were recognized as pressing by the politically conscious population, and were solved at least somewhat to their satisfaction, providing a layer of consensus on procedures of debate.[7] The Industrial Revolution, for example, though it had strong political implications, was mainly a transformation of the country from a fragmented agrarian society to a consolidated industrial state, and the resultant formation of a middle class from a socially stratified nation. No constitutional questions were at stake, nor were there questions as to what constituted the nation. However, African states became independent on short notice early in the 1960s, and issues had to be solved concurrently and argued among a varied number of dissident groups. Independence resulted in a sudden rise in expectations on the one hand, and on the other hand, the realization that the state coffers were depleted and could hardly satisfy these expectations. This did not allow for the creation of logical debate and made for weak constitutional consensus and weakened centralized authority.

Contrary to the popular argument, the above-mentioned crises have shown that a common enemy—the departing imperialist master—does not necessarily make for cohesiveness after he is dispatched, especially if his institutions are adopted with little alteration. Countries with many regional differences sought federalism as a solution to territorial as well as ethnic conflicts. Now federalism endeavours to square unity with diversity, but it can do so only on the supposition that the major diversities are territorially expressed. If the major diversities have no inclusive territorial base but traverse the whole society in the form of racial or communal conflict between intermingled communities, it is extremely doubtful if federalism can serve any useful purpose.[8]

African states have territorial bounds which coincide with ethnic diversities as well. But the expression of these interests and the source of political action is a very small middle class which traverses tribal differences in composition because of its urban base, but which has commitments to priorities as expressed in the rural areas. While this may be the case in any other nation, the difference may lie in the concept of nation as seen by the ethnic groups and therefore their commitment to it. This middle class powered the drive for independence, armed with the ideal that the black man should have the larger piece, if not all, of the cake. The number of problems they had to face were just as many as the alternative solutions to each one of them. Each group sought for an immediate solution, and, given the situation, perhaps federalism with its stratification of authority would not have been the ideal form of government.

It could be that the institution of the tribe, and its political, as opposed to its social, functions, does not fit well with the need for a well-ordered execution of priorities in a new state, which requires a strong central authority. A federation of states put together so as to recognize the political power of the tribe might reinforce political dissension and foster a sense of regional, rather than national, allegiance.

The African society has usually been considered in terms not of individual freedom, but of the individual as part of a group. The individual operated from a sense of social obligation. Wars were fought for the glorification of a tribe. Coming of age is usually a communal affair. The tribe in itself is a self-contained plural society. But it is a small unit, in many ways incapable of handling the problems that a pluralistic society today has to deal with. Nothing says that a simple straightforward aggregation of these distinct units will together form a viable whole consisting of independent parts. Several scholars have gone to great pains to point out how arbitrary the borders are in African countries, emphasizing this sawing of tribal units in half by boundaries as the source of most problems. It would seem that it is not the division of tribes between countries that is the persistent problem, because there is more internal disorder caused by complete tribal units than there are border wars. The identification of political personalities with the tribe they represent sometimes helps to illustrate how incongruous a modern state and tribal affiliations in politics are—the murder of Tom Mboya in Kenya in June 1969 is a case in point.

It may not be desirable or possible to upset the whole tribal system; but the nation-state is another and more powerful type of pluralistic society, and if the tribe can inspire a feeling of belonging and allegiance, then maybe the only way the nation-state can find to transfer this political allegiance to itself involves destroying recognition of the tribe as a political force. The process of building up the allegiance to the state and the form of government was not possible during pre-independence days. The primary concern was to get the power from alien hands. Now governments find they have to go through the process of educating the people about the system, something which very few were ready for, and something for which a federal state may not be suitable.

The task of the patriot in the generation preceding independence had been mainly that of teaching the people to defy the state, as represented by the metropolitan power. The aim was to grind the alien-controlled state to a halt. All this implied the notion that the nation had the moral claim to obedience—the nation as represented by the nationalistic political party.[9] When fighting for independence, therefore, governmental authority is not accepted as legitimate. The nation is the legitimate authority. One of the problems immediately after independence is achieved seems to be the definition of the nation and the extent of its authority, legitimacy, and claim to allegiances as seen by the new political elite, the traditional authority, and the urban and rural populations. The feeling of consensus during the colonial days has led to a rather unfortunate complacency about the need for this basic indoctrination of both the people and bureaucrats. The drawing up of a constitution does not guarantee that in the future straying politicians will be drawn back to constitutional propriety. Political passions or feelings of unity are not aroused by political institutions or forms of procedure.[10]

It is difficult to run a democratic institution to begin with, and the presence of poverty, war, or illiteracy makes it worse, for they lead to desperation, lack of political education and an unreal estimate of the consequences of political action.[11] This is not to say that an elected central government and underdevelopment are contradictory; but it does imply that no new government machinery can rely on sophisticated procedure for its existence. The institution can only be as sophisticated as the inhabitants, and to attain stability it may be necessary for the politically aware in the state to educate the population about its responsibility and stake in a stable and unified system during times of peace, rather than try to wield the big stick in times of stress.

The Nigerian and Congolese crises pointed out the difficulties of resolving tensions in a society which is passing through some form of transition. Most of the states experiencing the troubles are not static. The economies are slowly but surely growing, illiteracy, especially among the young, is slowly being overcome, and there is generally an air of rising expectations. But as conflicts of interest develop, the means of mediation become inefficient. There is a communication gap between the urban, Westernized elite, and the rural population they are supposed to govern. The result can be that the masses are manipulated to their own disadvantage by the different interest groups at the top. The coups and secession movements, rather than endangering the forms of government, have in general reinforced the status of the Western educated elites in African societies by staving off the complete collapse of governments threatened by the ineptitude of the politicians.[12] The movements have resulted in the rallying of the population to an elite clique promising reinstitution of the old and familiar order with different faces at the top, and generally serving to divert attention from the underlying causes by raising to the fore the issue of democratic freedom and constitutional procedure.

This difficulty of solving crises in a society in transition is very apparent in the efforts by the Organization of African Unity to secure peace. In the charter of the Organization the integrity of the national borders existing at the attainment of independence is assured. This ties the Organization's hands in any particular secessionist movement. In the Nigerian crisis the OAU, beginning with the Kinshasa meeting of the heads of state, prefaced its reports with its belief in a unified Nigeria as the goal of all the efforts, which Biafra consistently refused to accept as a precondition to peace talks. The fifteen heads of state who attended this meeting on September 11, 1964, agreed to send a consultative mission comprising the heads of state of the Congo (Kinshasa), Cameroon, Ethiopia, Ghana, Liberia, and Niger to the federal military government of Nigeria to "assure him of the Assembly's desire for the territorial integrity, unity and peace of Nigeria." [13] The consultative mission eventually met with General Gowon in Lagos on November 23. The official communique after the meeting had, among other things, the following recommendations: (1) As a basis for the return to peace and normal conditions in Nigeria, the secessionists renounce secession and accept the administrative structure of the Federation of Nigeria as laid down by the federal

military government of Nigeria in the decree Number 14 of 1967;
(2) General Ankrah of Ghana convey the text of the OAU
summit meeting in Kinshasa to the secessionists, as well as the
resolutions of the first meeting in Lagos, and report their reaction.
The purpose was to assure the Lagos government of the OAU's
support. There was no explicit attempt to impose or coerce both
sides into a cease-fire, or to try and negotiate the differences
between the two sides. General Gowon said it even more clearly
in welcoming the delegation: "Your mission here . . . in the
present circumstances . . . is to call on the rebel leaders to abandon secession . . ." [14]

The integrity of the present states is therefore considered non-
negotiable, even if the OAU is faced with the accomplished fact
of a split nation. While the OAU thus can be a very effective
mediator in cases of border disputes between states, its charter and
the fears of the member states tie its hands in the case of civil
conflict. At the same summit meeting, for example, it was possible to get Kenya and Somalia to agree to mediate their dispute
on the Northeastern province of Kenya and to meet in Lusaka.
Both states agreed to ensure peace at the border and cease hostile
propaganda against each other. Ethiopia and Somalia also agreed
to meet for a settlement of their border dispute. The head of
the state of Niger, announcing that he had succeeded in negotiating the border dispute, made two stipulations: "set up liaison
channels between their respective border authorities," and "establish a committee to study compensation for damages caused by
cross border raidings." [15]

It does not seem impossible for the arbitration committee of
OAU to set up similar procedures for cases of civil disorder, but
the idea seems to be to take the present state structures as
something firm enough to provide a base for tackling other problems. This is also in line with the principle of non-interference
in internal affairs of a state. With problems as pressing as illiteracy,
poverty, threats of neo-colonization, and the need to finance
liberation movements by the majority in southern Africa, it
would hardly be the time to question or tolerate the challenges
thrown at the legality or right to territorial integrity of any state.
Like the loyal opposition, such things almost seem to be luxuries.
Yet such challenges do arise, and for several reasons the OAU
is the only body that should and can effectively negotiate the
settlements. However, to affirm the integrity of a state and con-

stitution formulated in times of crisis, and without the participation of the people who called the whole thing to question to begin
with, would hardly seem the right way to achieve a long-lasting
settlement between warring factions.

Four member states recognized an independent Biafra–
Tanzania on April 13, 1968, Gabon on May 8, Ivory Coast on
May 14, and Zambia on May 20. They did so for what the leaders
separately termed humanitarian reasons; but President Nyerere of
Tanzania called attention to the whole process of the recognition
of states by the OAU. While affirming his belief in the necessity of
a federated Nigeria, he stressed the need of assuring the Biafran
people that their security and well-being would not be jeopardised
after the Civil War. Also, if the OAU could individually recognize
the right of Israel to exist because the people had not felt secure
anywhere else in the world, then why not Biafra, if, in the minds
of the secessionists, their very existence, let alone their desire to
determine their own future, was at stake? There are several
answers to this, but the point is that even if the OAU or the
federal military government saw them as obvious, there was no
neutral medium where the obviousness of a federal state could be
discussed.

The OAU as well as the individual states face a difficult position.
Even those states which recognize the existence of Biafra as an
entity realize the need for unity in this and the precarious situations they face in their states. But there is hardly any reason to
believe that the situation in Nigeria would influence events in
their own countries, despite assertions to the contrary. These
fears have resulted in the failure to bring about even a temporary
truce or a settlement short of military victory. Military intervention solved the Congo crisis. But what of the situation, like
the Nigerian Civil War, where intervention by United Nations
forces is unlikely and the military action is at a stalemate?

Although it is unpalatable now, someday the OAU will have
to discuss the question of when an entity can call itself a state,
and when a change of government is legitimate. South Africa
and Rhodesia, among others, are not recognized among the African
states because the majority in those countries do not have a voice
in their own future. They are representative of the past, where
the definition of who constituted the nation depended on the racial
background of the people in question. If a European violated an
African's territorial or civil rights, then this was not classified as

an illegitimate act. Secessionists regard their civil rights as having been violated. Traditional kingdoms not only regard themselves as coerced into an undesirable situation, but further claim their right to sovereignty by virtue of having been so for as long as they can remember.

In a rather direct fashion, both groups are calling to question the Western institution of a federal state. The answer may or may not lie in a modification of the institution or a simplification of its intricacies, so that the man in the street may see that the state is not against his particular interests, and that someone persuading him to put the interests of his tribe before those of the state is actually acting against the welfare of the tribe as well as the individual. The logical extension of the feeling of the expanded sense of self that Mazrui says developed after the colonial experience has not been exploited to the full. Tribes began to consider other adjacent tribes as part of self, and Mazrui argues that the Buganda would not now consider a ruler from the Banyora people as being foreigners.[16] This extension of self has crossed regional and other differences but it has not come to the point where it is a positive, all-embracing force, rather than just a nonexclusive, non-negative attitude. There is a "national consciousness," but this has not been developed to the most aggressive and assertive degree of national identity that is nationalism.[17] In the building of most nations the feeling of nationalism has resulted in the major group being the core around which the smaller tribes have been united, either willingly, or by force as in Germany. Once united, the general tendency has been to extend the influence to any other non-attached group nearby. There has been no time to develop a "social movement" which, though if altered in form and content over time is at any time larger and more amorphous than any single organization to permit this aggressive attitude to develop.[18] The OAU charter recognizes the presence of this dual identity, but also recognizes the need for large states in order to achieve the necessary self-control and prevent manipulation by outside forces. The charter is also against interference in the internal affairs of any state. Since the organization is important in helping define the relationship of the African states with each other as opposed to the world at large, it will have to consider the question of when a state ceases to be a state.

The current civil war has been just one more case of military ascendancy to political power. In several states the army has run the country after a coup, as in the Sudan, Ghana, and the Congo. In Nigeria two army officers were battling each other on a constitutional issue, the result of the political ineptitude of civilians. When the machinery of the state falls apart due to factionalism or failure to institute reforms, the army emerges as one of the country's distinct and united castes. Several reasons have been given to explain this military attitude. One has been the so-called colonial legacy, where the colonial power tried to keep tribal differences out of the army.[19] The emphasis on discipline, order, and obedience has also helped to promote the army's different outlook. With independence an intelligentsia emerged to lead the army, that is, a group of men with college degrees or some officer training at a metropolitan power's training center. Rightly or otherwise, they believe in the institution under which they were trained, and because they possess the only available physical force, they have acted to keep the status quo. In the Congo, General Mobutu shows no signs of ever leaving politics. In Ghana, the generals have restored the old order with a new constitution drawn up under their directions. General Gowon and Colonel Ojukwu have each drawn up their own respective constitutions.

The army has not shown any reactionary tendencies nor has there been a hardening of positions against politicians, primarily because the army itself has no long political tradition. The generals seem to be career men devoted to constitutionalism and order; as an institution the army did not take active part in the winning of independence. In fact, the army has been a catalyst in that it has preserved the old order by propping the system up and preventing it from total collapse when politicians failed. To the extent that the army has the potential to reshape the mood of the country's politics, the training of officers has become a vital quesiton. A revolt by the army which is uncontrolled by the officers, as in the Congo, can result in anarchy. If the politicians cannot control the generals, they might as well make them aware of the need for change, even if change entails some disorder, and also make them aware of the need for political adjustment in the army itself. It is not sufficient that only a few of them have any dictatorial tendencies: they have to see the need for economic and political change and the drastic measures sometimes necessary to bring about such changes, lest they act at every crisis to thwart painful but necessary adjustments. The intelligentsia in the army today, like in politics, is much more bureaucratic than it is innovative and is not large enough in numbers to coordinate state activities. The army officers were trained to run the army in states where the army's duties were to protect the country from external enemies and the government from disorderly elements. Much can be said for trying to attract talent to the army; if it is going to take the army to provide the proper atmosphere for progress, then the ideals of the army must be made to coincide with those of a progressive, civilian-run state.

Frantz Fanon attributes the failure of real revolutionary change to the inability of the national middle class to see into and explain the reasons for a popular act, its "intellectual laziness and spiritual penury." The middle class is devoid of any real power to bring about change and it has to rely on the former mother country to bail it out of trouble.[20] There is a risk that such an inept class will seize power in the army. Most, if not all the armies, rely on foreign powers for their equipment, training, and in some cases for part of their operational budgets. This manipulation by foreign powers is only one of the possible evils of military rule. The most important after-effect stems from the fact that an army is run by direct command from the general downward. There is an absence of dissent; primarily, orders are not to be questioned. A military government is more likely to put a similar halt to political activity, especially on the lower levels. To maintain their ideals of order and discipline even in the state, everything is done by presidential decree, and the usual legislative bodies become mere appendages if they continue to exist. Their actions may not serve to neutralize the national political figures and dissidents at whom the military rule is aimed, so much as they stymie political maturity at the regional levels by eliminating whatever degree of active participation by the public there was. The military government has the tendency to occupy itself with the preservation of national order, but does not have the wherewithal to provide for actual growth of the means to perpetuate this atmosphere after its departure; the longer a military rule remains, the greater, at least at the present time, the danger of this political atrophy. The atrophy is also encouraged by a false sense of change occurring with the coming to power of a different form of rule. If economic ills plagued the country under a civilian rule, the population might expect automatic change with a military government and relax their agitation for change. In the Congo, General Mobutu by unilateral decree passed constitutional changes on the organization of the provinces and their government, something which could be done in the course of political debate, but which the politicians had failed to do in 1962. The country might grow to expect such swift reaction to problems. In Ghana, the military overthrow of Nkrumah's government as a result of its economic and political failure has resulted in another civilian government; but the economic ills are as great as ever. The substitution of a military government for civilian authority does not always bring about changes in the structure of the political system either, or yield easy solutions for intractable problems.[21] On the other hand, it can lead to rifts appearing in the army just as in the political arena. A great deal of suffering can result when military methods are applied to political issues with army factions as members of the debating forum. The Nigerian Civil War could be the beginning of a shift of the battleground from the verbal but powerless civilian elite to the army. Local training of officers coupled with liberal doses of political education and propaganda could aid in increasing temperance and discussion when dealing with internal dissent.

The Congo crisis and the army mutiny in Uganda in January 1964, as well as the Nigerian Civil War, have shown the need for a strong army, and the dangers of a strong army which has no foreign threat to keep it busy. To allocate larger shares of the budget to the army in most African countries would mean greater costs in terms of development in other areas of the economy. Yet the army has to be strong if order is to be maintained. A government, which, despite massive foreign assistance, is not able to maintain order and security on its territory in the face of a revolutionary force, cannot be termed a national government.[22] The Congo government was never given a chance to develop its resources before chaos set in. On the other hand, one of the major problems in the Nigerian Civil war was the unwillingness of the federal forces to move swiftly and put an end to the conflict. The longer the conflict lasts, the more the secessionists are able to regroup and the more painful the effects of the war. Thus the allocation of a proportionately larger share of the national income to the defense budget at this stage of development, to enable swift deployment and action against disorder, might not really be a misallocation of resources. Economic development requires an atmosphere of vigorous but peaceful dissent and an assurance of internal order and stability, especially if it is imperative that foreign capital be attracted. Foreign investors attracted to the federation because of its promise of a large market should not have to look over their shoulders constantly for signs of dissolution. A strong military which is faithful to the concept of the state might act as a deterrent to any hasty action on the part of any region and, should anything happen, move quickly to restore order.

Mercenaries were one of the aftermaths of the Congo civil war. They became an important military factor in the Congo in September 1964 when they helped the Armée Nationale Congolaise to recapture the towns of Lisala, Boende, and later in November to seize Kindu. When eventually they were defeated and crossed into Ruanda they became an international political issue. The Congo government would have preferred that the disarmed men return for trial, while Ruanda was under pressure from overseas forces to grant amnesty and have them airlifted out of the country, as stated in the conditions for their disarming. In spite of the differences in opinions between the countries, the African leaders at the "Summit meeting of 12" in Kampala on December 15 sidestepped the issue of mercenaries. In due course the mercenaries were disbanded and some were repatriated. In the Nigerian Civil War, the Eastern Region was said to be aided by mercenaries from Portugal, and gunrunners of various nationalities have been making vast profits from the war. There are two different views on the use of mercenaries. In his advice to the prince, Machiavelli calls mercenaries cowardly, unreliable, and likely to bite the hand that feeds them. On the other hand, another viewpoint holds that the buying of mercenaries could be regaded as an act of independence.[22] Mazrui also regards it as a good thing in that after the conflict the nationals will have fewer atrocities to blame each other for, and therefore fewer causes for seeking revenge. They can become a unifying force by providing the nation with a common external enemy. To Machiavelli, the prince ought to make the art of war his primary concern and a science to be studied, the only science to study. If the prince could not lead his forces into combat, then command of the national army should be delegated to nationals. This had a lot to do with national prestige, cohesiveness, and the legitimacy of the claim to sovereignty by the prince in the eyes of his peers. Today the civilian prime minister would hardly look good in a saddle. In a civil war, more often than not, the very national leader to whom he should be delegating the command of the army is probably on the opposition. When a secessionist can purchase the services of a mercenary force, it is the sign of independence from the federation and also from the mother country to whom he is expected to run for aid. It is independence in that he and his followers can choose to whom they will delegate the defense of their lives and territorial integrity; it also shows a certain economic viability in that they can afford to support such an expensive form of defense. But such an exhibition of independence does not imply that the so-called state which substitutes purchased protection for national spirit, and the need for self-sacrifice that comes with this cohesiveness, has a right to exist as an independent entity. The actions of a group of leaders at the top do not imply the same liberty of choice for the general populace. The hiring of mercenaries can hardly be called an act carried out in the course of normal democratic action. There are no national referendums, no national contracts signed, nor are the legal agreements or terms of service made public. The Congo situation certainly proved that the mercenary in the end injures the state he is supposed to serve. As to being a unifying force by virtue of providing an exterior enemy and scapegoat for all the horrors of a civil war, this is an afterthought which sounds more logical than it really is. Mercenaries are only an agent. Though they may act outside their assigned duties, they are all the same invited in by the existing situation and at all times are a physical image of what the two sides actually feel for each other. They also display, in their ruthlessness, the contempt that the outside world might bear for the warring nation. Several politicians right now must be chagrined to read of proposed solutions to their country's problems suggested by the colonels Scrammes and Hoares in overseas newspapers, men whose only qualifications have been that of being highly paid soldiers of fortune invited by an ambitious secessionist. Nigeria can also pin all the tactical failure to end the long Civil War on the pilots and countries who bring guns into Biafra at a high profit; but the blame is more likely to fall even harder on the leaders of the secession for having exposed the country to public scrutiny and the resulting loss of national prestige. The presence of mercenaries, rather than helping heal the schism, contributes more toward destroying the national image and economy and sowing seeds for further friction.

The need for a strong military which backs the national government so it can determine its internal policy as well as protect itself has been shown in the Congo and Nigeria. In the Congo the national policy was to a large extent determined on the basis of how the United States, Belgium, and also the United Nations wanted events to turn out. The landing of Belgian and American paratroopers in the Congo on November 24, 1964, though for rescue purposes, demonstrated just how vulnerable the Congo was. At the beginning of the civil war in Nigeria, the federal military government gave bold deadlines for ending the Civil War, only to find their predictions fade away fast in the face of military aid to Biafra from various European and African countries—aid which could have been stopped by a powerful enough air force. This military helplessness is only an addendum to the economic dependence which prompted President Nyerere to say in a news conference that "the scramble for Africa has begun in real earnest and is going to be a much more dangerous scramble than the first one . . . this time African brother is going to slaughter African brother, not in the interests of Africa but in the interests of the imperialists both old and new." The Union Minière copper mining firm was caught right in the middle of the Congo crisis and largely for the company's interests Belgium had to indulge in a lot of political maneuvers. The oil companies are also in the middle of the Nigerian conflict. Each side has at one time or another accused the foreign oil consortiums of aiding the other side with funds. At the heart of the problem is the realization by both sides that they do not have the control of the economic situations in their areas, and that actually there is no viable national economy to control anyway, because of its dependence on the export sector. Most of the countries found it very difficult to marshal the economic resources of the country for the war effort. The country could be rich in copper, uranium ore deposits, or oil, but the conversion of this potential wealth to matériel lies in the hands of a foreign-owned and a foreign-government-influenced company. The states are learning that they have to eliminate the foreign corporation eventually and have control of the local economy in local hands as it grows. Development is likely to be achieved through large state-controlled enterprises, and not through small private concerns; for security reasons private foreign concerns are proving unsuitable. Nationalization might be the answer, or some other intermediate situation. There is no *a priori* reason why the concept of private enterprise as the mainstay of the country's economy should remain unquestioned. In the whole process of decolonizing there is a need for a complete evaluation of the colonial situation, and the big concern with monopolistic powers certainly has been part of the colonial experience. In nationalizing some of the copper interests in Zambia, President Kaunda noted that some of the companies had perpetual mineral rights in the country, an untenable situation. A representative of one of the companies involved was quoted in *The New York Times* as agreeing to the incongruency of having a rich foreign consortium operating in a poor country controlled entirely by foreign stockholders. A genuine nationalization drive with full participation by the local population could help bring about stability by giving the middle class a stake in the country's economic well-being and stability. Tanzania's attempt to carry out the Arusha Declaration by nationalizing the country's banks and large firms, including large export and import houses, has been the most ambitious move to date to control the country's economic route.

Does the problem of political instability and national solidarity of the states also pose a threat to the Pan African movement and the idea of an eventual political union of sorts of all the states? The federal military government of Nigeria has strongly pointed out that a successful Biafran secession attempt may lead to other Biafras elsewhere on the continent and destroy the OAU and with it any hopes of cooperation. It is not very clear how Katanga's attempt and failure influenced the then Eastern Region or the southern regions of Sudan. However, there is substance to the fear of the consequences of successful breakups; if present states find the going hard, twice that number would probably find even minimum dialogue almost impossible.

There are several economic as well as political reasons to support the need for some sort of African cooperation. For one, no single African state has any sizable control of the world trading situation. Since independence the states have remained divided and economically and militarily dependent on the mother country. They do not possess enough bargaining power when negotiating separately. Aid is extended only to those portions providing a market for exports of manufactured goods or to further the donor country's political interests. If the states bargained as an entity they could get better terms for their exports. At present the "sugar cube" policy used by metropolitan powers serves as bait to lure a country into more obligations and pull it into an almost scientifically refined combination of client states. The new state has to solicit new credit to balance its books and avoid political issues that conflict with the intentions of its benefactor. A case in point is the behavior of the former French West African states during the Algerian crisis. And in 1960 the Brazzaville Conference voiced opposition to those African states which directly supported the Congo (Kinshasa) government against Katanga, an idea more likely generated by a metropolitan power than by newly independent states. Besides economic reasons there is the advantage of establishing a common military establishment, a united front in international politics and combined efforts in combating illiteracy and other social problems. Those who regard such plans as impractical point to the diversity of the continent—different cultural backgrounds, colonial experiences, and ideology. Further, they claim it would be impossible to try and unify very different states some of which have difficulty preserving order in their own borders. The states are also said to cherish their new status and are not willing to release their sovereignty to any supranational organization. But attempts at various points in time to form some kind of organization show that Africans themselves hardly agree with this notion.

The Pan African movement outdates most of the independent African states. In its formative stage, it was a protest against racism in the Western Hemisphere and reached its peak with Marcus Garvey in the United States. Only at the sixth Pan African Conference of 1945 was there a strong African delegation. At that meeting strong support was expressed for nationalistic independence movements, primarily along the state lines already established by the colonists. When states started gaining independence in the late 1950s there was a shift towards reorganization along supranational lines with the formation of regional alliances, like the proposed Federation of East African States and the Organization Commune Africaine et Malgache (OCAM) in 1965. As far back as 1948 Nkrumah had ideas for a Union of West African States similar to the Soviet Union, an idea which was the object of the West African National Secretariat of which he was a member.[23] In 1959 the Federation of the States of the Sudan, Senegal, Upper Volta, and Dahomey was formed but it soon broke up and was followed by an entente by the Ivory Coast, Upper Volta, Niger, and Dahomey. Formation of regional alliances has continued, alliances which at times have been described as "patchwork compromise," making African unity nothing but an association of clients of a cooperative of consumers.[24] Nkrumah advocated a bold step into continental unity without regional alliances. The Organization of African States was formed in May of 1963 and though the eventual unity of the states was the aim, the Charter served the task of defining the relationships of the states with each other and with the other areas still under colonial rule. Since then political cooperation of the states has not been discussed.

The regional alliances have had growing pains and adjustments as well as some limited success. Some have started with political cooperation in mind and broken up over the issue; others have changed from political to economic agreements, and still other agreements have been formed as a reaction to the policies of other states. The East African Common Market represents favorable economic agreements, while the Ghana-Guinea-Mali union, the Brazzaville, Casablanca, and Monrovia groups represent political ententes.

In 1957, nationalist leaders from the territories of Kenya, Tanganyika, Uganda, and Nyasaland met to discuss their problems and agreed to the formation of a Pan African Freedom Movement (PAFMECA) which was to be a subgroup within the All Africa People's Conference. The organization was formally inaugurated at Mwanza in Tanganyika in 1958, shortly before the first meeting of the All Africa People's Conference at Accra in December of that year. Though considered only a subgroup within the AAPC to deal with local problems, PAFMECA soon developed an attitude of its own regarding the format of the proposed unity of African states. They supported the need to avoid hasty proposals and the development of regional associations as opposed to an all out union.[25] With the independence of Tanganyika in 1961, Dar es Salaam became the unofficial headquarters of the organization. At Addis Ababa in February of 1962 Ethiopia and Somalia were admitted to the organization, the former to ensure the support of Kenya on the Greater Somalia question and the latter for economic reasons. Nationalist organizations from South Africa and South West Africa were admitted as affiliates and the name was changed to the Pan African Freedom Movements for East Central and Southern Africa (PAFMESCA). There was equal representation of governments with nationalistic movements, and the primary concern of the organization was with the promotion of struggle against the colonialists in the territories. PAFMESCA played a vital part in the boosting of the United National Independence Party of Northern Rhodesia to the fore in the national elections of 1962. It helped unite the factions in Mozambique to form the liberation front, FRELIMO. With the formation of the OAU the task of promoting liberation movements was transferred to its committee and PAFMESCA was dissolved.

At about the time of PAFMECA there was talk of an East African Federation of Kenya, Uganda, and Tanganyika. Nyerere talked of demanding the freedom of the whole of East Africa as a political unit from the British. At his instigation negotiations for a federation resulted in the Nairobi declaration of June 5, 1963. The East African leaders pledged themselves to a political federation, upholding "the spirit of Pan-Africanism and the concept of nationalism as opposed to tribalism, racialism and inward looking policies." A working party was to be established to draft a constitution later that June and a full scale conference was to follow in August to discuss the proposals. Zanzibar was to be included in the organization soon after its elections in July of that year. The working party drafted a constitutional proposal, but the conference was not convened in August. Disagreement centered on the structure of the draft. Uganda thought the proposals too restricting and submitted an alternative which Kenya and Tanganyika felt was too loosely structured. Uganda boycotted a meeting called by the other two countries, effectively ending all talk of a political union.

In 1964, however, Tanzania and Kenya moved to establish an economic agreement, and signed an agreement with Uganda at Kampala in April. The purpose was to establish a uniform policy of industrialization; the allocation of industry was to be made through a system of licensing controls where the new industry would be "persuaded," through the mediation of a Licensing Board, to locate its plant in any of the three countries. A system of quota restrictions was established whereby the country with a trade deficit in intercountry trade could apply quota restrictions against the others, in effect forcing the industry affected to relocate. The plan ran into difficulties because prospective businesses sought to establish their plants in Nairobi where the market was. The reallocation plans only served to deter industry from basing its operations in the three countries, but the Kampala Agreement was considered some sort of compensation for Tanzania to remain in the East African Common Market which had been in existence since colonial days. Tanzania, however, embarked on a policy of self-reliance and placed several articles manufactured in Kenya on the list of prohibited imports in April 1965. This blocked the ratification of the Kampala Agreement. In November, the Phillips Commission was appointed to save whatever idea of the Common Market there was. The Commission emphasized cooperation rather than federation. Its work was partly complicated by the dissolution of the Common Currency Board and the adoption of separate currencies by all the countries in 1966. The outcome of the Commission's work, the East African Cooperation Treaty, was signed in Kampala on June 6, 1967, to become effective in December. The fifteen-year agreement provided, among other things, for the maintenance of a common tariff and an agreement not to enter into concessions with any foreign country unless the concessions were available to all three partners. Internal tariffs, with the exception of a revenue transfer tax, were to be eliminated. Conditions under which the revenue tax were applicable were well defined. An East African Development Bank, with headquarters in Kampala, was established to harmonize the fiscal incentives offered to industry by the three countries. It would also provide finances for development from contributions based on the members' ability to pay. More important, the treaty states that other countries could become members or associates by submitting applications. Zambia and Ruanda have since applied for membership.

Thus, although political union failed in East Africa, economic cooperation was achieved. The immediate economic benefits reaped from this cooperation could encourage further cooperation and hence provide necessary communication channels to facilitate new agreements. In West Africa, Ghana and Guinea tried to establish both political and economic unity when Guinea became independent. Because of disagreements with the French government, Guinea was cut from the French community when she obtained self-rule. Ghana came to her aid with a loan of £ 10 million, most of which was never utilised. The countries decided on a closer political tie and The Ghana–Guinea Union was formed on May 1, 1959. The declaration stated, among other things, that any African state could join and that each state would retain its own individuality and structure while surrendering some of its sovereignty to the Union. There was to be an Economic Council to study policy and to establish a Union Bank. Mali joined the Union to form the Union of African States (UAS). Disagreement over Ghana's policy towards the Congo and its economic agreement with Upper Volta stopped the Union from ever getting off the ground, and by 1962 it barely existed.

Three more political groupings are worthy of mention because they reflect the disagreements among states over the question of secession in another state. A group of states met in the Ivory Coast to discuss the possibility of former French colonies' negotiating a treaty between France and Algeria. The countries represented were Congo (Brazzaville), Ivory Coast, Senegal, Mauritania, Upper Volta, Niger, Gabon, Chad, Malagasy Republic (Madagascar), Cameroon, and the Central African Republic. The group strove to avoid a split with De Gaulle "who began French decolonization, granted independence to thirteen African states, including Madagascar." They also advocated negotiation in the Congo, opposed political union between states, and asserted the independence of Mauritania. The pro-Lumumba forces in the African states decided to regroup their power and held a conference at Casablanca in January 1961. Delegates came from Morocco, Ghana, Guinea, Mali, Libya, Algeria, and the United Arab Republic. The conference condemned France for establishing "the puppet State, the said Mauritania, against the will of the people concerned." They also condemned Belgium for dividing Ruanda Urundi into two states, and Israel for being "an instrument in the service of imperialism and neo-colonialism not only in the Middle East but also in Africa and Asia." Clearly, the group was against any further division of the continent, and would not have opposed the use of force to keep states intact. Ghana, for one, kept its forces in the Congo after all other African states had withdrawn theirs. The so-called moderates, in reaction to the Casablanca Conference, met in Monrovia in May 1961. In addition to the Brazzaville group there were representatives from Liberia, Nigeria, Sierra Leone, Ethiopa, Togo, and Libya. They reiterated their belief in the need for negotiation in the Congo but condemned hasty recognition of breakaway regimes in the Congo and taking sides with rival groups in any fashion, an obvious reference to the Casablanca powers. The two groups lost significance with the formation of the OAU in 1963.

Within a period of ten years several political and economic associations of one type or another have been formed, dissolved, modified, or expanded. All expressed a desire for the eventual inclusion of all independent African states. The idea seems to go beyond personalities or national politics. The effect of a secession movement on the idea of unity is both fluid and open to speculation. The Congo crisis is an example of the internal struggles of a state which became an issue between two opposing groups of nations. The Monrovia group wanted a negotiated settlement in the Congo, something which could have led to a sticky issue on the legality of Katanga. The situations in the Congo and Nigeria, however, are not quite the same; there seems to have been a clash of personalities involved in the former, something which is not evident in the present case. But political subdivisions could lead to more opportunity for similar clashes. A successful secessionist state would hardly be willing to give up some of its hard-won sovereignty to any supranational body without imposing some untenable conditions. After all, the whole point of seceding from a federation is to be able to hold all the cards in one's hands. The more states there are, the more likely the behavior of any regional grouping to become intransigent when they can claim a majority on their side. The Monrovia group claimed that the Casablanca group could not represent a general consensus because there were only five states in that union, while their group was composed of twenty states. This does not make for a peaceful solution of differences.

The states seem to face a conflicting set of choices which they themselves did not necessarily create. Does the present need for economic development, for instance, conflict with the concept of representative government? To sufficiently utilize their resources the states have to be large enough units to recognize economies of scale, full benefits of foreign aid, and comparative advantages. There is very little time for experimentation, for they are not operating in a vacuum. The rich are getting richer, often at their expense, and the gap widens with time. Political growth requires the populace to undergo an educational stage in the intricacies of institutions and gain practical experience in their workings. The process necessarily involves turmoil, in that the people themselves have to find the right form of government. Some would say that democracy is the only framework wherein men of different tribes, languages, and religions can live at peace with each other. They point out, however, that the uncertainties generated by the rapid change and the emotional temperature of independence gave unscrupulous men a chance to seize power. The political institutions adopted from the metropolitan mother country did not distinguish between democracy and license, on the one hand, and, on the other hand, failed to give minority and opposition groups enough representation.[26] That assumes that self-contained small units like tribes and religious sects are compatible not only with democracy but that such a democratic structure is compatible with the need for rapid economic change and even more rapidly rising economic aspirations. The idea of a democracy which recognizes ethnic differences by stratifying the state's power so that the small tribe has some control of its affairs sounds morally defensible, but it will operate only if the various levels recognize the necessity for the supratribal organization. Most African leaders seem to be denying this. Most organizations express a desire to transcend the feelings of tribalism, supposedly one of the legitimate subgroups in the state. There are countries with one-party legislative bodies and military governments, all of which restrict, to a degree, opinion. Whatever the expert opinion on this may be the African states and their populations will have to discover for themselves, through experimentation, the right format for their political institutions. Until now, the experimentation has involved military coups, assassinations, secession attempts, and various regional federations. These seem to be temporary situations; to expect stable political situations after only ten years of self-rule is to display political immaturity. Disorder is a necessary part of the development process, and occasionally violence becomes the unfortunate consequence of the disorder. It will subside only after the institutions have found their own equilibrium and the people are relatively satisfied with it. But can all this be consistent with the need to eliminate illiteracy, and poverty, and the need to industrialize? Economic development of an underdeveloped country now requires focusing all resources and manpower on that problem alone because of the inherent dangers of the whole process. It is incongruous with factionalism, disorder or a weak central government. Most countries just do not have the skilled manpower required to sufficiently man both the central and regional governmental machinery to make them function harmoniously. A small secessionist state would have even less. If local government is to mirror a democratic institution, a poorly run central government would be worse than no central government. The central government must be a strong one. Concentration of power, at least for the present, must be in the hands of the national body. When, or whether, this will ever be deemed unnecessary is another question; it also points out the conflict that may exist between economic and political goals in both long and short ranges. The situation seems to point to the concentration of efforts to solve the short-range problems lest there be no long run.

This conflict between the long range and the present also exists for the concept of Pan-Africanism. The idea will continue to influence the internal policy decisions of states, but on a lesser scale than the domestic strife in member states. As seen in the formation of the now defunct Monrovia and Casablanca powers, regional cooperation has been destroyed or built up depending on the alignment of the states towards a secession attempt. But such situations are as transitory as the events that cause them. To try and predict the future from the present situation would be as erronous as it would have been in 1961 if there had been an attempt to predict the future on the basis of the Monrovia–Casablanca split.

Disorder and internal strife on the present scale is not only to be expected, it is logical. It is one thing to expect the coups and secession attempts and try to find ways to learn from them; it is another to say they should not happen. For the only way to stop their instigation is by stifling free thought. Economic development requires a certain stability, but this cannot be used to repress an expression of grievances and expectations. Some middle-of-the-road solution has to be found, because the process of questioning the authority has to go on, and more vigorously than in any developed country, before people reach the stage of political apathy that is at times sparked by economic well-being. Africans have won the right to establish states, in the first instance, to establish and maintain their equality as men. But they have not as yet developed the nations for which the state is to become the external expression.[27] Nation-building will require a constant rearrangement of borders and minds as the scope and direction of the respective nations emerge and the gap between nation and state is narrowed. The definition of state boundaries has altered very little since they were set up during colonial days. The argument for the status quo would be that the definition of the state is inviolable, but that of the nation has to be altered until the two coincide. Secessionists, on the other hand, would have the definitions of both state and nation under fire. This questioning is an important issue in the long-range establishment of states everyone will at least respect. Just how much present state associations or prospects for federations now are affected depends on how the associations themselves react to the situation, their ability to distinguish between genuine grievances needing redress and political machinations of ambitious men who may also be getting external encouragement. The viability of an organization of this type depends primarily on its ability to exist as an entity without the need for force, its support by the member regions' realization that it is a necessary thing, and the ability to react effectively and swiftly to threats to its existence. Its challenge, as well as the state's, is to fashion a supranational organization that can widen the outlook of people who have been accustomed to thinking in terms of small units, to give them a broader political responsibility and make them want to delegate their power to it and protect it from disintegration. There is a lot to be said for the growth of national sentiment at the same time as the centralizing tendency.[28] But it is up to each state to inspect its own internal organization and adjust it to those implementations which are necessary to survive the existence of different ethnic groups and to achieve the desired wider associations. Although there is an African conciousness, there is not yet an African social "organization" on which we can focus our attempt to explain social facts, for social or political facts can only be explained by similar but lagged social or political facts in the focus of the political or social organization under which they occur. This permits a scientific approach that allows hypotheses formulation, speculation, and testing. Although African countries are living in a scientific age, little which has happened so far indicates the existence of a pattern or permits reliable, safe scientific speculation. It seems each event has to be considered separately for the moment since each is establishing a precedent. The sample is not large enough in each case, nor is it homogenous enough when looked at collectively, to make useful deductions.

Notes

1. A. Segal, "Ruanda—The Underlying Cause," *Africa Report,* April 1964, p. 5.

2. Donald S. Rothchild and M. Rogin, "Uganda," in *National Unity and Regionalism in Eight African States,* ed. Gwendolen Carter (Ithaca, N.Y.: Cornell University Press, 1966), p. 342.

3. Ibid., p. 341.

4. Edward Bustin, "The Congo," in *Five African States: Responses to Diversity,* ed. Gwendolen Carter (Ithaca, N.Y.: Cornell University Press, 1963), p. 119.

5. *La province du Katanga et l'Indépendence Congolaise,* Documents du Ministre des Affaires Etrangères, No. 1.

6. *U.S. Army Handbook for the Sudan* (Washington, D.C.: U.S. Government Printing Office, 1964), p. 306.

7. F. G. Carnell, "Political Implications of Federalism in New States," in *Federalism and Economic Growth in Underdeveloped Countries,* ed. Ursula Hicks (New York: Oxford University Press, 1961), pp. 22–23.

8. K. B. Collard, *Political Forces in Pakistan* (New York: Institute of Pacific Relations, 1959), p. 3.

9. Ibid., p. 9.

10. Ibid.

11. P. C. Lloyd, *Africa in Social Change—Changing Traditional Societies in the Modern World* (Baltimore: Penguin Books, Inc., 1967), p. 328.

12. Ibid.

13. *Africa Report,* November 1967, p. 36.

14. *Report of the OAU Consultative Mission to Nigeria,* September 1967, p. 6.

15. *Africa Report,* November 1967, p. 36.

16. Ali Mazrui, *Towards a Pax Africana—A Study of Ideology and Ambition* (Chicago: University of Chicago Press, 1967), p. 5.

17. I. Wallenstein, *Africa: The Politics of Unity* (New York: Random House, 1967), p. 225.

18. Helen Kitchen, ed., *Footnotes to the Congo Story* (New York: Walker and Co., 1967), p. 167.

19. Frantz Fanon, *The Wretched of the Earth* (New York: Grove Press, 1968), p. 135.

20. Kitchen, *Footnotes,* p. 172.

21. A. Tevoedjre, *Pan Africanism in Action—An Account of the UAM* (Cambridge, Mass.: Harvard University Press, 1965), p. 53.

22. Mazrui, *Towards a Pax Africana,* p. 206.

23. Ali Mazrui, *On Heroes and Uhuru Worship—Essays on Independent Africa* (London: Longmans, Green and Co., 1967), p. 126.

24. Tevoedjre, *Pan Africanism,* p. 6.

25. Colin Legum, *Pan Africanism: A Short Political Guide* (New York; Frederick A. Praeger, Inc., 1965), p. 73.

26. Arthur Lewis, *Politics in West Africa* (New York: Oxford University Press, 1967), p. 89.

27. David Currie, *Federalism and the New Nations of Africa* (Chicago: University of Chicago Press, 1964), p. 64.

28. Ibid., p. 83.

7

NIGERIA—CLASS STRUGGLE AND THE NATIONAL QUESTION

Jimoh Lawal

At a time when most of Africa is struggling against Western cultural and economic imperialism, Marxian concepts of analysis should be of crucial importance. For only a scientific analysis of the social dynamics and the nature of their evolution will allow the revolutionary and progressive forces to adopt a correct strategy. Yet there are those Africans who would argue that Marxian concepts have no relevance to Africa. (Marxism was developed in Europe and its application must be limited to Europe alone.) They even assert, as further proof, that African society is classless.[1] In the United States, where this kind of retrogressive thinking takes a different form—a form which smacks of paternalism—there is a group of American scholars who, because they have dabbled with some research in Africa, proclaim themselves "Africanists." These men would swear with a self-assurance that would surprise even their predecessors, the missionaries, that the most important struggle in Africa is tribalism—poor Africans!

Although Marx's study was based on his examination of the emergence or genesis of European capitalism, the method which he developed retains a universal validity. It emphasizes the importance of the forces of production to society showing how they determine the dynamics of production and beyond that the overarching framework of the societies. In human societies when a certain stage is reached in the development of the productive forces,

258

these societies break up into antagonistic social classes. In Nigeria, and in most of Africa, the development of the productive forces has obviously reached the stage where social classes have appeared already. Yet to expect the social classes of Nigeria to be identical with the classical European social classes based on slavery, feudalism, or capitalism is to commit a very serious mistake. No two societies are identical. Analyses, like revolutions, cannot be exported.

The Emergence of Social Classes in Nigeria

It would be safe to assume that by the seventh century, or certainly not later than the tenth century, the dominant mode of production in Nigeria was the village community. Of course there would have been a variety of village communities. It is equally true that the village community was a classless society, though certainly there was a form of social differentiation based on organizational division of labor. This social differentiation, though it had a well-defined hierarchy, was not antagonistic and therefore did not result in the formation of social classes. The traditional society possessed a form of egalitarianism sometimes called "communalism," as distinguished from tribal communism which may have existed at a much earlier period of social evolution. In this communal society a characteristic humanism reconciled individual advancement with group welfare. It is this spirit of communalism that has been idealized by some and imposed by others on contemporary African society.[2] This attitude ignores the objective historical evolution of the village community. It denies the dialectical process of social evolution, which demonstrates the movement of societies from a lower to a higher level, and it is therefore unscientific.

Nowhere in Nigeria has the village or tribal community survived in its original form. Its devolution began long before British colonialism; it began as early as the eighth century with the emergence of the Kingdom of Zaghawa, and later the Kanem and Songhai empires. Over the next ten centuries the process continued as other states emerged: the Bornu empire, the seven Hausa states in the North, and in the South, the Yoruba, Benin and Oyo states or what Crowder calls the "Kingdoms of the Forest."[3]

The new states could not have emerged without a change in traditional social organization of Nigerian communities. According to the theory of the evolution of societies the state only appears where class antagonisms exist, for the state is only the instrument by which one class dominates another. The states that developed in what was later to be called Nigeria do not escape this universal law of human evolution.[4] The processes of the establishment and development of social classes was slow, lasting centuries while the state existed only in an embryonic form.

The state comprised a few rulers, the king or oba or emir and his court. These rulers were either conquerors establishing their hegemony over the local peoples, as in the North, or the direct descendants of local rulers whose power had been increased by the strengthening of the traditional hierarchy, as was generally the case in the South. Their subjects were mostly peasants living in outlying villages and forming the only source of agriculture and craft production. At this stage feudalism proper had not yet developed, the state constituting merely a federation of villages. This situation was to change gradually, beginning with the influence of Islam and the slave trade.

This trade and the civil wars that were its result destroyed the ancient system. "Money-lust artificially introduced into black Africa, pushed the population into perpetual war to procure slaves to sell to the Arab and European traders." [5] This plague spread over Nigeria which, as part of the infamous slave coast, constituted the greatest source of "black gold." On the basis of this, trade states were formed and destroyed around forceful military leaders, thus the destruction of the ancient Oyo empire and the Yoruba civil wars of 1700–1850 and thus the eventual disintegration of the Benin Kingdom. The immense movements of the population because of the slave wars, the flight of the farmers before the slave raiders, brought about the emergence of new, unequal relationships between formerly friendly neighbors.

The influence of Islam in the Northern areas of Nigeria also affected the relationships of the different groups of people. The thrust of the military expeditions of Usman dan Fodio ended by 1850 in the establishment of the Fulani Islam empire over the whole of the Northern areas of Nigeria. In almost the whole area, with the important exception of the Middle Belt, a real feudality was instituted. This new arrangement destroyed the equitable balance between the herdsmen and farmers. The herdsmen, usually Fulani, were more powerful in war, better organized, and galvanized by religious appeal. Collectively they imposed themselves as the exploiters, collecting tribute from the farmers reduced to the state of peasantry. At the same time that the class differences among the farmers increased, the traditional rulers seized the herds of livestock which were formerly collectively owned.

We might safely say, therefore, that almost half a century before the establishment of British colonialism in Nigeria, the institution of class states had emerged. Its evolution was characterized by the unequal relationships between ethnic groups, the formation of a noble caste or privileged group imposing tribute on the farmers who had been reduced to the state of peasants and vassals, and the development of commercial exchanges and the appearance of a merchant class.

Class Struggle and British Colonialism

The establishment of colonial rule in Nigeria evolved in three stages. First, there was the period of the initial contact between the Europeans, in this case the Portuguese, and the coastal Nigerians in what was then the Benin empire. Then the direction of trade changed from the gold of the initial trading period to commerce in human beings. Closely following, with the abolition of the slave trade, came the so-called legitimate trade. From now on the march of British colonial interest had begun. Underlying all these stages, however, was the economic motive. In fact, these stages represented or reflected the changes that were taking place in the development of European capitalism. Capitalism arose in Europe on the basis of the wealth it seized from Africa, North and South America, Asia, and Australasia. The development of some of this wealth had led Europe to start the African slave trade. But with the advancement of industrial techniques by the nineteenth century, the growth of large-scale industry, and the concentrations of economic power in the hands of a few, Europe had moved from free competitive capitalism to monopoly capitalism and imperialism.[6]

The development of the slave trade came about with the discovery of the Americas and the colonization of North America by the British and French. The Africans, it was discovered, were capable of surviving working conditions which the aboriginal Indians were not. The real colonization of Africa developed as the European powers eventually decided to do away with the African middlemen and establish a monopoly over the colony.

The change in the British slavers' role from being the greatest plunderers to being the greatest advocates of the abolition of the slave trade involved no humanitarian change of attitude. With the development of the industrial revolution in Britain and cotton trade with America, interest in the slave trade was rendered obsolete. Abolition of the slave trade was therefore only one of the manifestations of the major changes from the era of mercantilism to that of the industrial revolution and aggressive free trade.

"The humanitarianism so widely advertized at the time was, in one sense, the reflection on the ideological plane of changes taking place in the economic sphere." [7] The abolitionist movement did not lead to a British policy of abandoning all economic contact with the coastal Nigerians. Abolitionism actually worked to the advantage of an economic circle of British capitalists in search of a dumping ground for their manufactured goods. It was in their interest to leave the Nigerian populations intact so that they would provide large markets.

From now on, the flag was to follow trade; and in this development the explorers of the African Association,[8] the missionaries,[9] and eventually the merchants of the Royal Niger Company,[10] all played their parts in the shady history of the establishment of British imperial rule in Nigeria. The British employed every trick in the book, from gun-boat diplomacy and outright military conquest to institution of a treaty system and the infamous indirect rule.

These tricks, however, were predicated by the very stiff resistance of the coastal—and later the Northern—Nigerians. The city-states that had grown up in response to the slave trade together with the older kingdoms of Benin and Yorubaland were eager to maintain their monopoly of the trade between the coastal and inland areas of Nigeria. The ruling classes of these states are truly the first modern comprador capitalists of Southern Nigeria, and their resistance forms perhaps the first chapter of the nationalist movement in Nigeria. By a curious twist of history the descendants of these rulers were destined to lead the nationalist movement in the 1940s and 1950s—a wry comment on the bourgeois nature of the Nigerian nationalist movement.

Suffice it to say that the resistance of these states lasted almost one century (1807–1906). Their eventual defeat resulted from a combination of factors: the ruthlessness of the British advance, the development of a new elite or ruling class whose interests were congenitally tied to the British exploiters, and the conversion of the old ruling class into agents of British imperial rule.

In terms of our analysis, how did the establishment of British rule influence the social class relationships? How did it affect the ethnic relationships in Southern and Northern Nigeria? Are there any direct links between this period and the present situation in Nigeria? It is our contention that, making allowances for local variations, the slave wars and skirmishes—especially the Yoruba civil wars—the British military expeditions, and the activities of the missionaries and merchants had a profound effect on the coastal societies. There followed the accelerated decadence of the village community and a reinforcement of traditional class differences. Colonization introduced and hastened the development of new class and ethnic differences both of which were linked with the exploitation of the country.

In the Northern part of the country the changes were less profound. The societies of the Hausa states that had emerged since the tenth century had changed very little. The Hausa aristocracy enjoyed a medieval ascendency over the Hausa peasant masses until Usman dan Fodio's Muslim jihad, when they were displaced by the Fulani aristocracy. It is doubtful to what extent dan Fodio Islamized these feudal masses, but they form what is certainly the most exploited class in Nigeria. The British, for all their liberal talk, did absolutely nothing to right the condition of the Northern peasantry. Aligning with the emirs and rulers, the British sought to convert these into willing instruments of British imperialism. A British official, precursor of Lord Lugard, evil genius of British imperialism, writes around 1890, "Our aim is to rule through existing chiefs, to raise them in the administrative scale, to enlist them on our side in the work of progress and good government." [11] It was, of course, in the interest of these sultans and emirs to act as tools and stooges of the British in order to maintain their age-old power over the peasants (the *talakawa*). In the next fifty years the descendants of this Fulani aristocracy were destined to be the best supporters of the British and the plague of the Nigerian polity. The peoples of the Middle Belt area of the North, whom we will discuss later, formed a group distinct from the rest of the North and, never having come under hegemony of the Fulani empire, have been the most progressive elements in this region.

In the South, the least hierarchical, most exploited area, the urbanized nonindustrial proletariat was developing. Its counterparts in the North were fewer and could be found in cities like Kano and Sokoto and Zaria, but these were generally isolated from the rural proletariat and peasantry. Along with the urbanized proletariat, the unemployed and unemployable lumpen-proletariat so glorified by Fanon was developing.[12]

Consequent to the liquidation of the former urban aristocracy of middlemen a more modern comprador class or infantile bourgeoisie has developed. This class includes the commercial and bureaucratic bourgeoisie and the intellectuals—the Ziks and the Awolowos, the groups that led the independence movement. In the countryside their counterparts consist of the rural bourgeoisie, the descendants of older hierarchized aristocracies, especially in Yorubaland; these are the owners of the huge cocoa plantations. Usually eager to maintain their privileges, they are always at loggerheads with the urban infantile bourgeoisie. Below them are the rural proletariat of seasonal, rural, and migrant workers. And at the very bottom of the scale, the Southern peasantry of small land farmers bears its exploitation in silence.

Superimposed on this hierarchy was British administration. British colonial interest aligned itself with the most reactionary forces of the Northern feudal lords and the Southern commercial comprador class; it enjoyed an undisputed monopoly of trade through its companies, preventing the development of any industry; it established Barclay's Bank and the Bank of West Africa to funnel in and out the funds of the finance capitalists of Britain; it organized local police forces to crush any opposition that might endanger the peaceful exploitation of the country.

For the next fifty years as the British sought to establish their control over the huge country, they used every means available to stem the rising tide of nationalism, not even refraining from bare-faced violence when they thought it necessary. But British colonial policy is too well known to need elaboration here.[13]

Meanwhile the class struggle continued on two fronts. Internally, the peasants, the working class and progressive members of the national bourgeoisie were aligned against the reactionary forces of the feudal classes and the comprador and bureaucratic bourgeoisie. At the national level those struggling for liberation opposed the British imperialistic goals manifest in the colonial exploitation of Nigeria. However, the two fronts were the two different aspects of the same class struggle of the oppressed Nigerian classes against the internal and external oppressors. In the end the fight for national liberation in Nigeria failed because it did not understand the Janus-like nature of the struggle; it failed to combine the overthrow of foreign political rule and foreign economic domination with the defeat of those traditional domestic forces, economic and political, which stand in the way of democracy and revolutionary change. In other words, "the anti-colonial struggle, to be complete, has to become a political, social and economic revolution, one that destroys imperialism and feudalism . . . and makes possible the full democratic participation of the people in running the affairs of the new state so that they can refashion their lives and ensure the building of a modern and prosperous society." [14] Nothing of the sort happened in Nigeria and the seeds of the present tragedy were sown then by the same class of people who now control the country.

Yet we cannot fail to wonder why this course of events took place, or what role the different classes played. Was civil war merely an accident, or was it made possible because of the class nature of Nigerian society?

National Liberation or Neo-Colonialism

Our struggle in Nigeria for national liberation and independence was not an easy one, though neither so protracted nor nearly so violent as the one our Algerian brothers fought against the French. But wherever the struggle took place, whether it was Nigerian women rioting in the East over tax or coal miners striking in Enugu, the British-educated "bourgeois" elite took credit for it, directing our people's sincere protest toward reformist goals. These intellectual bourgeois elements, more sophisticated in the ways of the Western world, inevitably emerged as the leadership of the national liberation movement. The urban proletariat and the peasantry were generally unconscious and unorganized and they became the tools of the bourgeois elements who were not interested in true national liberation nor in the revolutionary overthrow of the colonial system. True to their interest, they sought only to replace the British exploiters; thus the movement for national independence in Nigeria bore the marks of compromise from its birth.

Elsewhere we have talked about the nature of British colonialism. Here let it be reiterated that Britain had allied herself with certain economic and social strata of Nigerians which had an interest in supporting colonialism. Thus, colonial rule was in reality an alliance—an alliance between the occupying power and the internal forces of conservatism and tradition.

Yet as the century evolved, especially after World Wars I and II—themselves a result of the internal contradictions of the capitalist world—it became necessary for Britain to put colonial rule on a new footing to meet with the growth and development of the workers and the commercial and intellectual elite. Besides, the emergence of a world socialist system could not have gone unnoticed by the British.

Herbert Macaulay (a Nigerian despite his name), coming from the Lagos Yoruba bourgeois aristocracy, had since the early 1920s begun to form the fragments of a political body. At first the British ignored this movement, limited as it was to Lagos. However, gradually they began to see the advantage of directing this incipient nationalism. In the next three decades they imposed three different constitutions on Nigeria: the Richards, the Macpherson, and the 1954 constitutions.[15] All these constitutions were compromises. The Richards constitution established regional and ethnic chauvinism, the Macpherson constitution streamlined it, and the 1954, or independence, constitution consolidated it. The commercial and intellectual bourgeoisie, having had the initiative stolen from them, followed the British lead like stooges. Except for a few who made a feeble and futile whimper, they set about the business of forming regional parties based on the three biggest ethnic groups: the Hausa, the Ibo and the Yoruba. The parties created eventually became the Northern Peoples' Congress (NPC) in the extensive North, the National Council of Nigeria and Cameroons (NCNC) in the East, and Action Group in the West. The leadership of these parties were either the commercial and bureaucratic bourgeoisie or the feudal aristocracy of the major ethnic groups in each of the three regions. The rank and file of these parties, however, were, in the South, the urban proletariat, the petty bourgeoisie, and some of the peasantry; in the North, it consisted mostly of the peasantry and a minute proletariat.

Thus the British had perfected the modernization of colonialism in Nigeria, and by 1960 British imperialism had reached a new stage—the stage of neo-colonialism.[16] Thus 1960 was the year independence was won and lost around slogans and structures of Western liberal democracy imported wholesale to Nigeria. Others, understanding the nature of colonialism, have won their freedom, gun in hand, through armed struggle, but we in Nigeria because of our reactionary leadership had secured a phony independence through constitutional talks! One might well ask, as Egbuna does in his pamphlet, "How can you sit down at a table with your oppressor and ask him how best to get rid of himself? Unless he is an extremely foolish man, which no colonial power is or can afford to be, the best he can do is to give you a rope to hang yourself and save him the trouble of doing the job himself. That is precisely what has happened in Nigeria." [17] By 1960 neo-colonialism had ushered in a federal Nigerian government based on a coalition between the Eastern Nigerian commercial and bureaucratic bourgeoisie of the NCNC and the feudal masters of the NPC. The Action Group had to content themselves with being the opposition.

The NCNC, which had in the 1950s been the most progressive party, by the 1960s was more retrogressive. Under the leadership of Azikiwe, Mbadiwe and Okotie-Eboh it became the instrument of the Eastern and Midwestern commercial bourgeoisie. Aligned with the reactionary feudals, it fostered a neo-colonialist and servile policy abroad and one of outright and cynical oppression of the urban proletariat and peasantry at home. From the moment of independence it isolated its left-wing elements, eventually expelling Chike Obi from the party.

It was to the Action Group then that fell the mantle of the anti-imperialist struggle, as much as was possible within the neo-colonialist structure of the government. Within the party leadership there had always existed a left and a right wing. The right wing represented the rural bourgeoisie and the local wealthy class favorable to compromise with imperialism. The left wing represented certain sections of the progressive petit bourgeoisie and intellectuals and was generally favorable to the urban proletariat and the rural masses. It appears that from the mid-1950s the radical wing of the party had captured power and to a large extent succeeded in liquidating the rural bourgeoisie and remnants of the feudal chiefs. This radical wing numbered among its ranks intellectuals like Rotimi Williams, Anthony Enahoro, J. S. Tarka of the United Middle Belt Congress (UMBC), and the firebrand from the East, S. G. Ikoku. Under these men the Action Group came to be the one party that could truly be called "national," although it was basically still a nonrevolutionary party. It was the party that supported the formation of new states and tried to tackle the question of national minorities squarely. It supported the formation of a state for the Middle Belt and thus won a working alliance with the UMBC and threatened the Northern hegemony of the NPC. In the East the Action Group bolstered its image among the minorities by supporting the creation of the COR (Calabar–Ogoja–Rivers) states, thereby incurring the bitter animosity of the NCNC bureaucratic and bourgeois leadership. That the Midwest State was created in 1963, carved from the old Western Region, was perhaps no surprise, although the Action Group, in supporting this move, strove to weaken the state's support for the NCNC.

But the brightest star in the crown of victories of the radical wing of the Action Group appeared in 1960–1961 when it successfully spearheaded a national attack against the proposed Anglo-Nigerian defense pact. Britain was trying to put the finishing touches on its neo-colonial edifice by adding military to economic exploitation. The bourgeois-feudal coalition government had at first acquiesced to the British fraud, but backed down under public pressure including the dramatic action of the university students who, storming parliament, actually carried out members! However, from now on the reactionary forces began to strike back. The bourgeois-feudal coalition government had become increasingly fearful of the Action Group and the support it had begun to gain among the progressive anti-imperialist urban masses and the enlightened young people.

But the radical wing of the Action Group had lost its base in the West in the 1959 elections when Awolowo handed regional power over to Akintola. The split within the party deepened as Akintola sought to reinstate the Western Nigeria rural bourgeoisie, the feudal landlords and cocoa plantation owners. At the 1962 Action Group party convention the split came out in the open and the radical wing rallied behind the leadership of Awolowo and had Akintola expelled from the party. Adegbenro was announced his successor, but Akintola, a desperate man, led his supporters to riot in the Western House of Assembly. The bourgeois–feudal coalition had its chance. A state of emergency was declared in the West, Awolowo was arrested, and a commission of inquiry was instituted to study the finances of the Action Group administration.

Meanwhile, Awolowo and Enahoro were charged with treason and, after a flight to Britain and repatriation, were sent to jail. S. G. Ikoku escaped to Nkrumah's Ghana and to safety. For all intents and purposes the radical wing of the Action Group had been destroyed, and with it the aspirations of the Western bourgeoisie were quashed. Henceforth it would abandon any constitutional attempts at change, for it was now convinced that it had lost the parliamentary struggle. But this belief was not uniformly felt, and it did not dawn on most of the Western and indeed the Eastern bourgeoisie until the 1964 federal elections and the 1965 Western Nigeria elections.

The Action Group destroyed, Akintola had the go-ahead to organize his party, the United Peoples' Party (UPP). This outright reactionary party, the basis of the Western rural bourgeoisie and feudal landlords, teamed up with the NPC feudal-led party of the North to form the NNA—the Nigerian National Alliance of feudal lords and rural bourgeoisie. The NCNC commercial and bureaucratic bourgeoisie, realizing many years too late that its goals lay with the Western bourgeoisie teamed up with the remnants of the Action Group to form the UPGA—the United Progressive Grand Alliance of the Southern bourgeoisie. The bitter political struggle that ensued during the 1964 election campaign produced a flood of chauvinism. "In order to hold tight to itself the alliance of their peasantries, the Ibo and Yoruba bourgeois elites resorted to scaring the peasants with cries of domination. For its part the Northern feudal lords, hard pressed as they were by the Southern bourgeoisie, could find no weapon more useful than chauvinism. It appealed to the ethnic, religious, and historical (i.e., cultural) prejudices of the Northern peasantry of which it is by and large the traditional representative." [18]

In typical Nigerian bourgeois style the elections took place amid charges and countercharges of irregularities and intimidation. In the end, however, the NNA of feudals and rural bourgeoisie won the elections over the UPGA of Southern bourgeoisie. Tempers ran high and there was talk of secession by the erratic leader of the Eastern Nigeria NCNC, Dr. Okpara.[19] Finally, the NCNC walked sheepishly into an alliance with the Northern feudals to form a so-called broadly based government in which nearly one-third of the members were ministers or parliamentary secretaries.[20] Needless to say, the Akintola faction had a good representation in the federal government. Again the Action Group and a majority of the Western bourgeoisie were left out in the cold. From now on their supporters took towards organizing an armed rebellion in the West where conditions gradually deteriorated.

Yet while the bourgeois and feudal politicians squabbled among themselves and grumbled about despoiling the country, while abroad the coalition governments pursued the most reactionary foreign policy as sycophants of the British policy in Rhodesia and as outright supporters of United States imperialist interest and aggression in the Congo, the country was being bled by the monopoly of British commercial houses and banks. While foreign business bribed the politicians to get favorable contracts and the international Shell-B.P. and Gulf oil consigns pumped out the wealth of the country, prices ran high and the lot of the common peasant, the urban proletarian, and the petty bourgeois was becoming unbearable. This could not go on indefinitely, as had been indicated by the 1964 general strike. A new arrangement of the political superstructure was needed to take account of and resolve the economic and social class contradictions that had developed to the point of explosion.

In the West elections had been called in 1965. Akintola and his henchmen "won" in the most blatantly rigged election. The opposition took to the street in open rebellion, and law and order almost totally broke down. The weakened NCNC bourgeoisie watched from the side lines. Even the trade unions failed to see the opportunity offered by the mass uprising in the West. Without leadership and organization, the Western uprising remained mostly spontaneous. Whether it could have developed and spread to the rest of the country is difficult to say since an army coup early in 1966 made it impossible for the full potential of the armed uprising to be realized.

At the end of 1965 it was clear, therefore, that the class struggle and the national liberation struggle had reached a new stage. Neo-colonialism, aligned sometimes with the Southern bourgeoisie—though always with the feudal landlords—had succeeded in driving a wedge in the ranks of the Southern bourgeoisie, isolating the Western urban bourgeoisie from the petit bourgeoisie and small proletariat by crushing its parliamentary power. The Eastern bourgeoisie, hating competition from the Western bourgeoisie and resenting domination from the Northern feudals, had been unable to make up its mind whom to support. This position led it by 1965 to complete isolation from the Western bourgeoisie, placing it in a powerless vacuum. The feudals and Northern landlords have always had their goals clear—resistance of any and all change that would destroy their power. Turning South they teamed up with the least progressive forces of the feudals and rural landlords of the West, crushing the Action Group urban bourgeoisie and isolating their former ally, the bourgeois elite of Eastern Nigeria.

Thus at the end of 1965 the neo-colonialist and reactionary class forces were in the ascendancy. The Southern bourgeoisie was in retreat. In the East it still held power. In the West it had escalated the fight to a higher stage as it sought to liquidate the rural landlords. The proletariat, small, weak and unorganized, was not capable of any leadership, nor did it try to develop one. The peasantry, unconscious and unorganized, could not be mobilized. Meanwhile, the federal government of Balewa, watching the deteriorating situation in the West, remained unconcerned. Balewa even invited Harold Wilson and Commonwealth prime ministers, shaking hands with them when he should have been complying with the OAU resolution to break ties with Britain.

In January 1966, the army struck in the first coup.

Coup, Counter-coup and Secession

The struggle for the termination of the feudal-bourgeois alliance and the emergence of an absolute bourgeois dictatorship was first launched, like all bourgeois revolutionary struggles, under legalistic forms. The Action Group—then the most advanced sector of the bourgeoisie—had tried to dislodge the feudal nobles of the North in 1959, aligning with the UMBC. It failed disastrously. Another attempt at asserting an absolute bourgeois rule in the Federation as a whole led to a combination of all bourgeois elements in the UPGA. It, too, failed. An effort to increase the power base of the bourgeoisie by capturing power from the feudal-led NNA also failed in 1965 in Western Nigeria. "The bourgeois constitutionalists had been pressed to the wall." [21] Elsewhere in this analysis, it has been made clear that the proletariat and petit bourgeoisie, especially in the West, followed the leadership of the bourgeoisie. Hence, when the Southern bourgeoisie was pressed against the wall, they also felt powerless.

Thus, when in January 1966, Major Nzeogwu led the radical wing of the Nigerian army in a coup, it was in the interest of the Southern bourgeoisie—especially the disenchanted Western bourgeoisie and the progressive masses of Nigerians. This underscores the universal outburst of joy of most common Nigerians welcoming the coup that purportedly sent the old brood of corrupt politicians packing. But the forces of reaction struck quickly, and in a comeback loyal General Ironsi quelled the radical young army officers. A frightened Parliament handed him all powers, and the first coup had failed. However, the situation still retained some positive elements. Many felt that the corrupt bourgeois and feudal politicians should not be allowed back, and for a while they remained in the background.

What started, then, as a struggle on behalf of the oppressed classes in Nigeria ended with the emergence of Ironsi in a victory for the Southern bourgeoisie. One step further and the second counter-coup of July would have led to a complete turn of events, the victory of the class forces of reaction and neo-colonialism. The old forces of feudalism and corrupt politicians were to lurk behind General Gowon.

But meanwhile, Ironsi undertook the burden of unifying the civil service and removing the worst ills of the Balewa days. Ironsi's administration, although bourgeois-led and bourgeois-oriented, was certainly an advance over the feudal-led government of Balewa. We are not opposed to the progressive bourgeoisie where they can carry out progressive reforms against feudal and anachronistic sections of the society. We are not opposed to them when they are fighting for national and social goals which accord, however partially, with the aspirations of the proletariat and peasant masses. But where social and economic revolutionary goals are concerned, we believe the bourgeoisie, by its nature, to be unequipped and incapable of leadership. The Ironsi military-bourgeois regime failed to realize this (it could not do otherwise) and, before consolidating its victories and without establishing support among the masses, challenged the Northern hegemony. Thus Ironsi too hastily and very unwisely introduced Decree 34 nullifying the federal constitution and establishing a unitary government. He was virtually asking for a confrontation with the Northern feudal and rural bourgeois monarchs whose power, though reduced, was not completely diluted. True, Balewa was dead and Ahmadu Bello had been liquidated, yet a system is not made and another destroyed by eliminating a few of its leaders and instituting others.

The feudal remnants were now emerging; they alleged that the January coup was Ibo-dominated and was aimed at the Northern peoples. As proof they claimed that Balewa and Bello were dead while Okpara was safe. Decree 34 was merely a consolidation of so-called Ibo victory and was inimical to the interest of Northerners. They appealed to the prejudices of the Northern peasantry who, uninformed and subject to all kinds of intimidation, became the unwitting tools of their very opressors. In May disturbances broke out in a number of Northern towns in which some Southerners, mostly Ibos, were killed. The Ironsi regime, unprepared, had no solution to the problem. Had he consolidated his position, had he rallied the mass of the progressive people behind him, Ironsi might have been able to stand up against a renewal of Northern chauvinism. Perhaps it was too much to expect from a professional and ill-advised soldier.

In July he followed his predecessor, Balewa, to defeat in the counter-coup of reactionary Northern Nigerian army officers. Scores of Eastern Nigerian or Ibo army officers were killed and Gowon emerged as the leader of the ring of plotters. The betrayal of the progressive masses of the proletariat and peasantry was now complete. Behind Gowon were the old discredited politicians and all their feudal colleagues. They now came out into the open although their powers were visibly reduced.

The military governor of the Eastern Region, Ojukwu, refused to accept the authority of Gowon and allegedly began making arrangements for secession as early as August 9, 1966.[22] Secession of Eastern Nigeria was not, however, declared until May 1967. There was still to occur the massacre of Southern Nigerians, mostly Ibos, in September 1966 and a massive exodus of Southerners, mostly Ibo, to their regions of origin. The number of Easterners or Ibo killed in this communal slaughter may have exceeded 20,000.[23] Consequently a mass exodus of Easterners flowed back into the East in one of the saddest journeys Nigerians have ever made.

Meanwhile Gowon, weak and phlegmatic, did not (and could not) do much to alleviate the conditions of these Ibo indigenes. The constitutional talks that were going on at this time sounded indeed quite hollow. But while Ojukwu and Gowon continued their verbal battles, a third force, formally unrecognized, gradually emerged. This comprised the leaders of the minority groups of Nigeria, accounting for perhaps 40 percent of the total inhabitants. They were opposed to any form of government that would entrench the domination of the major groups, the Hausa-Fulani, the Yorubas, and the Ibos. Confederation was therefore vehemently opposed by these new leaders. They saw in the situation a chance to push forward the interest of the minorities, as, by some accident, they found themselves in a majority both in the top civil service and in the Federal Executive Council. "Under military rule," writes Legum, "it has been the civil servants exercising power behind the guns of the soldiers." [24]

They stood strongly against the Aburi Agreements of 1967 and were probably instrumental in preventing Gowon from implementing the agreement that would probably have reestablished a rather loose confederation. Ojukwu, presumably, had regarded Aburi as the last chance [25]—an opinion sheepishly piped by the bootlicking British correspondent, Frederick Forsyth.[26] Be that as it may, Gowon and Ojukwu moved further apart as the country quivered on the brink of total disintegration. The talk in Enugu and elsewhere was secession.[27] It was now only a matter of time. The arrangements and preparations that had been made had now gone too far.

One might now wonder in terms of our analysis what the alignment of the different class positions was just before Ojukwu's May 30 declaration of independence. What class of people did Ojukwu represent? What about Gowon—in whose interest was he working? Was secession an inevitable step?

Ojukwu's background is as elite as any to be found in Nigeria. Son of a millionaire father, he comes from a rather bourgeois family that made its wealth through commerce and real estate speculation. His father was therefore one of the most typical comprador bourgeois and landlords. Ojukwu, in relation to his class background represents that wing of the Eastern Nigeria bourgeoisie that is most typically capitalist in mentality and therefore most vehemently opposed to feudal autocracy and aristocracy.

The first coup pre-empted the realization of the potential of the Western popular uprising and was advantageous to the Southern bourgeoisie, primarily in the Eastern wing where they predominated. Ironsi's precipitate attack of Northern feudal hegemony by his May 24 broadcast was hasty and foolish although it was not without a purpose; its aim was to abolish once and for all Northern feudal power and reaction. A unitary form of government would probably have succeeded in doing this by giving power to the center and to the Southern bourgeoisie but it also would have sealed the doom of the national minorities and re-established the domination of the larger ethnic groups.

In the atmosphere of fear and uncertainty that followed this decree it was therefore easy for the dispossessed old feudal politicians to spread rumors to the effect that the January coup had been Ibo-inspired. It has been alleged that foreign elements were responsible for starting such rumors.[28] Whether this is true or not is hard to verify, yet we know that it is to the interest of neo-colonial forces to cultivate such rumors in order to deflect men's minds from the true issues. We might emphasize also that these neo-colonial forces, headed by Britain, have always been in alliance with the conservative feudal politicians. They worked together, therefore, to see that no meaningful change came over to the North.

The January coup had seemed to wrest the power from these reactionaries. They still controlled the situation from behind the scenes, however, since the old structures of oppression, the *alkali* courts and the local police, were still in operation. Moreover, their free movement had not been limited by arrests nor had they been publicly disgraced; a massive propaganda campaign in this direc- tion might have showed the people their true nature. As it was, Ironsi left them free to manoeuvre. Therefore, when the chance arose, they utilized the same weapon they had always used in the past—ethnic chauvinism.

The May slaughter of Southerners (mostly members of the Ibo ethnic group) was merely a foretaste of what was to come. We might say that the feudal chauvinists and their masters, the British, were trying out the reaction of the Southern bourgeoisie, besides testing their old weapon, ethnic chauvinism.

The gullibility of the Northern peasant masses was demonstrated by their slaughter of innocent Ibos who, mostly proletarian, should have been their true allies; Ironsi's and the Southern bourgeoisie's feeble reaction demonstrated to the feudal and neo-colonial North- ern reactionaries that the substance of their power had indeed not been squashed. They now prepared to destroy the weak and divided bourgeoisie of Southern Nigeria, although not before the Northern feudal bosses had toyed with the idea of leaving the Federation so that they would continue to oppress the peasantry without any bother by Southern progressives. Their British neo- colonial masters must have advised them against such a stupid move.

In the end, however, they decided to strike, and in July they initiated the counter-coup in which many Southern officers, mostly Ibo, were killed. For a while after there was confusion about the leadership of the coup as the British advised and prevailed on the feudal reactionaries and their military representatives to settle for a compromise. That compromise was Gowon.

One has no difficulty in associating Gowon with the British who trained him and who chose him as a compromise candidate. His failure to compromise for a confederate structure of government for Nigeria is probably due to advice from the forceful members of minority groups in the present government.

He has neither the flair, flamboyance, nor rhetoric of Ojukwu, himself a British-trained soldier. The "One Nigeria" which he advocates is not one in which the relations of the social classes would change substantially. Gowon's "One Nigeria" is the same that Britain wants—a Nigeria where exploitations of the country would continue, albeit within a "new" structure.

Ojukwu's resistance to Gowon had positive elements as long as he did not seek to secede. Indeed, after the September 1966 massacres, sympathy lay on his side, especially among the minority groups. Had Ojukwu aligned himself with these groups rather than declare his secession, perhaps the story would now be different. In any case, he showed his true intention by declaring secession. It was not an inevitable act nor did it have to happen. But Ojukwu, true to his bourgeois class background, is just as opportunistic as Okpara and Azikiwe, his predecessors. Okpara, as was already stated, had once threatened secession, while Azikiwe, the political prostitute and vacillating bloodsucker, has now crossed the line from being a "Biafran" to being a "true Nigerian" after he gained assurance he would receive his propertied assets in Nigeria. What a hoax!

Ojukwu has succeeded in doing to the common Ibo man what Ahmadu Bello did to the Hausa peasantry. He has succeeded in using the ethnic chauvinistic scare. He has used this to camouflage his true goal—to make himself and his class, the Ibo bourgeoisie, the exploiters of the oil-rich former Eastern Nigeria. Thus when he declared his secession, he declared it for "Biafra" to include the whole of the former Eastern Nigeria where other national minorities besides the Ibo people are to be found. Why does he refuse to others what he claims for himself? If he claims self-determination for the Ibo people, why does he refuse it to the Ibibios, the Calabaris, the Efiks and those other minorities of the so-called Biafra Republic? Or does he imagine that in the event of self-determination for the Ibo people, the Efiks would not ask it for themselves? Ojukwu and his bourgeois comrades have their eyes on the oil which lies in the minority areas of "Biafra" and his declaration of secession is only a tool towards achieving this objective.

Any attempts to deflect the true nature of the class struggle in Nigeria must be exposed and resisted. The introduction and injection of ethnic chauvinism is one such attempt and should be resisted. Nigeria is a multi-national state where for decades the largest national groups have used the ethnic scare to maintain their bourgeois or feudal hegemony over the national minorities, the proletariat, and the peasantry in Nigeria. We consider the struggle of national minorities as part of the democratic struggle of the exploited classes of Nigeria. The national question is therefore worth examining in the context of class struggle in Nigeria.

National Question and Self-determination

Consideration of nationality and self-determination, as of all other social questions, must be undertaken dialectically, for societies are dynamic wholes that are constantly changing. In investigating a social phenomenon, therefore, we must understand it in a general theoretical and historical framework, while recognizing the specific features that distinguish the social phenomena in the particular country from those in other countries in the same historical epoch. In this way we can be scientific.

We have already stressed the necessity of taking a class perspective in our discussion. In considering the national question and the emergence of nation-states, we intend to remain consistent with and true to our position.

The history of developing nation-states has been associated with the liquidation of feudalism, the rise of the bourgeoisie, and the development of capitalism. In terms of progress, this movement toward the formation of bourgeois-democratic states was an advance over feudal society and practice. The birth of the nation-states of Europe—Britain, France, etc.—occurred at this period of change in history. The rapid economic growth of these countries can be traced to the fact that they had established their nationality by the time they started the development of capitalism. Thus, unity had been achieved at a time "when capitalism was a progressive force in the fight against feudalism which was an obstacle to the formation of the national market." [29]

Capitalism, however, has now reached a second and final stage and we are witnessing the eve of its downfall. In its highest stage capitalism has emerged to be what Lenin called "imperialism" and what Nkrumah in recent years has called "neo-colonialism"—the last stage of imperialism.[30] In the industrial capitalist nations this has led to a sharpening of the class antagonism between the bourgeoisie and the proletariat; it has developed wars of aggression abroad and increased repression at home. Simultaneously, we also witness the emergence since 1918 of a world socialist block and a heightening in the Third World of the struggle for national liberation. Indeed we might say that the national liberation struggle in the Third World today forms the central and most active, sphere in the world revolution of the oppressed peoples and classes. Imperialism realizes this and therefore is waging a death struggle, using all means at its disposal.

In making the distinction between these two stages, we do not claim that either is totally exclusive of the other. We merely wish to state that an historical analysis that reveals the class relationships in these two stages and exposes the present state of international capitalism is necessary in determining what position to take on the nationality issue. Besides, it should help us to understand the forces, mostly external, that affect Nigeria.

What then should our position be on the issue of nationality in the era of socialistic achievement when capitalism is decadent and the bourgeoisie has outlived its usefulness?

In Africa we need not take the long and bloody route of capitalism in our movement towards rapid economic and social development. The capitalist path to development is closed in Africa, as elsewhere in the Third World, because the local national bourgeoisie, instrument of international capitalism, is not allowed independent development outside the framework of imperialism with which it maintains a parent-child relationship. Thus, imperialism confines the national bourgeoisie to commercial rather than industrial economic activity, which is retained for foreign investors and capitalists. It is only through socialism that nation-building can proceed without wars, conflict, and violent upheavals among us. We realize that the boundaries of African states have been inherited from foreign colonial governments and that they were fixed by the imperialists with little consideration of the aspirations and wishes of the people. Some of these states have been able to adjust their boundaries peacefully, as the Mali Federation did. Others have attempted to adjust these boundaries by force of arms, as is the present case in Nigeria. The fact that many African states are neo-colonial, led by reactionary feudal or national bourgeois classes whose interests are tied to those of foreign exploiters, only adds to the complexity of the situation.

In Nigeria, which reflects all these problems, the picture is further confused by the relationship between social classes and nationalities. Be that as it may, we believe that we should first ask what the true interest of the proletariat and the peasantry is. We do not believe that the reactionary nationalism of the Nigerian leadership or the opportunism of the Biafran nationalist bourgeois leadership is the answer.

We are opposed to any and all forms of oppression as much as we are against any system of privilege. We support the equality of all nations and in principle the *right* of all nations to self-determination. By this we mean the right of nations to secede. Lenin puts it well when he writes, "If we want to grasp the meaning of self-determination of nations, not by juggling with legal definitions, or 'inventing' abstract definitions, but by examining the historico-economic conditions of the national movements, we must inevitably reach the conclusion that the self-determination of nations means the political separation of these nations from alien national bodies, and the formation of an independent national state." [31]

Our support of the right to self-determination in principle does not mean, however, that we support any and all national movements without examination of their merits, based on specific features.

Nigeria is a multi-national state in which historically the three national giants—Hausa, Ibo, and Yoruba—have oppressed all the other national minorities that number many scores and form perhaps 40 percent of the entire population. All these national groups are at different levels of social and economic development. Within the boundaries that were inherited from the British imperialists in 1960, these politics were organized around ruling classes which used the three major political parties as tools for the exploitation of the impoverished masses. These three national giants—the Hausa-Fulani feudal lords, the Yoruba landlords, and the Ibo bourgeoisie—were tied in varying degrees to the British imperialist interests. The British employed these ruling classes to dampen the development of the progressive classes, to stifle the democratic aspirations of the national minorities, and to prevent any direct attack on British imperialist interests. Nigerian politics therefore has been basically a boring adjustment and readjustment of alliances between and among these three ruling classes. Behind them the British puppeteers, safe and secure, bled away Nigeria's wealth.

The oppression of the proletariat, the peasants, and particularly the national minorities stemmed on the one hand from the neo-colonialist nature of Nigeria and, on the other hand, from the injustice of the exploitation and oppression of the ruling classes of the three national giants. Thus in the old Nigeria before civil war, there were three ruling classes employing ethnic chauvinism to their own advantage while the national minorities were totally ignored.

In the former Eastern Region, for the whole of which Ojukwu has declared Biafran secession, there was a nationally heterogenous population of about 12 million. In this region the Ibo constituted a majority of 7 million while the other ethnic groups—Efiks, Ogojas, Ibibios, Bugumas, Kalagaris and others—comprised about 5 million. It is important to note that the Ibo national group lived in an area approximately 11,310 square miles in size, while all the other national minorities together occupied an area of 18,170 square miles. Eastern Nigeria was therefore neither geographically nor ethnically homogeneous. The Eastern Region, like all the other regions, was a British creation for administrative convenience.

In this old Eastern Region, the Ibo elite and the ruling class held a tight grip on the other ethnic groups whom, as a rule, they oppressed. Therefore, to announce self-determination for all these groups and call them "Biafran" smacks of opportunism—a thinly disguised attempt to continue the old oppression.

Hence, when Ojukwu claims that the Ibo national group has been the most oppressed as a group he is not doing justice to the facts. The national minorities were actually the most oppressed nationalities in the old Federation. We do not intend merely to compare who was more oppressed than the other. We only want to emphasize that all classes and nationalities were and are oppressed because of the reactionary and neo-colonialist nature of Nigeria. Ojukwu's separation of the Ibo national group from all the others only weakens the resistance movement against oppression.

However, in creating the twelve-state structure, the federal Nigerian leadership has stumbled onto a long overdue solution. It divides the old Northern Region into six states and slices the Eastern Region into three states, one for the Ibo national group and two for the Eastern national minorities. These new arrangements seem to establish the conditions for the exercise of self-determination, providing for the practice of local self-government for autonomous regions with special economic and social considerations. This solution has clipped the wings of the ambitious, bourgeois Ibo leadership. Even in their age-old preserve they now have to play a less important role.

We do not by any means condone the September 1966 slaughter of over 20,000 Ibos in the North nor do we fail to condemn an equally despicable massacre of 5,000 Northerners in Eastern Nigeria. We merely wish to give due consideration to the historical, social, and economic facts.

Ojukwu writes, "We have no territorial ambitions. We do not want to capture anybody or punish anybody. We just want to be left alone." [32] Yet in August 1967, he invaded and captured the Midwest, mostly inhabited by national minorities. His cry then was no longer "self-determination" but "Southern Solidarity." What outright opportunism!

Meanwhile on the Nigerian side, Gowon and his bourgeois advisors pursued a vicious war against the Biafran peoples crying their empty and barren slogans of "one Nigeria" and "unity." Having courted the national minorities by granting them some type of autonomy they seek now to liquidate the Biafran secession. Ironically, most of their weapons come from the same British imperialists who have contributed most to the present crisis.

Given these conditions then, what is the correct proletarian outlook? We should look beyond the immediate small gains in the organization of states and regions and ask these questions: who runs the economy of the country? Who benefits from the present crisis? Will the proletarian movement be advanced by the disintegration of the Nigerian federation?

We have already stated that our support for secession and self-determination is not unconditional. The proletariat supports secession when an oppressed nation seeks to separate from an oppressor nation. The Ibos as a national group have not been oppressed in Nigeria, and there is little evidence that they will be. At the time of this writing, already more than a million Ibos live in Nigeria. Some have even returned to Northern Nigeria.[33]

The claim that Biafra is more progressive than Nigeria does not affect our position; nor would the claim that Biafra is reactionary lead us to oppose her secession were the Ibos truly an oppressed people. "The answer to the question does not depend on the 'progressiveness' or 'modernity' of this or that group. The entire working class of the world supported the struggle of the Ethiopians against fascist Italy without reservation. This was irrespective of the fact that concretely Ethiopia was a backward, feudal monarchy in which the masses suffered slavery and oppression." [34]

Let us now pay tribute to the Biafran proletariat and peasantry who have borne the brunt of war for two years. Their fight is democratic by nature, for they fight a form of oppression. It is this democratic element that we support. However, we condemn the attempt (so far successful) of the national bourgeoisie of Biafra to lead the struggle to secede to national exclusiveness. This has led to the isolation of the Biafran proletariat and peasantry from their counterparts in Nigeria. Secession is too narrow a goal and plays into the hands of the national bourgeoisie. The Biafran masses have borne on their shoulders a struggle that should be national in character. Yet, we Nigerians are subject to the same criticisms we direct at the Biafrans. Neither the Nigerian working class nor the peasantry has come out in support of action independent of the Nigerian reactionary nationalists. We should not, however, discount the recent tax riots in the Western State and the student-worker agitation over the Biafran bombings of the Midwest State. The class struggle that has been for so long exploited and misdirected may now truly function according to its true nature.

On this basis, therefore, we condemn Nigeria's attempt to crush Biafra. We stand opposed to any attempt to find a purely military solution to the problem. The enemy is not the Ibos or the Biafran people. The enemy is Great Britain that seeks to keep us divided while it sells arms to us to strengthen her pound, increase her balance of payments, and steal the country's oil through Shell-B.P. The enemy is the reactionary classes in Nigeria that are allied with the Brittish exploiters. Graft, corruption, and nepotism continue under Gowon's military government; a profiteer class of military officers has developed and behind it the old faces— Awolowo, Enahoro—have reappeared.

Ojukwu and his bourgeois nationalists claim they are leading a revolution. But they are merely opportunists. Witness the behind-the-lines operations of the bourgeois profiteers who even in war demonstrate their selfish goals. Ojukwu recognizes their activities and has publicly acknowledged them, but he seems helpless.[35] These are the real internal enemies of the Biafran people. Indeed, while the war rages and millions starve, Ojukwu is sending envoys to SAFRAP, the French oil enterprise.[36] Ojukwu aligns himself with the French and even with the Portuguese who are suppressing Africans elsewhere. These, we reiterate, are the true foreign enemies of the Biafran people.

The deception of the Biafran bourgeoisie and reactionary Nigerian nationalists is now being exposed. We do not advocate the establishment of a bourgeois national state in the age of socialism when capitalism is on its way out. We advocate socialism, and the leadership of the proletariat, peasantry, and all progressives in the development of national democracy and socialism.

Conclusion

The struggle in Nigeria is a class struggle, since in class societies all struggles are along class lines. British colonialism's alliance with the reactionary local elements of the civil population had failed. This had become evident by the mid-1960's, first in 1964 when the labor unions called a successful general strike and again in 1965 when the popular Western uprising threatened to blow the lid off the corrupt system. Quite clearly the system could not continue as it was. An adjustment of the political superstructure had to be undertaken to contain or give room to the productive forces. Class antagonisms, especially between the Southern bourgeoisie and the Northern feudals, had reached the point of explosion. Something had to happen. The working class represented by the labor unions was unconscious of its role since the labor unions had fallen into squabbling factions following their presentation of a united front under the umbrella of the Joint Action Committee (JAC) during the 1964 general strike. The mass of the peasantry, without leadership from the proletariat, remained disorganized. It was therefore left to the progressive sections and elements of the petit bourgeoisie and the bourgeoisie to act. Nzeogwu's attempted coup was, in this circumstance, welcome.

From then the British acted quickly. Convinced beyond any doubt that politicians were discredited and fearful of a Nasser-type coup, they encouraged Ironsi's takeover in what might in the end have led to a popular coup. But even Ironsi was swept along by the popular fervor of the masses who asked for visible change. His subsequent actions may have made the British quite unsure of him even though Ironsi at best was simply a reformer. The second coup was certainly British inspired, and it established the former political alignment of Northern reactionary leadership. Behind Gowon the true power is Katsina, scion of the traditional feudal Northern leadership. All these men are in uniform, representing the same social class forces that ruled the old Federation. Behind them are the British who have merely replaced Balewa's golden voice with Gowon's smoky guns.

Ojukwu's refusal to recognize Gowon's authority for a while appeared to be a progressive act. But when he declared secession he showed his true nature. His inability or unwillingness to curtail or even control the bourgeois profiteers shows us in whose interests he was fighting. Externally he has made alliances with some of the most oppressive and reactionary imperialist and neo-colonial powers—France, Portugal, and South Africa—the same powers that oppress daily the black Africans of southern Africa. Ojukwu's claim that Biafra is the starting point of the black man's march to his destiny becomes groundless when we point to the powers he has chosen for his allies.[37] Ojukwu's rhetoric seems impeccable, but we now no longer judge men by their words. Only social practice is the criterion for truth. In this Ojukwu and his bourgeois friends have merely used secession to exploit the true nature of the struggle.

In more than two years of war, we have witnessed the devastation of the Nigerian and Biafran peasantry and working people. The antagonism within international imperialism has been imported into Nigeria and while Britain exploits the country, France and the Soviet Union are also trying to establish a footing. Having divided the country into two warring camps, world imperialism is attempting to subvert and destroy national consciousness and solidarity through the use of ideological weapons which wear the guise of humanitarianism. It is like soothing the dying moments of one's victim.

Thus humanitarian organizations like the Red Cross, Caritas, and others have rushed into the situation to "help" the poor, starving Africans. These are the modern missionaries and abolitionists. On the surface their activities seem laudable, but we in Africa are not deceived. The cultural weapons of imperialism, subtle and insidious, are more dangerous than arms.

The United States played a safe though a somewhat ambiguous role in the war. It allowed its citizens to supply clandestinely arms and money to Biafra. Groups like the American Committee to Keep Biafra Alive were encouraged to operate with the support of some prominent American citizens. At the same time the United States government officially supported a unified Nigeria. In this way it could switch its support from one side to the other at will.

The prospects for peace under the circumstances were quite dim. The British and French imperialists relished the crises created by the civil war. It was not they, of course, but the embattled people who bore the brunt of financing the war, who suffered, and who died. Even now there is no respite from their suffering. All political activity has been banned in Nigeria, and in Biafra also little criticism is allowed.

For hope, we must turn to the progressive elements on both sides, but more especially in Nigeria. This war and the past history of Nigeria have shown that the national democratic revolution and the struggle for national liberation cannot be fulfilled under the leadership of the national bourgeoisie. We must turn now to the more advanced forces representing the peasant, the proletariat, and sections of the petit bourgeoisie and the bourgeoisie.

We must continue, having now learned, if nothing else, who the internal and external enemies are and who are our friends.

Notes

1. See Kwame Nkrumah's incisive article on this subject entitled "African Socialism Revisited" in *Africa: National and Social Revolution; The Cairo Seminar, 1966* (Prague: Peace and Socialism Publishers, 1967), pp. 86–92.

2. See Leopold Senghor, *On African Socialism* (New York: Frederick A. Praeger, 1964), pp. 67–104.

3. Michael Crowder, *A Short History of Nigeria* (New York: Frederick A. Praeger, 1962).

4. "The Class Struggle in Africa," *Revolution* 1, no. 9 (1964): 23–49.

5. Ibid., p. 32.

6. V. I. Lenin, *Imperialism—the Highest Stage of Capitalism* (New York: International Publishers, 1939).

7. K. O. Dike, *Trade and Politics in the Niger Delta, 1830–1885* (London: Oxford University Press, 1956), p. 11.

8. Ibid., p. 14.

9. See J. K. Ajayi's *Christian Missions in Nigeria, 1841–1891* (London: Longmans, Green & Co., 1965) and E. A. Ayandele's *The Missionary Impact on Modern Nigeria 1842–1914* (London: Longmans, Green & Co., 1966).

10. John E. Flint, *Sir George Goldie and the Making of Nigeria* (London: Oxford University Press, 1964).

11. The official mentioned is Major Sharpe, quoted in Crowder, *Short History*, p. 193.

12. Frantz Fanon, *The Wretched of the Earth* (New York: Grove Press, 1966).

13. Kwame Nkrumah, *Towards Colonial Freedom* (London: Heinemann Educational Books Ltd., 1962).

14. Jack Woodis, *Introduction to Neo-Colonialism* (New York: International Publishers, 1967), p. 27.

15. Kalu Ezera, *Constitutional Developments in Nigeria* (London: Oxford University Press, 1960).

16. Kwame Nkrumah, *Neo-Colonialism, the Last Stage of Imperialism* (New York: International Publishers, 1965).

17. Obi B. Egbuna, *The Murder of Nigeria* (London: Panaf Publications, 1968), p. 10.

18. Eskor Toyo, *The Working Class and the Nigerian Crisis* (Ibadan: Oxford University Press, 1967), p. 15.

19. Okoi Arikpo, *The Development of Modern Nigeria* (Baltimore: Penguin Books, Inc., 1967), p. 138.

20. Ibid.

21. Toyo, *Working Class*, p. 15.

22. N. B. Graham-Douglas, *Ojukwu's Rebellion and World Opinion* (Apapa, Lagos: Nigerian National Press, 1968).

23. The number varies from 5,000 in Nigerian sources to 30,000 in Biafran sources.

24. Colin Legum, "Nigeria vs. Biafra: On Taking Sides," *Christianity and Crisis* 29, no. 9 (May 26, 1969): 151.

25. C. Odumegwu Ojukwu, *Biafra*, vol. 2, *Selected Speeches* (New York: Harper & Row, 1969).

26. Frederick Forsyth, *The Biafra Story* (Baltimore: Penguin Books, Inc., 1969), p. 79.

27. Graham-Douglas, *Ojukwu's Rebellion*, p. 7.

28. Egbuna, *Murder of Nigeria*, pp. 22–23.

29. Albert Zanolo, "African Unity Now," *The African Communist*, no. 36, 1st quarter (1969): 19. See also his article entitled "The National Question and Nigeria" in the same issue.

30. Nkrumah, *Neo-Colonialism*. See especially the Introduction.

31. V. I. Lenin, *National Liberation, Socialism and Imperialism: Selected Writings* (New York: International Publishers, 1968), p. 47.

32. Ojukwu, *Biafra, Selected Speeches*, p. 94.

33. Legum, "Nigeria vs. Biafra," p. 154.

34. Zanolo, "African Unity," p. 22.

35. C. Odumegwu Ojukwu, *Principles of Biafran Revolution*. Pamphlet published by the Biafra Review (Cambridge, Mass., 1969), pp. 14–15.

36. Ojukwu, *Biafra, Selected Speeches*, p. 137.

37. Ibid., p. 201.

8

THE SECURITY OF THE NIGERIAN NATION

Ogbemi Ola Omatete

Introduction

When the Nigerian Civil War came to an abrupt end in January 1970, the young Nigerian nation, like the young child, had successfully taken the first steps toward maturity. Like all other nations before it, and nations that will come after it, Nigeria will have to survive the hazards of growing up: hazards that can destroy or cripple the young nation, but hazards that must be faced. Few indeed are the nations that do not bear the ugly scars of growing up. Unlike man, however, a nation does not have the watchful eyes of parents to guide it through this turbulent period. The nation must rely on itself. This is why a vigorous national security program should be developed very early in the life of the nation. Failing this, the nation is apt to fall easy prey to international intrigue and power politics.

Has the end of the Civil War in Nigeria called for any change in the suggestions made in this article for strengthening the security of Nigeria? No. Definitely not. Instead, the end of the Civil War calls for urgency in defining Nigerian national interests and formulating appropriate national policies to preserve these interests. The suggestions in this article are neither exclusive nor definitive. They are simple suggestions made in the hope that they will stimulate discussions within the decision-making group in Nigeria.

The price of the Civil War has been high, and the lessons learned must be acted upon now while they are fresh in our minds. Nigeria's security must be defined and developed now.

Nigeria the Nation

Whatever the outcome of the Civil War, Nigeria has been born as a nation. The baptism of fire which many of its citizens have endured has strengthened their resolve to keep their nation strong and viable. To the extent that the bloody Civil War strengthens the concept of Nigeria as a nation, it will be a blessing in disguise. But one may justifiably ask how the Civil War has strengthened the concept of Nigeria as a nation—especially since Nigeria has been described as artificial, a product of British imperialism. (There has even been a book published entitled *Nigeria—The Tribes, the Nation or the Race.*[1]) Dr. Okoi Arikpo, the present Nigerian Commissioner for Foreign Affairs, in the preface to his book *The Development of Modern Nigeria* has replied to some of these criticisms by stating that

the central theme of the book is that Nigeria is neither a geographical expression nor a historical accident because, in spite of the bewildering variety of languages and customs found in the country, the people themselves are the progeny of two racial strains, negroid and hamitic, between which there has been continuous miscegenation for more than a thousand years, and because the physical features of the country—drainage system and vegetation zones—make it a single natural economic unit. Therefore, if British imperialism had not brought the inhabitants of the territory under one general government, some other social process could have accomplished the same end.[2]

In what ways has the Civil War strengthened the Nigerian nation? In any nation there is a relationship of responsibility and obligation between the nation and the citizen. The citizen owes some duties to the nation for the protection he receives—duties which include paying taxes and defending the nation. As a result of two coups in 1966, the nation's ability to protect all its citizens was weakened. All attempts to resolve the strained nation-citizen relationship peacefully failed, and the Civil War finally resulted. During the Civil War the nation called on its citizens to discharge their duties, and their response was strong. Citizens contributed to the war efforts, enduring great hardships. Heavy taxes were levied on individuals, and import and export duties were increased. Above all, there were but few families in Nigeria that were not called upon to make the supreme sacrifice—brothers, fathers, sisters, dearly loved ones were lost. The suffering was shared by both sides in the conflict.

Nigerians are human and ask themselves why they are required to make these sacrifices. The leaders on both sides of the Civil War have quickly come to their aid. The Federal Government of Nigeria (F.G.) has carried on all its publications "To keep Nigeria one is a task that must be done," and F.G. leaders in radio and television appearances talk about the duty of the citizen to fight for a united country. The secessionist leaders assured the loyalty of all their supporters by calling the Civil War a genocidal war (an allegation which has been proven untrue). In any case, the leaders have successfully rallied the citizens. Consequently, the citizens are more aware of the concept of the Nigerian nation, whether they have fought for its unity or for its disintegration.

If Nigerian leaders agreed on any single issue during the seven years after independence before the outbreak of Civil War, it was the creation of more Nigerian states. This could have been done before independence if Great Britain had not insisted that it would delay Nigeria's independence, a condition Nigerian leaders rejected. Although there was consensus on the division of Nigeria into more states, there was strong disagreement on how the boundaries should be drawn. During the emergency period before the outbreak of the Civil War, Nigeria was divided into twelve states instead of the existing four regions. Although this was followed immediately by the declaration of secession, the will of a vast majority of Nigerians had been fulfilled. Regardless of how the Civil War ends, there probably can only be more states created, definitely not less.

The creation of twelve states in Nigeria strengthens the Nigerian nation in three ways. First, it will reduce the number of people who feel neglected by the state capitals. Large populations in the present Southeastern State and Rivers State (formerly Eastern Nigeria), in the Midwest State (formerly administered from Ibadan, capital of Western Nigeria), and in the Middle Belt (formerly Northern Nigeria) will not feel left out. Second, since the states are now smaller, the Federal Government becomes more powerful even if the old constitution remains. Third and most important is that the creation of the twelve states in Nigeria will necessitate a new constitution. It is hoped that several of the mistakes of the First Republic will be avoided, mistakes listed by Dr. Okoi Arikpo.[3] Hopefully, the notion of politics as a winners-gain-all game will be modified; a national government similar to that advocated by Dr. W. Arthur Lewis in *Politics in West Africa* [4] might be included. Nigerians have been given a chance to write a new constitution that will strengthen the country.

The Civil War focused attention very clearly on the Nigerian nation, and it also indicated some of the responsibilities of nation-hood. Nigerian leaders now talk about not compromising the territorial integrity of the nation. They talk about defending their national airspace, their national waterways, and their national boundaries. A new nationalism is being born. The nationalism that resulted in independence for Nigeria is being replaced by one that identifies national responsibility.

National Interest

Foremost among the responsibilities a nation must bear is the preservation of the nation. Any policy or action that promotes the continued existence of the nation is of national interest.

From independence until the outbreak of the Civil War, Nigerian national leaders identified more strongly with subnational interests than with national interests. Two such subnational interests, political parties and ethnic groups, stand out in this respect. Party leaders were so interested in winning elections that they failed to realize that unfair election practices (which were known to all citizens) were actually destroying the nation. Youth lost respect for national leaders and saw little future in the nation. Healthy rivalry between the various ethnic groups in Nigeria could have resulted in a very progressive nation; instead, the rivalry degenerated to such a state that ethnic origin, rather than merit or need, qualified one for position, scholarships, and other benefits.

When political party and ethnic group interests merged, as in the case of the former Northern and Eastern regions of Nigeria, power always rested with the majority ethnic group, a situation not always in the best interest of the nation. Furthermore, since the three major political parties, National Council of Nigerian Citizens (NCNC), Action Group (AG) and Northern People's Congress (NPC), were based on the three majority ethnic groups (Ibo, Yoruba, Hausa-Fulani), Nigeria was defined primarily in terms of the interests of these groups, although they form barely half the population.

National interests and interests in political parties and ethnic groups can and do coincide, and such coincident interests should be encouraged and strengthened by adequate policies. Where national interests and subnational interests conflict, true national leaders would subjugate the latter to the former. Any action or policy that reinforces this subjugation is clearly in the national interest.

Nations also have international interests—for example, the right to sail the high seas—and sometimes national and international interests may conflict. A nation may define its territorial waters as twelve miles from its shores, whereas other nations would define it as just three miles. National interest may vary depending on the party with which the nation is dealing: what is of national interest when Nigeria deals with Dahomey may be quite different from what the nation considers of national interest in its dealings with Italy. National policies directed towards these two countries will consequently be different.

In the last analysis, national interest depends on the nation's decision-making group, which defines what is important in the maintenance of the nation. Defining national interest is only part of the role of the leaders of the nation; they must also be able to transmit their definitions to the citizens, so that the citizens are aware when their national interests are being threatened. In addition, the nation must maintain effective national security. After defining its national interests, the nation should be prepared to defend them by its national security policies.

National Security

A nation may be considered secure if there is a high probability of occurrence of its preferred values or national values. No nation is assured of full security all the time; all nations obviously work for foolproof security, but none can attain it. When a nation cannot influence events to favour its interests, it endeavors to limit the adverse effect of such events by manipulating the components of national security, which include military capability (to deter would-be enemies and to wage war to a successful end, if forced on the nation), economic potential (to influence an aggressor and to support a protracted war), intelligence system, both civil and military (to locate possible sources of threat to the nation), diplomatic capability (to make alliances and to publicize desirable national values), the national manpower (to man the administrative, industrial, technological, scientific, and military institutions), and finally, the national willpower (to show that the nation will not tolerate threats to its security). All these components are clearly interrelated. Each component will, however, be examined separately in order to see how Nigeria can employ it against security threats.

MILITARY CAPABILITY

In 1964, the total Nigerian armed forces numbered 8,000 men, out of a population of about 40 million.[5] This meant that there was one soldier for every 5,000 Nigerian citizens. This was the lowest ratio in all of Africa and, of course, in all of the world.[6] In 1966, the Nigerian population, according to a new census, was 55,600,000; the total armed forces increased to 11,500 men.[7] This still gave the 1964 ratio of one armed man for every 5,000 Nigerian citizens, still the lowest world ratio except in countries without any armed forces. The police force was 23,000 men strong in 1964, and this increased to 24,000 in 1966. The number of soldiers and police officers constitute only a small fraction of Nigerian citizens physically responsible for the security of the nation. The 1964 breakdown of the armed forces showed 7,000 men in the army, 850 men in the navy, and an air force that was being formed. The bulk of the military men was in the army. In 1966, 9,000 of 11,500 men were in the army, 1,500 men in the navy, and 1,000 men in the air force. (The air force was expecting a total of about 66 light planes, mainly from West Germany, but most of these planes were not delivered before the Civil War began.) Although there seems to be no criteria for defining the optimum armed forces strength for a given country, Nigeria, according to these statistics, had a very small proportion of its nationals engaged in protecting the nation from internal and external threats. Be that as it may, Nigerian leaders tolerated this small proportion, probably because they felt that there was minimal threat to their nation's security.

A civil war is the result of the complete breakdown of internal security. Since Nigeria was engaged in a civil war, the general conclusion that may be drawn is that the small proportion of Nigerians responsible for the security of Nigeria was insufficient. A detailed examination will indicate that this conclusion is only partly true. As a result of several political wrangles and two ensuing coups d'état, discipline within the armed forces virtually disappeared. The security of subnational groups replaced the security of the nation. The nation then had to seek ways to re-establish security within, or fall easy prey to external threats. Both of these alternatives actually did happen, although the latter has not yet led to a complete subordination of Nigeria to external domination.

During the Civil War the total armed forces strength swelled continuously as each side vigorously recruited. At the beginning of 1969, the total armed forces of the Federal Nigerian Government was estimated at between 80,000 and 120,000 men. The Biafran secessionist military forces were probably not less than half the Federal Government's average. Thus from 1966 to 1969, the total armed forces of all of Nigeria was from between 100,000 to 200,-000 men in a population now estimated at 60 million. The ratio of armed men to citizens had increased over tenfold and was only less than that of South Africa (ratio based on white population only), and of the United Arab Republic in Africa. This numerical break-down would still be similar to the pre-Civil War breakdown, where between 70 percent and 80 percent of the military were in the army; however, the air force and the navy have played a very important part in the Civil War, and their rate of increment is higher than the army's. Both forces have been important in the blockage of arms against the secessionist region in Nigeria, the navy more so than the air force. The enormous increase in total number of uniformed men has not necessitated any conscription by the Federal Government. The military service has remained completely voluntary. The secessionists initially used voluntary soldiers, although rumours now have it that some conscription is being carried out.[8] This indicates the large military potential of Nigeria primarily due to its relatively large population.

Arming the Military. The size of the armed forces is meaningless if the military cannot be supplied with the equipment required for defending the nation. Nigeria, like most developing nations, does not produce any of its own arms. Arms must therefore be bought with the hard cash so badly needed for a multitude of other important development programs. The sources from which arms may be bought also ties in with the security of the nation. A short history of arms supply will be traced.

The main source of arms and other military equipment, including know-how, to pre-Civil War Nigeria was from the Western nations. The United Kingdom, in the main, provided the army and navy with equipment until about 1964. (There was no air force before 1964.)[9] In 1964, the navy had one patrol boat, two mine-sweepers, and one landing craft, all built in Britain. In 1966, Britain was still largely responsible for the equipment of the army, which then had two reconnaissance squadrons with Ferret armoured cars. The navy had now acquired a frigate from the

Netherlands, which also donated a submarine chaser. The air force was supposed to have had sixty-six planes—twenty-six Piaggio trainers, thirty Dormier communications aircraft, and ten Noratlas transports—all to be delivered by Western Germany; however, these planes did not seem to have been delivered by the outbreak of the Civil War. Personnel was trained either in countries that supplied the equipment, or officers from these countries were sent to Nigeria to help train the Nigerians.

In January 1962, after the cancellation of the Anglo-Nigerian defense pact of November 1960, Nigeria looked towards the middle powers for help in training personnel. Although a large number of the officers still trained in Britain, by 1964 Nigerian cadets were training in India, Pakistan, and Canada. India could not help in training the Nigerian air force. By 1966 there were cadets of all three arms of the military training in Australia, Canada, Ethiopia, India, and Pakistan, besides those in Britain and Germany. There was also some military assistance from the United States, but this was quite small.

The Civil War completely changed the pattern of arms supply, and in so doing strongly indicates the importance of the source of arms in the security of a nation. As stated above, before the Civil War Nigeria had obtained all its weapons from Western nations, largely Britain, some European countries, and, to a very small extent, the United States. At the outbreak of the Civil War these countries refused to sell arms to Nigeria. This refusal was particularly irritating to the Federal side, since Biafra had managed to obtain two American-made B–26 bombers. By refusing, the Western nations left a vacuum which was quickly filled by arms dealers called "Private Entrepreneurs, All!" by Thayer and by governments which had had very little influence in Nigeria.[10] Gunrunners specialized in bringing arms into Biafra, with the direct help of France and Portugal and their former or present colonies, and of South Africa.[11] Whereas Nigeria received all her planes from the Soviet Union, Biafra obtained hers from French and Swedish sources. Both sides bought arms from various countries. Nigeria obtained arms from Russia and Czechoslavakia and later from Britain, which claimed to have reversed its policy in order to counter Soviet influence in Nigeria. Biafra, on the other hand, obtained Spanish-, French-, Czechoslavakian-, and American-made arms through gunrunners. Nigeria now buys its arms from both the East and the West, whereas Biafra obtains its arms primarily from the West, via Portugal, France and South Africa.

What would have happened to Nigeria if the Soviet Union had not supplied it arms when all the Western nations refused to grant an export license for it to buy planes, whereas Biafran American-made B–26 bombers were harassing Nigerian citizens? It is difficult to speculate since it is possible that Nigeria could have bought planes from "private entrepreneurs" too. If Nigeria could not have purchased planes from these private sources, would the secessionist attempt have succeeded, leading to the disintegration of Nigeria? Whether this question is answered affirmatively or negatively, the lesson of the relation between the source of a nation's arms supply and the security of the nation cannot be lost on Nigeria leaders. They must consider ways of making the source of arms in a post-Civil War Nigeria a little more reliable.

ECONOMIC CAPABILITY

The military capability of a country depends directly on its economic capability. Men in uniform must be paid and equipment purchased. These expenditures take a large chunk from the national wealth. The bigger the military services, the larger the amount of national wealth ploughed into the military. If a fixed percentage of a nation's gross national product (GNP) were spent on the military, then the more rapidly the GNP grows the more national wealth can be used for military expenditures. A large military can be maintained if the GNP forms a large base and there is rapid economic growth.

The military expenditure in a country where all the equipment is produced within that country and the personnel are trained within goes directly into the national economy. The expenditure circulates within the country, producing multiplier effects. In such a country, the debate over military spending generally raises questions of efficiency of expenditure or of national priorities. In Nigeria, however, and countries like Nigeria, where all the equipment is imported and most of the high-level personnel are trained in foreign countries, a high bulk of the military expenditure is outside the country. This made many politicians in the First Republic (1960–1966) argue for a small military force. The Nigerian intellectuals maintain that such spending depletes the small foreign exchange needed for development and results in a negative multiplier effect. Thus the money spent on arms abroad can only be justified as expenditure for procurement of national security.

In 1964 the total military expenditure in Nigeria was $33.6 million which was 1 percent of the GNP of Nigeria. This percentage was in the lowest third for all African nations. In 1966, it was then about $54.0 million, which was about 0.9 percent of the country's GNP, and 9.9 percent of the total government budget. In terms of percentage of GNP, Nigeria was still in the lowest third for all African nations, and in the lower half in terms of percentage of government expenditure. By 1969, the Civil War was costing Federal Nigeria about $18.0 million per month.[12] Although no estimate is known for the Biafran side, probably both sides of the Nigerian Civil War must have spent about $25.0 million per month on the war. This comes to $300 million per year. This huge sum, used primarily for purchase of equipment and hiring of personnel from foreign countries, contributes very little to the Nigerian economy. What a boost to the economy it would be to spend this much money within the country! Nigerian leaders must begin to plan how this much money (or part of it) may be invested in the national economy, at the same time maintaining a tolerable level of national security.

Good financial planning and the growth of petroleum and traditional exports have helped Federal Nigeria to raise her share of the military expenditure.[13] Duties on imported consumer items, such as cars, refrigerators, and textiles, were raised enormously, resulting in a virtual cessation of imports of items not produced in Nigeria, while the local industry for items produced in Nigeria, such as textiles, has boomed. Heavy machinery is needed for the economical development of the country. A postwar Nigeria must consider import substitution for many of the imported items, beginning with light industries. But before any major industrial processes can operate and completely use components from within Nigeria, starting from raw material to finished products, a steel mill or some basic industry to manufacture raw material for machinery must be established. This priority cannot be long neglected.

The part played by foreign interests in the national economy influences the security of the nation. Here two distinctions may be made: the role of the foreigner outside Nigeria and within Nigeria.

Nigeria, a developing nation, earns all her foreign exchange from the primary industries, agriculture and mining. The goods produced from these industries are exported to more developed countries, from which Nigeria imports manufactured goods. However the raw materials seem to purchase less and less manufactured goods, so that the developed countries are always in a favourable position relative to Nigeria. Also the price of these raw materials seems to fluctuate enormously in the markets of these consumer nations. Nigeria buys her arms with money from her exports. If the foreign countries that import these raw materials can manipulate the prices, then they can influence Nigeria's security. There is a possibility that they do manipulate prices of raw material. It may be fortuitous that cocoa prices rose sharply after Nkrumah's overthrow in Ghana, although the price of cocoa—Ghana's main foreign exchange earner—had been very bad during the latter part of his regime. Maybe not. Again, such foreign influence would be minimal if the arms needed for national security were obtained within the country.

The foreign influence upon Nigeria is very strong. Most of the businesses in Nigeria are owned by foreigners, mainly the British. If Nigerian and British interests conflicted on certain issues and the British businesses in Nigeria supported their government, could Nigeria ensure that her national interest could prevail in the face of British business opposition? If the answer is negative, what are the steps the country is taking to ensure the occurrence of her preferred national values? It is doubtful that Nigerian leaders will nationalize any foreign businesses in the near future. Recently a decree was issued by the federal military government requiring all foreign companies operating in Nigeria to register in Nigeria.[14] This raised a furor with many companies and governments, as if this were not a normal requirement in most countries, though it appears that they are now complying with the decree. Foreign investment is needed, but Nigerians must weigh carefully how concessions they now make to foreign business may affect the security of their nation.

In talking about business, one must not fail to mention the role labour plays. Nigeria has had trade unions which predate independence. Trade unions were very active in the fight for independence and the strike of about 30,000 workers in 1945 is a case in point.[15] After independence in 1964, the trade unions demonstrated their strength when a general strike paralysed the country and forced the government to negotiate with them. Except on these two occasions, the labour unions in Nigeria have seldom been unified. There was a split in the labour movement in 1960; as a result, there is the Trade Union Congress of Nigeria (TUCN), which affiliated with the Western-controlled International Confederation of Free Trade Unions (ICFTU), and there is the Nigerian Trade Union Congress (NTUC), which leans to the Eastern-controlled World Federation of Trade Unions (WFTU).[16]

The split occurred because the trade unions could not decide on which international organization to join. Both factions receive money from the international group to which they lean and fight frantically to win control of the Nigerian trade unions for the respective group. The fight is continuing, evidenced by the allegation that the Central Intelligence Agency (CIA) is spending "half a million dollars to split the Nigerian workers." [17] All attempts by the Nigerian government to pressure these factions into unifying has so far met with little success. Yet can such domination or control of Nigerian trade unions by foreign interests, East or West, be in Nigerian national interest? For instance, a trade union leader who had been invited to visit China, Russia, and other Eastern bloc nations, was later invited to visit Western nations. At one of the Western capitals, he talked with a colleague and found out that a resolution passed at one of the international meetings of trade unions was not being acted on by the union in that Western nation. When he asked why the union had failed to act, his colleague promptly answered that it was not in their national interest to do so. This example is not used to point a finger to Western double-dealing—the same things may occur in Eastern nations—but is cited to illustrate what seems to be missing in trade union leadership in Nigeria, the national interest. Have Nigerian labour leaders really defined Nigerian national interests before plunging the Nigerian labour movement into the international arena?

Since most of the foreign investments in Nigeria come from Western countries, such countries definitely have a stake in ensuring that Nigerian labour unions do not ally with Eastern trade unions. Thus a British labour delegation has been sent to Nigeria to help organize work shops. This is to counter the Soviet influence in certain trade unions whose leaders are alleged to have helped the Nigerians in securing the deal to supply Nigeria with Soviet planes. More such delegations are planned. One cannot see an end to such interferences in the Nigerian trade union movement unless the leadership decides to exert its independence more overtly. They must make this decision soon for the security of their nation.

INTELLIGENCE

National security depends strongly on the capability of the intelligence system, which consists of the whole apparatus for collecting and evaluating information vital to national security: "collectors (including spies), researchers, compilers, evaluators, relators, estimators, writers, disseminators, and a host of others, together with all their gadgets, communication systems, libraries, laboratories, files and production plants." [18] Intelligence is divided into military and civilian intelligence, although the distinction between the two is unclear, especially in peacetime. In wartime, the military intelligence operates actively, collecting information about the enemy's movements, numbers, morale, and so on, information essential for immediate tactical decisions. In peacetime both civilian and military intelligence function to identify possible trouble spots both within and without the country.

The intelligence system collects all the information required to make decisions that are vital to the national interest, including how the various national security components may be used to influence other nations. Most of the information about a country's components—military, economic, intelligence, diplomatic, and manpower—can be obtained in the open in peacetime. Thus peacetime intelligence is over 80 percent in the open. But national interest may require more information than can be obtained openly; it is then that spying becomes necessary.

The intelligence system must operate effectively within the nation, too. There may be citizens who for diverse reasons may not want the existence of the nation. Such citizens should be known before they may do damage. When national identity has been well developed, such citizens are few and the danger from them is minimal. Consequently, in older countries, detailed information is kept more on foreigners than on nationals. In young, unstable countries, where a national image is just being forged, the intelligence system has to have information on citizens as well as foreigners, for such countries are vulnerable to danger from within and from outside the country. An intelligence system capable of keeping such a catalogue of information is expensive, requiring both manpower and economic inputs that a developing nation can ill afford; yet the security of the nation requires that an attempt be made to secure such an intelligence system.

Since over 80 percent of peacetime intelligence is obtained openly, an intelligence system does not require highly paid secret agents or spies to be effective. How does a nation obtain this open information? First there are the diplomatic missions (embassies, consulates, information agencies, and so on) within which there is a section responsible for information gathering. A second way is at the university level, where special institutes or departments are set up to study specific areas in the world. Here scholars work in various fields such as diplomatic history and strategic studies, and acquire as much information as possible about their specific area or country. Third, there is the foreigner in any nation who gets to know the citizens and the way they react under given situations. The amount of information such people acquire depends on their profession and the people they meet within the country. The missionary, the foreign educator, the foreign businessman, and the foreign student accumulate information at different levels in the society, commonplace information that may be useful in decision-making. Foreigners are restricted in their movements in many countries, because they may obtain information that a nation may not want them to know. Intelligence gathered in this way is a far cry from spying and is not very expensive. However, Nigeria does not seem to have organized itself to acquire this type of information. It is doubtful that there are Nigerian scholars who study the diplomatic history of countries with which Nigeria deals, or scholars who specialize in strategic studies. Even if there are, are they being used in the formulation of policy? Intelligence gathering is too important to be left to chance. Post-Civil War Nigeria must develop an inexpensive and efficient intelligence system.

DIPLOMATIC CAPABILITY

Diplomacy is a strong component of national security that must be used along with the other components to achieve national goals. Diplomatic capability will be dealt with in two aspects—the diplomacy that helps the nation to secure allies (not only military allies, but also allies that give moral support to a nation), and the diplomacy that succeeds in projecting a highly favourable national image in a foreign country.

If the Civil War is considered from the diplomatic aspect, it would seem that secessionist Biafra has been very successful in projecting a highly favourable image of its struggle in the mass media of all Western nations and in some African countries. Nigeria, on the other hand, has done poorly in this respect. How did Biafrans become so successful? They seem to have realized very early the role the mass media plays in influencing the thoughts of people in Western nations. Accordingly they acquired public relations firms in Europe (Geneva) and the United States (New York and Los Angeles). These men saturated the mass media with news favourable to the Biafran cause. Nigeria was always put on the defensive, trying to explain Biafran accusations. For example, all the news media reported that Nigeria was waging a genocidal war against Biafra. Such words as "genocide" evoked all the emotions of the Nazi atrocities of World War II and won ample sympathy for the Biafrans—sympathy that Nigeria is still fighting in terms of economic and moral support for the secessionist cause. By the time Nigeria had neutral military observers to report that no such attempts were being made it was too late, and only a very few news media even bothered to report it. Another example is the claim that Nigeria is deliberately trying to starve Biafran children. Pictures of starving children filled all the mass media, and again Biafra won sympathy and support. No news media bothered to mention that in the history of civil wars, Nigeria is the first country that has agreed to allow food to be sent to the secessionists, requiring only that the food be checked to ensure that no arms are being sent along. It is possible to give several examples of excellent secessionist Biafran propaganda that have put Nigeria on the defensive.

Why has Nigeria apparently failed to project a credible image of her action in the Western news media? One answer is that Nigerian diplomatic missions did not acquire enough information about the role of the news media in the thought processes of people in Western nations, and if they did acquire this information, then they did not act quickly enough to use it. It seems as if Nigeria assumed that it was doing what any nation would do if there were a secessionist movement within its boundaries. Nigeria did not realize that, with the enormous influential power of public relations firms and the mass media, such actions must be explained and justified to all friendly countries.

Whether one considers that Nigeria has done well or poorly in securing allies depends on one's viewpoint. Despite the very strong propaganda for the Biafran cause, no Western nation at the time of this writing has officially recognized Biafra, although Portugal and France covertly support it. Only four African nations, Tanzania, Zambia, Ivory Coast, and Gabon, have recognized Biafra. This number of countries is fewer than those that recognized Katanga during the Congo civil war. South Africa and Rhodesia give covert support, as might be expected. That some countries recognize Biafra at all may be considered a victory for Biafran diplomacy, and hence a failure for Nigerian diplomacy. But since the Organization of African Unity (OAU) has been solidly behind Nigeria, one might say Nigeria has done very well. Indeed Nigeria has moral support from many Western governments and, surprisingly, from Eastern governments with which Nigeria was not very friendly before the Civil War.

The realization of the role that diplomatic capability can play in national security will definitely shape Nigeria's postwar diplomacy. Nigeria will have to use the mass media to project a favourable image—an image of justice, dynamism, and progress.

NATIONAL MANPOWER

The large population of Nigeria gives it a large potential supply of manpower. This is evidenced, for example, in the ease with which the armed forces have been increased from 11,500 to about 200,000 within two years, without any conscription. But national manpower requires more than people; it requires that these people be trained to fill the various institutions in the country. National strength is not numbers alone, but also the patriotism of the people and the skills they possess with which to build the nation. The dissemination and the development of these skills, including patriotism, are the primary responsibilities of the educational institutions in the country. Nigerian educational institutions have done fairly well in developing certain skills in the country. Granted that much, these institutions could have been used to better advantage if Nigerian leaders were willing to adapt these foreign institutions to Nigerian needs. There is still a preponderance of classical teaching, which was initiated by the British. Although Britain is reviewing her educational system, Nigeria still sticks to the old system. The output of graduates in the arts and humanities still far outnumbers those in science and technology, contrary to the proclaimed goals of Nigerian leaders.

If Nigerian educational institutions have had moderate success in developing skills in their students, they have failed hopelessly in developing patriotism within them. This failure is due to the fact that the educational institutions which the British left have not been modified. The British were not particularly interested in teaching Nigerian patriotism to Nigerians, for obvious reasons. The missionaries who operated a substantial number of the primary and secondary schools were not interested in Nigerian patriotism either; their primary interest was in winning converts to their various denominations and making them "good" Christians. It was common practice to make all students in a mission school become members of the church operating the school, regardless of the student's previous faith. In some cases, a failure in the Scriptures meant a failure in the whole examination no matter how well the student scored in other subjects. Yet it is the educational system, especially the primary and secondary schools, that can build within the children the concept of the Nigerian nation and the sacrifices that must be made to preserve it. An adequate national manpower supply must have, in addition to administrative, scientific, and technological skills, and other skills for nation-building, a strong national commitment, a commitment which the educational systems do not now develop. Not until Nigeria reorients its educational system to cater to the Nigerian interest, will the system be able to produce true Nigerian nationalism. This reorientation should commence immediately.

NATIONAL WILLPOWER

National willpower, though an intangible, is one of the strongest components of national security. It is what determines how much sacrifice a nation will be willing to make if its security is threatened. In this respect, Nigeria has confounded numerous "experts" who predicted that it would soon collapse and disintegrate under the economic and political pressure of the Civil War. What was disregarded was that during Nigeria's young history the will to survive had been acquired. It is now exemplified in the sacrifices that are being made during this Civil War by both sides. The national willpower does not just occur; it is developed and built by a nation. The citizen must have such a favourable image of his nation that no sacrifice would be too great for him to make for the nation. How does he acquire this image? First, his study of the history of the nation must make him proud to belong to that nation. This is where the Nigerian educational systems have failed. The history of Nigeria that Nigerians study is still flavoured with European tastes. For example, to the European, Mungo Park discovered the River Niger; but to the millions of present-day Nigerians, whose ancestors have lived on the banks and sailed the waters of the River Niger for centuries before Mungo Park was born, such history is incorrect. There are many similar foreign interpretations of Nigerian history being fed to Nigerian children, even when the history books are written by Nigerians. Such interpretations do not give the Nigerian a favourable image of his country. It takes a very minimal effort to remedy this situation, but that effort is still to be made by Nigerians.

Second, as a result of colonialism, an outlook often called colonial mentality has developed. It is really an inferiority complex, understandable, but still an inferiority complex. It makes former colonials believe all information that emanates from the metropolitan countries. As a result, current information about the nation that is carried in foreign mass media is taken as the truth, rather than information from internal sources. Again the Civil War has helped to weaken this attachment to news from Britain and Western countries. The credibility gap between what Nigerians experience daily during the Civil War and what is alleged to exist in the foreign mass media has clearly opened the eyes of thinking Nigerians. When Nigerians begin to believe in their own sources of information, then the national self-image will become more sharply focused.

Another offshoot of colonial mentality that badly needs pruning, if not complete weeding, is the tendency for Nigerians, especially the leaders, to trust foreigners more than citizens. Every Nigerian who tries to get information for research purposes knows how nearly impossible it is to do so, whereas if a foreigner doing the same research asks for such information, he gets it readily. In most cases, it is better for the Nigerian to work through foreigners or their organizations to obtain information about his own country. This attitude is changing, but it must be completely reversed if Nigeria is to have any national secrets at all. This irresponsible attitude definitely gives the Nigerian who has encountered it a poor image of his nation, an image that does not make him proud to be its citizen.

After the Civil War, Nigerian leaders must re-evaluate the national image. Changes must occur. If changes do not occur, Nigeria may not withstand the challengers to its national willpower that may arise in a post-Civil War Nigeria.

THREATS TO THE NATION

We have been examining national security and its components, but we have not considered what the nation should be secure against. The nation must be secure against threats to its existence: external threat, which is an attempt, originating from outside the nation, either to destroy the nation or to force on it a line of action contrary to its interests, and internal threat, which is conflict between groups in the country endangering the country's existence. External threat results from conflict between the nation and another nation or an international organization. Both threats are not combatted equally effectively by the various components of national security; a nation tries to use the most efficient mix of the components to annul the threat. Moreover, there is not a clear demarcation between external and internal threats. The classification has been based on the source of the threat, but it is possible, and indeed quite common, that threats are both external and internal. This is the case, for example, when a foreign nation works overtly or covertly with a group within the nation to destroy or weaken the nation. The external component of such a threat will be considered with external threat, and the internal component with internal threat; security against internal threats shall be called internal security, and against external threats, external security. For Nigeria to assert itself in the community of nations, it must not only be cognizant of both types of threat, but must also be prepared to confront them.

INTERNAL SECURITY OF NIGERIA

In a young nation like Nigeria, intergroup conflicts are the rule rather than the exception, with various interest groups struggling to share the limited national wealth. Nigeria is especially susceptible to these conflicts because of the pluralistic nature of the nation. Conflict may arise between political groups, ethnic groups, or religious groups, each group defining national interests in terms of the group's interest only. The conflicts manifest themselves in various forms: disruptions, sabotage, subversion, guerrilla war, and finally, civil war. Nigeria, between 1964 and the outbreak of the Civil War in 1967, went through all these manifestations of internal conflicts except for guerrilla war, and the Civil War may yet be reduced to guerrilla war.

To be internally secure, Nigeria must reduce these internal conflicts to levels that will not affect the security of the nation. Conflicts must exist within the nation, but the nation must ensure that there are instruments to settle them peacefully. The internal conflicts in Nigeria between 1960 and 1967 were of three types. First, there were conflicts between political parties. In many cases, the party in opposition felt the elections were rigged by the ruling party so as to exclude the opposition from power. Second, there was the accusation of ethnic favoritism. People from the same

ethnic group enjoyed an unproportionate share of the national
"pie." Third, there was conflict over loss of civil liberties due to
the "political police system." The instruments to settle these
conflicts can be written into the constitution; however the constitution is of limited use if Nigerians are not educated about it, so that
they can check not only the excesses but also the inefficiencies of
their leaders.

Here internal security must rely on the awareness of the citizens.
This awareness has not been developed and will not be developed
until the educational system is adapted to a Nigerian format. A
postwar Nigeria must give top priority to an overhaul of the educational system. In doing so, considerable thought should be given
to such elementary requirements as the teaching of civics at all
primary and secondary schools, the relegation of religion to its
proper perspective in missionary schools, and the reviewing and
rewriting of books used in these schools, especially books in the
arts and humanities. With such changes, Nigerian schools may
begin to produce Nigerian citizens instead of educated Nigerians
with anti-Nigerian values. The educational system should produce
Nigerians who not only are constructively critical of their country,
but also believe enough in it to be willing to defend it if need be.
An educational system that develops a strong national willpower
will enhance internal security.

Internal security depends on the economic resources of the
nation. Conflicts over sharing of the national wealth would not
disappear if the national wealth were larger. However, increased
national wealth would diminish the occurrence of acrimonious
struggles over its distribution. A post-Civil War Nigeria must
pursue economic policies that increase the national wealth.

The "political police system" poses a very grave danger to
internal security. By "political police system" is meant those law
enforcement agencies that derive their power from other than the
central government. These include native-authority policemen,
customary court policemen, and the like. Many Nigerians believed
that police officers from these agencies made several political
arrests in their law enforcement duties. Consequently they felt that
their civil liberties had been curtailed. This is a very volatile
situation and can be blown up any time into riots or other disturbances. Along with the police system was the so-called customary judiciary system, which defined law by what is customary
within the locality. Such laws left too much to the people in power

and were easily used to victimize dissenters and people with opposing points of view. Nigerian leaders must now realize that a nation cannot have different judiciary systems for different sections of the nation. If citizens must move freely within the nation, the laws they have to obey should be uniform. The police system will therefore have a uniform basis for law enforcement activities. This does not preclude arbitrary arrest, but it will reduce such arrests. Law enforcement officers from the federal police system in the First Republic were more highly respected by all Nigerians than any of the local officers. A central police system in post-Civil War Nigeria will most likely win similar respect. Such trust between citizen and police officer is conducive to internal security. A post-Civil War Nigeria should therefore unify both the judiciary system and the police system to reduce internal threats to the nation.

The national intelligence operation is a very essential part of the internal security. The identification of latent trouble spots in a nation is vital to the security of that nation. As the Nigerian crisis developed, it became clear that the Nigerian intelligence system was very weak. For example, the Federal Government considered that only a police action was necessary to quell the intransigence of the Eastern Region of Nigeria. It is now clear that what was needed was definitely more than a police action. The secessionist Biafrans actually captured nearly all of Southern Nigeria before they were checked. They took over and held the Midwestern Region for about eight weeks. They moved into the Western Region before they were stopped at Ore. Apparently, the intelligence report must have indicated that the Biafrans were inadequately armed, and hence a military action would not be needed. The initial Biafran success and subsequent actions negate any such claims. Biafra was probably better armed initially than Nigeria, and police action was definitely an inappropriate response to its secession declaration. If Nigerian intelligence had correctly assessed the situation and responded accordingly, perhaps the ensuing tragedy of the Civil War might have been averted. An efficient intelligence system is, therefore, an essential prerequisite for the internal security of Nigeria.

Nigeria is a young nation in flux. Disturbances and riots may break out suddenly. Guerrilla war may even result. It is hoped one civil war is enough for the nation. However, a nation cannot base its security on hopes only. Consequently, to achieve credible internal security, Nigeria must take steps to prevent disturbances, riots, guerrilla war, and civil war, and if the preventive measures fail, it must be prepared to quell them most efficiently. The preventive steps, no doubt, will include constitutional changes, changes in the judiciary system, and a better distribution of national wealth. In addition, however, the police and military must be prepared to move fast to trouble spots in the country. This would require more efficient movement of the police and military around the country. Traditionally, people prepare for what they have experienced. Nigeria may prepare for her future security from the experience of the Civil War. This will not be sufficient. Nigerian leaders have to be more imaginative and be able to prepare the country against threats not encountered during the Civil War, in addition to those brought about by the Civil War.

A Nigerian proud of his country will fight against the destruction of Nigeria. However, pride in one's nation has to be cultivated, since it is not innate. The educational system has been suggested as an institution for cultivating such pride. Another avenue for cultivating this pride is through mass communications: radio, television, films, and printed material. Here again, the citizens would be receiving education about their country and why they should be proud of it. This education reaches more of the people much faster than the conventional system. Every village or hamlet in Nigeria has at least one radio set and so can be reached. Once national pride is developed its effect is catalytic. The television producer who is a proud Nigerian will televise shows that project such pride. This is why older countries appear not to make conscious efforts to build national pride; it is there and it snowballs. Young countries like Nigeria must build it. In Nigeria, it is essential that the leaders realize that they are building a nation for their children and grandchildren, for the younger generation. If this is realized, then the opinion of the younger Nigerians should be consulted on occasion. Otherwise, the youth may be alienated from the nation. In this regard many educated young Nigerians have complained that their talents are not fully employed. This is expensive both economically, and with regards to internal security. This is not to suggest that youth should have its way, but merely that the eagerness of youth to serve the nation should be utilized and reinforced. Youth will then be more strongly committed to the Nigerian nation.

The internal security of Nigeria depends on Nigerians. If Nigerians are satisfied with their country and will criticize constructively so as to improve the ills of the country, then Nigeria will be secure internally. If there is discontent prevalent in the country, and no avenue for criticism is open, Nigeria will remain internally insecure. The best internal security for a country is its citizens' loyalty to that country.

EXTERNAL SECURITY OF NIGERIA
In contrast to internal security, external security depends to a large extent on non-Nigerians. External security is security against external threats, made against the Nigerian nation by other nations. If Nigeria is to survive in the amoral international community, it must not only be capable of deterring external threats to its security, but also be able to defend the nation if the deterrence fails. Nigeria may face external threats from three types of nations: neighbouring nations or any other African nation, the major powers, and the middle powers.

There may be conflict between Nigeria and any of its immediate neighbours. Such conflicts may arise over international boundaries or over the sharing of some natural resources. A good example is the use of the River Niger. Any of the countries (for example, Mali or Niger) through which the Niger flows before entering Nigeria may decide to dam or divert it. If the damming or diversion could in any way damage the river before it enters Nigeria, this would be a grave threat to Nigeria's security. The Niger is so vital to Nigeria for agriculture and transportation (besides the fact that Nigeria derived its name from the Niger) that the nation would fight this threat with all its resources to protect its interests, including physical force if needed. Conflicts may arise over several other problems, such as harbouring political prisoners of one nation by another and, possibly, meddling in each other's internal matters. These types of interference will probably result if the Civil War is ended in the battlefield rather than on a conference table, and any neighbouring country is very sympathetic to the side that loses. Nigeria should develop avenues to settle such conflicts.

Similar conflicts may arise between Nigeria and nations which are neither neighbours nor share common natural resources like the River Niger. A section of Africa spells danger to any black African nation—the southern part of the continent where white minority governments hold down the black Africans to second-class citizenship. Nigeria has always been against these nations, if not ideologically, at least pragmatically. As younger, more nationalistic black Africans come to the helm of government, harsher measures against these countries may be used. Nigeria, because of its population and size, may be required to be more militant than it has been. Consequently there will be reciprocal threats between South Africa, Rhodesia, Mozambique, and Angola on the one hand, and Nigeria and other black nations on the other. This is a very real threat that Nigerian leaders must be prepared to face.

The threat from the big powers hangs dangerously over the heads of young nations like Nigeria. By big powers are meant countries with nuclear weapons and their immediate allies in NATO and the Warsaw groups. These big powers control the world economies and world arms production and sales, and hence can control the security of a small nation like Nigeria. If Nigeria took any of them on in a conventional war, Nigeria would be destroyed. In addition, there is the possibility, though remote now, that such powers may use their nuclear weapons to blackmail Nigeria. Nigeria's ability to protect its interest is consequently limited in this case, but the country must use this limited ability most efficiently, while exploring avenues to increase its options.

The middle powers include all other nations that do not fall in the two categories above—many Middle Eastern, Asian, and South American countries. Some of these countries share common problems with Nigeria such as dependence on foreign exchange from sales of primary goods in the world's markets, importation of military hardware and manufactured products, and instability because of the youth of the nation. Others have stabilized and may be excellent sources from which to obtain aid during our period of national reconstruction. The threat to Nigerian security from such nations is negligible at the present.

An effective deterrence to all nations who may threaten Nigeria is the Nigerian national willpower. Nigerians, through their leaders and through ordinary citizens, should make it known to all nations that they will not tolerate encroachment by other nations on their rights and interests. Nigerians will be willing and prepared to defend their national interests if threatened by any nation. Such projection of the national willpower will influence the policies and intentions of all nations towards Nigeria. Nigeria's willpower is more important in the country's relationship with the big powers than with other nations. Nigeria would probably be capable of defending itself militarily against African nations and the middle powers. But as was noted earlier, Nigeria cannot militarily defend itself against the big powers in a full-scale war. Nigeria must therefore impress on these nations that they can gain nothing if they force a war on Nigeria and Nigeria loses. Every Nigerian will remain their enemy. These powers realize that there is little they can do with a conquered nation with hostile citizens. National willpower must be not only a deterrence, but a credible one, and must be projected as such if it is to be effective.

Diplomacy is another component of national security that is effective against external threat. Nigerian diplomacy should aim at creating a favourable image of Nigeria in all foreign countries and winning strong allies where possible. Nigeria should join all international organizations in which it can define and protect its national interests. With regard to black African nations, Nigeria should pursue very diligently the policy of strengthening the Organization of African Unity (OAU). A strong OAU enhances Nigerian external security in many ways. It serves as a forum for negotiating disputes between Nigeria and other members at the conference table, thus diminishing the desire to settle disputes on the battlefield. A strong OAU would deter the interference of big powers in Nigerian affairs as well as in the affairs of other member states. Concerted effort against South Africa, both at the diplomatic and military levels, would be possible and more effective. Because of the benefits which a strong OAU may provide, there will be forces which will work for a weak OAU, and Nigeria should be prepared to counteract their influence (South Africa and Portugal, for instance, would like a weak OAU). Nigeria should cooperate with other African nations in areas not covered by the OAU Charter. Cooperation and mutual assistance between Nigeria and neighbouring African countries, like the Congo, that have had experiences similar to Nigeria's, will be beneficial to all parties involved—for example, exchange of students and scholars, integrated infrastructure where possible, and exchange and loan of high level manpower. By cooperating in this manner, mutual trust replaces the unfounded suspicions planted during the colonial era, and the threat to Nigeria from these nations is minimized.

Nigerian diplomacy, with regard to the middle powers, should aim at reliable friendship with them. Nigeria has already been aided by these powers in its military development programs, as outlined earlier, and there are men from these powers in medicine, education, and other professional fields now serving in Nigeria.

This type of mutual friendship and cooperation between Nigeria and these nations should be continued. Nigerian diplomats in these countries should aim at projecting the image of Nigeria as a young, dynamic, and progressive country.

Among the weapons Nigeria has to protect its interests against threats from the big powers, diplomacy is second only to national willpower. Nigeria should develop dependable and harmonious relations with these countries. However, Nigeria cannot afford to go into any military alliance with big powers. The experience of the Civil War shows that the country's national interests necessitate keeping open its options by remaining friendly with powers on all sides of the cold war. Friendly relations with big powers, however, will not deter them from interfering with Nigerian affairs in ways detrimental to Nigerian national interests. Nigeria must not only be capable of identifying these planned interferences very early, but more important, it must make the whole world aware of the intended threat to its security from big powers. Dissemination of such information will depend on the effectiveness of Nigeria's publicity and propaganda machinery. In alerting the world to the sinister plan against a small defenseless nation by a big power, Nigeria may force several lines of action on the accused nation. The nation may proceed to execute its threat and face the censure of world public opinion. The nation may try to defend itself, and if it cannot, it may back down from its planned course of action. Nigeria may win the support of another big power which would make it known to the threatening nation that it will not stand idle if Nigeria is unduly molested. Publicity and propaganda are strong weapons if Nigeria can locate the threat to its interest before the threat is executed. This calls for capable information gathering and processing, which the intelligence operations should supply.

The diplomatic mission must help in the collection of information that will be used in decisions affecting the nation. Nigerian diplomats, therefore, must be well-trained and capable men, not merely recipients of such positions as political favours. All of Nigeria's representatives in any nation should be knowledgeable about that particular nation and speak that nation's language fluently. As a start, it should be Nigeria's policy that a fraction of its representatives, say one-third, meet the above requirements. How can diplomats operate effectively in a nation whose major language they cannot speak and whose culture they do not understand? It has been rumoured that such a situation did exist in a Nigerian diplomatic mission in an important European country. The educational institutions can help in training these men. Departments specializing in area studies or major country studies should be initiated; departments of Asian studies, Russian studies, American studies or European studies, and an Institute for Strategic Studies should be developed, perhaps in preference to African studies departments. The need to understand other black African nations is important, but commonly shared experiences and the improbability of grave threats from one to another relegate their study to secondary importance. These special departments would produce men who would be effective diplomats in the nations to which they are sent, men who would be able to feed information routinely into the national intelligence system and use the feedback from the system for making important decisions. The significance of an efficient intelligence system for Nigeria's national security cannot be overemphasized. Enough has been said about it. It is hoped that Nigerian leaders will develop one as a matter of national urgency.

Post-Civil War Nigerian diplomacy should give highest priority to improvement of the Nigerian image, which has been badly damaged during the Civil War. Nigeria would need all the information it can acquire about the various nations where this important public relations work must be pursued and should begin to collect the requisite information now. A reliable intelligence system would be of great help, but in the absence of such a system, Nigeria must carry out the public relations program while it is building one.

An external threat to Nigerian security may call for economic actions by Nigeria. It is hoped that Nigeria will not have to use any economic actions against any black African nations, but rather, will be seeking ways for stronger economic cooperation among all these nations.

Nigeria currently has very little economic relations with middle powers, since most of the middle power countries, so defined, produce goods similar to Nigeria's. In an effort to increase its trading partners, Nigeria should seek trade with these powers; where economic interests coincide, such as in the sale of agricultural products to the world market, Nigeria should cooperate with them, with a view to improving their position vis-à-vis the consumer.

Nigeria's economic dependence on the big powers, especially the Western powers, puts it in a very weak bargaining position economically. Nigeria should cooperate with other nations producing raw materials in securing a favourable position in dealings with world consumers. Nigeria should also pursue policies that will improve the Nigerian economic position with respect to the big powers. These policies include the development of a large internal market within Nigeria and neighbouring African countries, rapid industrialization so that industrial consumer items are no longer imported, and development of export trade in industrial products. While Nigeria is doing this, it should endeavour to trade with all nations in the world. This will alleviate its dependence on certain nations and thus enhance its position. Neo-colonialism has been defined as "political independence without economic independence." Since no nation is completely economically independent of other nations, independence in this definition is a relative one. A desirable goal for Nigeria is the ability to maneouver within economic constraints. The preceding policy suggestions should lead towards this maneouverability.

Nigeria's armed forces are the most potent element of its national security and should be a strong deterrence to nations that may want to influence Nigerian interests adversely. If this deterrence value fails, then the armed forces become Nigeria's defense against aggression. An estimated 200,000 men are now in the Nigerian armed services, which would be too large a standing military service in peacetime. But Nigeria will not go back to the 11,500 men of 1967, before the Civil War. Some realistic number should be agreed on and the rest could return to civilian life. There should, however, be a large reserve to back up the standing forces, a reserve obtained by a system of national service. Nigerian youth should be required to demonstrate their national commitment by serving the nation in some capacity, either through military service, or other services, such as the building of roads, schools, and hospitals; this service will bring together Nigerians from diverse backgrounds, thereby reducing unfounded prejudices. At the same time, the standing military would be given continuous training to raise its skill and effectiveness. Furthermore the military could be used to produce an intermediate-level manpower, a level of training which Nigerian education has almost completely neglected.

Although the total number of men in uniform would decrease, the Nigerian air force and Nigerian navy should increase both in number and effectiveness. Nigerian leaders now define Nigerian airspace, but the Nigerian air force, which is doing an excellent job so far, has not been able to defend the airspace completely. Nigeria should not consider itself secure until it can defend its airspace against intrusion; if the cost of military planes is prohibitive, Nigeria could use local commercial planes that can be quickly converted to simple military planes. The Nigerian navy, small in relation to the size of the Nigerian coastline, has not been put to very severe test in the Civil War. It has had to defend only a very small section of the Nigerian waterways. The country should now consider having a navy that can challenge intruders along its coastline. In sum, Nigeria should build a balanced military force where the army, navy and air force share appropriate responsibility, instead of a force dominated by the army.

Nigeria should be working within the context of the OAU and should not have to employ its armed forces against neighbouring African states or member states of the OAU. If the need arises, however, Nigerian armed forces should be able to defend the Nigerian airspace, territorial boundaries, and waterways against any African nation.

Nigeria's dealings with the middle powers should not lead to military confrontation. Nigeria has received generous offers of military training from these nations and has used the offers in certain cases. In striving for military maneouverability, Nigeria should emulate some of these middle powers and should also continue to expand its suppliers of military hardware to include as many nations as possible in order to reduce its dependence on any one country. The Civil War has proven how dependence on a certain few suppliers can be nearly fatal. Nigeria, like India and Israel should also obtain licenses to produce some of the arms within the country. The advantages of such a policy are that some money spent on military hardware would circulate within the national economy, and Nigerian technical know-how would improve. Another policy that some middle powers pursue that might be beneficial to Nigeria is to negotiate, along with the purchase of heavy arms, the sale of machines for making spare parts for these arms. Nigeria is already manufacturing very simple arms, so that the policies recommended here should enhance Nigeria's reliance on itself. Nigeria should continue to use officers from these middle powers in developing its own military schools until it becomes self-sufficient.

Nigeria cannot compete with the big powers in terms of modern weaponry; however, it can match them in the determination to defend itself against aggression. With the advent of modern technology, big powers have found it unnecessary to take over small countries like Nigeria for economic necessity; technology creates prosperity without imperialistic expansion. If, in spite of this, big powers would still wage aggressive war on Nigeria, the country should not throw its glove into the ring and quit. Instead it should settle down to wage the type of war a big power would detest—avoiding conventional open war confrontation and thus prolonging the conflict. Meanwhile Nigeria should use its diplomacy to win allies and, through its publicity and propaganda outlets, should force world opinion against such a big power. If all these fail, the Nigerian willpower should be strong enough to resist the aggression successfully.

Conclusion

In a brief examination of the Nigerian Civil War, we have concluded that the Nigerian nation can only gain strength from it, rather than be weakened by it. Now that the concept of the Nigerian nation has been established, we argue that Nigeria must be prepared to protect its own national interests, especially the continuance of its existence. This will call for an adoption of efficient national security programs, which should include military capability to defend the nation, economic potential, a capable intelligence system, diplomatic ability, national manpower pool, and national willpower.

We maintain that to achieve the objective of internal security, an educated and politically aware citizenry is essential. We suggest that the Nigerian educational system be overhauled in order to adapt it to Nigerian realities. We argue that the educational system and mass media be employed to create an image of Nigeria which will make the citizen proud. The constitution should be framed so as to bring forth desirable political, economic, and judiciary changes in Nigeria.

External security will depend on Nigeria's ability to project a national willpower that will brook no interference from foreign nations. Nigeria should employ a capable intelligence system and an efficient diplomatic corps to attain this objective. Although prepared to engage in open conflict, Nigeria should wage war only when all other efforts have failed and the aggressor still threatens Nigeria. Economic and military policies should be developed that will reduce Nigeria's dependence on any one nation or national alliances. These policies, we argue, will enhance the possibility of Nigeria's survival in the political jungle of world power struggles.

In the final analysis, all major decisions in a nation are political. Nigeria must develop and use able political leadership and must endeavour to employ all its indigenous talents before importing foreign ones. Nigerian leadership must not only be sensitive to the nation's needs, but also be cognizant of international demands and limitations. It is hoped that such leadership will emerge in Nigeria, and that it will lead the country from the destruction and chaos of a civil war to the path of purposeful progress.

Notes

1. F. A. O. Schwartz, Jr., *Nigeria: The Tribes, the Nation or the Race—The Politics of Independence* (Cambridge, Mass.: The M.I.T. Press, 1965).

2. Okoi Arikpo, *The Development of Modern Nigeria* (Baltimore: Penguin Books Inc., 1967).

3. Ibid.

4. W. Arthur Lewis, *Politics in West Africa* (New York: Oxford University Press, 1965).

5. Institute for Strategic Studies, *Adelphi Paper*, no. 21 (London), August 1965.

6. Institute for Strategic Studies, *The Military Balance 1967–1968* (London, 1969).

7. Institute for Strategic Studies, *Adelphi Paper*, no. 27 (London), April 1966.

8. *Daily Times* (Nigeria), June 1969.

9. Institute for Strategic Studies, *The Military Balance 1967–1968* (London, 1969) and Institute for Strategic Studies, *Adelphi Paper*, no. 15 (London), December 1964.

10. George Thayer, *The War Business: The International Trade in Armaments* (New York: Simon and Schuster, 1969).

11. Ibid.

12. "Nigerian Budget, 1969–1970," *Daily Times* (Nigeria).

13. *U.S. News and World Report*, 16 June 1969.

14. Federal Government of Nigeria, *Company's Decree*, 1969.

15. Colonial No. 204 (London: H.M.S.O., 1946).

16. Claude S. Phillip, *The Development of Nigerian Foreign Policy* (Evanston, Ill.: Northwestern University Press, 1964).

17. *Sunday Times* (Nigeria), 24 August 1969.

18. Allison Ind, *A History of Modern Espionage* (London: Hodder and Stoughton, 1965).

9

THE ECONOMICS OF THE NIGERIAN CONFLICT

Victor P. Diejomaoh

The outbreak of civil war in Nigeria in July 1967 was the culmination of multifarious events having sociocultural, political, and economic dimensions. The course of the Civil War itself was determined by a complex of factors. The place of economics in the understanding of the conflict is therefore partial. It will be particularly difficult to determine the primacy of sociocultural, political, or economic factors as explanatory variables of the conflict. These factors have been particularly interlinked so that it is difficult to determine what factors were truly fundamental. However, it is easy to identify economic factors that were closely related to the genesis of the crisis and the progress of the conflict itself. Without necessarily being a dogmatic proponent of economic determinism, it can be demonstrated that economic factors were particularly significant in explaining the origin and course of the conflict in Nigeria. This will be our task in this chapter.

Economic Background of The Conflict

EDUCATIONAL DIFFERENTIALS AND THEIR REPERCUSSIONS

A major underlying factor to the conflict is the large differential between the level of economic development of the former Northern Region of Nigeria and Southern Nigeria. Although there are no reliable per capita income figures to demonstrate this income differential, an examination of partial economic indices, such as per

318

capita levels of human resource development, government expenditures and revenues, provision of health and transport facilities, and export levels, show quite clearly the differential in per capita income levels between the North and the South. While per capita

TABLE 1
Indices of Relative Regional Levels [a] of Public Services
(North = 1.0)

	North	East	West	Midwest	Lagos
Education 1965					
Enrollment in					
1. *Elementary school*	1.0	5.1	4.71	8.1	8.6
2. *Secondary school (Grammar)*	1.0	8.0	b	b	28.9
3. *University output of students*	1.0	11.5	9.5	10.7	1.9
Transportation 1965					
Length of all					
1. *Roads*	1.0	1.7	1.4	3.1	3.1
2. *Tarred roads*	1.0	1.2	3.4	4.1	2.0
Health 1964					
1. *General hospital beds*	1.0	2.1	1.2	2.5	4.8
2. *All medical institution beds*	1.0	3.1	2.8	3.5	12.3
Regional government expenses 1965–1966					
1. *Total current*	1.0	1.4	2.11	2.5	—
2. *Total capital*	1.0	2.2	2.4	3.8	—

[a] To obtain these indices, divide data of each region by that of the North. Divide the population of the North by that of the relevant region. Multiply the two results together.

[b] The secondary school data for the West and Midwest are not comparable with those of other regions because Western and Midwestern figures are inflated by modern school students.

SOURCE: Calculated from Federal Office of Statistics, Lagos, *Annual Abstract of Statistics,* 1966.

income differentials are traceable to a large number of factors, differentials in the level of modern educational attainments between the North and the South are largely responsible for the differentials in per capita incomes of Northern and Southern Nigeria.

These differentials in education were related to the conflict in many ways. As a result of the differences in the level of human resource development, the number of educated manpower in the different categories in the South substantially exceeded that of the North. Southerners, particularly Ibos and Yorubas, dominated the federal Civil Service, federal government corporations, and universities as well as positions in private industry throughout the whole Federation. By dint of their superior educational attainment, Southerners felt that they too should dominate the federal government and its policy-making. However, the constitutional arrangements of universal suffrage and the large population of the North which exceeded that of the South gave control of the federal government to Northerners. Given the constraint of tribal organization of parties and intolerance of opposition parties, it seemed that without a break-up of the North, a remote possibility under existing conditions, the Northern Region would perpetually dominate the federal government. This was considered undesirable by most Southerners who felt that the relatively less educated Northerners would not provide a sufficiently progressive government. There was also increasing dissatisfaction with the practice of placing some less qualified Northerners over their more qualified Southern colleagues. When it seemed that the prospects of a peaceful end to the rule of the North and its ally, the Nigerian National Democratic Party in the Western Region, were remote, a military coup took place in January 1966. The coup was almost exclusively organized by Ibo officers.

The difference in education between the South and the North was largely responsible for the failure of the first attempt at unitary government established by Decree Number 34 under the Ironsi regime. The Northerners were certain that under a unitary form of government, with jobs given out on the basis of educational qualifications, they would be hopelessly disadvantaged. Southerners and, most probably, Ibos would have dominated not only the central government but the North itself, and therefore the hopes of Northerners for rapid economic advancement would have been shattered. The fear of economic domination of the North by Southerners, particularly Ibos, was responsible for the counter-coup led by Northern officers in July 1966 in which Lt. Col. Yakubu

Gowon, now Major General Yakubu Gowo, was brought to power. It should be stressed that this fear of economic domination of the North was so great, that the Northern officers after their counter-coup of July 1966 seriously contemplated taking the Northern Region out of the Nigerian Federation, despite the serious economic problems that would have accompanied such a decision. The communal riots in the North in September and October of 1966, in which numerous Ibos as well as other Southerners such as Yorubas, Edos, and Efiks were killed and forced to flee the North, were a reaction of Northerners against economic domination by Southerners. These Southerners were able to entrench themselves in a dominating position in the North largely by dint of their relatively higher levels of educational attainment.

The disparity in educational levels also figured in the secession strategy of Ojukwu. The assumption was that since so many Ibos were employed throughout the Federation in all ranks and institutions because of their educational attainment, if they were withdrawn from their positions in the Federation and asked to return to Eastern Nigeria, the Nigerian economy would collapse.[1] This assumption turned out to be false. After the exodus of Ibos, the Nigerian economy, far from collapsing because of manpower shortages created by the exodus of Easterners, particularly Ibos, held up particularly well. More will be said about this later. This assumption failed, because there is a substantial supply of educated manpower in Southern Nigeria even without the Ibos. The educated manpower in the rest of Southern Nigeria and in the North rose to the task and was able not only to maintain a relatively stable economy but to provide personnel for conducting a military campaign that has been impressive by most standards. This fact should refute an erroneous impression circulated in the Western press about the Ibos being the only educated people in Nigeria and that the Nigerian Civil War has been a conflict between the highly educated, dynamic, and civilized Ibos and hordes of Nigerian barbarians and vandals.

Since in the Nigerian setting economic advancement and educational attainments are highly correlated, and because of the problems created in the past that are likely to continue in the future because of differentials in educational attainment, it will be instructive to trace briefly the genesis of the existing differentials between the North and the South.

The advent of modern education in Nigeria can be traced to the middle of the nineteenth century as a result of Christian missionary activity. Although Christian missions visited Benin and Warri in Midwestern Nigeria in the late fifteenth century and early in the sixteenth century, these early missionaries did not use schools for their proselytizing activities. It was only after the rise of evangelism in the nineteenth century, and the realization that schools were critical as instruments of conversion, that the modern educational enterprise began in Nigeria. The first school was a mission school established in Badagry, Western Nigeria, in 1845 by the Church Missionary Society. Schools were also established early in Eastern Nigeria at Calabar in 1851 (by Presbyterians) and at Onitsha in 1857 (by the Church Missionary Society). As early as 1859, the Church Missionary Society had opened a secondary grammar school in Lagos. The Presbyterians opened a secondary school in Eastern Nigeria in 1895 (Hope Waddell Training Institution in Calabar). It should be stressed that in the early development of education, the colonial government played a relatively passive role. By 1900, only two elementary schools could be credited to the government (these were established in Southern Nigeria). The government did not establish a secondary school until 1909 (King's College, Lagos).

From the foregoing it will be seen that formal institutions of learning were started in Southern Nigeria in the nineteenth century. Progress in Northern Nigeria was however extremely slow, because of two major factors: the slow pace of Christian missions in opening up schools in the North and the passive role of the colonial government in expanding education in the early decades of contact with Northern Nigeria. The Christian missions were slow in founding schools, because the bulk of Northern Nigerians were Muslims and were not willing to be converted to Christianity. Actually there was an agreement with British colonialists to restrict the activity of Christian missions in Northern Nigeria. Christian missions were, however, allowed into non-Muslim areas of the North and did open schools in these areas. Also in Muslim areas, schools were opened for Southern Nigerians who had migrated to the North.

These qualifications notwithstanding, the pace of progress in modern education was quite slow in the North. The first Christian Mission School was opened in the North after 1902, and the first government school near Kano in 1909. In 1912, there were only 34 primary schools in the North, 5 government and native administration schools, and 29 unassisted voluntary agency schools. Average attendance in all primary schools was only 954 pupils. Secondary education was particularly slow in developing. By 1937, there was only one secondary school in all of Northern Nigeria with an average attendance of 65 students. In the realm of teacher training institutions there was only one such institution by 1926, with an average attendance of 55 students. In contrast to the North, by 1912, the southern provinces of Nigeria had more than 200 elementary schools, with an average attendance of 35,716 pupils. By 1937 the average attendance in secondary schools in the South had reached 4,275. In the area of teacher training institutions, the South had 14 by 1926 with an average attendance of 265 students.

As shown in Tables 2 through 4 the gap in educational development between North and South had been considerably reduced by the beginning of the Crisis in 1966. However, very wide gaps still existed between the North and South at this time. In the development of primary education, the Northern Region had established 2,714 schools with an enrollment of 518,864 pupils. This was considerably below the southern performance. Although the popu-

TABLE 2
Total Regional Average Attendance

	Primary School	Secondary (Grammar) School	Teacher Training
1912			
Southern provinces	35,716	n.a.	n.a.
Northern provinces	983		
1937			
Southern provinces	218,500	4,285	857
Northern provinces	20,269	65	218
1947 [a]			
Southern provinces	538,391	9,657 [b]	3,046
Northern provinces	70,962	251	740

[a] Data for 1947 are for enrollment.
[b] Does not include enrollment in unassisted voluntary agency schools.
SOURCE: Compiled from O. Nduka, *Western Education and the Nigerian Cultural Background,* Tables II, III, and IV (Ibadan: Oxford University Press, 1964).

TABLE 3
Total Regional Enrollment

	Primary School	Secondary (Grammar) School	Teacher Training
West [a]			
1955	811,432	10,935	6,743
1959	1,080,301	22,374	10,392
1966	741,832	48,146	3,410
East			
1955	641,205	10,421	4,008
1959	1,378,403	15,792	11,765
1966	1,236,872	68,737	9,093
North			
1955	168,521	2,671	1,946
1959	250,912	4,683	3,254
1966	518,864	17,700	12,687
Lagos			
1955	37,636	3,720	43
1959	66,320	4,804	424
1966	98,511	14,088	
Midwest			
1966	384,877	16,272	3,647

[a] It should be noted that between 1959 and 1966 the West was divided into two regions, the West and the Midwest. The actual division occurred in 1963.

SOURCE: Statistics Division, Western Nigeria Ministry of Economic Planning, *Western Region Statistical Bulletin,* June 1959; Statistics Division, Midwest Ministry of Finance and Economic Development, *Midwest Statistical Notebook,* July 1968; Federal Office of Statistics, Lagos, *Annual Abstract of Statistics,* 1960, 1961, and 1967.

TABLE 4

University Population by Regions–1966

Universities	Regional Population				
	North	East	West	Midwest	Lagos
Ahmadu Bello	74	38	18	10	2
Nsukka	2	395	54	72	6
Ibadan	4	166	204	27	2
Ife	2	61	130	24	—
Lagos	1	15	13	13	—
Total	83	675	419	146	10

SOURCE: Federal Office of Statistics, Lagos, *Annual Abstract of Statistics*, 1967.

lation of the North exceeded that of the Eastern, Western and Midwestern regions and Lagos Federal Territory put together, the number of primary and secondary schools and their enrollment in the West and East respectively substantially exceeded those in the North. In 1966, there were in the East 5,925 primary schools with enrollments of 1,236,872; in the West, 4,380 primary schools with enrollment of 741,832; in the Midwest, 1,750 schools with 384,877 pupils; and, in the Lagos Federal Territory, 129 primary schools with an enrollment of 98,511. The gap in secondary education was even larger than in primary education. In contrast to the 17,700 students enrolled in secondary grammar schools in the North in 1966, there were 68,737 in the East, 48,146 in the West, 16,272 in the Midwest, and 14,088 in Lagos.

The earlier and more massive development of primary and secondary education in the South compared to the North was bound to show up in large gaps in educational attainments at the university level. Graduates of secondary schools in the South who had money or were adventurous went to the United Kingdom or United States for university education. While there were university graduates in the South in the first decade of this century, it was not until the early 1950s that there was a university graduate in the whole of the North. As in the other areas of education, there has been considerable progress in university education in the North.

However, in 1966 when the Nigerian Crisis started, the gap between the North and South in university education was the largest of all the gaps in educational development. Of all the graduates from Nigerian universities in 1966, there were only 83 from all of the North compared to 675 from the East, 419 from the West, 146 from the Midwest, and 10 from Lagos. A large number of Nigerians also graduated from foreign universities in the same year, and although detailed information on such graduates is not available, it is certain that the North was poorly represented among such graduates.

We have so far concentrated our attention on the annual rate of development of enrollment in schools without information on the supply, of manpower at different levels of skills. We can, however, obtain this information (in the absence of global information on regional distribution of manpower supplies) from the annual rate of development of educational institutions. The relatively earlier and larger enrollment of Southerners in all levels of educational institutions must have translated itself after some years into a relatively larger supply of manpower at all the different levels of the skills.[2] Since there was a relatively large stock of educated persons in the South compared to the North, there were considerable opportunities for rapid economic advance for Southerners who chose to migrate to the North. The migration of Southerners to the North eventually created a situation in which Northerners felt that their economy was being dominated by foreign elements (given the strong ethnic feelings under prevailing conditions) whom they had to expel.

INTERREGIONAL MIGRATION

Although the pull of opportunity in the North resulting from the different development of North and South was partly responsible for the South to North migration, the push of necessity also contributed to this migration. This latter contention can be borne out by an analysis of the relative distribution of land resources between the various regions of Nigeria. This analysis is important in throwing some light on the particular nature of some events in Northern Nigeria during the communal riots there in May, September, and October of 1966. It will be remembered that in these riots more Ibos were injured and killed than any other Nigerian ethnic group resident in the North. Of all the ethnic groups in Southern Nigeria who had migrated to the North, the Ibos were far more numerous, outnumbering all other groups put together. Southern economic domination of the North, therefore, seemed to the Northerners to be Ibo economic domination. The overwhelming predominance of Ibos in Northern Nigeria cannot be traced only to educational gaps. It can be seen from Tables 2, 3, and 4 that the level of educational development and economic development in the East, West, and Midwest are quite comparable. Hence differential development between the East and the North does not fully explain the overwhelming presence of Ibos in the North compared to other ethnic groupings in the South.

The explanation is largely due to the unfavorable land/man ratio in the Ibo parts of the former Eastern Region. As agriculture is the main occupation in Nigeria, and especially since the level of technology is low and land rotation is prevalent in Nigerian agriculture, extensive amounts of land are necessary for agricultural purposes. The population density in the Ibo areas of Eastern Nigeria, now known as the East Central State, was 712 persons per square mile (1963 census figures for population) compared to only 156 persons per square mile for the whole of Nigeria. The population density of other relatively densely populated areas in Nigeria, (Kano State, 347 per square mile, Southeast State, 337 per square mile and Western State, 326 per square mile) was considerably below those of the Ibo areas. In southern Onitsha, and northern Owerri (Ibo areas) density exceeded 800 per square mile; in some parts it was over 1,000 per square mile. There, inadequate fallowing practices had produced progressive land degeneration, the conversion of forest land to grassland and serious erosion. Food production was insufficient to meet the needs of the local population and there was considerable emigration to the cities and other parts of Nigeria.[3]

Although Ibos migrated to other parts of Nigeria, the North provided the best opportunity in terms of the land/man ratio, to say nothing of the opportunity created by the educational vacuum. The population density in the Northern Region was only 106 per square mile (1963 census figures) compared to 337 per square mile in the West, 170 per square mile in the Midwest, and 24,639 per square mile in Lagos Federal Territory. It can be seen from these figures that the need for emigration from the West and Midwest was considerably smaller than in the Ibo areas of the East. Since the West and Midwest were on a comparable level with the Ibo areas in educational development, Ibo migrants would have encountered greater competition in these areas as far as education was concerned. In fact, many Ibo immigrants did menial jobs and were never considered to be dominating the economy of these areas.

The mass migration of Ibos to the North is an important factor in understanding the Nigerian conflict. After Ibo military plotters had killed their leaders, the Northerners felt that the Ibos were planning to dominate them in perpetuity and were planning a unitary state in which they would lose a great deal. Consequently, the Northerners vented their spleen on Ibos who were to be found in large numbers throughout the North. Ibo immigrants in the North were so numerous that when forced to flee back to the East, they imposed a very major economic burden on the economy of the Eastern Region. In order to create job opportunity for these refugees, Ojukwu expelled all non-Easterners from the Eastern Region even before secession was declared. It is reported that nearly every Ibo family had relatives who were refugees from the North and for whom they had to care. The return of the Ibo refugees therefore had a pervasive effect throughout the Ibo East. Also the injuries with which these refugees returned and the reported death of others inflamed the entire Ibo population. It was on this anger that Ojukwu and his collaborators capitalized in planning their strategy for secession. A major factor in the support of many Ibos for the secession bid was the consideration that if they could not be guaranteed safety in jobs outside of the East, then there was no point in remaining in the Federation, making financial contributions for maintaining central services from which Easterners could not benefit. The issue of migrants from one region or state to another is of great importance for the future of the Nigerian economy. We shall discuss this later.

ECONOMIC DISCRIMINATION

Biafra was originally intended to cover all of former Eastern Nigeria, comprising the Ibo areas (now the East Central State) and the minority areas (now the South East State and River State). In explaining the federal Nigerian victory in the Civil War, it should be stressed that the victory was possible because people in the minority areas were opposed to secession and strongly supported the federal government.[4] Had these people supported secession, the military campaign in their area would have been particularly difficult and long, because of their hostility and the difficult terrain. There are indeed reports of the local population giving federal forces secret help against the secessionist forces. The federal forces of the Third Division, in fact, used these minority areas as a base for advancing into the so-called Ibo heartland.

The opposition of the minority areas to secession was based on their fear of economic subjugation to the Ibo majority. They feared that their natural resources would be exploited for the benefit of the Ibos who would control political power indefinitely in the new republic of Biafra. These fears were not altogether unfounded. In Nigeria there was a tendency for minority areas to be neglected by the majority which controlled the government. In developing countries like Nigeria, the rate of economic development is closely related to the enthusiasm of the government to pursue developmental policies. Hence if the government is not interested in an area, its prospects for development are dim. This is exactly what happened in the minority areas of the former Eastern Region. These areas were the least economically developed parts of the former Eastern Region, largely because of poor government initiative. As a result of this economic neglect by the government, leaders in these areas had long sought their own state (Calabar-Ogoja-Rivers State) in the hope that greater control of their own affairs would enhance their prospects for more economic development. As a recognition of the gross neglect of the Niger Delta parts of the former Eastern Region, a colonial commission of enquiry recommended the creation of a Niger Delta Development Board to accelerate the development of the area.[5]

The issue of economic discrimination has relevance not only for the minority areas of the former Eastern Region, but also for the whole of the Federation of Nigeria. Under the civilian regime and with the arrangement of three regions (i.e., before the creation of the Midwest State in August 1963), the majority ethnic groupings of Hausa-Fulani, Ibos, and Yorubas dominated the various minorities in their areas. The majority groups always distributed government expenditures in order to favour their areas. Also areas controlled by parties in opposition were usually discriminated against in the provision of public services. Under these circumstances, the minority groups which often formed the political opposition in the regions as well as the opposition groups at the central level were always restive. The dissatisfaction of these groups created a destabilising factor throughout the country.

We have said that it was fear of perpetual domination of the South by the North that led to the coup of January 1966—a coup engineered largely by Ibo officers. At the time of the coup, political control at the federal level (and hence power to distribute federal government expenditures) rested mainly with Northerners and their ally, the Nigerian National Democratic Party of the Western Region. The Ibos feared that, having been edged out of political control, they would be heavily discriminated against, and this was, no doubt, a factor in the largely Ibo coup of January 1966. While the Ibos shared largely in power at the federal level (i.e., before January 1965), they had used their position to allocate a disproportionate amount of federal government jobs and federally sponsored projects for the benefit of Ibos. This was widely known in Nigeria. After the Ibo-led coup in January of 1966, which brought an Ibo to the head of the federal government, it was widely alleged that the military government was allocating jobs and influence to Ibos disproportionately. This factor greatly dampened the initial nationwide acclamation for the coup. The Northern counter-coup, as stated earlier, resulted from fear of perpetual economic domination by Ibos and Southerners. The Northerners were certain that the government, controlled largely by Southerners, would not distribute government expenditures equitably. Therefore, because of this mistrust, disadvantaged groups, which felt they could not redress their grievances by peaceful means, were ready to use and did use forceable means to ensure that they could control the distribution of public expenditures—either in the whole Federation, in their own autonomous states, or even in sovereign states. These considerations lie behind the coups and counter-coups of 1966, the decision to create more states in 1967, and the secession attempt of the Ibos in 1967.

The Economic Viability of Biafra and the Centrality of Oil in the Nigerian Conflict

So far we have concentrated on historical economic factors underlying the coups, counter-coups, the communal riots in 1966, and eventually the secession of 1967. It is now necessary to examine more immediate economic considerations which might have led to the decision to pull the former Eastern Region out of the Federation of Nigeria and create from it the independent Republic of Biafra. It is also important to understand why the new Republic of Biafra was supposed to encompass not only Ibo areas of the former Eastern Region but the non-Ibo minority areas as well.

A major factor in the creation of any state, especially a sovereign one, must be the economic viability of the state. The disgruntled Ibo leadership in Eastern Nigeria must have grappled with this problem in developing their strategy for secession. A sovereign Ibo state would have suffered from severe economic disabilities. We have shown earlier that the population density of the Ibo-speaking areas was very high and that under existing agricultural technology, some parts could not provide enough food to sustain the population. It should be pointed out that with the population further swollen by refugees, estimated at about 2 million, from Northern Nigeria and other regions, the economic situation had become even more untenable. It was this inadequacy of resources which had given rise to Ibo migration not only to other parts of Nigeria but to neighbouring foreign countries like the Cameroon Republic, Gabon, and Fernando Po (now part of Equatorial Guinea).

There were no important exports from the Ibo-speaking areas of the former Eastern Region. Of the estimated £25 million worth of agricultural exports (mostly palm produce) from the whole of Eastern Nigeria before the Civil War, only £9 million came from the Ibo-speaking areas. Exports and the prospects of exports of nonagricultural commodities were modest. The export of coal (produced in Ibo area) mostly to Ghana for use in their railways was declining and brought in less than £0.1 million just before the Civil War. The Ibo-speaking areas of the East accounted for only 2.8 percent of Nigeria's total crude petroleum exports, although boundary areas between the Ibo and Rivers State areas also accounted for another 5.5 percent. Exports of crude petroleum from Nigeria in 1966 amounted to £92 million. Total exports from Ibo areas just before the Civil War were therefore substantially less than £20 million out of the Nigerian total of £283 million.

The prospects for industrialization in the Ibo-speaking areas were also dim. With an agricultural sector that could hardly meet food needs, there would have been poor prospects for supplying agricultural raw materials. The textile mills in the East, for example, depended on cotton from the North. Moreover most of the industries in the Ibo East were set up with the anticipated demand of the entire Nigerian market. These industries would have become unviable with the loss of markets outside the Ibo areas. In any case with such inadequate export earnings, foreign exchange would have become a major constraint on further industrialization. Finally, it should be pointed out that a sovereign Ibo state would have been completely landlocked and most probably surrounded by hostile Nigerian neighbours. Foreign trade, so essential to developing countries in particular, would have been very difficult for an Ibo state.

Considerations of this nature were clear to the Ibo leadership. An Ibo state would have been economically unviable. Accordingly, it was necessary to take the non-Ibo areas along (even against their wishes) to provide the economic resources for the new state of Biafra. Captured rebel documents[6] show that the secessionists had designs not only on the minority areas in the former East but also on the Midwest State (the invasion and occupation of the Midwest in August 1967 proves the point) and if possible the Western State and other areas south of the Niger and the Benue rivers. In any case, if they could hold only Biafra, i.e., the whole of the former Eastern Region of Nigeria, Biafra would have been eminently economically viable. The major element in the viability of Biafra was the petroleum resources of the former Eastern Region.

It is important to stress the significance of oil. Before the initiation of petroleum exports from eastern Nigeria in 1958, the Eastern Region contributed the least of all the regions to the foreign exchange earnings of Nigeria. She was actually dependent on foreign exchange earnings from other regions.[7] Since Nigerian governments, like those of most other developing countries, depended largely on foreign trade taxes, the Eastern Region was the poorest region in terms of government revenues in the days before oil was exported. The financial plight of the East was so serious in those days that the East was not able to start its 1955–1960 development program on schedule and had to cancel some aspects of its compulsory and universal free primary education (unlike the West) because of financial stringency. The East was then a staunch advocate of the principle of need (with its implication of national unity) and an opponent of the principle of derivation in the revenue allocation formulae for Nigeria.[8] Thus in the days before oil, the East under its Ibo leadership was a strong advocate of a united Nigeria with strong powers for the central government. So long as the East had a major interest in the resources of a federal Nigeria, there was no need to threaten secession. However, with the discovery of oil in the East and its economic implications, the picture changed. The Eastern leaders, according to an authoritative source,[9] started contemplating secession as early as 1962. When the Binns Fiscal Commission was appointed in 1964, the submission of the Eastern Region was strongly in favour of the principle of derivation, which they had previously opposed, so that it could obtain the maximum returns from oil tax revenues.

It is important to state briefly the attractions of the oil industry in the former Eastern Region and in Nigeria generally. In 1966 before the outbreak of the Civil War, Nigeria exported 146,635,195 net barrels or 19,890,150 long tons of crude petroleum valued at £91,950,489. The Eastern Region accounted for 62.9 percent of this total. The Midwest accounted for the other 37.1 percent. The net contribution of the petroleum industry to Nigeria's balance of payment in 1966 was £43.4 million, i.e., after allowance for service payments and net inflow of capital for further development. £15.5 million was paid by oil companies as licenses, mining rents, and royalties, and a profit tax of £2.9 million on their operations in the fiscal year 1966–1967. Under revenue allocation formulae current before the Civil War, the East would have obtained 50 percent of the mining rents and royalties paid on the operations of oil companies in the East and another 10.5 percent of the total oil amounts paid throughout Nigeria for mining rents and royalties from its share of the distributable pool. The profit tax on oil companies went to the federal government.

But the static picture for 1966 does not tell the whole dynamic story of Nigerian oil. Oil production and export had been growing at phenomenal rates since the beginning of exportation, increasing from £1 million in 1958 to £92 million in 1966. According to one projection, production of crude petroleum in Nigeria in 1970 would reach 40 million metric tons, about twice the 1966 level and by 1980 would triple to 120 million metric tons.[10] Proven reserves of crude oil are estimated at about 400 million tons, probable reserves at 600 million tons, and possible reserves at 1,200 million tons. These oil resources are accompanied by vast reserves of natural gas. Possible reserves of gas are estimated at over 800 thousand million m^3($1m^3 =$ 35 cubic feet). It is conservatively estimated that in the 1969–1974 period, tax revenues from oil would amount to about £600 million.[11] While the above figures may not be exactly accurate, they give the right orders of magnitude and indicate the bright future which lay ahead of the petroleum industry in Nigeria.

The Ibo leadership in Eastern Nigeria was well aware of these bright prospects. If it could include the minority areas (the Rivers State accounted for 57.1 percent of Nigerian oil production before the war) in their Biafra, they would have control of this vast oil production. With these oil resources, Biafra would not only have been economically viable but it would have become, apart from Libya, the wealthiest state in Africa. If Biafra had succeeded in holding the Midwest, as its leaders had contemplated, then Biafra would have controlled all of Nigeria's oil resources, and it would have become even more wealthy. Ibo leaders of Biafra were in fact hoping that Biafra would become the leading black nation in Africa and held out bright hopes for its rapid economic development. It is therefore clear that when circumstances arose in 1966–1967 which the Ibo leadership found unpleasant, they knew that if they could successfully pull Biafra out from the Federation, good economic prospects lay ahead. If there had been no oil resources, the economic case for secession would have been very weak. The existence of oil in Eastern Nigeria was largely responsible not only for the secession attempt of the Ibo leadership, but also for including the minority areas (who were opposed to secession) in their Biafra.

The oil question was very critical in the progress of the Nigerian conflict. When the rebels declared secession, they hoped that the oil companies would pay taxes to them. These taxes would have provided valuable foreign exchange resources to purchase arms. The oil companies operating in the East were, however, by law expected to pay their taxes to the federal government which was still the recognized government for all Nigeria. Shell-BP, the major oil producer in Nigeria, was caught between the demands of the rebel regime to pay taxes to them and their legal obligation to pay taxes to the federal government. Shell-BP could not openly flout the Nigerian federal government because, at the beginning of the war, the federal side still controlled Midwest production of oil which was being largely done by Shell-BP. In any case the outcome of the war was not certain. On the other hand Shell-BP could not altogether ignore the Biafrans, since at the beginning of the war, they effectively controlled the oil installations in the Eastern Region of Nigeria. Shell-BP therefore decided to pay a token amount to the Biafran government.

The dilemma in which Shell-BP found itself was largely responsible for the ambivalent attitude of the British government at the beginning of the Nigerian conflict. The British government not only owned interests in the British Petroleum Company (BP) but also the Royal Dutch Shell Company. Both companies were collaborating as Shell-BP in the Eastern Region. The investment of Shell-BP in the East exceeded £ 100 million.[12] British investments outside the rebel zone were also quite substantial. The danger of losing British investments either in Eastern Nigeria or the rest of Nigeria, if she took sides, was largely responsible for Britain's initial decision to remain neutral in the Nigerian conflict and to refuse to sell arms to federal Nigeria as she had before the conflict. The British neutral posture changed, of course, when Nigeria's military forces quickly captured the oil terminal at Bonny in July 1969 and blocked all oil exports from the Eastern Region. The swift action of federal forces in neutralising the effect of oil in the conflict was, of course, based on federal Nigerian awareness of the potential benefits of oil to Biafra.

The economic nonviability of Biafra without oil became quite clear after the federal capture of Bonny which meant that Biafra could not get any foreign exchange or tax resources from oil. After the initial foreign resources and foreign currency obtained by selling Nigerian currency abroad had been exhausted around April of 1968, the Biafran resistance began to collapse rapidly. After the fall of Port Harcourt in May 1968, many other towns fell in relatively quick succession just falling short of Umuahia. This was during the period when rebel resources had almost run out and poorly equipped rebel forces could not match the much better supplied federal Nigerian troops. It was when the rebels were almost on their knees that the French came to the rescue, late in July 1968, although substantial aid began to flow in only after September 1968.

The involvement of the French in the Nigerian crisis is the result of a multiplicity of considerations, some having nothing to do with economics. However, it seems that the French involvement in the Nigerian conflict is closely tied up with the oil issue. The French saw in the Nigerian conflict a chance to edge out the large British oil interests in Nigeria. The French oil company, SAFRAP, which was operating in the former Eastern Region was responsible for only a very small proportion of total oil production there. If the Biafrans won their independence struggle, they would have thrown out the British who, after hesitations, decided to back Nigeria fully. This would have left the field open to the French. There are authenticated reports that Ojukwu and his government mortgaged all of Biafra's mineral resources for a ten-year period to the French Bank of Rothschild in exchange for a grant of £6 million.[13] French President Georges Pompidou, the former French Prime Minister, is a leading official of the bank. It is therefore clear that French support for Biafra must have been in exchange for something substantial. All that Biafra had to offer was the promise of oil.

It should be stressed that French intervention in the Nigerian Civil War was very critical in extending the course of the war. Just before the French intervened, the Biafrans were almost at the end of their rope. It is highly probable that without French assistance, the Nigerian Civil War would have ended or should have been reduced to very manageable proportions by the end of 1968. However, with the intervention of the French, Biafra's fire power was so substantially increased that the end was postponed to January 1970. We have shown that this prolongation of the war as a result of French intervention was related to anticipated oil concessions to the French.

We have attempted to show in the foregoing paragraphs that oil has been a central consideration in the Nigerian conflict. It is highly probable that without oil in the area originally claimed by Biafra, there would have been no secession. Secession without oil would have involved fewer international intrigues, and the duration of the Civil War would have been greatly reduced.

The Economic Case for the Unity of the Nigerian Federation

Many commentators, international do-gooders, and even some Nigerians at one time or other, felt that the cost of a civil war was so high that it was unadvisable to engage in one, and that the former Eastern Nigeria should be allowed to secede as the Republic of Biafra. It is, therefore, important to state, albeit briefly, the economic considerations for unity in Nigeria and why the federal government of Nigeria had to forcibly thwart the secession bid of Biafra. The main economic argument is simple. The integrity of the Nigerian federation greatly enhances its prospects for economic development—the major obsession of all Nigerians. Economic development is desirable for not only anticipated better standards of living, but also for political power and independence which go with an economically advanced country. These points are too well accepted to need further elaboration.

Nigeria, as constituted before the secession attempt, had considerable economic advantages (and fairly bright prospects for self-sustaining economic growth). Although its true population is not known, all available estimates of its population, ranging from 45 million to 56 million in 1963, indicate that it has the largest population of all African countries. It, therefore, provided (despite its relatively low per capita income) one of the largest markets in Africa and hence was a major attraction for foreign investments. Its large market also meant that it could more easily exploit the economies of scale attendant on a large market. The need for a large market for sustained economic development is critical. If the market is too small, prospects for long-run economic development are slim. This is true, because after import-substitution industrialization concentrating on the manufacture of consumer goods is exhausted, further development is stunted. Even the maximum advantages from import-substituting consumer industries cannot be obtained if markets are small. To accelerate growth further, it is necessary to move into a stage of industrialization concentrating on the production of capital goods. The markets required by capital goods industries in order to ensure viability are normally so extensive that many small countries cannot produce capital goods economically and therefore have to import them. However, the import capacity of small countries is so limited that they cannot import sufficient machinery for their industrialization, and in any case their small markets cannot support extensive industrialization. Prospects of rapid economic development by concentrating on primary production are dim because of the declining terms of trade for primary producing countries. The prospects for development of small countries, except the mineral-rich ones, are therefore very bleak. It is considerations of this nature which have stimulated the United Nations Economic Commission for Africa to urge African countries to form larger economic units in order to escape from the vicious cycle of poverty.

The economic prospects of the Nigerian Federation were not only dependent on its large size. The Nigerian Federation had a diversity of resources. Exports from the Federation were composed of many different commodities, such as cocoa, groundnuts, palm oil and palm kernel, tin metal and ore, raw cotton, rubber, timber and crude petroleum. Since the prices of these commodities do not all move in the same direction at the same time, the instability of Nigerian export earnings was much less than those of countries which depend on one major export commodity, such as Ghana for example. If Nigeria had been allowed to disintegrate, the country would have been split into small states in which one export crop would have predominated. Export earnings would therefore have been subject to considerable fluctuations. Since domestic incomes, government tax revenues, and the import capacity are closely related to export earnings, the individual states would have been subjected to severe economic strictures, with the exception of the oil-rich Rivers and Midwest states. It should be noted that the Western State produces mainly cocoa; the Southeastern State, palm produce; and the Northern states, groundnuts or cotton. In a united Nigeria, and with the centralized control of foreign exchange, states deficient on foreign exchange earnings could always count on the central pool of foreign exchange. The foreign exchange constraint would thus have been less binding on the development of different regions. In fact, taking Nigeria as whole, foreign exchange is not the most binding constraint on Nigerian economic development.[14]

Apart from these advantages of unity, it should be noted that several facilities had been developed with the whole Nigerian federation in view, namely, the road and rail transport networks, the harbour facilities, and electrical, postal, and telecommunication services. The economies obtained through the centralized administration of these facilities would have been lost with the disintegration of the Federation and the consequent duplication of these facilities. Moreover, most of the new states resulting from disintegration would have been completely landlocked, and with the current feelings of suspicion and hostility, transportation especially for foreign trade purposes would have become extremely difficult.

If Biafra had been allowed to secede it is more than likely that the whole Federation would have disintegrated. The Western Region was making its own plans for secession in the event of Biafran secession. It is unlikely that the North would have held together. The Midwest would also have opted for a separate existence. It is not certain how many independent states would have emerged out of the ruins of the Nigerian Federation. The prospects for economic development of these independent states would have been considerably dimmer than those of a united

Nigeria. Furthermore, the disintegration of the Nigerian economy would in all probability have been followed by those of other African countries. The trend in Nigeria and Africa would have been towards disintegration at a time when moves are being made towards integration and larger economic units (for example, the European Common Market, the European Free Trade Association, the Central American Common Market, the Latin American Free Trade Association). To pursue this trend toward disintegration would have been to condemn Nigerians and Africans to perpetual economic deprivation and subjugation to economically more advanced nations. The very future of Africa was in the balance and it was definitely necessary for the Nigerian government to forcibly put down the secession attempt.

Somewhat less important, to allow Biafra to secede was to allow it to carry away the wealthiest part of the Nigerian Federation—the oil-producing areas of the Rivers State and the agriculturally rich areas of the Southeastern State. We have shown earlier that these parts of the former Eastern Region were not interested in secession and were being forced to be part of Biafra against their will. It is also likely that if Biafran secession were not checked, Biafra would also have attempted to seize the oil-producing Midwest State (as was in fact the case in August 1967). No sovereign and self-respecting state allows its territory to be seized without putting up military resistance. Moreover, once the wealthy minority areas of Biafra were liberated, the rest would be economically unviable and since not all Ibos wanted secession, it would have been necessary for the federal government to liberate them from perpetual economic deprivation in an economically unviable independent Ibo state.

Finally, it has been argued in some quarters, that all Nigeria needed for satisfactory economic performance was a common market.[15] Biafrans and their supporters had argued for a confederation or a loose federation with economic cooperation. However, the economic advantages from a fairly strong federation are considerably greater than those from a common market. It has been difficult to coordinate economic policy even in the existing Nigerian Federation. Most of the regional governments had sought to create a degree of self-sufficiency which tended to negate the advantages of the federation, and this was because the regional governments had considerable autonomy. If their autonomy was increased to the extent allowed for in a confederation or in a common market arrangement, it is more than likely that greater effort would have been toward self-sufficiency with consequent waste and dissipation of economic potentials resulting from unity. Moreover, the present slow progress towards common market arrangements in Africa shows that would have been a silly gamble to throw away a united country in exchange for an uncertain common market arrangement. Finally, it is not unlikely that a confederation or common market could itself have disintegrated in the long run.

Economic Impact of the Conflict

THE ECONOMIC POLICY BACKGROUND

In order to understand fully the changes in various economic sectors during the Nigerian crisis, it is important to indicate the economic policy background against which the changes have occurred. Some of the economic changes which have taken place would most probably have been different if the economic policy that was followed had been different. After the first coup in January 1966 there was no significant change in economic policy, other than Decree No. 34, requiring a unitary government for Nigeria, which was a direct result of the coup. However, after the July 1966 counter-coup and the subsequent mass return of emigrated Nigerians to their regions of origin, some readjustment in policy became necessary.

The major readjustment in economic policy took place in Eastern Nigeria, which received an influx of returned emigrants estimated at slightly over 2 million people. In order to be able to create jobs for some of these returned emigrants, the Eastern government ordered all people of non-Eastern origin (except Midwest Ibos) who had been resident in the East out of the Eastern Region. The Eastern government was, however, able to create jobs only for the civil servants and high level professionals. Although some expenditures were undertaken to resettle some of the lower skilled refugees, those settled were necessarily few because of limited resources. The others either became dependent on their relatives in the rural areas or swelled the ranks of the unemployed in the cities, where they provided a situation receptive to mass propaganda, hysteria, and extreme political leadership.

In pursuance of its policy of playing for time while the foundations for secession were laid, the Eastern Nigerian government spent the early part of 1967 haggling for more funds from the federal government. When the funds were not provided on the scale demanded, the Eastern Region government confiscated all the revenues that were payable to the federal government from Eastern Nigeria.[16]

Federal government corporations in the East were seized by the Eastern Region government. Some planes of the Nigerian Airways were seized, along with rolling stock and wagons of the Nigerian Railways. In retaliation, the federal government denied the Eastern Region government access to Nigerian foreign exchange, postal, and telecommunication facilities.

In anticipation of the impending secession of the East, the federal government decreed the creation of twelve states on 27 May 1967. This action, as we shall see later, has raised and will continue to pose a number of economic problems. The question of revenues for the new states from federal sources was an immediate problem. This was resolved by maintaining the essential features of the existing revenue allocation arrangements, with the new states having the powers of the old regions. However, the eastern and northern states were to divide between them the distributable pool shares normally allowed to the former Eastern and Northern Regions respectively. The percentage share of the new states in the distributable pool were to be as follows: Lagos State, 2 percent; Western State, 18 percent; Midwest, 8 percent; East Central, 17.5 percent; Southeast, 7.5 percent; Rivers, 5 percent; and each of the Northern states, 7 percent.[17]

When the Eastern Region declared secession on 30 May 1967, the federal government's first strategy was to use economic blockade. The whole of the former Eastern Region was put under a total blockade, in hopes that it would bring so much distress that the rebel government would either renounce secession or be overthrown by dissidents in the East. Although these hopes proved false, the effects of the economic blockade were recognized to be very unpleasant in the East, and this probably hastened their decision to use military force to settle the conflict quickly. The Civil War broke out in July 1967. When the rebels occupied the Midwest from 9 August to 9 October 1967, the Midwest State was also put under total blockade by the federal government.

From the outbreak of the war in July 1967 to October 1967, no other special economic measures were undertaken. The effect of this was to put heavy pressures on government finances and the international balance of payments. In October 1967, the following measures were undertaken by the federal government to assist in raising resources for the war and maintaining a measure of financial stability:

1. the 1 percent savings in expenditure by all ministries except Defence and Internal Affairs;
2. postponement of capital projects to which the government had not irrevocably committed itself;
3. the establishment of two committees—one to advise on how to effect economies in the running of overseas diplomatic missions and the other to ascertain how public corporations can be made more viable." [18]

Other measures introduced included raising the rates of import and excise taxes and introducing a national reconstruction surcharge of 5 percent on tariff rates, with the exception of a few necessary import items. A super tax of 10 percent on company profits in excess of £5,000 or a tax of 15 percent of the issued and paid up share capital, whichever was larger, was introduced. A compulsory national savings scheme was introduced which required all wage and salary earners as well as self-employed people (other than flat rate taxpayers) to contribute 5 percent of their incomes for one year starting 1 December 1967. Flat rate taxpayers were expected to contribute 10 shillings. These sums were to be refunded with interest in 1977. Finally, the importation of a few commodities was completely restricted.

These measures proved inadequate to curtail domestic demand for imports, and with inadequate export performance as will be discussed later, it became necessary to introduce massive import restriction and tighten up foreign exchange control. In January 1968 the following items were placed on specific import license and their importation was declared suspended until further notice: packing containers of paper, chains (all materials), domestic and office furniture, wood and plywood (semi-worked), textile piece goods, made-up tarpaulin, passenger cars, carpets and rugs, domestic washing machines, refrigerators, and air conditioners, radios, electric hair dryers, television sets, radiograms, tape recorders, gramophones, pleasure boats, enamelware, electric cookers, porcelain or china housewares, other ceramic housewares, domestic utensils of aluminum and other metals, flasks, food preparations (not elsewhere specified in the *Nigerian Trade Summary*), stock fish, cereals, flour and starch for foods, wines and spirits, beer, cigarettes, rice, vegetable roots and fibres, edible nuts, pastry biscuits and cakes, confectionary excluding chocolates, tomato puree, envelopes, exercise books, fountain pens (especially ball-point pens), developed films, unissued postal and similar stamps, bank notes and similar documents of title, outer garments, socks, shorts, handbags and wallets, imitation jewelry, beads, common toilet soap, toys, and indoor games.

The total approximate value of these items was £61.5 million or about 25 percent of all imports in 1965, the last year of normalcy before the outbreak of the Nigerian crisis.

The economic situation necessitated further strengthening of economic policy in April 1968. The import surcharge was raised from the 5 percent (imposed in October 1967) to 7.5 percent, affecting all imports. A 10 percent import duty was imposed on raw materials used in local industry, a category not hitherto taxed. A 10 percent excise tax was imposed on certain domestic manufactures that were previously tax free. There were further increases on the excises on beer, soft drinks, and cigarettes. For one year only, the tax free privileges of pioneer companies were revoked for those earning profits above £5,000 and seventeen more items were placed on specific licensing, including cement, corrugated iron sheets, metal doors, windows and frames, roofing nails, assembled domestic sewing machines, electric generators, buses, furniture and fixtures, matches, umbrellas, and bulbs. Many of the items placed on specific licenses in January and April 1968 were manufactured in Nigeria but an overwhelming majority of them were not. The extensive list given earlier shows the wide scope of the import restrictions which affected not only consumer goods but also raw materials and capital goods.

The Economic Cost of the Conflict

It is impossible to give in a neat summary figure the cost of the Nigerian conflict. The economic repercussions of the conflict are vast and varied. Among the obvious costs are the increase in government expenditure required to compensate for the social dislocations of 1966 and after, and the subsequent Civil War after July 1967. Due consideration must also be given to reductions in gross national product and the implications of the reduced output for future production. Important, but difficult to estimate accurately, is the destruction to capital. There are also the missed opportunities and the general hardship of life in a war situation. The most colossal loss, however, is the destruction to human life that the conflict has engendered. Despite the attempt by economists to quantify the economic worth of a human life, the effort is still subject to serious limitations. Even if these limitations are removed, it is not known how many lives have perished in the Nigerian conflict although conservative estimators will agree that it runs into hundreds of thousands. The best we can do on a fairly accurate basis in the following paragraphs will be to give rough estimates of the financial cost of the Civil War and the effects of the war on various sectors of the economy.

It is obvious that a civil war will necessitate vast expenditures to supply the substantially expanded armed forces with their requirements. Estimates around October 1968 put the Nigerian army strength at about 80,000–90,000 men, and the rebel army at 50,000 men.[19] These numbers compare with 8,000 which was the strength of the total Nigerian army before the coup of January 1966. On the federal Nigerian side, a leading government official estimates that from 1 September 1967 to 31 March 1969, direct expenditures to sustain the Nigerian military amounted to £300 million. Of this amount, about £60 million was incurred in foreign exchange.[20] If allowance is made for a normal peacetime military expenditure of about £30 million, it means that during the above period £270 million was spent to support the military as a result of the conflict.

Estimates of destroyed capital as measured by capital expenditure necessary to replace the destroyed capital will probably be subject to great error. This is because it is difficult to identify all destroyed capital, private as well as public, and because prices are far from stable. However, for what they are worth, estimates by various government officials of expenditures necessary to replace destroyed capital and resettle displaced people range from £250 million to over £400 million. Since this estimate was made before the war was ended, it can be assumed that the cost of the total conflicts in terms of capital replacement and resettlement now that the war has ended will probably substantially exceed £500 million. The amount that was spent on supporting the military during the conflict and in replacing destroyed capital and resettlement will probably not exceed £1,200 million. This amount is only about 75 percent of the estimated gross domestic product of 1967. The most liberal estimates after including military expenditure will probably not top £1,600 million, or about Nigeria's gross domestic product of 1966. These figures indicate that the financial loss occasioned by the war will not exceed one year's gross domestic product for Nigeria. If adequate economic policies are pursued after the war, and the Nigerian Federation achieves self-sustaining economic development, the cumulative increases in future incomes will more than compensate for the loss. It should be noted that we have so far made no effort to estimate the lifetime income streams of Nigerians slain as a result of the conflict. On the basis of very conservative estimates, it can be concluded that the amount involved cannot be less than £2,500 million. Even if the correct figure turns out to be four times the estimated, it can still be concluded that the total economic loss can be more than covered in the long run if economic development continues unabated in the Nigerian federation.

It should be expected that the growth of the national economy during a civil strife as in Nigeria will be adversely affected. This is because output is seriously disrupted in areas of active conflict. The Nigerian experience since 1966 proves no exception to the rule. In the 1960–1965 period, the gross domestic product in real terms increased at the rate of 5 percent per year. However, in the 1966 fiscal year encompassing most of the first year of the crisis, the growth rate of gross domestic product in real terms was only 2.6 percent. Some of this decline can be traced to the restrictive credit policy of the Central Bank in 1965 and 1966 and a decline in capital formation at the federal level of government. However, uncertainty generated by the coup and counter-coup of 1966, and the mass movement of population in the second half of 1966 with their consequent disruptions to production, account in great measure for the slowdown. In 1967, gross domestic product is guesstimated to have increased by only 2.4 percent. It should be remembered that the Civil War started in July 1967 and that output was largely disrupted in the main theatres of conflict, the Eastern Region and the Midwest. In 1968, with the whole of the former East virtually dislocated, with farmers turned into refugees, and production substantially affected not only because of the war itself but also because of the effect of the economic blockade, import restrictions, and higher taxes, it can be safely assumed that gross domestic product fell below the level of 1967 (there were no official figures to confirm this conclusion). Since the Nigerian population was growing at an average annual rate of 2.5 percent, it follows that per capita income levels at the end of 1968 were slightly lower than those of 1965. However in 1969, with life returning to normal in most parts of the former Eastern Region, and in most of the Midwest, gross domestic product must have surpassed the 1968 levels. The Nigerian economy had therefore entered an expansionary phase in 1969 that is likely to be intensified as normalcy is restored.

In examining the effect of the war on various economic sectors, we turn first to an analysis of exports, the pacesetter of economic growth in Nigeria. As can be seen from Table 5, total exports increased substantially by almost £20 million in 1966. The political crisis did not have much impact on exports in 1966. Although some of the traditional exports, such as cocoa, palm kernels, palm oil, and groundnut oil and cake, showed declines in export value in 1966, this was due largely to declines in quantity exported and lower export prices. These factors were unrelated to the Nigerian crisis. In 1967 the Nigerian crisis began to adversely affect total exports. Total exports fell substantially from £283.1 million in 1966 to £238.1 in 1967. Apart from cocoa which was enjoying unusually high prices in 1967 and which was produced primarily in the Western State, an area largely unaffected by the Nigerian crisis, all major exports suffered substantial declines. The most adversely affected commodities were in the active war zones where exports were not only disrupted by the war but were also restricted because of the blockade imposed on the war zones. For example, exports of palm kernels and palm oil (coming mostly from the East) fell from £22.4 million and £11 million respectively in 1966 to £7.8 million and £1.3 million. Crude petroleum exports fell from £92 million in 1966 to £72.1, and rubber exports, largely from the Midwest, fell from £11.5 million in 1966 to £6.4 million in 1967. Groundnut exports from the North fell slightly because of increased transport difficulties.

The Civil War raged throughout 1968 and had further adverse effects on exports which fell to £211 million, according to revised estimates. The decline in petroleum exports was largely responsible for the decline in total exports. This occurred because there had been some recovery in some of the traditional export commodities, such as palm kernels, palm oil, and groundnuts and its derivatives, because of partial dismantling of the blockade. Despite the recovery in some of the traditional exports, their values in 1968 were still below the 1966 levels. In 1969, preliminary indications showed that the exports for 1969 would exceed the peak levels of

TABLE 5

Exports of Major Commodities for Selected Years, 1959–1968

(£ millions)

Year	Cocoa	Palm Kernels	Palm Oil	Ground-nuts	Ground-nut Oil and Cake	Petro-leum	Rubber	Raw Cotton	Other	Grand Total
1959	38.29	25.97	13.81	27.47	6.32	2.70	11.61	7.30	27.04	160.51
1962	33.35	16.89	8.94	32.43	8.63	16.74	11.36	5.86	29.81	164.01
1965	42.69	26.54	13.59	37.81	15.26	68.10	10.99	3.30	45.06	263.34
1966	28.26	22.43	10.96	40.82	14.4	91.97	11.47	3.42	n.a.	283.13
1967	54.69	7.80	1.26	35.41	11.41	72.11	6.35	6.51	42.56	238.10
1968	51.57	10.20	14.20	38.00	14.40	37.00	n.a.	3.30	n.a.	211.0

SOURCE: Federal Office of Statistics, *Annual Abstract of Statistics*; Federal Ministry of Information, *Nigeria Trade Journal.*

1966. Provisional figures issued in 1970 confirmed this. It was estimated that crude oil production (which resumed in the last quarter of 1968) would hit a peak of 600,000 barrels a day. However, because of rebel air raids the 1 million barrels a day mark was reached only in April 1970 after the war had ended. Total exports for the first half of 1969 were estimated at £170 million. It will be seen, therefore, that the upward march of Nigerian exports had resumed in 1969.

As a result of the Nigerian conflict, imports were substantially reduced. Like exports, imports were not significantly affected as a result of the crisis of 1966. Although imports fell that year from £275.3 million to £256.4 million, the decline was due largely to continuing import substitution, increased import duties, credit restrictions, and lower federal government capital formation. It must be recognized, however, that because of the uncertainties created in 1966, some plans for expansion in the private sector were shelved, and thus imports were kept at a lower level. However, by 1967, the effect of the crisis became significant. The economic blockade of the East and later the Midwest shut off large imports, while the increased import taxes and restrictions of October and November 1967 further affected the situation. Offsetting these retarding factors were increased imports for war purposes. The military and other imports by the rebel regime are not included in the figures after 30 May 1967. Accordingly, the £222.5 million given in official sources understate total Nigerian imports. It is likely, however, that after correction is made for rebel imports, that total Nigerian imports for 1967 were below those of 1965 if not those of 1966.

The decline in imports was accentuated in 1968. As indicated in the discussion of economic policy, massive import restrictions were imposed in 1968 in addition to various tax devices to curb consumer demand. The effect of these factors is reflected in the low level of total imports in 1968 estimated at £192.7 million. As most of the areas under the rebels' regime had been liberated by the end of 1968, the error factor in not including rebel imports is smaller. There is no doubt that even after allowance is made for these imports that total imports declined still further in 1968. However in 1969, with resumed and expanded production of the oil industry, the trend of imports was upwards. Moreover, the federal budget proposal of May 1969 ended the import restrictions on the following items: motor vehicle tires and tubes, milk, sugar, salt, petroleum products and lubricating oils, spare parts, wheat, food items not already restricted, coffee, cocoa and tea, natural and manufactured gas, certain medicaments, industrial requirements of oil producers, some medical instruments, portable personal effects, cement and motor vehicles other than passenger cars. As a result of the freer import situation in addition to normal expansion of items not previously restricted, imports in 1969 substantially exceeded those of 1968. As normalcy is established in the remaining war zones and reconstruction and development programmes are implemented, it can be expected that imports will continue their upward trend.

In concluding our analysis of the external sector, mention should be made of the effects of the crisis on capital inflows and foreign exchange reserves. It is to the credit of the Nigerian economy that despite the Nigerian crisis with all its uncertainties, there has been no net capital outflow from Nigeria. It is not surprising that the levels of net capital inflow have declined as a result of the crisis. Foreign investors in the war zones, whose output was interrupted or completely stopped, could not be expected to expand their productive facilities with new capital inflow. Investors outside the theatres of war had some doubts about the future of their markets and therefore were cautious about expansion. When the Civil War broke out, some foreign aid donors and international aid agencies refused to make new commitments to the Nigerian government. Net inflow of private capital (if the oil industry is excluded) fell from £19.6 million in 1965 to £6 million in 1966, and to £5 million in 1967. With restoration of confidence in 1968, when it became clear that the rebels could not win, net inflow of capital increased to £16.4 million. Net capital inflow of the oil industry increased from £17.4 million in 1965 to £28.9 million in 1966, £45.5 million in 1967 and declined to £39.6 in 1968 when oil output was at its lowest levels. With economic recovery getting underway in 1969, it can be expected that the trend in net capital inflow will be upward after 1969.

The foreign exchange reserves of Nigeria have been greatly depleted as a result of the Nigerian conflict. Inadequate capital inflow and substantially increased service payment of the oil industry combined to create a loss of foreign exchange reserves of £8.8 million in 1966, with total foreign exchange reserves falling from £93.2 million in 1965 to £84.4 million in 1966. Prompt action was not taken to conserve foreign exchange reserves in 1967 with the outbreak of the war and the need for large imports of armament. Accordingly, there was a large drop in foreign exchange reserves from £84.4 million at the end of 1966 to £51.1 million at the end of 1967. Largely because of the measures to hold down imports in 1968, the foreign exchange reserves at the end of that year stood at £51 million, about equal to the level at the end of 1967.

Nigeria's management of her external financial position has been able indeed judging by the standards of developing countries. In a period of civil war, she managed to maintain a stable exchange rate, although numerous foreign exchange restrictions were in operation. Other developing countries even in peacetime resort to similar measures. This compares particularly well to the experiences in the Congo and South Vietnam, two countries that have recently experienced a civil war. For example the Congolese franc was devalued from 50 francs per dollar in 1960 to 180 francs per dollar in 1963, while the South Vietnamese piastre was devalued from 35 piastres per dollar in 1960 to 117.5 piastres per dollar in 1966. The Nigerian government was also able to maintain enough foreign exchange reserves to finance about three months worth of imports in 1967 and 1968. It, therefore, met conventional standards of international financial prudence which most developing countries cannot do even in peacetime.

AGRICULTURAL PRODUCTION

Coming now to the domestic front, the absence of data on total agricultural production makes it difficult to discuss here the effect of the Nigerian crisis on this important sector. However, it can be assumed that the trend for total agricultural production is similar to the trend for gross domestic product already discussed.

INDUSTRIAL PRODUCTION

The Nigerian conflict did not have a significant adverse effect on industrial production in 1966. The Central Bank index of industrial production actually shows a substantial increase in 1966 rising from 185 in 1965 to 236.2 in 1966 (1963 = 100). The increase in industrial production was broadly based, with substantial increases being scored in mining, manufacturing, and electricity production (see Table 6). In 1967 following the outbreak of the war, with data for the Eastern Region omitted for the second half of 1967, the index of industrial production showed a substantial fall from

TABLE 6

Index of Industrial Production
(Base: quarterly average 1963 = 100)

	Total all industries	Mining	Total manufacturing industries	Beer (including stout)	Vegetable oil products	Soap (including detergents)	Paints, varnishes and lacquer	Soft drinks	Roofing sheets	Vehicle assembly	Cotton textiles	Footwear	Cement	Natural rubber	Electricity
								Manufacturing Industries							
Weights	1,000.0	317.0	571.0	109.9	44.3	16.7	4.5	21.8	9.6	8.3	51.4	7.0	40.5	29.5	112.0
1964	127.5	138.9	123.5	118.0	122.3	96.1	146.3	122.6	168.4	134.4	113.3	129.7	159.5	108.2	116.4
1965	185.0	271.9	146.9	121.3	136.5	158.6	202.0	183.3	59.9	188.7	198.2	106.4	188.9	96.5	133.6
1966	236.2	391.5	165.9	133.7	94.1	141.7	243.2	138.2	118.0	95.4	338.9	185.4	192.6	109.6	154.5
1967 [a]	210.4	303.3	174.7	128.3	91.7	130.4	455.6	136.3	94.2	119.2	446.9	219.3	141.0	85.8	129.6
1968 [b]	163.0	161.0	172.1	149.1	132.0	93.3	206.0	132.0	84.9	106.0	419.5	237.0	107.0	78.1	122.2

[a] Production figures for establishments located in the three Eastern states are included only up to the first half of the year when these figures were available.
[b] Excludes production figures of establishments located in the three Eastern states.
SOURCE: Central Bank of Nigeria, *Monthly Report, March 1969.*

236.2 in 1966 to 210.4 in 1967. However, even with the exclusion of Eastern states from manufacturing production figures in the second half of 1967, total manufacturing production increased from an index of 165.9 in 1966 to 174.7 in 1967. In 1968, with data for the Eastern states excluded for the whole year, the index of manufacturing production stood at 172.1. This shows that without the Eastern states, which accounted for 30 percent of total Nigerian manufacturing output before the war, manufacturing output in the rest of Nigeria in 1968 surpassed that for the whole country, including the East, in 1966. Obviously, manufacturing output increased very rapidly outside the war zones throughout the period of the Nigerian crisis. This rapid expansion of manufacturing output was stimulated largely by the heavy import restrictions. Some producing units, notably tire manufacturing, went into twenty-four hour production and still could not satisfy internal demand. One of the benefits of the conflict has been the realization that the domestic manufacturing sector could substitute for a large number of imports.

It should be pointed out, however, that although total manufacturing has increased rapidly, some manufacturing sectors remained depressed compared to pre-war levels, for example, soft drinks, soap and detergents, paints, varnishes, and lacquer, roofing sheets, and natural rubber. Mining production fell in 1967 and again drastically in 1968. However, an examination of the quarterly indices of mining production shows that mining production had been rising rapidly throughout 1968 and that by the fourth quarter the level of production had exceeded 1965 levels and was about 80 percent of the 1966 peak levels. Since petroleum dominates mining production and its level of production in 1969 topped pre-war levels, it can be concluded that mining production in 1969 exceeded the pre-war peak levels of 1966. Electricity generation declined in 1967 and again in 1968, but with the opening of the Kainji Dam in 1969 and the restoration of electrical services in war-torn areas, electricity production in 1969 reached and probably surpassed pre-war levels. Hence in industrial production we see again that expansion was firmly under way in 1969.

PUBLIC FINANCES

The disruptions of 1966 and the Civil War and its aftermath had a considerable adverse impact on the public finances by increasing expenditure requirements and reducing sources of government

TABLE 7

Nigerian Public Finances
(Values in £ millions)

	Current Revenues	Current Expenditures	Surplus (+) Deficit (−)
1964–1965			
Federal	86.8	76.5	+10.3
North	33.5	30.1	+ 3.4
East	27.0	26.1	+ 0.9
West	20.9	21.1	− 0.2
Midwest	8.2	6.8	+ 1.4
1965–1966			
Federal	97.1	94.4	+ 2.7
North	32.6	35.9	− 3.3
East	30.5	24.9	+ 5.6
West	22.6	24.4	− 1.8
Midwest	9.2	7.8	+ 1.4
1966–1967			
Federal	101.0	100.5	+ 0.5
North	33.6	34.9	− 1.3
East (e)[a]	30.7	29.6	+ 1.1
West	23.1	20.8	+ 2.3
Midwest	12.0	8.1	+ 3.9
1967–1968			
Federal	84.3	102.1	−17.8
North (e)[a]	33.3	37.3	− 4.0
West	19.5	19.2	+ 0.3
Midwest	10.1	9.2	+ 0.9
1968–1969			
Federal	93.1	91.0	+ 2.0
West	20.1	19.9	+ 0.2
Midwest	11.1	9.7	+ 1.4
North Central	5.3	5.9	− 0.6
North East	4.7	7.0	− 2.3
North West	3.6	5.6	− 2.0
Kano	6.9	5.4	+ 1.4
Benue-Plateau	4.3	5.6	− 1.3
Kwara	2.5	5.4	− 2.9
Total Northern States	27.3	35.0	− 7.7
Rivers	4.2	6.5	− 2.3
Lagos	10.5	10.3	+ 0.2

[a] e = Estimates

SOURCE: Federal Office of Statistics, Lagos, *Digest of Statistics*, July–October 1967; *Annual Abstract* 1966; Federal and State Budgets 1968–1969.

revenues. In many cases expenditure levels either fell or were brought closer to actual revenue yields by a reduction in rate of growth. As indicated in the section on economic policy, the rate of taxation was increased on a smaller tax base in order to increase tax revenues. Even so, as can be seen from Table 7, the current revenues of the federal and all state governments fell substantially either in the 1967–1968 or 1968–1969 financial year or in both years. The main sources of current revenues, import and export taxes, suffered significant declines because of the drop in exports and imports which we discussed in the section on foreign trade.

The effect of reduced revenue yields after the 1966–1967 financial year and fairly rigid current expenditure levels was an increase in the current account deficits of some governments, the creation of deficits where there had previously been surpluses, and the reduction of surpluses. The stringent financial situation led to increased government borrowing from the banking sector. Net credit to the government sector increased from £27.2 million in December 1965 to £47.2 million in December 1966 and rose further to £80.3 million and £155.6 million respectively for December 1967 and December 1968. Government borrowing from the Central Bank rose from £21.7 million in December 1965 to £56.9 million in December 1968. Despite increased government borrowing, all governments found it necessary to curtail capital expenditures, with emphasis being placed on the completion of essential works in progress and the initiation of projects deemed essential for the war effort. However the budgets of 1969–1970 showed that pre-war levels of revenue and expenditures were to be exceeded.

It should be remembered that the Nigerian crisis precipitated the creation of more states. With the creation of the states, the financial viability of a number of governments had to be determined. Because of the active military campaign in the Eastern states, the finances of these states were thrown into complete disarray. Taxpayers were turned into refugees, and not only could they no longer pay taxes, they now imposed greater expenditure requirements. The Rivers State, for example, in its 1968–1969 budget estimated that all its anticipated revenue would have to come from federal sources. There was not even an attempt to draw a budget in the East Central State until after the war ended. The three Eastern states, however, under normal conditions, would be quite viable financially, especially the Rivers State with ample oil revenues. However, until reconstruction expenditures are successfully completed, they will need considerable financial assistance from the federal government. The 1969–1970 budgets of the Southeastern State not only reflect the return to normalcy in these areas, but also the need for financial assistance from the federal government.

Despite the rebel incursion in the Midwest State and the decline in current revenues in 1967–1968, the finances of the Midwest are basically sound (notice the current account surpluses and the favorable outlook of the oil industry in the Midwest). Recovery in government revenue and expenditures actually began in the 1968–1969 financial years. The 1969–1970 budget estimates reflected still further that expansion was well under way and that total government expenditures and revenues for the year would substantially exceed pre-war levels. The Western State like all others suffered some declines in 1967–1968, but like the Midwest State, its government revenues and expenditures began to recover in 1968–1969, and the 1969–1970 estimates indicated that government revenue and expenditure levels for that year would substantially top pre-war levels. The finances of Lagos State, which came into existence on 1 April 1968, are basically sound. The high income base in Lagos State ensures the highest per capita levels of government revenues and expenditures in the Nigerian federation. The 1968–1969 and 1969–1970 budgets reflected the sound financial position of the state. There is, therefore, no question as to the viability of these three states discussed.

The financial positions of the Northern states, however, leave a great deal to be desired. The Northern Region, before the creation of the six states, was in the worst financial position in the federation. In the fourteen-year period between 1953 and 1967, the current budget of the North was in deficit eight times, and the combined budgets of the Northern states in 1968 showed a substantial deficit. These persistent deficits imply, of course, that either government revenues must be increased or the growth of current expenditures must be reduced. Since the North has the lowest levels of per capita provision of government-supplied services, a curtailment of the growth of government expenditures would mean a further widening in the gap between the North and the South. The creation of six state governments in the North with their increased administrative expenditures means that lesser revenues would be available for development. Under existing financial arrangements the Northern states will be faced with persistent financial problems. The 1968–1969 budget estimates showed a deficit for each of the

Northern states except Kano State. While the six Northern states are viable in the sense that they can maintain minimum basic government services, they cannot without federal assistance pursue a vigorous development policy that is essential to bridge the gap between the North and the South.

Before concluding our remarks on the public finances, let us examine briefly the financial position of the rebel regime. It should be fairly obvious that fully accurate information on this subject cannot be available for security reasons. However, some information is available, and it is important that it be presented for an understanding of the conflict.

The ability of the rebels to wage the war and maintain some semblance of a government depends, of course, on the government's finances. Since the rebel regime had planned secession for about a year before its actual declaration, it had taken care to conserve some reserves which were transferred to European bank accounts. This provided foreign exchange for the purchase of arms and the support of rebel external propaganda and diplomatic envoys at the initial stages of the war. The rebel regime also obtained revenue by attempting to sell abroad Nigerian pound notes seized from the Central Bank branches at Enugu and Benin and commercial banks in the territory controlled by the rebels. The federal government later foiled the rebels' financial strategy by bringing out a new issue of currency in January of 1968 and declaring that the old currency was no longer to be legal tender. After the exhaustion of these initial reserves, the rebel government ran into serious financial problems. It commandeered all private possessions of foreign currency and precious metals. This did not significantly improve matters. By the end of April 1968, Biafran reserves were exhausted, and the rebel regime found it difficult to continue its importation of arms and payment of foreign pilots and cargo plane transportation changes. It will be remembered that the period of financial stringency for the rebels (i.e., April to September 1968) marked their period of rapid reverses ranging from the loss of the whole of the Rivers State, much of the Southeastern State, and important centers in the East Central State such as Aba and Owerri. During this period of financial stringency the main sources of finance were the payment of relief organizations for local materials and donations from "Biafrans" abroad and Aid Biafra groups. However, after September 1968, the rebel regime's financial position was substantially improved as financial assistance from French sources increased. This assistance leading to increased imports of arms significantly increased the rebel opposition in the battle-ground.[21]

PRICE LEVELS

A usual characteristic of economies involved in war is a rapid in-crease in price levels, as aggregate demand exceeds supply. The rate of inflation, however, depends on the ability of the government to curb private demand. On the whole, the Nigerian government has been rather successful in holding down the rate of inflation. Official statistics indicate a rate of inflation in 1967 and 1968 for the Nigerian regions outside rebel control which is not significantly greater than in the pre-war years when prices were almost stable.[22]

Although official data show a 7 percent increase in 1966 in the consumer price index of low income groups (i.e., earning below £400 per annum), this increase cannot be traced to the effects of the Nigerian conflict. The increase was the result of a drop in agricultural output in 1966, but this decline could not have re-sulted from the disturbances of 1966, since most of the disruptions were in urban areas. The consumer price index for lower income groups rose only from 122 (1960=100) in 1966 to 124 in 1967 and remained unchanged at 124 in 1968. For the middle income group (earning £400–£700 per annum), the consumer price in-dex was relatively stable rising from 118 (1960=100) in 1965 to 120 in 1966, to 122 in 1967, and to 125 in 1968. Since the low and middle income groups comprise about 95 percent of all income groups, it will be seen that prices were almost stable for all income groups during the worst periods of the Nigerian conflict.

Although the official statistics may have understated the degree of consumer price increases, the results indicated are theoretically defensible. Food production in federally controlled areas was not affected adversely by the conflict; actually output increased. How-ever demand was lower than in the pre-1966 period because the East is a food-deficient area. Sales of food to the East ceased with the blockade of 1967. The exodus of Ibos from areas outside the East further reduced the demand for food. The demand for housing also declined with the departure of Ibos from several Nigerian cities. Since food and housing are the major determinants of the cost of living of lower and middle income groups, it will be seen that these results are plausible.

The cost of living of upper income groups increased more

rapidly, although the extent cannot be precisely stated because there is no official index of consumer prices for higher income groups. Upper income groups depend more on imported items and domestically manufactured products. The prices of imported items rose sharply in 1968 following the restriction of imports and higher import taxes. Prices of domestic manufactures also increased because of excessive domestic demand. Transportation costs and higher excise duties also rose sharply with the banning of car imports and higher excises on petroleum products. The effect of these price increases was limited, however, because of the small size of the upper income group.

The rate of inflation in rebel-controlled areas or areas recently liberated from rebel control has been quite high, as may be expected, because these areas were the main centers of fighting, and output and distributive channels were severely disrupted there. While no precise quantitative information is available to indicate the rate of overall inflation in rebel areas, partial information is available. After the liberation of Owerri in October 1968, it was found that a cup of garri which would have cost about 2 to 3 pennies before 1966 now cost 16 pennies (1/4d) indicating a price rise of 400 percent to 700 percent.[23] A yam was said to be costing £2 indicating a price rise of close to 2000 percent.[24] The situation in Owerri was reflective of what was happening in rebel areas. Since garri and yams are basic foodstuffs, it can be surmised the overall rate of inflation must have been very high because of the predominance of food in determining total consumer costs.

On the whole, however, the performance of the Nigerian economy with respect to price inflation has been highly creditable. The rate of price increase in federally controlled territories was lower than that of most developing countries not engaged in any civil war or not experiencing any serious political disturbance. This reflects the inherent stability of the Nigerian economy because of its vastness, diversity, and rich resources. It also testifies to the wisdom of the economic policy pursued and the determination of Nigerians to make sacrifices for the integrity of their nation.

Conclusions

In the preceding pages we have undertaken a wide ranging analysis of the economic historical background and economic impact of the crisis. In conclusion, it is important to analyse the implications of the foregoing for the future of the Federation.

In order for the Federation of Nigeria to realize fully its economic potential, it is essential that there be no repetition of the sort of crisis in which the country has found itself. A basic cause of the current conflict has been the wide gaps existing between the North and South in levels of per capita income and especially in human resource development. We have shown that the Northern states without external assistance do not have the resources to bridge the gap between the North and South. So long as this economic gap exists there will be the temptation for the Southerners to take advantage of the Northerners and for Northerners to be suspicious of Southerners. Also, so long as the gap remains, it would be difficult for jobs and development projects to be allocated strictly on the basis of efficiency. If this were done, the poorer states of the North and other relatively less developed states in the South would always lose out, and the economic distance between them and the more developed states would increase. Under these circumstances disequilibrating forces would increase in the Federation and endanger the political and economic stability of the country.

It is therefore essential that in the interest of stable future development, the Nigerian governments both at the federal and state levels, must adopt a positive and conscious policy of reducing the gaps between the less developed and more developed parts of the country. At the federal level, this would probably involve the increased use of conditional matching grants to stimulate expenditures, particularly in the area of education in the Northern states. Since the widest gaps are in the areas of secondary, and particularly university, education, the federal government will have to develop a special scholarship and loan programme for the Northern states and the less developed states in the South such as the Rivers, Southeastern and Midwest states. It will also be advisable to locate more development projects in the less developed states even if the economic rate of returns on such projects would be lower than those in the more developed regions. These principles should also be applied within individual states. This is because there is also a need to avoid the disequilibrating forces at state levels which accompany wide differentials in development levels until a definite policy is introduced for reducing the gaps between more developed and less developed regions in Nigeria. As long as the heterogenous character of the Federation remains, it is certain that future stability within the country will be endangered.

A policy of reducing development gaps between states implies that government expenditures in the less developed states must be permitted to grow at a more rapid pace than in the more developed states. It does not mean that there should be stagnation in the more developed states as has been the fear in certain Nigerian quarters. However, to permit a relatively faster rate of growth of government expenditures particularly in the Northern states, there must be a change in the revenue allocation formulae of the Federation. More emphasis will have to be placed on the principles of need and balanced development in working out a definitive formula. However, there cannot be an abandonment of the principle of derivation as has been urged by prominent figures in Nigeria.[25] This will amount to a negation of the principle of autonomy involved in any federation. Complete abandonment of the principle of derivation would also antagonise wealthier states and sow the seeds of future disintegration. Finally, in any future revenue allocation exercise, it will be necessary to ensure that the federal government is in a sufficiently strong financial position to be able to come to the assistance of the states and to shoulder heavier responsibilities which will be necessitated by the fact that the new smaller states will be less capable of undertaking sizeable projects.

Another issue closely related to the question of development gaps, which has contributed to the current crisis, is that of economic discrimination. There has been a tendency in the past for ethnic groups in control positions to reserve job and government projects for their areas. At the federal level of government, the Ibos and the Yorubas in particular, and lately the Hausa-Fulani group, were guilty of these charges. These practices, of course, led to an intensification of ethnicity with its centrifugal implications. Since most states are not ethnically homogenous, economic discrimination was also practiced at the state level with its consequent danger to stability. If stability is truly desired in Nigeria, there must be a reversal of this policy of economic discrimination. It leads not only to an inefficient allocation of resources, but also poses a serious threat to the very existence of the country. In a diversified country like Nigeria all elements must be made to see that they are not being cheated and that the Federation exists for the benefit of all. If the principle of efficiency is not too badly violated, it will be desirable to adopt a system of quotas in job and government expenditure allocation in the transitional period after the war ends. This will enable all the disparate elements in the Federation to see that they have a stake in the government and will enhance the spirit of nationalism and cohesion.

Another major issue that must be resolved in the interest of future stable development is that of interstate migrations in search of jobs and investment opportunities. In any true federation, there must be a free mobility of the factors of production. This usually results in more rapid economic development of the whole federation. However, it is essential that these migrating factors of production be identified with their areas of residence, for otherwise they may constitute enclaves of quasi-foreign investments which will not only be regarded as exploitative but will probably actually be exploitative. Under these conditions it is apparent that such migrating factors of production will either be ejected or expropriated. This interpretation is fairly reflective of what happened to Ibos and other Southerners in the North.

It must be stressed, however, that Nigerians must be free to work and invest wherever they please in the Federation. The federal and state governments must guarantee the safety of such Nigerians and their property. Many state governments have an overt or covert policy of discouraging other state residents from holding jobs in their states. If this policy is not reversed, we would be making nonsense of the Federation. If the individual states were to become watertight compartments for their citizens, most of the advantages of the Federation would be lost; it is doubtful that true loyalty to the Federation can be developed or expected under such circumstances. There would, of course, be no incentive for the wealthier states to subsidize the poorer states, if their residents cannot work there. Negation of the right to free flow of factors of production would eventually intensify demands for separatist movements.

The foregoing remarks are of topical significance for long-run stability. The more immediate considerations, however, are the repair of economic damage occasioned by the war and the institution of a firm foundation for future economic development. Since this could constitute a separate study, our remarks here will be very summary. Considerable damage has been done to roads and bridges. Some undamaged roads, such as the Lagos-Ibadan road, have been heavily overworked because of disruption of other transport routes. The railway system has been under severe strain because of manpower shortages, and the inability to use the Eastern wing of the rail network. Schools have been destroyed, electricity and water supply interrupted, and hospital facilities substantially overloaded. Apart from these public facilities, substantial damage has been done to private properties in urban areas. It has been estimated that damage to real estate in Onitsha, Awka, and Ikot-Ekpene is about 70 percent.[26] Damage has also been done to industries. In rural areas, farmers have been driven away from their farms and homes, and their capital has been completely lost. A large number of refugees have been created in the war-affected areas of the Eastern states and the Midwest State.

It is in the light of this information that policy can be formulated for reconstruction and rehabilitation. Nigerian governments are well aware of these problems and steps are being undertaken to identify damages to public facilities. Steps have already been taken to restore some of the damaged public facilities in the Midwest, Rivers, Southeastern and Central Eastern states. A national plan for reconstruction and development for 1969–1974 has been launched. Much of the government planning, however, has been in terms of reconstruction and extension of public facilities. Considerable attention will have to be given to the provision of capital and advice to displaced persons who were previously self-employed and cannot now secure employment with the government or private firms. Unless this is done on a substantial scale, the level of unemployment will be very high and this could create further instability in the nation. In refloating major industrial enterprises in the war affected areas, it will be necessary to consider the granting of subsidized loans or outright cash grants to firms restarting their businesses. Many of these firms, having suffered substantial losses, may be more in need of cash grants and subsidized loans than higher capital allowances as indicated in the federal budget of 1969–1970.

A major factor in ensuring stability and harmony in the future is the provision of jobs to Ibo intellectuals. Many of these were recalled to the East from their jobs throughout the Federation. It is essential that if they are to identify with a united Nigeria, they must be restored to jobs commensurate in status to jobs they previously held. Although the federal government has promised that Ibos can return to their jobs at the end of hostilities, returning Ibo intellectuals are meeting some opposition from those who were holding their jobs in their absence. Considerable care needs to be taken to avoid friction on this issue in the future. The intransigence of the Ibo leadership has been greatly related to the fear that they had no future in a united Nigeria. Future developments in Nigeria must prove that this fear was injustifiable and unfounded. To ensure this, there must be careful planning to ensure that Ibo intellectuals are placed in adequate jobs. If this is not done, it can be expected that they will be a disgruntled group that would seek not only to sabotage government efforts but possibly to rekindle the flames of open rebellion.

Finally the economic stringency imposed by the war has shown that Nigerians are willing to make significant economic sacrifices for a cause they consider worthy. The import restrictions have also indicated the potential of the nation for import substitution and the nation's ability to do without certain categories of imports. These factors, which have made it possible to release substantial resources in a non-inflationary way for war purposes, could well be put to use for reconstruction and development purposes. There is need for considerable publicity of the necessity of reconstruction and development and that continued sacrifices will be called for in order to release the required resources for these ends. It is therefore essential that there should not be a hasty dismantling of economic measures introduced in support of the war effort. The surcharges on imports and excise duties should remain a permanent feature of the tax structure. Judging from the high prices people were willing to pay in order to consume imported goods, particularly consumer durables like cars, it will be advisable to increase import taxes on these articles now quantitative restrictions are withdrawn. The restrictions which are likely to affect adversely the rate of economic development should, however, be withdrawn. Finally, while the import restrictions have given rise to a great number of import substituting industries, some of these will never be viable in a less restricted market situation. It is therefore essential that there should be a careful reappraisal of the import substituting strategy of the country.

Notes

1. For more details on Ojukwu's secession strategy, see N. B. Graham-Douglas, *Ojukwu's Rebellion and World Opinion* (Apapa, Lagos: Nigerian National Press, 1968?).
2. For more detailed discussion on the development of education and the Christian impact, see J. F. Ade Ajayi, *Christian Missions in Nigeria, 1841–1891, The Making of a New Elite* (London: Long-

364 VICTOR P. DIEJOMAOH

mans, Green & Co., 1965); O. Nduka, *Western Education and the Nigerian Cultural Background* (Ibadan, Nigeria: Oxford University Press, 1965); and O. Ikejiani, *Nigerian Education* (Ikeja, Nigeria: Longmans, Green & Co., 1964).

3. G. K. Helleiner, *Peasant Agriculture, Government and Economic Growth in Nigeria* (Homewood, Ill.: Richard D. Irwin, Inc., 1966).

4. The fact of their support of the federal government is not only indicated by the current enthusiasm of these people for their state, it was admitted by Ojukwu himself. For more on this, see Graham-Douglas, *Ojukwu's Rebellion* and L. B. Ekpubu, "The Minorities and the Nigerian Crisis" (Paper presented at the Social Science Conference, Makerere University College, Kampala, December 1968).

5. British Colonial Office, *Report of the Commission Appointed to Enquire into the Fears of Minorities and the Means for Allaying Them* (London: H.M.S.C., 1958).

6. Federal Ministry of Information, Lagos, "Nigeria, the Dream of a Rebel?"

7. For more details on this, see O. Olakanpo, "Federalism and the Foreign Trade Sector," *Journal of Business and Social Studies* (Faculty of Business and Social Studies, University of Lagos, March 1969).

8. See the submission of the Eastern Region government in *Nigeria, Report of the Fiscal Commissioner* (London: H.M.S.C., 1958).

9. Graham-Douglas, *Ojukwu's Rebellion.*

10. Mourtada Diallo, "Energy Resources and Utilization" (Paper presented at the Conference on National Reconstruction and Development, Ibadan University, 25 March 1969).

11. *West Africa* (London), 29 March 1969, p. 347.

12. These statistics are from the Manchester *Guardian,* 2 June 1967.

13. Federal Ministry of Information, Lagos, "Foreign Meddlers in the Nigerian Conflict."

14. See, for example, Victor P. Diejomaoh, "Financing Development Expenditures, Nigerian Experience Since 1950" (Ph.D. diss., Harvard University, 1968).

15. See, for example, W. Arthur Lewis, *Reflections on Nigeria's Economic Growth* (Paris: O.E.C.D., 1969), p. 5.

16. It should be stressed that the seizure of federal government revenues and properties in the East was part of a conscious strategy to take the former Eastern Region out of Nigeria in stages, and not because the demanded revenues were not given. Dr. Graham-Douglas, who was Attorney General of the Eastern Region at the time, has indicated in the publication already cited that Ojukwu and his close

advisors had declined to secede in 1966 and were just playing for time in early 1967 while they built up their military strength. The demand for more money from the federal government and other demands were part of the delaying tactics they chose to employ.

17. For a summary of Nigerian revenue allocation arrangements up until 1965, see O. Teriba, "Nigerian Revenue Allocation Experience, 1952–1965," *Nigerian Journal of Economics and Social Studies* (November 1966).

18. Central Bank of Nigeria, *Annual Report, 1967,* p. 56.

19. *West Africa* (London), 12 October 1968.

20. Permanent Secretary of the Ministry of Economic Development A. Ayida, "Development Objectives" (Paper presented at the Conference on National Reconstruction and Development in Nigeria, Ibadan University, 24 March 1969).

21. Kennedy Lindasy in his article, "Financing Biafra's War," *West Africa* (London) 19 October 1968, estimates that the local expenditure of relief groups, donations from Biafrans and Aid Biafran groups amounted to £1,153,000 from April to September 1968. He also estimates in the *Nigerian Observer,* 12 June 1968 that French sources supplied the rebels £2 million and relief agencies £3.5 million in 1968. The sums were supposed to have been increased in 1969.

22. Figures from the Federal Office of Statistics and the Central Bank of Nigeria.

23. *West Africa* (London), 12 October 1968.

24. Ibid.

25. See, for example, Chief I. O. Dina, "Fiscal Measures" (Paper presented at the Conference on National Reconstruction and Development, Ibadan University, 29 March 1969) and *Report of the Interim Revenue Allocation Committee* (Apapa, Lagos: Nigerian National Press, 1969).

26. U. Asika, "Rehabilitation and Resettlement" (Paper presented at the Conference on National Reconstruction and Development in Nigeria, Ibadan University, March 1969).

10

NIGERIA TODAY: THE DILEMMA OF PEACE

JOSEPH OKPAKU

Winding one's way through the busy streets of Lagos, jumping in and out of sometimes brand new, sometimes rickety (but always somehow running) taxi cabs, as much in cozy government offices as in the crowded roadside shops, one question continues to haunt the casual observer: What is the future of Nigeria? This immediately provokes another question: What is the present state of Nigeria? Which in turn provokes the inevitable question: How has the war affected the country and the lives and dispositions of its people?

It is summer 1971. More precisely, it is early July. And as one goes through the immigration lines at Ikeja Airport, four years to the minute from when the war broke out, the immense importance of those questions, and the potential impact of their answers on the lives of the people and the future of the country strike with a kind of brutality that is comparable only to the feelings experienced in the period immediately preceding the war. Now, as it did then, the question embodies in itself the anxieties, the dreams, and the fears of a people facing yet another moment of truth.

Nor should it have been less dramatic, since sixty million people in one way or another had jointly and individually committed a period of their lives—a not insignificant period at that—to the resolution of a nation's dilemma, the responsibility for which was certainly attributable, at least in part, to the judgment, the actions, and the idiosyncrasies of its leaders and public servants.

Following all these sacrifices, all the pain and sober experiences that turned out to be their share of the responsibilities and duties of citizenship, it was only to be expected that the Nigerian people would no longer view the manipulation of their future (otherwise called national politics) with disinterest or blind faith. Rather, they would now demand of their leaders, their public servants, and their fellow citizens a responsibility and sense of duty that would reassure the citizens that the sacrifices of the past were worthwhile and that the nation would be so run as to guarantee against a repetition of the woes of the past.

As one participated in group conversations, chatted with brief acquaintances or perfect strangers, or indulged in semi-social, semi-political reminiscences, a picture emerged of what Nigeria has been, what it is, and what its future most probably will be. The following is a summary of those impressions. Needless to say, some of the observations, especially those which anticipate future behaviour, are subject to differing opinions. Such differences are not only inevitable but desirable, especially in the areas in which the consequences of pursuing present policies are likely to be undesirable.

Post-War Nigeria

Several weeks of taking mental snapshots of the diverse segments of Nigeria's complex life result in a picture of a nation that has proved itself in battle and in so doing has acquired a great sense of self-pride and self-confidence.

Nigeria, the land of highlife music and happy-go-lucky people, found itself plunged into civil war when it least expected it. Just when it needed to rely on the assurances of established international relationships, Nigeria found itself confronted with a realignment of hitherto supposedly unflinching alliances and commitments. Caught in a civil, military, and diplomatic crisis with no time to spare for weighing the pros and cons of the various options, Nigeria had to turn away painfully from the turned backs of former suitors, the empty stares of former friends, and the indifference of former eager ears, to face the equally harsh options of new overtures that were bound to have a profound permanent influence on the future of the country. But somehow, considered miraculous by many, Nigeria, the nation whose ability to blunder through its problems was second only to that of the United States, and whose almost naïve belief in the fundamental goodwill of nations was bound ultimately to teach it some profoundly painful political lessons, rose up to face the onerous demands of the situation and performed to the end with remarkable bravery and strength. This was due partly to the awakening patriotism of its people, partly to the great survival instinct of an injured and misused nation, and partly to the resilience of a fundamentally solid and healthy culture and society. This bravery was true of all parties to the conflict—Biafrans, federalists, the nonchalants, and the large proportion of those in the middle who neither understood nor cared for the goings on, but had to make the sacrifices all the same.

When 1969 finally drew to a close, taking along with it the last shots of this fractricidal conflict, Nigeria had fought an expensive civil war in the face of the formidable diplomatic and military forces of some powerful nations without owing one penny to anybody for the purchase of ammunition. Besides proving—to its own surprise—that its economy was substantial enough to stand it in good stead in the cut-throat arena of international political economics, Nigeria had also proved to African and non-African governments the truth of the crucial maxim in international diplomacy: the only way to guarantee a nation's emergence from war with independence from its friends and foes alike is to pay for all goods in hard cash. This, of course, is most often impossible to do. Ironically, the result has been that Nigeria fought a civil war, and, in the process, achieved its first real and true functional independence.

The end of the civil war brought with it an event of historical importance, the first completely negotiated surrender and end of hostilities in the history of modern warfare that was without punitive reprisals against, or psychological humiliation of, the militarily defeated parties. It was a humane end to a war bitterly fought by equally proud peoples. It was humane, that is, to the extent that one can use the word when talking about wars. The Nigerian people on both sides of the conflict set an example of common sense and judgment, seriously ignored in the West, that placed in unfavorable perspective the endless bickerings and absurd egocentric and ethnocentric silliness of the Vietnam peace talks and the resultant continuing unnecessary loss of lives at a time when there is no longer a point to be made or a principle to fight for.*

* A distinction, albeit a debatable one, may be made between a war in which both parties are motivated by equally genuine and equally

While Americans continued to fight a useless war in Vietnam, Nigeria effectively brought to a close a bitter moral war. It could be said, without much risk of error, that both the Biafrans and the federalists had a genuine reason for going to war. In other words, the war was essentially inevitable after the moral position of both sides had been established. There may be controversy as to the results of the end of the Biafran war. Some may even argue that the Biafrans did not achieve an honorable peace, contending that a defeat in itself is dishonorable. But it is reasonable to say that the facts reveal a degree of rapprochement substantial enough to be at least moderately convincing, which Nigerians—Ibos and non-Ibos alike—can be very proud of.

The end of the war in 1970 brought with it a new sense of relief, and a new hope. A new hope. A new dream. And what happens to that hope and that dream will determine whether or not the war was worth the sacrifices, and whether or not the new leaders have carried out the obligation of their legacy.

The components of this hope can be listed quite simply:

1. Termination of all physical hostilities.

---

valid objectives, and one in which the motives of at least one party to the conflict are ulterior or otherwise morally unconvincing. In the former the battle can cease when the objectives have been achieved, the points made, or the anger assuaged, or when it is clear that there is a stalemate. In the latter, the very absence of genuine motivation in itself eliminates the existence of precisely those factors that are crucial in continuously assessing the results of the conflict in order to determine when the objectives have been achieved or when it is clear that they are unachievable. When the stated reasons for the conflict (sometimes a political excuse comes to be believed as original genuine motivation) continue to change with new governments or the changing demands of equally changing expedience, it is no longer possible to compare the real results with a substantive objective. The result is, first, endless continuation of the conflict—in other words, a war for its own sake. Thus, the former may be described as a moral war and the latter as an amoral war. Alternatively, the former can be called a "useful war" and the later a "useless war." (This terminology does not contradict the position that all wars are undesirable.) Second, a "useful war" will end when it has outlived its "usefulness"; a "useless war" will not end (although it may change from physical conflict to other forms), because it cannot establish a logical end without having established a pre-determined goal.

2. Termination of all psychological hostilities, including the end of aggressive talk or propaganda.

3. Renewal of former friendships.

4. Rehabilitation of former Biafrans and other displaced people into the mainstream of Nigerian society with minimum distinction between one Nigerian and another.

5. Rebuilding of war-ravaged homes and institutions.

6. Conversion of a wartime economy to a peacetime economy, with the social changes this implies.

7. The consequent redeployment of military priorities to a peacetime situation, including the disarming of recruits and the reduction of the size of the armed forces. The economy simply cannot support close to 300,000 men in uniform; the military government's unwillingness to reduce this number is fiscally rather irresponsible and could be an Achilles heel.

8. Development of the primacy of individual civil rights over the necessity of wartime patriotism, especially the return of police powers to unarmed policemen and the limitation of the soldier's authority to issues of national security and not to the policing of routine civilian behaviour.

9. The improvement of the general standard of living, especially public services such as health, housing, and transportation.

10. The control of individual and organized practices to stop the unfair or illegal use of official advantage for the exploitation of the public.

11. Guarantee of the self-respect and self-pride of every citizen, and his protection from abuse or misuse by private, government, civil, or military personnel.

12. The creation of a healthy atmosphere and a stable political situation that will encourage the enthusiastic participation of all citizens in the national development, and the prevention of the re-creation of the same situation that led to the conflict in the first place. This would include preventing a situation of disillusionment, especially among the young, and putting an end to the arrogant use of power by leaders and their staffs and the underestimation of the powers of the ordinary citizen.

13. The obliteration of all corruption, especially in high places, among public figures and officials who consider themselves untouchable.

The first six items of priority have, to some degree, been accomplished. All physical and psychological hostilities have more or less been terminated and former friendships seem to have been renewed. It is of course true that there is still some anger or resentment here and there, which is to be expected, but it amounts to very little and will disappear if the other priorities are achieved.

It can also be accurately said that most people displaced during the war have been rehabilitated, at least physically, and that much progress has been made in the direction of staving off starvation and creating new jobs. Here again, as in other instances, there are shortcomings in the area of speed and efficiency, but the overall achievement is reasonably good.

As for the economy, the necessary shift from wartime to peacetime priorities may be said to have been made, except for the fact that the military budget is so fantastically disproportionate in comparison with the allocations for civilian priorities that this threatens, more seriously than the military government seems to realize, the peace that the military itself fought so hard to achieve.

To criticize obvious aspects of poor judgment on the part of the military is not to find fault unduly or to detract from the praise and honor probably due it in the light of its position in the life of the country today. Rather, not to honestly criticize the military is to fail to give it the benefit of insight that it should appreciate and welcome. This is doubly important in light of the fact that Nigerian intellectuals cannot but admit that their failure to offer honest criticism, either out of fear or for personal advantage, at the early stages of the Nigerian crisis contributed to the precipitation of the war.

Present Challenges

One must examine, quite frankly and fearlessly, though sympathetically, the strengths and weaknesses of the present authorities, in the belief that honest criticism is a *sine qua non* for effective functioning of a dedicated government. For this reason, the following observations can be honestly deduced from an assessment of the country today. It might also be said that these observations are held by a wide segment of the people and therefore are worthy of attention.

MILITARY VERSUS POLITICAL

It is not merely academic to reexamine the definition of the term "political." In pre-war Nigeria, the distinction between the politician and the civil servant was based, in part, on the fact that the former made the policy and the latter carried it out faithfully. The politician was the man who ran the country, and the civil servant the man responsible for the running of the country. In terms of those who run the country, the difference between pre- and post-war Nigeria is not the distinction between politicians and non-politicians but between civilian politicians and military politicians. Therefore, when the military shifts or expands its area of operation from national security to national government and policy making (as it does during periods of military rule), it changes its area of authority, and, accordingly, its responsibilities. The politician owes certain responsibilities to the public by virtue of the *privilege* of governing, and the soldier does not (because the former is elected and the latter is not), but the soldier loses his immunity from political and policy responsibilities and criticisms the moment he functions as a politician.

It is therefore most useful to examine the virtues and short-comings of the military government in Nigeria and the concept of the soldier-politician. This is not such a strange idea since the military seems to have made the transformation with little difficulty. While in the past politicians drove around in black or green American Pontiacs and Chevrolets, the military politicians now drive around in green German Mercedes Benzes. While politicians went on foreign tours with large entourages, now military politicians go abroad with equally large entourages. (It should be noted, however, that the head of state, General Yakubu Gowon, has restricted his trips to the African continent.) While before there were overt signs of rich and wealthy civilian politicians, now there are signs or rumors of signs of rich and wealthy military politicians. When two people wear the same clothes, people soon begin to say the same thing about them. Just as there used to be talk about the corrupt civilian politician, now there is talk about the corrupt military politician. Remarkably, the picture is so similar that just as Nigerians used to say that the civilian head of state, the late Sir Abubakar Tafawa Balewa, was one of the few honest politicians, they are also beginning to say that the military head of state, General Yakubu Gowon, is one of the few honest military politicians. In other words, because any group that runs a country is subject to charges of corruption and mismanagement, the military, otherwise untouchable when functioning purely as the military, becomes subject to the same charges when it assumes the role of government.

It is of course possible that, just as was the case under civilian rule, some of these rumors and suspicions are inaccurate. But in politics rumors are as important as facts, if not more so. It is, therefore, important that the military government earn the confidence of the public just as any civilian government must. It is not a serious condemnation to suggest that it is quite obvious that there are pockets of corruption in some echelons of the military government (this is true of most governments), or that the public image of some military politicians leaves something to be desired. What is important is that the government work to convince the public of its integrity. This is doubly important because the military's justification for coming to power was its ethical position that the civilian government and its first military successors suffered from a fair amount of moral ineptitude. The military government cannot afford to run the risk of having similar charges raised against it; that would mean forefeiting its moral and political *raison d'être*. Every soldier must make himself a symbol of integrity and avoid creating the image of one whose strength depends on his gun. (It could be said, without being facetious, that it is a long way from the wild wild West of America, where the gun was law, to present-day Nigeria.)

ARMED ROBBERY AND PUBLIC EXECUTION

What then does one make of the public executions in the country and the military decrees that created them? The response might be another question: How can you ask the military to clean up its ranks and yet be opposed to deterrent public executions? The simple answer is that public executions do not act as a deterrent. Years of study throughout the world have shown this to be true. Public executions, especially those handled with the distressing and disheartening blood-thirstiness that has been the case in Nigeria, only serve to brutalize the public sense and to destroy the respect for the supremacy of life. To take life in public at playgrounds and stadiums where people are used to going to clap for soccer fans or laugh at straggling long-distance runners is to destroy the value of life for the Nigerian. To destroy the value of life and the fear of taking it in the Nigerian mind is to destroy the fundamental basis of his culture. One hardly needs to argue further, as it should be clear by now both from the increase in armed robbery and growing disinterest—if not disgust—of the Nigerian public to these mid-afternoon tragedies that it is time to abandon this public brutality.

To say so is not in any way to defend crime or the threat of it. Rather, it is to put the convicted defendant back in his right place as a man who must be reformed by society, not used as a scapegoat to cleanse society's conscience.

Because most Nigerian papers are national and because armed robbery is new to Nigeria, one or two armed robberies a day among a population of about 50 to 60 million people can make the entire society panic. Anybody who has lived in Europe or America cannot help but be simultaneously impressed and amused by the Nigerian response, when one recalls that in such cities as New York or Chicago there are scores of armed robberies, murders, and other homicide cases everyday. Furthermore, it is not the theft of ten pounds or fifteen pounds, even at gun point, that is the major corruption problem in the country, it is mismanagement of thousands of pounds by people never likely to go on trial, that constitutes the public threat.

There is also the question of the legality or wisdom of declaring a man guilty so swiftly that before there is time to discover errors on the part of the prosecution the defendant may have been hanged. Nigeria has lost many people in the war and does not need to take any more lives. Furthermore, if the original intention was to convince the people or the world of the honesty of the military politician it should be obvious by now that nobody will be convinced this way and it should be stopped. It is certainly not a mark of weakness to fail to take life. Such unduly harsh measures, which do violence to the prestige of the legal profession and the penal system of the country, do not contribute anything whatsoever to the well-being of the state. They should be abandoned quietly and honorably.

ETHNOCENTRIC POLITICS

The continuation of ethnic favours without regard to competence and qualification is another threat to the well-being and stability of the country. This situation exists in practically all echelons of the society and, most embarrassingly, even among the educated and enlightened men at the universities. Nigeria shall have fought a war of unity in vain if qualified scholars are passed over in favour of less qualified or even untrained individuals because such scholars are not Yoruba or whatever other ethnic qualification is required at a given Nigerian university.

FOREIGN SERVICE

The Nigerian foreign service has always left a lot to be desired, not only in terms of its unduly large staff but also in terms of the caliber of some of the country's diplomats. While it is true that a fair number of Nigeria's representatives abroad compare favorably with diplomats from other countries, the Nigerian foreign service suffers substantially from the use of obviously untrained—if not uneducated—"political types." Such appointments are often made out of misguided favoritism. Just as it is not an insult to tell an engineer that he cannot perform a medical operation, it is not an insult to emphasize that foreign service requires a certain level of education and training, or at least experience. Nigeria has so many highly trained young men who speak several languages in practically every country in the world that there is no reason whatsoever for Nigeria to be represented by someone who embarrasses Nigerians the moment he opens his mouth.

BUREAUCRACY

Nobody has ever praised the British for efficiency. The addition of clumsiness to the excessive bureaucracy that was Nigeria's colonial legacy has made the functioning of everyday life and business in Nigeria an absolutely terrifying experience—things that should be settled in five minutes taking three months. Part of the problem is that whereas in some places the public servant sees his responsibility as pleasing the customer or the citizen, in Nigeria every little Tom, Dick, and Harry who sits behind a desk thinks that he is the Prime Minister and does not hesitate to show his displeasure at the audacity of the ordinary citizen's coming to bother him. In most cases these people do not seem to see any connection between the salary they get at the end of the month and the job they do. Besides the unnecessary irritation of the situation, this clumsy misguided petty arrogance costs the country thousands of man-hours daily.

CORRUPTION IN THE CIVILIAN SECTOR

It would be misleading to suggest that in Nigeria only the military is corrupt. Corruption is also widespread in the civilian sector. The average American earns at least fifty times more money than the average Nigerian, but the Nigerian pays much more than the American for most services and products because of all the bribes involved. An additional problem is the fact that the Nigerian tends to be so impressed by wealth, no matter how it is acquired, that his only reservation is that he wished he had the wealth himself. In this respect, as in many others, Nigeria is like America. Odd as it might seem, one suspects that the only solution to corruption in Nigeria is to legalize it. Thus, a building inspector whose official monthly salary is thirty pounds should be officially regarded as earning one hundred pounds a month (seventy pounds in *jara* or dash or bribes) and should be made to pay tax on the one hundred pounds. The salaries of those whose jobs do not offer any opportunity for bribery (it is hard to think of one) should be increased accordingly.

ESTABLISHMENT AND PROTECTION OF CIVIL RIGHTS

At the time of national emergency, emphasis is placed, of necessity, on the duty and obligations of the citizen to the state. In fact, such periods are said to be periods of emergency precisely because certain rights and privileges of citizenship are suspended in order to be able to function effectively under the pressures of crisis. At the end of such emergencies, however, it is important to return to the normal situation in which the rights and privileges of citizenship are of primary importance and therefore carefully protected. Among these rights is the protection of the citizen against any abuse or arbitrary treatment at the hand of any public official, police officer, or soldier. Too often the so-called average citizen, the one to whom all public officials owe their positions, is unduly ill-treated. He is kept waiting at the post office while the tellers carry on private conversations. He is shoved off the bus by some unjustifiably impatient conductor. He is often insulted and sometimes brutalized by the soldier, and generally made to feel irrelevant. There is no space here to go into the origin of this; it derives partly from the false sense of authority that the British established (they always seemed to feel that they had to shout at all Nigerians) and partly from the officiousness that results from a new and often unnatural sense of authority. Nevertheless, this problem substantially affects the attitude of the average Nigerian to those in authority.

Unfortunately, this is compounded by the fact that with all the emphasis on the ordinary man's duty to country he has hardly been told about rights of citizenship. There is very little talk about laws that protect the individual from the excesses of government, which is unhealthy if only because it makes the average Nigerian feel that he is not part of the process of government. Every Nigerian should be taught the limitations on the powers of the government, the public official, the soldier, the policeman, and the man next door. This can be done in schools, through newspapers and radios, and in adult educational classes. For example, a citizen should know that he cannot be searched indiscriminately by anyone, that he cannot be insulted or struck by any policeman or soldier, that there are certain things his landlord cannot do to him, and that even the big bosses have certain limitations on their behavior.

Such knowledge would create a healthy sense of belonging in the mind of the average citizen and put the validity of the responsibilities of citizenship into the proper perspective. In other words, the Nigerian should be convinced that he makes sacrifices for his country in return for certain guarantees from the country. Citizenship is reciprocal. Since the civil war the average Nigerian, after having seen violence, is less afraid of power (which is as it should be since citizens should respect rather than fear the law) and is therefore less likely to stand for arbitrary authority or the misuse of power. It is probably a hard fact to face but it is necessary for every policeman, soldier, or public official to be taught that his job is to serve the average citizen, out of whose tax money he is being paid.

One does not need to emphasize that Nigeria has all it takes to be a great and influential nation. The very greatness of the potential, however, makes the job of the government and the people that much greater. Nigeria can easily develop a society in which everyone is reasonably happy, the leaders and public servants humble, the citizens proud and kind. This may mean some people having less booty than they now have. But unless fundamental changes are made in the thinking in the country and unless priorities are rearranged to put public interest before private profit, Nigeria could easily develop into a modern-day America, in which the disparity between the rich and the poor, the haves and the have-nots, is so great that nothing short of continuous suffering, strife, utter misery in ghettos, and paranoia and repressive heavy-handedness on the part of the frightened and guilty rich can develop. The choice is up to the leaders and the people. The leaders must learn to earn their honest living and let others earn theirs. The citizen must learn to do his duty without demanding more than his salary; he must learn to accept "thank you" as the only appreciation for doing his job well; and, in the final analysis, he must change his present belief that there is nothing wrong with corruption as long as the corrupt live in grand style. He must learn that to be rich at all costs is no virtue.

If the government of Nigeria takes a cold look at its responsibilities and shows sensitivity to the reservations of its people, no matter how mildly or faithfully expressed, it will win the respect and admiration of its people. In so doing, Nigerians today might go down in history as those who built a great nation. If, however, the leaders throw away their opportunity, and the citizens show interest only in their immediate benefit, then all the lives of precious citizens shall have been lost in vain. This does not need to be so. One can only hope and trust that it will not be so.

APPENDICES

A

CHARTER OF THE ORGANIZATION OF AFRICAN UNITY

We, the Heads of African States and Governments assembled in the City of Addis Ababa, Ethiopia;

CONVINCED that it is the inalienable right of all people to control their own destiny;

CONSCIOUS of the fact that freedom, equality, justice and dignity are essential objectives for the achievement of the legitimate aspirations of the African peoples;

CONSCIOUS of our responsibility to harness the natural and human resources of our continent for the total advancement of our peoples in spheres of human endeavour;

INSPIRED by a common determination to promote understanding among our peoples and co-operation among our States in response to the aspirations of our peoples for brotherhood and solidarity, in a larger unity transcending ethnic and national differences;

CONVINCED that, in order to translate this determination into a dynamic force in the cause of human progress, conditions for peace and security must be established and maintained;

DETERMINED to safeguard and consolidate the hard-won independence as well as the sovereignty and territorial integrity of our States, and to fight against neo-colonialism in all its forms;

DEDICATED to the general progress of Africa;

PERSUADED that the Charter of the United Nations and the

Universal Declaration of Human Rights, to the principles of which we reaffirm our adherence, provide a solid foundation for peaceful and positive co-operation among States;

DESIROUS that all African States should henceforth unite so that the welfare and well-being of their peoples can be assured;

RESOLVED to reinforce the links between our states by establishing and strengthening common institutions;

HAVE agreed to the present Charter.

ESTABLISHMENT
Article I

1. The High Contracting Parties do by the present Charter establish an Organization to be known as the ORGANIZATION OF AFRICAN UNITY.
2. The Organization shall include the Continental African States, Madagascar and other Islands surrounding Africa.

PURPOSES
Article II

1. The Organization shall have the following purposes;
     a. to promote the unity and solidarity of the African States;
     b. to co-ordinate and intensify their co-operation and efforts to achieve a better life for the peoples of Africa;
     c. to defend their sovereignty, their territorial integrity and independence;
     d. to eradicate all forms of colonialism from Africa; and
     e. to promote international co-operation, having due regard to the Charter of the United Nations and the Universal Declaration of Human Rights.
2. To these ends, the Member States shall co-ordinate and harmonize their general policies, especially in the following fields;
     a. political and diplomatic co-operation;
     b. economic co-operation, including transport and communications;
     c. educational and cultural co-operation;
     d. health, sanitation, and nutritional co-operation;
     e. scientific and technical co-operation; and
     f. co-operation for defence and security.

PRINCIPLES
Article III

The Member States, in pursuit of the purposes stated in Article II, solemnly affirm and declare their adherence to the following principles:
1. the sovereign equality of all Member States;
2. non-interference in the internal affairs of States;
3. respect for the sovereignty and territorial integrity of each State and for its inalienable right to independent existence;
4. peaceful settlement of disputes by negotiation, mediation, conciliation or arbitration;
5. unreserved condemnation, in all its forms, of political assassination as well as of subversive activities on the part of neighbouring States or any other States;
6. absolute dedication to the total emancipation of the African territories which are still dependent;
7. affirmation of a policy of non-alignment with regard to all blocs.

MEMBERSHIP
Article IV

Each independent sovereign African State shall be entitled to become a Member of the Organization.

RIGHTS AND DUTIES OF MEMBER STATES
Article V

All Member States shall enjoy equal rights and have equal duties.

Article VI

The Member States pledge themselves to observe scrupulously the principles enumerated in Article III of the present Charter.

INSTITUTIONS
Article VII

The Organization shall accomplish its purposes through the following principal institutions:
1. the Assembly of Heads of State and Government;
2. the Council of Ministers;

3. the General Secretariat;
4. the Commission of Mediation, Conciliation and Arbitration.

THE ASSEMBLY OF HEADS OF STATE AND GOVERNMENT
Article VIII

The Assembly of Heads of State and Government shall be the supreme organ of the Organization. It shall, subject to the provisions of this Charter, discuss matters of common concern to Africa with a view to co-ordinating and harmonizing the general policy of the Organization. It may in addition review the structure, functions and acts of all the organs and any specialized agencies which may be created in accordance with the present Charter.

Article IX

The Assembly shall be composed of the Heads of State and Government or their duly accredited representatives and it shall meet at least once a year. At the request of any Member State and on approval by a two-thirds majority of the Member States, the Assembly shall meet in extraordinary session.

Article X

1. Each Member States shall have one vote.
2. All resolutions shall be determined by a two-thirds majority of the Members of the Organization.
3. Questions of procedure shall require a simple majority. Whether or not a question is one of procedure shall be determined by a simple majority of all Member States of the Organization.
4. Two-thirds of the total membership of the Organization shall form a quorum at any meeting of the Assembly.

Article XI

The Assembly shall have the power to determine its own rules of procedure.

THE COUNCIL OF MINISTERS
Article XII

1. The Council of Ministers shall consist of Foreign Ministers or such other Ministers as are designated by the Governments of Member States.

2. The Council of Ministers shall meet at least twice a year. When requested by any Member State and approved by two-thirds of all Member States, it shall meet in extraordinary session.

Article XIII

1. The Council of Ministers shall be responsible to the Assembly of Heads of State and Government. It shall be entrusted with the responsibility of preparing conferences of the Assembly.
2. It shall take cognisance of any matter referred to it by the Assembly. It shall be entrusted with the implementation of the decision of the Assembly of Heads of State and Government. It shall co-ordinate inter-African co-operation in accordance with the instructions of the Assembly and in conformity with Article II (2) of the present Charter.

Article XIV

1. Each Member State shall have one vote.
2. All resolutions shall be determined by a simple majority of the members of the Council of Ministers.
3. Two-thirds of the total membership of the Council of Ministers shall form a quorum for any meeting of the Council.

Article XV

The Council shall have the power to determine its own rules of procedure.

GENERAL SECRETARIAT
Article XVI

There shall be an Administrative Secretary-General of the Organization, who shall be appointed by the Assembly of Heads of State and Government. The Administrative Secretary-General shall direct the affairs of the Secretariat.

Article XVII

There shall be one or more Assistant Secretaries-General of the Organization, who shall be appointed by the Assembly of Heads of State and Government.

Article XVIII

The functions and conditions of services of the Secretary-General, of the Assistant Secretaries-General and other employees of the

Secretariat shall be governed by the provisions of this Charter and the regulations approved by the Assembly of Heads of State and Government.

1. In the performance of their duties the Administrative Secretary-General and the staff shall not seek or receive instructions from any government or from any other authority external to the Organization. They shall refrain from any action which might reflect on their position as international officials responsible only to the Organization.

2. Each member of the Organization undertakes to respect the exclusive character of the responsibilities of the Administrative Secretary-General and the staff and not to seek to influence them in the discharge of their responsibilities.

COMMISSION OF MEDIATION, CONCILIATION AND ARBITRATION
Article XIX

Member States pledge to settle all disputes among themselves by peaceful means and, to this end decide to establish a Commission of Mediation, Conciliation and Arbitration, the composition of which and conditions of service shall be defined by a separate Protocol to be approved by the Assembly of Heads of State and Government. Said Protocol shall be regarded as forming an integral part of the present Charter.

SPECIALIZED COMMISSIONS
Article XX

The Assembly shall establish such Specialized Commissions as it may deem necessary, including the following;
1. Economic and Social Commission;
2. Educational and Cultural Commission;
3. Health, Sanitation and Nutrition Commission;
4. Defence Commission;
5. Scientific, Technical and Research Commission.

Article XXI

Each Specialized Commission referred to in Article XX shall be composed of the Ministers concerned or other Ministers or Plenipotentiaries designated by the Governments of the Member States.

Article **XXII**

The functions of the Specialized Commissions shall be carried out in accordance with the provisions of the present Charter and of the regulations approved by the Council of Ministers.

THE BUDGET
Article **XXIII**

The budget of the Organization prepared by the Administrative Secretary-General shall be approved by the Council of Ministers. The budget shall be provided by contributions from Member States in accordance with the scale of assessment of the United Nations; provided, however, that no Member States shall be assessed an amount exceeding twenty percent of the yearly regular budget of the Organization. The Member States agree to pay their respective contributions regularly.

SIGNATURE AND RATIFICATION OF CHARTER
Article **XXIV**

1. This Charter shall be open for signature to all independent sovereign African States and shall be ratified by the signatory States in accordance with their respective constitutional processes.
2. The original instrument, done, if possible in African languages, in English and French, all texts being equally authentic, shall be deposited with the Government of Ethiopia which shall transmit certified copies thereof to all independent sovereign African States.
3. Instruments of ratification shall be deposited with the Government of Ethiopia, which shall notify all signatories of each such deposit.

ENTRY INTO FORCE
Article **XXV**

This Charter shall enter into force immediately upon receipt by the Government of Ethiopia of the instruments of ratification from two thirds of the signatory States.

REGISTRATION OF THE CHARTER
Article **XXVI**

This Charter shall, after due ratification, be registered with the Secretariat of the United Nations through the Government of

Ethiopia in conformity with Article 102 of the Charter of the United Nations.

INTERPRETATION OF THE CHARTER
Article XXVII

Any question which may arise concerning the interpretation of this Charter shall be decided by a vote of two-thirds of the Assembly of Heads of State and Government of the Organization.

ADHESION AND ACCESSION
Article XXVIII

1. Any independent sovereign African States may at any time notify the Administrative Secretary-General of its intention to adhere or accede to this Charter.
2. The Administrative Secretary-General shall, on receipt of such notification, communicate a copy of it to all the Member States. Admission shall be decided by a simple majority of the Member States. The decision of each Member State shall be transmitted to the Administrative Secretary General, who shall, upon receipt of the required number of votes, communicate the decision to the State concerned.

MISCELLANEOUS
Article XXIX

The working languages of the Organization and all its institutions shall be, if possible African languages, English and French.

Article XXX

The Administrative Secretary-General may accept on behalf of the Organization gifts, bequests and other donations made to the Organization, provided that this is approved by the Council of Ministers.

Article XXXI

The Council of Ministers shall decide on the privileges and immunities to be accorded to the personnel of the Secretariat in the respective territories of the Member States.

CESSATION OF MEMBERSHIP
Article XXXII

Any State which desires to renounce its membership shall forward a written notification to the Administrative Secretary-General. At the end of one year from the date of such notification, if not withdrawn, the Charter shall cease to apply with respect to the renouncing State, which shall thereby cease to belong to the Organization.

AMENDMENT OF THE CHARTER
Article XXXIII

This Charter may be amended or revised if any Member State makes a written request to the Administrative Secretary-General to that effect; provided, however, that the proposed amendment is not submitted to the Assembly for consideration until all the Member States have been duly notified of it and a period of one year has elapsed. Such an amendment shall not be effective unless approved by at least two-thirds of all the Member States.

IN FAITH WHEREOF, We, the Heads of African State and Government have signed this Charter.

Done in the City of Addis Ababa, Ethiopia this 25th day of May, 1963.

ALGERIA
BURUNDI
CAMEROUN
CENTRAL AFRICAN REPUBLIC
CHAD
CONGO (Brazzaville)
CONGO (Leopoldville)
DAHOMEY
ETHIOPIA
GABON
GHANA
GUINEA
IVORY COAST
LIBERIA
LIBYA
MADAGASCAR

MALI
MAURITANIA
MOROCCO
NIGER
NIGERIA
RWANDA
SENEGAL
SIERRA LEONE
SOMALIA
SUDAN
TANGANYIKA
TOGO
TUNISIA
UGANDA
UNITED ARAB REPUBLIC
UPPER VOLTA

PROTOCOL OF THE COMMISSION OF MEDIATION, CONCILIATION AND ARBITRATION

PART I   ESTABLISHMENT AND ORGANIZATION
Article I

The Commission of Mediation, Conciliation and Arbitration established by Article XIX of the Charter of the Organization of African Unity shall be governed by the provisions of the present Protocol.

Article II

1. The Commission shall consist of twenty-one members elected by the Assembly of Heads of State and Government.
2. No two Members shall be nationals of the same State.
3. The Members of the Commission shall be persons with recognized professional qualifications.
4. Each Member State of the Organization of African Unity shall be entitled to nominate two candidates.
5. The Administrative Secretary-General shall prepare a list of the candidates nominated by Member States and shall submit it to the Assembly of Heads of State and Government.

Article III

1. Members of the Commission shall be elected for a term of five years and shall be eligible for re-election.

2. Members of the Commission whose terms of office have expired shall remain in office until the election of a new Commission.

3. Notwithstanding the expiry of their terms of office, Members shall complete any proceedings in which they are already engaged.

Article IV

Members of the Commission shall not be removed from office except by decision of the Assembly of Heads of State and Government, by a two-thirds majority of the total membership, on the grounds of inability to perform the functions of their office or of proved misconduct.

Article V

1. Whenever a vacancy occurs in the Commission, it shall be filled in conformity with the provisions of Article II.

2. A Member of the Commission elected to fill a vacancy shall hold office for the unexpired term of the Member he has replaced.

Article VI

1. A President and two Vice-Presidents shall be elected by the Assembly of Heads of State and Government from among the Members of the Commission and hold office for five years. The President and the two Vice-Presidents shall not be eligible for re-election as such officers.

2. The President and the two Vice-Presidents shall be full-time members of the Commission, while the remaining eighteen shall be part-time Members.

Article VII

The President and the two Vice-Presidents shall constitute the Bureau of the Commission and shall have the responsibility of consulting with the parties as regards the appropriate mode of settling the dispute in accordance with this Protocol.

Article VIII

The salaries and allowances of the Members of the Bureau and the remuneration of the other Members of the Commission shall be determined in accordance with the provisions of the Charter of the Organization of African Unity.

Article IX

1. The Commission shall appoint a Registrar and may provide for such other officers as may be deemed necessary.
2. The terms and conditions of service of the Registrar and other administrative officers of the Commission shall be governed by the Commission's Staff Regulations.

Article X

The Administrative expenses of the Commission shall be borne by the Organization of African Unity. All other expenses incurred in connection with the proceedings before the Commission shall be met in accordance with the Rules of Procedure of the Commission.

Article XI

The Seat of the Commission shall be at Addis Ababa, Ethiopia.

PART II GENERAL PROVISIONS
Article XII

The Commission shall have jurisdiction over disputes between States only.

Article XIII

1. A dispute may be referred to the Commission jointly by the parties concerned, by a party to the dispute, by the Council of Ministers or by the Assembly of Heads of State and Government.
2. Where a dispute has been referred to the Commission as provided in paragraph 1, and one or more of the parties have refused to submit to the jurisdiction of the Commission, the Bureau shall refer the matter to the Council of Ministers for consideration.

Article XIV

The consent of any party to a dispute to submit to the jurisdiction of the Commission may be evidenced by:

(a) a prior written undertaking by such party that there shall be recourse to Mediation, Conciliation or Arbitration;

(b) reference of a dispute by such party to the Commission; or

(c) submission by such party to the jurisdiction in respect of a dispute referred to the Commission by another State, by the

Council of Ministers, or by the Assembly of Heads of State and Government.

Article XV

Member States shall refrain from any act or omission that is likely to aggravate a situation which has been referred to the Commission.

Article XVI

Subject to the provisions of this Protocol and any special agreement between the parties, the Commission shall be entitled to adopt such working methods as it deems to be necessary and expedient and shall establish appropriate rules of procedure.

Article XVII

The Members of the Commission, when engaged in the business of the Commission, shall enjoy diplomatic privileges and immunities as provided for in the Convention on Privileges and Immunities of the Organization of African Unity.

Article XVIII

Where, in the course of Mediation, Conciliation or Arbitration, it is deemed necessary to conduct an investigation or inquiry for the purpose of elucidating facts or circumstances relating to a matter in dispute, the parties concerned and all other Member States shall extend to those engaged in any such proceedings the fullest co-operation in the conduct of such investigation or inquiry.

Article XIX

In case of a dispute between Member States, the parties may agree to resort to any one of these modes of settlement: Mediation, Conciliation and Arbitration.

PART III MEDIATION
Article XX

When a dispute between Member States is referred to the Commission for Mediation, the President shall, with the consent of the parties, appoint one or more members of the Commission to mediate the dispute.

Article XXI

1. The role of the mediator shall be confined to reconciling the views and claims of the parties.
2. The mediator shall make written proposals to the parties as expeditiously as possible.
3. If the means of reconciliation proposed by the mediator are accepted, they shall become the basis of a protocol of arrangement between the parties.

PART IV CONCILIATION
Article XXII

1. A request for the settlement of a dispute by conciliation may be submitted tó the Commission by means of a petition addressed to the President by one or more of the parties to the dispute.
2. If the request is made by only one of the parties, that party shall indicate that prior written notice has been given to the other party.
3. The petition shall include a summary explanation of the grounds of the dispute.

Article XXIII

issues in dispute and to endeavour to bring about an agreement with the parties, establish a Board of Conciliators, of whom three shall be appointed by the President from among the Members of the Commission, and one each by the parties.
2. The Chairman of the Board shall be a person designated by the President from among the three Members of the Commission.
3. In nominating persons to serve as Members of the Board, the parties to the dispute shall designate persons in such a way that no two Members of it shall be nationals of the same State.

Article XXIV

1. It shall be the duty of the Board of Conciliators to clarify the issues in dispute and to endeavour to bring about an agreement between the parties upon mutually acceptable terms.
2. The Board shall consider all questions submitted to it and may undertake any inquiry or hear any person capable of giving relevant information concerning the dispute.
3. In the absence of agreement between the parties, the Board shall determine its own procedure.

Article XXV

The parties shall be represented by agents, whose duty shall be to act as intermediaries between them and the Board. They may moreover be assisted by counsel and experts and may request that all persons whose evidence appears to the Board to be relevant shall be heard.

Article XXVI

1. At the close of the proceedings, the Board shall draw up a report stating either:
   (a) that the parties have come to an agreement and, if the need arises, the terms of the agreement and any recommendations for settlement made by the Board; or
   (b) that it has been impossible to effect a settlement.
2. The Report of the Board of Conciliators shall be communicated to the parties and to the President of the Commission without delay and may be published only with the consent of the parties.

PART V   ARBITRATION
Article XXVII

1. Where it is agreed that arbitration should be resorted to, the Arbitral Tribunal shall be established in the following manner:
   (a) each party shall designate one arbitrator from among the Members of the Commission having legal qualifications;
   (b) the two arbitrators thus designated shall, by common agreement, designate from among the Members of the Commission a third person who shall act as Chairman of the Tribunal;
   (c) where the two arbitrators fail to agree, within one month of their appointment, in the choice of the person to be Chairman of the Tribunal, the Bureau shall designate the Chairman.
2. The President may, with the agreement of the parties, appoint to the Arbitral Tribunal two additional Members who need not be Members of the Commission but who shall have the same powers as the other Members of the Tribunal.
3. The arbitrators shall not be nationals of the parties, or have their domicile in the territories of the parties, or be employed in their service, or have served as mediators or conciliators in the same dispute. They shall all be of different nationalities.

Article XXVIII

Recourse to arbitration shall be regarded as submission in good faith to the award of the Arbitral Tribunal.

Article XXIX

1. The parties shall, in each case, conclude a *compromis* which shall specify:
    (a) the undertaking of the parties to go to arbitration, and to accept as legally binding, the decision of the Tribunal;
    (b) the subject matter of the controversy; and
    (c) the seat of the Tribunal.
2. The *compromis* may specify the law to be applied by the Tribunal and the power, if the parties so agree, to adjudicate *ex aequo et bono,* the time-limit within which the award of the arbitrators shall be given, and the appointment of agents and counsel to take part in the proceedings before the Tribunal.

Article XXX

In the absence of any provision in the *compromis* regarding the applicable law, the Arbitral Tribunal shall decide the dispute according to treaties concluded between the parties, International Law, the Charter of the Organization of African Unity, the Charter of the United Nations and, if the parties agree, *ex aequo et bono.*

Article XXXI

1. Hearings shall be held in *camera* unless the arbitrators decide otherwise.
2. The record of the proceedings signed by the arbitrators and the Registrar shall alone be authoritative.
3. The arbitral award shall be in writing and shall, in respect of every point decided, state the reasons on which it is based.

PART VI   FINAL PROVISIONS
Article XXXII

The present Protocol shall, after approval by the Assembly of Heads of State and Government, be an integral part of the Charter of the Organization of African Unity.

Article XXXIII

This Protocol may be amended or revised in accordance with the provisions of Article XXXIII of the Charter of the Organization of African Unity.

IN FAITH WHEREOF, We the Heads of African State and Government, have signed this Protocol.

Done at Cairo, (United Arab Republic), on the 21st day of July, 1964.

ALGERIA	MALI
BURUNDI	MAURITANIA
CAMEROUN	MOROCCO
CENTRAL AFRICAN REPUBLIC	NIGER
CHAD	NIGERIA
CONGO (Brazzaville)	RWANDA
DAHOMEY	SENEGAL
ETHIOPIA	SIERRA LEONE
GABON	SOMALIA
GHANA	SUDAN
GUINEA	TOGO
IVORY COAST	TUNISIA
KENYA	UGANDA
LIBERIA	UNITED ARAB REPUBLIC
LIBYA	UNITED REPUBLIC OF TAN-
MADAGASCAR	GANYIKA AND ZANZIBAR
MALAWI	UPPER VOLTA

FUNCTIONS AND REGULATIONS OF THE GENERAL SECRETARIAT

PART I THE GENERAL SECRETARIAT
Rule 1

The General Secretariat, as a central and permanent organ of the Organization of African Unity, shall carry out the functions assigned to it by the Charter of the Organization, those that might be specified in other treaties and agreements among the Member States, and those that are established in these Regulations.

Rule 2

The General Administrative Secretariat shall supervise the implementation of decisions of the Council of Ministers concerning all economic, social, legal and cultural exchanges of Member States:

(i) keeps in custody the documents and files of the meetings of the Assembly, the Council of Ministers, of the Specialized Commissions and other organs of the Organization of African Unity;

(ii) within its possibilities, the General Secretariat shall place at the disposal of the Specialized Commissions the technical and administrative services that may be requested. In case a session of a Specialized Commission is held outside the Headquarters of the Organization, at the request of a Member State, the General Secretariat shall conclude agreements or contracts with the Government of the Member State on whose territory the Session of the Specialized Commission is being held, to guarantee adequate compensation of the disbursements incurred by the General Secretariat;

(iii) receives communications of ratification of instruments of agreements entered into between Member States;

(iv) prepares an Annual Report of the activities of the Organization;

(v) prepares for submission to the Council, a report of the activities carried out by the Specialized Commission;

(vi) prepares the Programme and Budget of the Organization for each Fiscal Year, to be submitted to the Council of Ministers, for its consideration and approval.

Rule 3

The General Secretariat of the Organization of African Unity is the Secretariat of the Assembly, of the Council of Ministers, of the Specialized Commissions and other organs of the Organization of African Unity.

Rule 4

The Organization of African Unity has its Headquarters in the City of Addis Ababa.

Rule 5

The Headquarters is for the official use of the Organization, for objectives and purposes strictly compatible with the objectives and purposes set forth in the Charter of the Organization. The Administrative Secretary-General may authorize the celebration of meetings or social functions in the Headquarters of the Organization when such meetings or functions are closely linked, or are compatible with the objectives and purposes of the Organization.

PART II THE ADMINISTRATIVE SECRETARY-GENERAL AND THE ASSISTANT ADMINISTRATIVE SECRETARIES-GENERAL

The Administrative Secretary-General

Rule 6

The Administrative Secretary-General directs the activities of the General Secretariat and is its legal representative.

Rule 7

The Administrative Secretary-General is directly responsible to the Council of Ministers for the adequate discharge of all duties assigned to him.

Rule 8

The appointment, term of office and removal of the Administrative Secretary-General are governed by the provisions of Articles XVI and XVIII of the Charter and of the Rules of Procedure of the Assembly.

Rule 9

The participation of the Administrative Secretary-General in the deliberations of the Assembly, of the Council of Ministers, of the Specialized Commissions and other organs of the Organization shall be governed by the provisions of the Charter and by the respective Rules of Procedure of these bodies.

Rule 10

The Administrative Secretary-General shall submit reports requested by the Assembly, the Council of Ministers and the Commissions.

Rule 11

The Administrative Secretary-General shall furthermore:

(i) carry out the provisions of Article XVIII of the Charter, and submit Staff Rules to the Council of Ministers for approval;

(ii) transmit to Member States the Budget and Programme of Work at least one month before the convocation of the sessions of the Assembly, of the Council of Ministers, of the Specialized Commissions and of other organs of the Organization;

(iii) receive the notification of adherence or accession to the Charter and communicate such notification to Member States, as provided in Article XXVIII of the Charter;

(iv) receive the notification of Member States which may desire to renounce their membership in the Organization as provided in Article XXXII of the Charter;

(v) communicate to Member States, and include in the Agenda of the Assembly, as provided in Article XXXIII of the Charter, written requests of Member States for amendments or revisions of the Charter;

(vi) establish, with the approval of the Council of Ministers, such branches and administrative and technical offices as may be necessary to achieve the objectives and purposes of the Organization;

(vii) abolish, with the approval of the Council of Ministers, such branches and administrative and technical offices as may be deemed necessary for the adequate functioning of the General Secretariat.

The Assistant Administrative Secretaries-General
Rule 12

The appointment, term of office and removal of the Assistant Administrative Secretaries-General are governed by the provisions of Articles XVI and XVII of the Charter and the Rules of Procedure of the Assembly.

Rule 13

The Administrative Secretary-General shall designate one of the Assistant Administrative Secretaries-General who will represent him in all matters assigned to him.

Rule 14

One of the Assistant Administrative Secretaries-General shall exercise the functions of the Administrative Secretary-General in his absence, or because of any temporary incapacity of the Administrative Secretary-General, and shall assume the office of the Administrative Secretary-General for the unexpired term in case of a definite vacancy. In case of definite vacancy, the Council will designate one of the Assistant Administrative Secretaries-General who will replace the Administrative Secretary-General provisionally.

PART III ORGANIZATION OF THE GENERAL SECRETARIAT
Rule 15

The General Secretariat has the following departments:
  (i) the Political, Legal and Defence Department;
  (ii) the Economic and Social Department;
  (iii) the Administrative, Conference and Information Department.

The Administrative Secretary-General shall create divisions and subdivisions, as he may deem necessary, with the approval of the Council.

PART IV FISCAL RULES
Rule 16

The Administrative Secretary-General shall prepare the Programme and Budget of the Organization as provided in Article XXIII of the Charter, and shall submit it to the Council of Ministers for scrutiny and approval during its first ordinary session.

Rule 17

The proposed Programme and Budget shall comprise the programme of activities of the General Secretariat of the Organization. It shall include the expenses of the Assembly, of the Council of Ministers, of the Specialized Commission and of other organs of the Organization.

Rule 18

In formulating the Programme and Budget of the Organization the Administrative Secretary-General shall consult the different Organs of the Organization of African Unity.

The proposed Programme and Budget shall include:
  (i) a list of contributions made by Member States in accordance with the scale established by the Council of Ministers and by reference to the provisions of Article XXIII of the Charter;
  (ii) an estimate of various incomes;
  (iii) a description of the situation of the Working Fund.

Financial Resources
Rule 19

Once the budget is approved by the Council of Ministers, the Administrative Secretary-General shall communicate it to the Member States, with all pertinent documents, at least three months before the first day of the Fiscal Year. The budget shall be accompanied by a list indicating the annual contributions assigned by the Council to each Member State. The annual contribution of each Member State becomes due on the first day of the Fiscal Year.

Rule 20

The Administrative Secretary-General is the Accounting Officer of the Organization and shall be responsible for the proper administration of the Budget.

Rule 21

The Administrative Secretary-General shall submit to Member States a quarterly statement on payments of contributions and outstanding contributions:

Rule 22

There shall be a General Fund, in which the following amounts will be entered:
(i) annual contribution of Member States;
(ii) miscellaneous income, unless the Council of Ministers determine otherwise;
(iii) advance from the Working Fund.
From such General Fund all expenditures established in the budget shall be set.

Rule 23

The Administrative Secretary-General may establish fiduciary funds, reserve funds and special funds with approval of the Council of Ministers. The objectives and limitations of these funds shall be defined by the Council of Ministers. These funds shall be administered in separate accounts, as provided in special regulations approved by the Council of Ministers.

Rule 24

The Administrative Secretary-General, may accept, on behalf of the Organization, gifts, bequests and other donations made to the Organization, provided that such donations are consistent with the objectives and purposes of the Organization, and are approved by the Council of Ministers.

Rule 25

In the case of monetary donations for specific purposes, these funds shall be treated as fiduciary or special funds, as provided in Rule 22. Monetary donations for no specific purposes shall be considered as miscellaneous income.

Rule 26

The Administrative Secretary-General shall designate the African Banks or Banking Institutions in which the funds of the Organization shall be deposited. The interests accrued by such funds, including the Working Fund, shall be entered as miscellaneous income.

Accounting
Rule 27

The accounts of the Organization shall be carried in the currency determined by the Council of Ministers.

Financial Supervision
Rule 28

The Council of Ministers shall be responsible for the supervision of the finances of the Organization.

Rule 29

The Administrative Secretary-General shall submit to the Council of Ministers any matter relating to the financial situation of the Organization.

PART V MISCELLANEOUS
Rule 30

The Administrative Secretary-General shall submit to the Council of Ministers for its approval, at the earliest possible moment, the complete Regulations governing the Accounting Method of the Organization, in accordance with established international accounting practices.

Amendments
Rule 31

These Regulations may be amended by the Council of Ministers by a simple majority subject to the approval of the Assembly.

B

THE O.A.U. CONSULTATIVE MISSION

In the second week of September, 1967, the Fourth Summit meeting of Heads of State of the Organization of African Unity was held in Congo (Kinshasa). One of the unscheduled matters which cropped up towards the end of this meeting was the Nigerian crisis. An earlier meeting of the Council of Ministers which prepared the grounds for the Summit did not include this topic in its agenda because the Federal Military Government had taken a positive stand, and the Council in turn had clearly recognized, that the crisis was purely a domestic affair of Nigeria. As such, it would have amounted to a violation of the O.A.U. Charter to bring it up for open discussion at the Kinshasa meeting.

However, out of a brotherly concern for the future peace and stability of African States in general, which can be affected by the outcome of the Nigerian crisis, the African Heads of State decided at the end of their scheduled discussions to express their genuine desire for an early and peaceful solution. The opportunity to give this expression came when nine African States sponsored and presented to the Conference an eight-point Resolution on the Nigerian crisis. The sponsoring states included Ethiopia, Niger, Ghana, Cameroun, Zambia, Congo (Kinshasa), Uganda, Liberia and Sierra Leone.

Text of the resolution which was unanimously carried ran as follows:

406

(*i*) The assembly of heads of state and government meeting at its first ordinary session in Kinshasa from 11th to 14th September, 1967;

(*ii*) Solemnly reaffirming their adherence to the principle of respect for the sovereignty and territorial integrity of member states;

(*iii*) Reiterating their condemnation of secession in any member state;

(*iv*) Concerned at the tragic and serious situation in Nigeria;

(*v*) Recognizing the situation as an internal affair, the solution of which is primarily the responsibility of Nigerians themselves;

(*vi*) Reposing their trust and confidence in the Federal Government of Nigeria;

(*vii*) Desirous of exploring the possibilities of placing the services of the assembly at the disposal of the Federal Government of Nigeria;

(*viii*) Resolves to send a consultative mission of six heads of state to the head of the Federal Government of Nigeria to assure him of the assembly's desire for the territorial integrity, unity and peace of Nigeria.

Arising from the last point of the Resolution, a team of Six African Heads of State, headed by His Imperial Majesty Emperor Haile Selassie of Ethiopia, was delegated to visit Nigeria as early as possible for the purpose of consulting with the Federal Military Government on the possibility and prospects of ending the crisis. Other members of the team included President Tubman of Liberia, President Hamani Diori of Niger Republic, President Ahmadu Ahidjo of Cameroun, President Joseph Mobutu of Congo (Kinshasa) and Lt.-General Joseph Ankrah, Chairman of the National Liberation Council of Ghana.

A period of nearly two months passed, yet the team did not visit Nigeria to discharge their assignment. The Federal Government, for its part, had welcomed the appointment of the consultative mission and had promised to co-operate with them whenever they arrived. This assurance was repeated in several public statements and conveyed to the Heads of State concerned.

At last the team arrived in Lagos on Wednesday, 22nd November, but only four Heads of State came, out of the six originally appointed by the O.A.U. President Tubman of Liberia and President Mobutu of Congo (Kinshasa) were held back by important state duties. In a series of talks which continued into the late hours of Thursday evening, 23rd November, the four-man team consulted the Federal Military Government on the terms and conditions for a cease-fire in the current war to crush the rebellion in the eastern parts of Nigeria. The meeting had been officially declared open on Thursday morning by Major-General Yakubu Gowon, Head of the Federal Military Government and Commander-in-Chief of the Armed Forces.

In his opening address, the Nigerian Head of State made a brief but enlightening review of the background to the crisis; for the consultations with his Government, he pointed out, can be fruitful only if the true nature of the crisis was clearly recognized and understood. He was a man of peace, he assured the mission, but he was also a soldier with honour. And his oath of honour as a soldier 'is to defend and preserve the territorial integrity of Nigeria.' General Gowon reiterated the two essentials for an end to the war, namely, the renunciation of secession and the acceptance of the division of the country into twelve states as a guarantee of future stability and peace in the country. When these have been observed a new leadership from the Central-Eastern State can come forward to join other Nigerian leaders in the search for lasting peace.

The pages which follow contain texts of the address of the Nigerian Head of State and the reply of Emperor Haile Selassie on behalf of the visiting team. Also reproduced in full is the text of the final Communique issued by the Consultative Meeting at the end of the discussions.

By this Communique the African Heads of State reaffirmed the original stand of the Kinshasa Resolution which brought the Consultative Mission into existence. It recognized that the crisis is purely an internal affair of Nigeria and that no solution is possible except within the context of the national unity and territorial integrity of the Federation. Further, the Mission is in complete agreement with the Federal Military Government's insistence that, as a prior condition for an end to the war, the rebel regime must accept the administrative structure of twelve states as a basis for permanent peace and stability in the Federation. For the enlightenment of the reader the text of Decree No. 14 promulgated by the Federal Government on 27th May, 1967, and dividing the country into these twelve states, is also reproduced in the pages which follow.

WELCOME ADDRESS TO THE O.A.U. CONSULTATIVE MISSION BY THE HEAD OF THE FEDERAL MILITARY GOVERNMENT, COMMANDER-IN-CHIEF OF THE ARMED FORCES, MAJOR-GENERAL YAKUBU GOWON

Your Imperial Majesty and
Your Excellencies,

We are very happy to welcome to Nigeria Your Imperial Majesty and Your Excellencies. You have all been in Lagos before in happier days. We believe that your visit can bring hope and happiness to all Nigerians in their search for national unity and lasting peace.

Despite the doubts expressed abroad about the value of your Mission, the Federal Military Government is convinced that our friends in Africa can be of assistance in our determination to maintain the integrity of Nigeria.

We have, however, always insisted that our friends are only those who are firmly committed to the maintenance of the territorial integrity and unity of Nigeria. Our true friends are those who publicly and genuinely condemn the attempted secession by a few who have imposed their will on the former Eastern Region of Nigeria. The Kinshasa Resolution of the O.A.U. Summit on the Nigerian situation proves that all African States are true friends of Nigeria. I wish to take this opportunity to express formally our appreciation of the brotherly spirit of the O.A.U. Summit in recognizing the need for Nigeria to be preserved as one country.

It is in the interest of all Africa that Nigeria remains one political and economic entity. The O.A.U. has rightly seen our problem as a purely domestic affair and in accordance with the O.A.U. resolution, your Mission is not here to mediate. I consider, however, that we should briefly outline to you the background to the current situation in the country.

I have, both personally and through my accredited representatives, explained to your Imperial Majesty and Your Excellencies the course of events in this country and the various steps taken by the Federal Military Government to secure a peaceful settlement. I made concession after concession to the former Military Governor of the then Eastern Region of Nigeria; some of you have personal experiences of how I was rebuffed on each occasion. I later discovered that the only concession which could satisfy Mr. Ojukwu and his clique was for me to agree to the disintegration of Nigeria.

This I could not and will never agree to, and I am happy that my firm stand on this fundamental question has now been vindicated by the whole of Africa in the clear commitment in the Kinshasa Resolution, to the maintenance of the territorial integrity añd unity of Nigeria.

Your consultations with the Federal Military Government can be fruitful only if we all recognize the nature of our crisis. There was fear of domination by one Region over the other and by one ethnic group over the rest. The only way to remove this fear and the structural imbalance in the Federation is by creating more states. There was widespread demand throughout the country for the creation of states. The Federal Military Government accordingly reorganized the country into twelve states. It is just not possible to ·avoid friction through any arrangement based on the four former Regions. The former Northern and Eastern Regions had to be split up in order to remove the imbalance in the country's political structure. Moreover, the former Eastern Region had to be split up to satisfy the aspirations of the five million non-Ibos who had been agitating for their own states under the civilian regime and even since the colonial days. These five million non-Ibos in the East definitely want to remain within Nigeria. It must also be pointed out that the Mid-West was created out of the former Western Region to meet the desires of the minorities in the then largely Yoruba West.

The creation of the twelve states has been enthusiastically received in all parts of the country, especially by the minority groups in the former Eastern Region of Nigeria. If the masses of the Ibo people were given an opportunity to express their views, the majority of them would have welcomed the creation of states and their chosen leaders would have participated in the subsequent discussions on how the crisis could be resolved on the basis of the new States.

I wish to restate the position of the Federal Military Government. Federal forces are not fighting the Ibos as a people. The Federal Military Government believes that the Ibos as a people need the rest of Nigeria just as the rest of Nigeria needs the Ibos. We also firmly believe that the Ibos have the same rights as other ethnic groups and that the legitimate needs of each ethnic group can be fully met within a Federal Union of Nigeria.

I am aware that all African countries are trying to come together in a desire for unity. It would be a betrayal of this African search for unity if we in Nigeria were now to break up the ties and bonds developed among the Nigerian peoples over several decades.

I have taken the liberty to review the political background to the Nigerian crisis so that Your Imperial Majesty and Your Excellencies might appreciate fully the reasons for the insistence by the Federal Military Government on certain essential conditions for the cessation of military operations. We cannot cease the current military operations to end the rebellion in the Eastern parts of Nigeria until the rebels renounce secession. Rebel forces must lay down their arms. A new leadership of the East-Central State must accept the new structure of the Federation based on twelve states. After the cessation of operations on these terms, representatives of the Federal Government and of the States will then discuss the form of a new Constitution (including the issue of state powers *vis-a-vis* the Central Government, the precise form of Governmental institutions, the system of revenue allocation and arrangements for ensuring free and fair elections in the future)—and other matters. The Federal Government, in consultation with the State Governments, will arrange for the resettlement of victims of the upheavals of 1966 and 1967 and the rehabilitation of damaged areas.

I am a man of peace, but I am a soldier with honour. My oath of honour is to defend and preserve the territorial integrity of Nigeria. Once the so-called secession was declared, the Federal Military Government had no alternative but to use force to end the rebellion. There is no peaceful means of ending secession, especially where the secessionist leaders are not prepared to listen to the voice of reason. I know the tragedies of war and the hardships that war inflicts on innocent citizens. I saw action in the Cameroons and the Congo and can therefore speak from experience. That is why I did so much to prevent the situation in Nigeria from developing into war.

I wish to reaffirm that the Federal Military Government welcomes your Mission. We will listen very carefully to whatever you have to say. I believe that the most valuable contribution the Mission can make in the present circumstances is to call on the rebel leaders to abandon secession.

There is no peaceful alternative to keeping Nigeria as one country. If we in Nigeria fail, there is no guarantee that other African leaders can contain secessionist movements in their own parts of the continent. As Your Imperial Majesty and Your Excellencies know only too well, it was the Democratic Republic of the Congo and Tshombe yesterday, it is Nigeria and Ojukwu today. Who knows which African country will be the next victim of secessionist forces?

Your Imperial Majesty and Your Excellencies, may I end this address by thanking you most sincerely for the highest motives and the brotherly love which have brought you to Lagos. We deeply appreciate the moral support and confidence which the Heads of States and Governments of the O.A.U. have expressed in the Federal Military Government in its resolve to keep Nigeria one. The entire people of Nigeria appreciate your visit. We are hopeful that your visit will enable you to understand more fully the nature of our problem and the correctness of the measures taken by the Federal Military Government.

FULL TEXT OF HIS IMPERIAL MAJESTY, EMPEROR HAILE SELASSIE OF ETHIOPIA'S REPLY TO THE WELCOME ADDRESS OF HIS EXCELLENCY, MAJOR-GENERAL YAKUBU GOWON, HEAD OF THE FEDERAL MILITARY GOVERNMENT AND COMMANDER-IN-CHIEF OF THE ARMED FORCES TO THE O.A.U. CONSULTATIVE MISSION TO NIGERIA

Today undoubtedly all of us recall that the peoples of Africa, and those who support the freedom of man, rejoiced on that October day in 1960 when Nigeria emerged triumphant and achieved its freedom and became an independent state thus joining the then small family of independent African countries. That occasion will forever be remembered by Nigerians as well as by the rest of Africans for it marked a big step forward in the struggle of Africans to be masters of their own destiny. And with the advent of freedom and independence of Nigeria, there came along the task and the responsibility of building a strong nation. All of Africa was pleased to see a stable Nigeria racing vigorously along the path of national development. For more than half a decade, the Nigerian people and its leadership worked in concert and understanding to produce a vigorous Nigeria.

However demanding the task of national development is in terms of time and resources, Nigeria never faltered in her commitment to Pan-Africanism. Together with her sister African States, Nigeria has always been in the forefont of the struggle for African liberation and unity.

This Nigerian stability and climate of co-operation has now unfortuately been interrupted for some time. We have all been distressed to see the power and the resources of Nigeria being taxed by internal differences and strife since January, 1966.

Excellencies, as you are all familiar with the details of the present Nigerian crisis, we deem it unnecessary to delve into them. None the less, we wish to state here that the situation is grave for Nigeria as well as for the rest of Africa and we should do all that is in our power to help the Federal Nigerian Government to bring peace to Nigeria nation.

Excellencies, the Assembly of Heads of State and Government, in its last session in Kinshasa, established this Mission with a view to consulting with the Federal leaders of Nigeria in order to find an amicable solution to its problem within the context of the Federal Republic of Nigeria as one unit.

The Organization of African Unity is both in word and deed committed to the principle of unity and territorial integrity of its Member States. And when this Mission was established by our Organization, its cardinal objective was none other than exploring and discussing ways and means together with and the help of the Federal Government, whereby Nigerian national integrity is to be preserved and innocent Nigerian blood saved from flowing needlessly. This great responsibility entrusted to this Mission by the Organization of African Unity requires, for its success, from all concerned, whole-hearted co-operation and sacrifice in the interest of one Nigeria and the well-being of Africa.

Ethiopia, as a founding member of the Organization of African Unity, fully subscribes to all the principles enshrined in the Charter. The national unity and territorial integrity of Member States is not negotiable. It must be fully respected and preserved. It is our firm belief that the national unity of individual African States is an essential ingredient for the realization of the larger and greater objective of African Unity. It is precisely because of this that we oppose any attempt at national fragmentation on religious and/ or ethnic grounds. That is why Ethiopia unreservedly supports Nigerian national unity and territorial integrity.

We wish to appeal to the patriotic sense of all Nigerians to put aside their differences and work in unison for their mother country —Nigeria. The world is watching whether Nigerians would rise above their present difficulties and reconstruct their country so that Nigeria will continue to play its full role in African and World

Affairs. We are certain that the people of Nigeria will overcome their present crisis and uphold their unity.

We feel that the fratricidal war that is going on in the country will only weaken the sister State of Nigeria by depleting her valuable human and material resources and by denying her a climate of peace and co-operation which is so essential for nation building. In view of this we believe that a solution needs to be urgently sought— a solution which will accommodate the varying interests in Nigeria but specific enough to ensure the steady development of the Nigerian State.

We shall commence our consultations with the expectation that we shall achieve the objectives of our Mission with the co-operation and understanding of all Nigerian brothers.

May Almighty God Bless our Work.

COMMUNIQUE ISSUED AT THE END OF THE FIRST MEETING OF THE O.A.U. CONSULTATIVE MISSION WITH THE FEDERAL MILITARY GOVERNMENT OF NIGERIA IN LAGOS ON 23rd NOVEMBER, 1967.

The O.A.U. Consultative Mission under the chairmanship of His Imperial Majesty Haile Selassie I, Emperor of Ethiopia, and comprising H.E. the President of the Federal Republic of Cameroun, El Haj Ahmadu Ahidjo, H.E. the President of the Republic of Niger, Monsieur Hamani Diori and H.E. Lt.-General Ankrah, the Chairman of the National Liberation Council of Ghana held consultations with H.E. Major-General Yakubu Gowon, Head of the Federal Military Government of Nigeria, today, pursuant to the resolution on the Nigerian situation adopted at the Fourth Session of the O.A.U. Summit Conference in Kinshasa on the 14th September, 1967.

The Mission reaffirmed the decision of the O.A.U. Summit embodied in its resolution condemning all secessionist attempts in Africa. The Mission also reaffirmed that any solution of the Nigerian crisis must be in the context of preserving the unity and territorial integrity of Nigeria.

The Mission considered the terms of the Federal Military Government for the cessation of military operations.

The O.A.U. Consultative Mission agreed that as a basis for return to peace and normal conditions in Nigeria the secessionists should renounce secession and accept the present administrative structure of the Federation of Nigeria, as laid down by the Federal Military Government of Nigeria in Decree No. 14 of 1967.

H.E. Lt.-General Ankrah was mandated by the Mission to convey the text of the O.A.U. Kinshasa summit resolution as well as discussions and conclusions of the first meeting of the Mission in Lagos to the secessionists and report back to the Mission urgently the reaction of the secessionists. The Mission will decide on the next course of action on the receipt of His Excellency Lt.-General Ankrah's report.

It was also agreed that the O.A.U. Consultative Mission will remain in constant touch with the Federal Military Government.

The Federal Military Government was in complete agreement with the conclusions reached at the meeting and the action to be taken to ensure the unity, territorial integrity of, and peace in Nigeria.

LAGOS.
23rd November, 1967.

INDEX

Abayomi, K. A., 17–18
Abubakar, Sir Tafawa Balewa, 60
Acholonu, Alexander D., 167–169, 172
action, vs. philosophy and history, 152–227
Action Group (AG), 20–21, 23–27, 54, 271, 290; "abundant life" and, 40; anti-imperialism of, 267; coalition government and, 55; crisis in, 57–58; Democratic Socialism and, 32, 40; destruction of, 268–269; eleven-year "rule" by, 25; Federation and, 56; Ibadan element and, 25; NCNC and, 39–41; 1962 census and, 121; rivalry with NPC, 30; strength of, 88; victories of, 268
actor, 213, 219
actor-philosopher matrix, 157
Adamawa emirate, 32
Adebo, Chief Simeon, 182
African actor, 5, 164, 214, 219
African-American Institute, 7–8
Africanist: American, 162, 258; O'Connell as, 194–207; vs. Machiavellianism, 199
Africanization, process of, 144–145
African problems: African actor and, 159–161; African view of, 13; philosophical misunderstanding in, 159–160
African states, divided nature of, 233–234
agricultural exports, 331
agricultural production, 350
Ahmado Bello Youth Organization, 168

air force, size of, 293–294, 314–315
Akinsanya, Samuel, 17–18
Akintola, Chief Samuel, 40, 268–269
Alafin of Oyo, deposing of, 25
Alakija, Sir Adeyemo, 19
Algeria, intervention by, 143
Almond, Gabriel A., 14, 81
Ambedkar, B. L., 89
American Africanists, 162, 258
American Civil War, 119, 127
Amoda, Moyibi, 14–69, 152–227
Anglo-Nigerian defense pact, 268
Ankrah, Gen. Joseph A., 238
Anti-Colonialist Party, 50
anti-imperialism, 267
anti-Ibo coup, 193
Anuforo, Maj. C. I., 177
Apter, David E., 205
Arab-Israeli War, 129
Arendt, Hannah, 206
Arikpo, Okoi, 94, 102–103, 288
armed robbery, 373–374
Armée Nationale Congolaise, 244
arms supply, source of, 293–294
army revolts, 241, 243. *See also* Nigerian army
Associated Press, 4
Awolowo, Obafemi, 17–18, 21, 25, 40, 52, 55, 88–89, 102, 107, 268
Awolowo Youth Organization, 168
Azikiwe, Dr. Nnamdi, 17–19, 28–29, 31, 40, 53, 56, 267

Balewa, Sir Abubakar Tafawa, 58, 60, 175, 192, 271–273, 372
Banfield, Edward C., 81